LA Sports

DAVID K. WIGGINS, SERIES EDITOR

Other Titles in This Series

*Making March Madness:
The Early Years of the NCAA, NIT,
and College Basketball Championships, 1922–1951*

*San Francisco Bay Area Sports:
Golden Gate Athletics, Recreation, and Community*

*Separate Games:
African American Sport behind the Walls of Segregation*

*Baltimore Sports:
Stories from Charm City*

Philly Sports: Teams, Games, and Athletes from Rocky's Town

DC Sports: The Nation's Capital at Play

Frank Merriwell and the Fiction of All-American Boyhood

Democratic Sports: Men's and Women's College Athletics

Sport and the Law: Historical and Cultural Intersections

*Beyond C. L. R. James:
Shifting Boundaries of Race and Ethnicity in Sports*

*A Spectacular Leap:
Black Women Athletes in Twentieth-Century America*

Hoop Crazy: The Lives of Clair Bee and Chip Hilton

LA Sports

Play, Games, and Community in the City of Angels

**Edited by
Wayne Wilson and David K. Wiggins**

Copyright © 2018 by The University of Arkansas Press

All rights reserved
Manufactured in the United States of America

ISBN: 978-1-68226-052-4
eISBN: 978-1-61075-629-7

22 21 20 19 18   5 4 3 2 1

Designer: Jamie McKee

∞ The paper used in this publication meets the minimum requirements of the American National Standard for Permanence of Paper for Printed Library Materials Z39.48–1984.

Library of Congress Control Number: 2017947017

To Jan, a true LA athlete

Contents

Series Editor's Preface   ix
Acknowledgments   xi

Introduction "I Love LA":
The Sporting Culture of Los Angeles   3
Mark Dyreson

1. The Life Cycles of Sports Venues in Los Angeles:
   Sports and Local Economic Development   19
   Greg Andranovich and Matthew J. Burbank

2. On Los Chorizeros, the Classic, and El Tri:
   Sports and Community in Mexican Los Angeles   37
   Luis Alvarez

3. Pitches Less Than Perfect:
   Notes on the Landscape of Soccer in Los Angeles   55
   Jennifer Doyle

4. Figure Skating in Southern California:
   From Frontier to Epicenter   71
   Susan Brownell

5. Sports Car Paradise: Racing in Los Angeles   93
   Jeremy R. Kinney

6. Professional Football in the City of Angels:
   The Game Moves West   109
   Raymond Schmidt

7. The 1932 Olympics:
   Spectacle and Growth in Interwar Los Angeles   129
   Sean Dinces

8. "Never Go Back": Pasadena Racial Politics
   and the Robinson Brothers   149
   Gregory Kaliss

9. Reel Sports: Hollywood Stars at Play in LA   167
   Daniel A. Nathan

10. Behind the Curtain: Leadership, Ingenuity,
    and Culture in the Making of Earvin "Magic" Johnson,
    Showtime, and the Laker Dynasty   183
    Scott N. Brooks

11. The Golden Games: The 1984 Los Angeles Olympics   201
    Matthew P. Llewellyn, Toby C. Rider, and John Gleaves

12. Shaping the Boom:
    Los Angeles Surfing from George Freeth to Gidget   219
    Tolga Ozyurtcu

13. The Halcyon Days of Muscle Beach: An Origin Story   239
    Jan Todd

14. I Was Standing There All the While:
    Jim Murray and the Birth of a Sports Mecca   255
    Ted Geltner

15. Vin Scully: The Voice of Los Angeles   275
    Elliott J. Gorn and Allison Lauterbach Dale

    Notes   291
    Contributors   341
    Index   347

Series Editor's Preface

Sport is an extraordinarily important phenomenon that pervades the lives of many people and has enormous impact on society in an assortment of different ways. At its most fundamental level, sport has the power to bring people great joy and satisfy their competitive urges while at once allowing them to form bonds and a sense of community with others from diverse backgrounds and interests and various walks of life. Sport also makes clear, especially at the highest levels of competition, the lengths that people will go to achieve victory as well as how closely connected it is to business, education, politics, economics, religion, law, family, and other societal institutions. Sport is, moreover, partly about identity development and how individuals and groups, irrespective of race, gender, ethnicity, or socioeconomic class, have sought to elevate their status and realize material success and social mobility.

Sport, Culture, and Society seeks to promote a greater understanding of the aforementioned issues and many others. Recognizing sport's powerful influence and ability to change people's lives in significant and important ways, the series focuses on topics ranging from urbanization and community development to biographies and intercollegiate athletics. It includes both monographs and anthologies that are characterized by excellent scholarship, accessible to a wide audience, and interesting and thoughtful in design and interpretations. Singular features of the series are authors and editors representing a variety of disciplinary areas and who adopt different methodological approaches. The series also includes works by individuals at various stages of their careers, both sport studies scholars of outstanding talent just beginning to make their mark on the field and more experienced scholars of sport with established reputations.

LA Sports: Play, Games, and Community in the City of Angels provides important information and insights into the development of sport in a city known for its sunshine, beaches, palm trees, crowded freeways, glamorous lifestyles, and movie stars. Edited by Wayne Wilson and myself, the collection of essays is written by well-known scholars with long publication lists and expertise on various aspects of sport in Los Angeles. Although space limitations did not allow for coverage of every topic, the essays that are included in the anthology furnish details about the pattern of sport in a sprawling and diverse urban community through cogent analysis and interpretations. To a large extent, there is something for everyone in this collection, from essays that are biographical and cover specific sports to those that analyze the Olympic Games and evolution of sports venues. The story of legendary sportscaster Vin Scully is included here, as are the careers of renowned sportswriter Jim Murray, the indomitable Jackie and Mack Robinson, and a host of other men and women who contributed to the growth and popularity of bodybuilding, surfing, ice skating, soccer, car racing, football, and basketball in one of America's most iconic cities.

David K. Wiggins

Acknowledgments

This anthology has been a pleasure to put together. Like all anthologies, however, it has been a time-consuming task and has required the patience and expertise from a number of different people to bring it to fruition. As with all the books in the Sport, Culture, and Society series, a special thanks should be extended to Mike Bieker, David Scott Cunningham, Deena Owens, and all the other staff at the University of Arkansas Press for their unwavering support and enthusiasm for this project. Thank you to Shirley Ito and Michael Salmon, of the LA84 Foundation Sports Library, for their remarkable dedication and expertise. We also would like to thank Jon SooHoo, Mark Langill, and Oscar Delgado for providing us wonderful images of the Los Angeles Dodgers and Los Angeles Lakers. Finally, but certainly not least, we would like to thank and extend our sincere appreciation to all the contributors to this book. Each of the contributors, all of them very knowledgeable in their chosen fields, has been a pleasure to work with. They have added immeasurably through their individual essays to our understanding of sport in one of America's most important and intriguing cities.

LA Sports

INTRODUCTION

"I Love LA"

The Sporting Culture of Los Angeles

MARK DYRESON

When Los Angeles sport franchises win games, the strains of "I Love LA" frequently fill stadiums and arenas. Since the iconoclastic songwriter Randy Newman released the tune in 1983, this unofficial anthem of Los Angeles has heralded victories by the Dodgers, Lakers, Clippers, Kings, and Galaxy.[1] Though recently replaced at Kings and Galaxy games by the more raucous tune "This Is LA," written by the Los Angeles–based Celtic punk band, The Briggs, "I Love LA" remains the traditional anthem of many Los Angeles sports fans.[2] Indeed, when the Rams returned to Los Angeles from twenty-one years of exile in St. Louis in 2016, the chords of "I Love LA" coursed through the Los Angeles Coliseum as 90,000 people attended the first preseason game of the National Football League's (NFL) restoration in the city.[3]

"I Love LA" has become a tribal custom at a multitude of sporting events in SoCal, the region that is coterminous with the greater Los Angeles megalopolis. In particular, it heralds wins by the Dodgers and Lakers.[4] "From the South Bay to the Valley," Newman's distinctive voice blares over stadium loudspeakers. "From the West Side to the East Side," Newman warbles. "Everybody's very happy," he cheers. Or, at least those who stayed until the end of the game are very happy, as Los Angeles fans are notorious for being fair-weather front-runners who arrive late and exit early, to get to the beach or their favorite nightspot or just to beat the massive traffic jams that plague the city.[5] "'Cause the sun is shining all the time," Newman trills, taking a shot at urban rivals in lesser climes, New York, Chicago, Boston, Detroit, and others. "Looks like another perfect day," he gloats. "I love LA," Newman's canned voice chirrups. "We love it," respond his canned backup singers.[6]

Los Angeles is like other American cities in some ways. Sporting contests and sports teams provide possibilities for building communal bonds and defining civic identity.[7] In Los Angeles, however, molding commonweal presents special challenges. "Los Angeles is 72 suburbs in search of a city," the early twentieth-century manufacturer of witticisms, Dorothy Parker, herself a lifelong New Yorker, once famously quipped.[8] Los Angeles indeed lacks the centuries of urban history, prominent architectural anchors, and clear geographical determinants that many other American metropolises enjoy. Inhabited by indigenous peoples for millennia, a village of Los Angeles sprang into existence in this Pacific coastal basin when in the eighteenth century the imperial overlords of New Spain decided to plant several pueblos in the wilderness of Alta California to support the military *presidios* they had already built in the region. These new villages, Los Angeles, Santa Barbara, and San Jose, were settled by Spanish pioneers from Sonora in the 1770s and 1780s.[9]

The official founding date of Los Angeles was 1781, the same year that the army of the brand-new United States effectively ended at Yorktown, Virginia, the British campaign to quell its rebellious North American colonies, thus guaranteeing the survival of the fledgling American republic.[10] During the Spanish period the population of Los Angeles counted only a few hundred inhabitants. After Mexico revolted from New Spain, the hamlet grew to a few thousand. In the 1840s the expanding republic of the United States, now a regional power with ambitions of stretching from the Atlantic to the Pacific, seized Los Angeles and millions of square miles of Mexican territory and incorporated the lands into its continental designs. By the 1870s, the US town of Los Angeles had 5,000 residents. By the 1890s Los Angeles had exploded into a city of more than 50,000. Over the next century it grew at even more astounding rates, appearing on the list of the top-ten American cities for the first time in 1920 with over 500,000 residents and climbing to the second-largest city in the nation with over 3.4 million inhabitants by 1990.[11]

In a nation with an urban history characterized by the sudden and rapid appearance of boomtowns, Los Angeles stands out as the newest and largest megalopolis—and from many vantages, the most rootless and transient. Los Angeles represents a dichotomy, a city at the same time both exceptional and ordinary, a one-of-a-kind urban structure and a commonplace urban space.[12] Los Angeles has also developed a sporting culture that is both unique and exaggerated as well as conventional and mundane, as the essays in this collection on the sporting life of the "City of Angels" reveal. On the one hand, Los

Angeles has all the regular sporting traditions available in any US city, including a thriving intercollegiate sporting scene at the University of Southern California (USC), the University of California at Los Angeles (UCLA), as well as at more than fifty other institutions that dot the city, large and small, public and private, secular and sectarian.[13] Los Angeles also sports franchises in all the "big four" American national pastimes, baseball, basketball, hockey, football. Other customary sports, from golf, tennis, and track and field to horse racing, sailing, and swimming thrive in greater Los Angeles.[14]

In terms of distinctiveness, Los Angeles serves as the cradle for "action" or "lifestyle" sports. Beach volleyball, mountain biking, triathlon, snowboarding, skateboarding, surfing, windsurfing, BMX biking—each traces a lineage to the Los Angeles basin.[15] Los Angeles also has a special connection to the Olympics, having produced more Olympians, hosted more Olympic Games, and developed more training infrastructure for Olympic sports than any other urban region in the United States. The city remains convinced that it plays a special role as the Olympic backup location, ready to step in and take over should any host city falter in its duties.[16] In the interim, urban boosters dream of a third shot at formal hosting duties. As of this writing, that dream seems likely to come true in 2028.[17]

"I Love LA" has a connection to the city's Olympian aspirations, serving originally in an "unofficial anthem" role for the 1984 Olympics. As Los Angeles in the early 1980s geared up to host its second Olympic Games, songwriter Randy Newman penned this catchy, sardonic tune about his native city. Newman later explained that the idea sprang from a conversation he had on an airplane flight with Don Henley, the leader of the iconic 1970s and 1980s rock group, The Eagles. Henley, a native Texan who had relocated to Southern California in order to make his career at the center of the American popular music industry, mentioned to Newman that everyone in the business seemed to be writing songs about urban angst and social collapse set in Newman's native Southern California. The Eagles, Henley related, had contributed "Hotel California" (1977) to the genre. As an indigenous Angeleno, Henley contended, Newman was in a perfect place to contribute to the growing number of popular songs that painted Los Angeles as a false paradise.[18]

Taking but twisting Henley's cue in his own inimitable style, Newman wrote "I Love LA" as the opening track of his *Trouble in Paradise* album, a compilation that debuted in 1983 to enduring critical acclaim and won a spot on *Rolling Stone* magazine's "100 Greatest Albums of the 80s" list.[19] Though the song certainly skewered the image of Los Angeles as an unadorned nirvana, juxtaposing images of vagrants vomiting in the streets with depictions of perfect weather and perfect landscapes, "I Love LA" became something that Newman never intended—an anthem for his native city. The tune has been employed repeatedly in soundtracks to invoke the ambiance of Los Angeles, beginning when it was first released and placed in a time capsule to promote John Carpenter's Southern California–based science fiction drama *Starman* (1984).[20]

Newman's original music video, played endlessly on Music Television (MTV) and other cable-music channels in the 1980s and 1990s, featured the songwriter cruising the streets of greater Los Angeles in a red 1955 Buick Super Convertible with, as his lyrics chronicled, "a big nasty redhead" cuddled next to him.[21] The music video evoked images of Southern California sprawl and car culture, motifs that Hollywood films borrowed in cruising scenes from *Down and Out in Beverly Hills* (1986) to *Naked Gun* (1988) to *Chips '99* (1998).[22] The tongue-in-cheek quality of the song lent itself especially to the Los Angeles disaster movie genre, movies in which epic calamities destroy huge swaths of the city. "I Love LA" played while lava and fire covered the city in *Volcano* (1997), while the British comic Rowland Atkinson bumbled through several cataclysms in *Bean: The Ultimate Disaster Movie* (1997), and while earthquakes, floods, crime sprees, political catastrophes, and decadence turn the city into an apocalyptic island prison in the campy science fiction thriller *Escape from LA* (1996).[23]

Since Newman penned "I Love LA" in 1983, other, darker songs about Los Angeles have hit the airwaves and become symbolic canticles of the Los Angeles experience. Some of these songs grew from the emerging Southern California "hip-hop" culture and highlighted the deep racial and social divisions that plague the city, including NWA's "Straight Outta Compton" (1988), Dr. Dre's "Let Me Ride" (1992), and Tupac Shakur's "To Live and Die in LA" (1996). Punk and metal bands from the same era produced their own dark (but white, in contrast to hip-hop) and dystopian homages of the city's underbelly, including Guns N' Roses' "Welcome to the Jungle" (1987) and the Red Hot Chili Peppers' "Under the Bridge" (1991). None of those memorable songs, however, became embedded in Southern California's sports culture in the way that "I Love LA" has burrowed into the production of Los Angeles sporting events. "I Love LA" has been even more popular at Los Angeles sporting events than it has been in Hollywood schlock. The song blares when the Dodgers triumph in a baseball game at Chavez Ravine and when the Lakers or Clippers won a basketball game at the old Great Western Forum—and now when they win in the new Staples Center. In the short-lived early twenty-first-century challenger to the NFL's dominion, the XFL, the Los Angeles Xtreme cranked up "I Love LA" every time they scored a touchdown.[24]

While "I Love LA" has become a popular anthem for the city, the song remains controversial in Southern California. While some see it as a catchy pop tune that showcases the glamour, pleasures, and sparkle of Los Angeles, others understand it as an acidic commentary on a community that is vapid, shallow, and illusory. Like other trinkets that adorn Los Angeles, including the nickname "tinseltown," Newman's lyrics cut both ways, celebrating and condemning his hometown in the same breath. "Everybody's very happy," Newman cackles about his fellow Angelenos. "Looks like another perfect day," he croons. But are they happy, amid the palm trees and beaches, and is endless sunshine a recipe for perfect days? Those questions rest at the heart of the Los Angeles conundrum. Is the city an American paradise, or does the glitter mask harsh, dream-killing currents that lure the foolish to certain disappointment?

In the world of sports, Los Angeles has always been a bit of both. The City of Angels is the only American metropolis to host two Olympic Games, and frankly the only Olympic site that the American public remembers and celebrates. Olympic venues, such as the Los Angeles Coliseum, remain tourist attractions because of their Olympic heritage. Few recall that only two decades ago Atlanta hosted an Olympics. Tourists rarely pilgrimage to Atlanta to relive Olympic memories. Even more forgotten is St. Louis, the city that hosted the first Olympics on American soil in 1904, and in which visitors would have to search diligently for any remnants of past Olympian glories. Everyone remembers, however, that Los Angeles is an Olympic city.[25]

Not only did Los Angeles host two Olympics but both Games transformed the world's most popular sporting contests in enduring ways. The 1932 Olympics cemented the nascent link of sport, politics, and mass entertainment as Hollywood's dream factories turned the Games into a spectacle of beautiful and youthful athletic bodies battling for national glory in thrilling competitions. After 1932, no questions remained about whether or not the Olympics was a significant global event.[26] The 1984 Olympics transformed the spectacle again. In an era in which the Olympic movement seemed bound for extinction as taxpayer-funded boondoggles and political controversies threatened to drive even the most confident or delusional cities out of the hosting business, Los

Angeles stepped in when not a single other municipality in the world was willing to provide a home for the Games. The 1984 Olympics created a blueprint for successfully funding and promoting the Olympics that restored the luster of the Olympic brand. Olympic host cities have been duplicating the Los Angeles model ever since.[27]

In many ways Los Angeles became a paradise for the Olympics, and the Olympics showcased the fleeting dreamland that Los Angeles could become during global mega-events, as the essays in this volume by Sean Dinces on the 1932 Games and Matthew Llewellyn, John Gleaves, and Toby Rider on the 1984 Games illuminate.[28] Those two Olympics remain in civic memories moments in which the diverse neighborhoods that make up the city became, if only momentarily, a united community rather than a mostly geographic collection of sprawling parts. The two Olympic spectacles also showcase the city's enduring sporting architecture that contributed a great deal to the unique financial success of both of those events.[29] Los Angeles has done a far better job, as the essay in this collection by Greg Andranovich and Matthew J. Burbank demonstrates, of building and maintaining and refashioning and repurposing stadiums and arenas that by modern standards have exceptional life cycles.[30] No other host of multiple Olympics (London—1908, 1948, 2012; Paris—1900, 1924; Tokyo—1964, 2020) has ever used the same main venue, as Los Angeles has with the Coliseum in 1932 and 1984—and plans to do once again should it win the 2024 Games.[31] In many other host cities even recent Olympic venues have become empty "white elephants." Los Angeles, however, seems to be the repurposing king of athletic facilities, as the histories of the Coliseum and its sister site, the Rose Bowl, for everything from football, soccer, and Olympic events to rock concerts, religious revivals, and action sports contests reveals.[32]

The architecture of sports has left its marks on Los Angeles, and not only through monumental buildings that hosted athletic events. The iconic palm trees that line Wilshire Boulevard and other major streets were planted to prettify Los Angeles for the 1932 Olympics and revitalized again for the 1984 Games.[33] The Olympic structures occupy a special place in the city's civic culture. The 1992 riots following the Rodney King trial verdict witnessed the destruction of a great deal of property in parts of the city, yet spared not only the area around the Coliseum but the LA84 Foundation headquarters built to memorialize the heritage of the Olympics in the south-central neighborhoods that stood at the epicenter of the racial unrest.[34]

In American culture, sport has long been used as an emblem to promote visions of racial and ethnic harmony and integration. Sport supposedly highlighted the virtues of meritocracy, a unique space in American society where talent and not heritage or background triumphed. Of course, not only in Los Angeles but everywhere else in the nation, sport also revealed racial and ethnic discrimination and division. Sometimes urban boosters in Los Angeles used sporting events or iconic athletes to promote images that Los Angeles was a paradise of racial harmony. Certainly the organizers of both Olympic pageants sought to portray the city as a racially progressive oasis where whites, blacks, Latinas/Latinos, and Asians lived amicably. Commentators frequently offered the city's embrace of the Mexican-born Dodger pitcher Fernando Valenzuela in the 1980s, the much ballyhooed "Fernandomania," as a counterpoint to the long history of discrimination and hostility toward the large Latina/Latino community in the city.[35] In his essay for this volume, Luis Alvarez dissects the roles sport played in the community-building endeavors of Mexicans and Mexican Americans in the frequently hostile environs of the city, revealing moments of connection that appeared amid enduring patterns of segregation.[36]

This volume also offers an examination of the African American experience in Los Angeles from the vantage of one of the most well-known figures in the struggle for civil rights on playing fields and in the broader realms of American life, as well as from a key figure who lived largely in the shadow of the more famous athlete. Jack "Jackie" Roosevelt Robinson stands as one of the central figures in the dismantling of legalized segregation in the twentieth-century United States. Many historians regard his pioneering challenge of the color line in the undisputed national pastime of his era, baseball, a crucial first assault on segregation that paved the way over the ensuing decades to integrate almost every realm in the American public square. As the well-known folktale reveals, the story has an important Los Angeles connection. An infant Robinson escaped the rigid apartheid of the Deep South—Cairo, Georgia—and grew up in the allegedly vastly more racially progressive environs of greater Los Angeles. In the suburban neighborhoods of Pasadena, he attended schools and played on teams with whites, matriculating to more integrated success first at Pasadena City College and then UCLA. In Southern California he seemed to have escaped the scourges of racism, rising to stardom not only in baseball but in football, track and field, and a host of other endeavors. Indeed, some chroniclers of Robinson's story imply that only after he signed his first major league contract and he and his wife took their first trip from Los Angeles to the spring training grounds of the then Brooklyn Dodgers to Daytona Beach, Florida, a town in the deepest recesses of the Jim Crow South, did Robinson for the first time experience the unvarnished venom of racial hostility.[37]

However, as Gregory Kaliss reminds the readers of this collection in his contribution, in spite of his multitude of opportunities to compete on the playing fields of Los Angeles, Robinson routinely felt the sting of racism in the supposedly more enlightened climate of Southern California, as did his older brother, Matthew "Mack" Robinson. Kaliss rescues from obscurity the important narrative of the lesser-known Robinson brother, a world-class athlete himself who earned a 200-meter silver medal in the 1936 Berlin Olympics behind Jesse Owens, and pairs Mack Robinson's narrative of perseverance in the face of decades of persistent racism in Southern California with the more celebrated tale of Jackie's triumphal rending of the color line in baseball that helped to spark the modern civil rights movement.[38] Los Angeles emerges in Kaliss's and Alvarez's accounts as less than the racial paradise that it often posed as, and more the conflicted and divided city that Newman captured in "I Love LA."

In spite of those ethnic and racial divisions and the myriad other social conflicts that rent Los Angeles and, indeed, sometimes because of them, the city has produced two iconic chroniclers of the Southern California sports scene who have sometimes united the local masses across ethnic, class, and even generational gaps and at other times illuminated the fractures that divided the metropolis. Jim Murray, the legendary columnist and correspondent for Los Angeles dailies and national magazines, arrived in the city from the East Coast in the midst of the boom times of the Second World War and spent the next five decades exploring the transformation of the city into a "sports mecca," as Ted Geltner in his essay for the collection aptly labels both the place and the era.[39] Murray, like Randy Newman, always sensed trouble lurking in paradise. He challenged local and national racial and sporting sensibilities, championed civil rights causes and decried pugilism as an unconscionable vice that brutalized the participants in the ring to sate the bloodlust of the masses.[40] Like Murray, Vin Scully, the legendary radio and television voice for the Dodgers, migrated from the East Coast to Los Angeles. Indeed, Scully began his career with the Dodgers in 1950, when they still resided in Brooklyn. He migrated with the team to their new home in 1958, and altogether in Brooklyn and then Los Angles spent sixty-seven years broadcasting Dodger baseball. Unlike Murray, Scully tended to soothe social fissures rather than shining a light into the dark underbelly of the Southern California wonderland. Still, he provided a remarkable symbol of continuity to a notoriously transitory and ephemeral city, linking together generations of Angelenos, newcomers and old-timers alike, as Elliott Gorn and Allison Lauterbach Dale reveal in their treatise on Scully in this volume.[41]

Other elements of the sport history of Los Angeles reveal more trouble in paradise and illuminate the fragility of communal bonds in the city. While Los Angeles is the only American city to host two Olympics, it is also the only American city to lose two of its franchises in what for the past half century has been the dominant national pastime in the United States, professional football. In 1995, the Los Angeles Rams and the Los Angeles Raiders both fled the city, in large part due to their failure to get public funding for refurbishing their homes in the old Olympic venue, the Los Angeles Coliseum, or securing guarantees for public financing on new stadium sites. The Rams had been in Los Angeles since 1946 when city boosters purloined the team from its original home in Cleveland, while the Raiders had relocated from Oakland to Los Angeles in 1982. In the hardball world of professional sports economics, Los Angeles has hardly been a paradise for local fans or entrepreneurs seeking riches in the booming goldfields of professional football. Professional football teams, as Raymond Schmidt divulges in his contribution to this collection, have come and gone more frequently in Los Angeles than most fans remember.[42]

When it comes to *fútbol*, the version of football Americans call soccer and the rest of the world adores, Los Angeles has been a much more beneficent climate. While other cities, St. Louis and Philadelphia in particular, claim a longer soccer lineage, Los Angeles has been since the mid-twentieth century the most fertile American soil for the growing importance of *fútbol* in US culture. In 1994, the Rose Bowl staged the final in which Brazil beat Italy on penalty kicks in the only World Cup held in the United States. In 1999, the Rose Bowl housed another iconic soccer moment that ended with Brandi Chastain stripping off her jersey to warm the hearts of sports bra manufacturers everywhere following her winning goal in the penalty kick shoot-out in front of the largest crowd in American history to witness a women's sporting event as the United States beat China in the women's World Cup final.[43]

Fútbol has flourished in Los Angeles in part because Latin American immigration has made the city a haven for Latinos and Latinas. Since the mid-twentieth century Latinas/Latinos have become the largest ethnic group in greater Los Angeles. Migrants from Mexico, Central America, and South America have brought their Latin American soccer cultures with them, fusing their passion for *fútbol* with a strong native interest in the game to make the city into a soccer hotbed. When the US national team meets "El Tri," the Mexican national side, in "friendlies" or in the more hostile conditions of World Cup qualifiers, stadiums in Los Angeles fill to overflowing and Mexican partisans sometimes outnumber US partisans. So deep is the Mexican fan base in Los Angeles that for a decade from 2005 to 2014, Chivas, a powerful Mexican soccer club from Guadalajara, opened a Los Angeles branch in the US-based MSL.[44]

Soccer in Los Angeles, however, has evolved from more than just Latin American roots. White fans flock to games to see global stars such as David Beckham, the premier English player of the early twenty-first century who spent his twilight years playing for the Los Angeles Galaxy and cultivating his celebrity as well as facilitating his wife's brand, the British pop-star Victoria Beckham ("Posh Spice" of the Spice Girls), in the entertainment capital of the world. European clubs regularly tour and train in Los Angeles. The city has a huge contingent of white players and a long history of cultivating the sport among the Anglo middle classes. The American Youth Soccer Organization, a leader in the mid-twentieth-century mainstreaming of the game, was founded in 1964 in Los Angeles.[45] The city's ethnic, class, and social frictions frequently emerge in the collisions between soccer and *fútbol*, as Jennifer Doyle demonstrates in her keenly observed reminiscences of pick-up and recreation-league games for this collection.[46]

Newman's "I Love LA" video did not capture any images of local soccer but it did pay homage to the ubiquity of cars and beaches in the sporting life of Los Angeles. Newman's song and video highlight the significance of the automobile in the history and culture of Los Angeles. "Rollin' down the Imperial Highway," Newman croons, "With a big nasty redhead at my side." He feels the "Santa Ana winds blowin' hot from the north," and declares, "we was born to ride." Cruising in his car becomes the ultimate symbol of freedom in Newman's LA anthem. In his contribution of this volume, Jeremy Kinney recovers the surprisingly lost history of auto racing in the region. Though Indianapolis or Daytona Beach come more quickly to mind when fans ponder the power of race cars in American life, no city has had a more profound impact on the history of the automobile than Los Angeles.[47] Angelenos were born to ride—and to race, as Kinney reveals in his essay for this anthology.[48]

Newman's evocation of the unique climate and geography of Los Angeles inspire other sporting motifs in his video montage of the song. New York City and Chicago are routinely frosty and frigid, not exactly places for year-round cruising in a convertible or regular trips to the beach. The paradisical landscapes of the Pacific strand have long been iconographic sites for selling the Los Angeles dream to the rest of the world, as well as important sporting habitats that give Los Angeles its own unique niche in the American landscape. The seashores of greater Southern California have given the world beach volleyball and triathlon. Those famous coastlines also serve as the epicenter of the American surfing scene—a recreation that Los Angeles cannot claim to have invented but which the region can argue that it transformed into a global industry that has had a tremendous influence on everything from fashion to linguistics. Tolga Ozyurtcu's essay for this collection provides insights into the history of surfing in Los Angeles, a sporting culture that has perhaps most deeply indulged in the mythology of the city as a paradise.[49]

Newman's "I Love LA" video bursts with depictions of beautiful young surfers playing on the beaches, and also with the corps of bodybuilders who have made the Pacific shores into their alfresco theaters. American weightlifting and muscle shaping might have first emerged in less edenic climes, such as York, Pennsylvania,[50] but as Jan Todd's meditation for this volume chronicles, multitudes of Americans for whom the cultivation of the body was the highest priority soon deserted harsher climates for the sun-kissed sands of "Muscle Beach." At the Santa Monica location that served as the original "Muscle Beach" and at a myriad of locations around greater Los Angeles, including indoor palaces such as Gold's Gym, they sculpted their bodies and made the city into the capital of producing beautiful exteriors.[51]

Of course, Los Angeles is home to huge enterprises that require beautiful human exteriors—the motion picture and television industries. Weightlifters and bodybuilders who trained in the city not only dominated international competition circuits but crossed over into the entertainment markets. The original Muscle Beach and its countless offspring in Los Angeles trained and tuned bodies to appear in front of the cameras. A few devotees even made the leap from bodybuilding to Hollywood stardom, most famously Arnold Schwarzenegger, who was born in Austria but had his major breakthroughs when he relocated to Los Angeles.[52]

While beaches and buff bodies immediately summon visions of Los Angeles, figure skating rarely conjures up images of Southern California. Indeed, skating would seem better suited to the cities Randy Newman disparages in "I Love LA," "cold" and "damp" New York or the Chicago he suggests be left to the "Eskimos." Surprisingly, in spite of its balmy climate, Los Angeles has become a major center for ice skating, as Susan Brownell documents in her essay in this volume.[53] As she notes, the entertainment industry has played a major role drawing ice skaters to Los Angeles, serving as a staging ground for at least a century of ice shows and as early as the 1930s drawing skating ingénues such as Sonja Henie with the prospect of Hollywood stardom. Ice skaters have, like Henie, relocated to Los Angeles in the quest to garner world-class coaches and training opportunities as well as to chase stardom.[54] The city has also produced homegrown champions including Olympic silver medalists Michelle Kwan and Linda Fratianne.[55]

The unexpected history of ice skating in Los Angeles reveals a crucial reality about the city's sporting scene. More than any other metropolis in the United States, sport, celebrity, and the entertainment industries comingle and combine in Los Angeles. Figure skaters leap from Olympic ranks onto silver screens and bodybuilders with thick European accents can become Hollywood action heroes. One of the greatest American football players of all-time, Jim Brown, abandoned his athletic career while still in his prime for a series of mediocre film roles.[56] A mediocre football player named Marion Morrison, who was born in Iowa and grew up in Southern California, lost his spot on the mighty USC Trojans roster after he broke his collarbone at a Los Angeles beach in a body-surfing accident, then quickly abandoned football, changed his name to John Wayne, and became one of the biggest superstars in the history of American cinema.[57]

Celluloid storytelling and sporting lore mix regularly in Los Angeles. In his contribution to this anthology Scott Brooks chronicles the rise and cultural cachet of the "Showtime" Los Angeles Lakers that developed in the late 1970s and dominated the National Basketball Association with their star-studded teams and their collection of starlets and stars who had to sit courtside at their games. From "A" list movie stars such as Jack Nicholson to "B" list staples such as Arsenio Hall, the Hollywood glitterati turned out to watch players who themselves were stars of such a magnitude that the public know them by a single moniker, from the era of "Magic" and "Kareem" to the epoch of "Shaq" and "Kobe."[58]

Hollywood's moviemakers have long been fascinated with sport. The sports film genre dates all the way back to the late nineteenth century when British and American filmmakers first turned to the world of sport for subject matter and directed their cameras to record prizefights and cricket matches, baseball games and football contests.[59] In the early twentieth century as American filmmakers began to congregate in the Los Angeles area, Hollywood began to make sport films. Among the first was *The Champion*, a pugilistic comedy starring Charlie Chaplin that hit American theaters in 1915, shortly after the studio that produced the film moved from Chicago to Southern California.[60] Since then, as Dan Nathan chronicles in his essay on Hollywood and sport, Los Angeles studios have made hundreds of sport movies.[61] Some of these movies have been great, like *Eight Men Out* (1988). Others have been good, like *Tin Cup* (1996). Some have been bad, like *The Mighty Ducks* (not only the 1992 original but also all of the sequels). Some have been just plain ugly, like *Kingpin* (1996).[62] Some have even fantastically transformed the Rams—in their Los Angeles not their St. Louis incarnation—into Super Bowl champions, like *Heaven Can Wait* (1978), a cinematic trick that has yet to be performed in mere real life.[63]

"I love Los Angeles," the comedian Billy Connolly once remarked. "It reinvents itself every two days."[64] Reinvention might in fact be what Los Angeles is best at and what sport most contributes to the cultural fabric of the city. The Rams appear and disappear—and then reappear again. The Olympics come and create an ephemeral sense of community and then depart, a magical zephyr that lasts for only a fortnight every half century. Skaters thrive in a city where the temperature rarely falls below the mark necessary to turn liquid water into solid ice. Most celebrities come and go, but a few seem to endure forever, like Vin Scully. Hollywood and Burbank's dream factories produce multitudes of trends and fads and occasional cultural touchstones. "I love LA," Randy Newman warbles. "We love LA," his fellow Angelenos warble back—at least in the music videos that promoted the song.[65]

The unofficial anthem of the city and its sporting culture represent this defining penchant for reinvention. Newman initially intended it to skewer the vacuous smugness that cloaked his city like a pesky smog. While some musicologists have incorrectly inferred that Los Angeles organizers asked Newman to write a theme song for the 1984 Olympics, his quirky canticle did serve as the unofficial soundtrack for the Olympian spectacle when a blossoming American corporation with global ambitions used the tune in its scheme for pirating Olympic glory away from the International Olympic Committee's (IOC) official corporate sponsors.[66] Nike, the global shoe giant, repurposed "I Love LA" as the centerpiece for its 1984 Olympic marketing campaign. Nike had lost the competition to become the "official" cobbler of LA84—the shorthand nickname of the second Los Angeles Games, when it balked at the $4 million price that rival Converse paid to the IOC for that privilege. A cabal of clever Nike marketers then huddled with the advertising geniuses at Chiat/Day, the Los Angeles firm that a few months before the 1984 Olympics made Apple's iconic "1984" commercial for the Super Bowl, an advertisement that the industry's experts unanimously concur revolutionized the medium. For roughly $100,000 Chiat/Day's virtuosos produced what advertising experts consider the first "ambush" commercial in history, an innovation still celebrated in case studies at American business schools. Nike hijacked the Olympics away from official sponsor Converse and put LA84 into the service of its own "Swoosh"-marked products.[67]

The Nike spot, played incessantly throughout the Olympics, begins with Randy Newman at the wheel of his big red Buick Super Convertible, the "nasty redhead" back at his side, tooling through the same classic Southern California scenes his song and video had originally evoked. Surfers stroll into epic waves; palm-fringed boulevards roll by; neon signs flash from the same familiar buildings that inhabit thousands of movies and television shows; roller skaters preen along the trails at Venice beach; high-end sports cars flash by. The ad celebrates the city's racial and ethnic diversity without a hint of the divisions beneath the veneer of paradise. Low riders prance; African Americans dance; white biker gangs pose; and the LAPD pulls over not some scary gangbanger but Gary Shandling, a white, Jewish comedian who made a career lampooning mainstream, middle-class, middle-aged angst.[68]

Sporting celebrities appear prominently in Nike's "I Love LA" spot. A Dodger resplendent in blue and white, smiles before adoring crowds; a clutch of Raiders (then in Los Angeles) posture in the back of a convertible; a cabal of body sculptors wave to the cameras at one of Muscle Beach's many progeny; Moses Malone plays basketball with joyous children at an outdoor playground; beautiful California girls jog along pristine beaches. To aid in the campaign Nike erected massive billboards that rose for many stories on the sides of Los Angeles buildings that featured Nike's talented pool of sponsored athletes. Newman and his red-headed friend drive by a giant billboard of Bo Jackson, the Raiders football star as well as a major league baseball phenom whom Nike featured in multiple campaigns during the 1980s. Nike had also wisely signed several American Olympic favorites. Carl Lewis, who would match Jesse Owens legendary feats from the 1936 Olympics in Berlin and win four gold medals in the 100 meters, 200 meters, 4x100 meters relay, and long jump at Los Angeles, practices for the long jump among a bevy of bikini-clad distractions on one of the city's sparkling beaches. Mary Decker, a gold-medal favorite who instead found heartbreak in a Los Angeles Olympic collision in the 3000 meters with Zola Budd, appeared in a much happier moment in the Nike commercial, flying gracefully down a Los Angeles street in front of a ten-story poster of herself.[69]

Throughout the commercial, "I Love LA" provides a soundtrack for the Nike promotion, the perfect background tune for summoning the spirit of Los Angeles sport and culture. "I love LA," Newman shouts. "We love it," the surfers and Raiders, bodybuilders and Dodgers, joggers and posers, Lewis and Decker, shout back.[70] Who could resist Newman's siren call, even with his sarcasm about his native city's unbridled hedonism so explicitly foregrounded? Certainly not the team of authors who will guide you throughout the rest of this anthology on an illuminating journey through the sporting life of Los Angeles.

CHAPTER ONE

The Life Cycles of Sports Venues in Los Angeles
Sports and Local Economic Development

GREG ANDRANOVICH AND MATTHEW J. BURBANK

Introduction

After nearly every Super Bowl, rumors begin to circulate in the media of teams moving and new cities getting National Football League (NFL) franchises. Los Angeles, a city without a professional football team since the Raiders moved back to Oakland in 1995, is seemingly always part of the rumor mill. The rumors in 2015 seemed more plausible than in past years because there were three teams that potentially could move to LA. These teams would leave their home cities of St. Louis, San Diego, and Oakland, in part, because the owners want newer NFL stadiums that would enhance profitability. The sale of the Los Angeles Clippers National Basketball Association (NBA) franchise in 2014 for $2 billion and the Los Angeles Dodgers in Major League Baseball (MLB) in 2012 for $2 billion enhanced the prospective value of locating professional sports franchises in LA. For city leaders, sports franchises are tied to the image of being a major league city. The costs of developing a new NFL-quality stadium, however, are substantial, with the price estimated to be nearly $2 billion in 2015. Although cities are finding it more difficult politically to underwrite the costs of building sports venues, Los Angeles has two existing stadium proposals, one in downtown LA and another in the City of Industry, and three new ones on the drawing boards, one in Inglewood, one in Carson, and a third in downtown LA for the city's newest Major League Soccer (MLS) team.

Sports plays an important role in LA's development and restructuring into a global city. There are twenty-four arenas, twenty-eight stadiums, and eighteen specialized facilities across the Los Angeles region and these venues generated an estimated $4.1 billion in regional economic impact.[1] While these sports facilities represent the apex of sports infrastructure in the region, they also recall an impressive palimpsest of public and private facilities, and quotidian, collegiate, and professional sports that goes back to LA's earliest days, reflecting and influencing not only changing societal values and mores, but also the spatial practices that underpin the city's economy and its politics.[2] For example, Agricultural Park was just beyond the city limits of Los Angeles in the 1870s and was used for horse, bicycle, and automobile racing. The park was also used for animal fighting and was a center for vice and prostitution. As the area surrounding the park developed and a university opened across the street, residents demanded an end to these activities. The state of California acquired the land in 1908 and reopened it as Exposition Park in 1913.[3] The national pastime, baseball, has a long history in Los Angeles. Professional baseball teams began to use LA for winter practice in 1886, and minor league baseball was popular for many years in venues such as Gilmore Field (and adjacent Gilmore Stadium) and Wrigley Park, home fields for the city rivalry between the Hollywood Stars and the Los Angeles Angels of the Pacific Coast League. When the Brooklyn Dodgers owner bought Wrigley Field and the Angels and their territorial rights, Wrigley Field was swapped for land in Chavez Ravine to build a major league stadium.[4] The opening of LA's Dodger Stadium in 1962 effectively ended the reign of minor league baseball in the city. Other notable venues that have closed include Ascot Park in 1990, which was known for auto racing and called the "busiest dirt track in America for 33 years"; the Olympic Auditorium, which was home to numerous boxing matches but repurposed as a church in 2005; and the Hollywood Park horse track in 2013.[5] These venues illustrate Los Angeles as a sports mecca, showing off the best sports talent of the times across a variety of sports in a style that spectators flocked to see while paving the way for contemporary sports development. Many of LA's top sports venues have played important roles in the city's development.

Santa Anita Park remains a top sports venue in thoroughbred racing, but it also once was used as a staging area for Japanese Americans being transported to internment camps during World War II.[6] Other important Los Angeles sports venues include Pauley Pavilion, home of the UCLA college basketball dynasty during the 1960s and 1970s but also a place where world leaders gathered, and more recently the StubHub Center, home of the MLS LA Galaxy and a site for international soccer matches.[7] Finally, the Staples Center anchors a downtown sports and entertainment district where professional basketball and ice hockey are played and top entertainment acts perform. The district includes theaters, a museum, residences, and a luxury hotel.[8] In his assessment of using sports and culture as tools for economic development, Rosentraub notes that decisions on where to place infrastructure should be made strategically in that attracting attention to a particular place via spectator sports and cultural activities can leverage future economic and community development opportunities.[9] These opportunities do not exist outside of the place where the sports venue is located and, as a strategic policy decision, sports venue location becomes a contested process potentially pitting various sports boosters, business boosters, local government officials, and community members against one another over the meaning of place and the use of public money in supporting one vision of the city over others.

This chapter examines the concept of a sports venue from the standpoint of civic infrastructure. Our interests are in what sports tells us about the relationship between people and their government. Civic infrastructure refers to those projects that are publicly funded for public purposes and are central to urban economic development policy making. We examine the politics of civic infrastructure in the context of Los Angeles. We use "Los Angeles" broadly to reflect the regional identity in the metropolitan area, even though a number of the stadiums that exist or are being proposed are outside of Los Angeles proper. First, we briefly examine the history of public investment in civic infrastructure. Then, we provide an overview of the histories of two iconic sports venues: the Los Angeles Memorial Coliseum and the Rose Bowl in Pasadena. The choice of these venues reflects an important public policy question addressed in the concluding section: whose interests should large-scale public investment support?

Life Cycles of Public Infrastructure

Nearly all cities in the United States want sustained economic growth, but city governments are not in a position to control whether or not economic growth occurs. What city governments can try to do, however, is to provide the infrastructure such as transportation, communication, housing, education, utilities, and recreation to enable and encourage economic growth. Public investment in infrastructure, then, is a central component of urban economic development policy making. But infrastructure is not a monolithic category for making policy choices, the politics of infrastructure policy making are not uniform, and the politics change over time following changes in the purpose of the infrastructure. We provide a brief overview of these characteristics to illustrate the different roles local governments have taken in infrastructure policy making especially as it relates to sports venues. Sports venues are today a widely used feature in urban economic development policy making, but sports in the United States are organized differently from sports in most other nations. A key differentiating factor is that sports are more like cartels in the United States, with team owners assuming a key role in determining the rules of the business of sports.[10] For local governments this feature of American sports can be problematic. The pattern of activity in sports venue development, however, is similar to that of public infrastructure more generally, featuring decisions around an initial investment, renewal costs, operations costs, and maintenance costs; sports venues have become an important component of city building projects in the current era of global economic restructuring.

Altshuler and Luberoff identify four eras of the production of public infrastructure by purpose, level of government, and impacts.[11] The first era, prior to 1950, began with the canals and railroads that built the nation, but in terms of urban outcomes the late 1800s were characterized by large private investments underwritten by the urban political machines that saw political opportunities in blending profit making with patronage. For the political machines, politics was seen as another form of business activity and political coalitions were formed for practical convenience.[12] During the Progressive Era, these large projects were a focus for change. The two city-level officials who had the greatest impact on infrastructure development—the city engineer and the comptroller—were generally outside of the machine dynamics.[13] Fogelson describes the changes in transportation and water delivery that occurred during the Progressive Era reforms undertaken in Los Angeles as shifting power and authority from private providers toward the public sector, with municipal, county, and state agencies all benefiting.[14] For example, railway companies yielded power to highway departments and control of water passed from small corporations to municipal boards and regional water districts. In part, these institutional changes stemmed from the new progressive reforms that gave local governments chartering authority.[15] Under this new authority, LA's two largest port cities—Los Angeles and Long Beach—created semiautonomous proprietary harbor departments, modeled on the successes of the LA's Department of

The Sports Arena was demolished in 2016 to create space for a new stadium to host Los Angeles Football Club of Major League Soccer. Photo courtesy of LA84 Foundation.

Water and Power, to spearhead the development of the ports and later airports. These projects were catalytic in LA's transformation into a metropolis.[16] As a prelude of things to come, in 1919 publicity-seeking boosters also wanted to have a landmark stadium in Los Angeles to rival Yankee Stadium, and this led to the construction of the Los Angeles Memorial Coliseum.[17] At the time, most investments in sports facilities were privately financed.[18]

The second era, the "great mega-project era," started after World War II and lasted into the late 1960s. This era saw massive infrastructure investments by the federal government that remade many large American cities by building roadways out to new suburban housing and clearing land for office construction and amenities.[19] Eisinger notes that this was the beginning of major investments in a tourism infrastructure, indicating a new pattern of investment and urban restructuring—away from the interests of local residents in favor of visitors and investors.[20] During this time, public support for the construction of venues for professional sports franchises grew rapidly starting in 1953 with the relocation of baseball's Boston Braves to Milwaukee, the first such move since 1903.²¹ Following that move, Baltimore, Kansas City, and Minneapolis built publicly funded stadiums. At the end of the 1950s, the Giants and Dodgers baseball teams moved from New York to California. Dodger Stadium in Los Angeles, which opened in 1962, was privately funded on publicly provided land that, due to the shift in sentiment regarding public housing and the success of a Community Redevelopment Agency lawsuit to prevent redevelopment, displaced the residents of the poor Chicano Chavez Ravine neighborhood and gave the land to the Dodgers free of charge.²² The Los Angeles Sports Arena was built with public money in 1959 to lure the NBA Minneapolis Lakers to Los Angeles in 1960.²³ These venues were built in urban locations that often resulted in residents of poor neighborhoods being displaced in favor of building tourism and leisure infrastructure.

The third era of infrastructure projects was a period of transition from the mid-1960s to the early 1970s. The successes of civil rights and environmental movements at the national level and the shock of widespread urban riots in 1965–1968 led to the adoption of new federal laws that changed the legal standing of citizen and community groups that ultimately changed the politics of large-scale infrastructure development.²⁴ In Los Angeles, this shift was reflected in the election of Tom Bradley as mayor. The Bradley electoral coalition grew from the neighborhoods, but Bradley's agenda of reshaping LA into a global city saw business interests, especially downtown developers, become increasingly important in policy making.²⁵ This period coincided with the beginning of locally felt impacts of global economic restructuring, and the zenith of this transformation was the hosting of the 1984 Olympics with limited new infrastructural expenditures by the city of Los Angeles.²⁶

In the fourth and present era of infrastructure development, cities have sought new investment strategies that are less controversial and less disruptive to neighborhoods.²⁷ In this period, amenities have become more important with public investments in rail rapid transit, festival retail markets, convention centers, sports facilities, and airport terminals becoming ubiquitous. Except for rapid transit, these investments no longer required or utilized federal support. Altshuler and Luberoff note that there are key differences between infrastructure projects in this period, which they call the era of "do no harm," compared to those in earlier periods.²⁸ Among these key differences are location (nonresidential and relatively compact locations preferred), urban design (low rise to entice the public), and the use of public-private partnerships. Santo's analysis of cities' investments in sports divides this era into "subsidies writ large"

(1960–1989) followed by "escalation and extravagance" (1990–present).[29] The major professional sports leagues expanded during this period and some of the older privately financed stadiums were replaced using public financing. Some stadiums were moved into suburban locations following the fan base that had moved out of central cities much earlier. The need for massive parking lots and the trend toward multiuse venues meant that costs increase as the footprint of the facility was larger to accommodate different uses. In the period since the 1990s, governments spent "over $15 billion on sports facilities, up from a total public expenditure of $11 billion in the previous 30-year era."[30] The newest venues are back to being single sport facilities and most are replacements for stadiums built in the 1960s and 1970s. Thus, "the median age of facilities in use dropped from 21 years in 1989 to 13 years in 2009."[31] These changes have occurred in parallel with the rise of sports-as-entertainment, where the value of a sports franchise is unbundled into the many revenue-generating components, with television broadcasting, parking, and concessions now figuring into the price of entertainment and requiring additional components that increase complexity and cost.

It is in this broader context of global economic restructuring that we use the term civic infrastructure to differentiate the sports facilities today from those of the past. As a serious component of urban redevelopment and regeneration to enhance a city's competitive position, sports plays a role in cementing certain investment trajectories that critics argue tend to rebuild cities in the interests of visitors not residents, and sports team owners not the public.[32] When publicly financed facilities end up supporting private interests, it raises important questions about urban outcomes and about democracy in urban America.

LA Memorial Coliseum

The Los Angeles Memorial Coliseum is located in the University Park community of the city of Los Angeles. The stadium features an iconic colonnaded or peristyle eastern entrance marked by the Olympic torch, the Olympic rings, and two bronze headless nude statues of male and female Olympians that were added prior to the 1984 Olympics. The field runs east to west and features a press box on the south side of the stadium. The Coliseum has served as the Olympic stadium for both the 1932 and 1984 Olympics, the host stadium for the 1967 and 1973 Super Bowls, and was home field for the Los Angeles Dodgers during the 1959 World Series with the Chicago White Sox.

The Coliseum has served as the home stadium for several professional sports teams including the NFL Rams (1946–1979), the NFL Raiders (1982–1994), and the MLB Dodgers (1958–1961).[33] The Coliseum is perhaps best known as the home field for two well-known college football programs, the University of California, Los Angeles (UCLA, from 1933 to 1981) and the University of Southern California (USC, from 1921 to present). The Coliseum has hosted a variety of other sports, including international soccer matches, motocross, and even ski jumping.[34] The Coliseum also has been used as the site for a number of important occasions in US popular history including the acceptance speech for the Democratic nomination for president by John Kennedy in 1960, evangelist preacher Billy Graham drawing a record crowd of over 134,000 people in 1963, the Wattstax Music Festival in 1972, the 1976 Bicentennial Spectacular, a papal mass conducted by Pope John Paul II in 1987, and a public celebration for Nelson Mandela after his release from prison in South Africa in 1990. The Rolling Stones, The Who, U2, Bruce Springsteen, and the Grateful Dead have all performed in concert at the Coliseum. Just before the opening ceremonies for the 1984 summer Olympics, the Coliseum was declared a National Historic Landmark.[35]

The stadium was originally conceived as a memorial to veterans of the First World War from Los Angeles and as part of a plan to attract the Olympics Games to the city.[36] Ground was broken for the facility in 1921 and the completed Coliseum hosted its first competition, a USC football game, in November 1923.[37] The stadium cost $2.5 million ($34.8 million in 2015 dollars) to build and was financed by a Community Development Association (CDA) under an agreement with the city and county of Los Angeles that provided the city, county, and the CDA equal access to the facility with the city and county to assume full ownership of the stadium over a period of years.[38] The Coliseum originally seated about seventy-four thousand people. In 1930, the stadium was expanded for the upcoming 1932 Olympics to a capacity of just over one hundred one thousand people and the torch was added to the east entrance. The expansion cost $950,000 ($13.5 million in 2015 dollars).[39]

The Coliseum and Sports Arena are jointly owned by the city and county of Los Angeles and state of California. Currently, operations are managed by USC under a long-term lease with the public agency that oversees the facilities, the Los Angeles Memorial Coliseum Commission. The Coliseum Commission was established in 1945 as a Joint Powers Authority and has nine members. Three members are appointed by the governor, three members by the LA County Board of Supervisors, and three members by the mayor of Los Angeles.[40] The Coliseum and Sports Arena are situated on land owned by the state in Exposition Park and administered by the board of the nearby California Science Center, just south of the main campus of USC.[41] For many years, the Coliseum and Sports Arena were operated directly by the Coliseum Commission, which hired professional staff to manage both facilities. In July 2013, however, the commission modified its existing lease arrangement so that USC would take over the day-to-day operation of both facilities. The terms of the new lease arrangement require USC to pay an annual rent of $1 million, which increased to $1.6 million in 2016 and is adjusted for inflation thereafter. USC agreed to pay for improvements to the Coliseum, estimated to cost between $70 and $100 million, in return for keeping all the ticket and concession revenues from USC football games as well as other events held in the Coliseum or Sports Arena. USC can sell the naming rights to the Coliseum, estimated to be worth $4–6 million a year, and keep 95 percent of those revenues while paying the state 5 percent. The lease deal specifies that if USC's management of the stadium becomes more profitable over time, the state will get a small share of those profits.[42]

For USC, maintaining the competitiveness of its position as a college football power nationally means having quality facilities available. The Coliseum's last major renovations were in 1993, when the running track was removed and seats were added to bring fans closer to the field, and locker rooms and public restrooms were updated. Following the 1994 Northridge earthquake, the stadium was repaired and retrofitted at a cost of $93 million and in 1995 a $6 million press box was constructed. Beginning in 2008, USC's renovations have included replacing the field turf and upgrading the drainage, replacing the main video board, enhancing the sound system, adding sixteen hundred seats, and upgrading concession services and adding two new clubs for fans.[43]

The difficulties and costs of updating a 1920s-era stadium to meet the demands of contemporary college football programs has led to some unhappiness even among loyal USC supporters. Then-USC athletic director Pat Haden visited twenty college and NFL stadiums to see what others were doing and then USC hired an architectural firm to provide additional ideas. USC surveyed the public and donors beginning in 2013, but the survey generated controversy because many took it as a marketing device. Haden addressed this controversy by noting that, in addition to basic maintenance and new amenities, one of the reasons for updating the Coliseum was to provide "long term revenue generation" that might, or might not, rely on the use of personal seat licenses.[44] Still, this controversy served to highlight the pressures that even a highly successful football program such as USC feels as it attempts to compete with other programs in its conference and with national rivals such as Notre Dame.

Critics of the new lease deal have indicated that it is overly generous to the interests of USC and have charged that the terms were essentially negotiated in private between members of the Coliseum Commission and university officials without regard for the public interest.[45] The new lease deal, however, came about after a scandal involving the management of the Coliseum during a time when both the Coliseum and the Sports Arena were facing serious financial problems. The origins of the scandal begin in 2010 after a fifteen-year-old girl died of a drug overdose while attending a rave held at the Coliseum promoted by a local company. The *Los Angeles Times* began an investigation that led to a series of reports of financial irregularities in 2010 and 2011. These stories prompted a criminal investigation that resulted in charges against the former general manager of the Coliseum and Sports Arena, the former events manager, and the former technology manager, as well as a Coliseum contractor and the chief executives of two local firms that regularly held events at the facilities. In essence, the general manager of the Coliseum, Patrick Lynch, was charged with allowing the events manager, Todd DeStefano, to work for the two companies promoting raves at the Sports Arena and Coliseum while also serving as the government official overseeing how these companies used the facilities. Lynch and DeStefano were charged with accepting bribes from company officials, conflicts of interest, and making unrecorded cash payments to union officials. An audit conducted by the city of Los Angeles found such dysfunction in the management of the Coliseum and Sports Authority that the operation was "void of essential formal policies, procedures, and protocols."[46]

As a result of the scandal and poor management of the facilities, the Coliseum Commission was unable to pay for upgrades to the stadium that it had promised to USC under their lease arrangement in 2011 and found itself in a greatly weakened financial position, leading to discussions to renegotiate the lease terms.[47] During this renegotiation, there were forty stakeholder meetings and four public meetings held over two years to discuss the new lease arrangement and its impact on the residents of University Park and other neighborhoods surrounding Exposition Park.[48] The commission sought to solve its problems by seeking a new long-term lease deal that essentially turned over the management of the Coliseum and Sports Arena to USC and let the university pay for the required improvements to the Coliseum. Part of the new lease, which went into effect in 2013, allowed USC to negotiate for the replacement of the Sports Arena.[49] In 2015, a deal was announced that would result in the demolition of the Sports Arena and the construction of a new outdoor soccer stadium to be the home field for a second Major League Soccer team in LA, the Los Angeles Football Club. The $250 million cost of constructing the new soccer-specific stadium, conference center, and soccer museum is to be privately financed, but the deal still requires the approval of the Coliseum Commission, the Los Angeles City Council, and LA's mayor.[50]

The Rose Bowl

The Rose Bowl is located north of Los Angeles in Pasadena. The stadium is situated in an area of Pasadena known as Arroyo Seco, which the stadium shares with the Brookside Golf Course. The south entrance to the stadium features the iconic scripted "Rose Bowl" name under a red rose. The stadium was originally designed as a horseshoe with an open south end that was later filled to create a complete bowl. The Rose Bowl is best known as the location and namesake of the first college football bowl game in 1900 and for the Tournament of Roses parade traditionally held on New Year's Day.[51]

The stadium serves as home field for the UCLA football team since the team moved from the LA Memorial Coliseum for the 1982 season. The Rose Bowl was also the home stadium for the MLS Los Angeles Galaxy from 1996 to 2002 when the team moved to a soccer-specific stadium, the StubHub Center, in Carson. The Rose Bowl has been the host stadium for five NFL Super Bowls (1977, 1980, 1983, 1987, and 1993), the men's World Cup soccer final in 1994, the women's World Cup soccer final in 1999, the gold medal soccer match in the 1984 summer Olympics, and the 2011 CONCACAF Gold Cup soccer match. The stadium served as a venue for competition in both the 1932 and the 1984 Olympic Games. The Rose Bowl also has been the venue for a number of concerts featuring performers such as the Rolling Stones, the Eagles, Guns N' Roses, U2, and One Direction. The stadium was designated as a National Historic Landmark in 1987.[52]

The permanent stadium for football was constructed in 1922 to replace temporary stands put up each year for the college football games held in

Tournament Park. The stadium was completed in 1923 and named "The Rose Bowl" at that time. The original horseshoe design had a seating capacity of fifty-seven thousand seats and cost $272,000 to build ($3.8 million in 2015 dollars). The open end of the stadium was filled in 1928, raising the seating capacity to seventy-six thousand seats.[53] The Rose Bowl stadium was built in the post–World War I period when a number of cities, including San Diego and Los Angeles, were constructing "huge outdoor sports facilities to encourage athletics and promote the reputation of their cities."[54] At the time, college football was becoming more popular and a number of colleges were building large stadiums.[55] Unlike college stadiums, however, the Rose Bowl was not built by a college nor did it serve as the home stadium for a college team. Instead, the stadium was built by the city of Pasadena as a place to host a yearly end-of-season college football game. In large part because of the popularity of the games hosted in the Rose Bowl, these games became collectively known as "bowl games."

The stadium has been expanded or reconfigured a number of times since the seating bowl was completed in 1928.[56] In 1931, the original wooden sections of the stadium were replaced with concrete and the seating expanded to accommodate 83,000 spectators. In 1949, the stadium was enlarged to 94,400 seats at a cost of $335,000 ($3.3 million in 2015 dollars). The first press box was added to the stadium in 1961. Improvements were made to the seating in 1982 for UCLA's home football games at the Rose Bowl and in preparation for the 1984 summer Olympics when the stadium would host soccer matches. In the 1980s, the stadium was retrofitted to improve resistance to earthquakes. In the 1990s, the media facilities were improved and luxury seating was added. The stadium underwent a $21.5 million renovation ($32.9 million in 2015 dollars) to the sound system, scoreboards, and restrooms as part of the deal to make the stadium home to the LA Galaxy in 1996. The stadium's locker rooms were renovated in 2006 at a cost of $43 million.[57]

The Rose Bowl stadium is owned by the city of Pasadena and for many years was operated directly by city employees. This arrangement proved to be workable because the stadium was primarily used to host the Rose Bowl game, which was run and organized by the Tournament of Roses Association. The Tournament of Roses Association was responsible for organizing the Tournament of Roses parade and the Rose Bowl game and was largely staffed by volunteers. While the stadium generally lost money, the professionally managed Brookside Golf Course usually made enough money to cover the costs of both facilities. After 1982 when the stadium became the home for the UCLA football team, there was increased pressure on the city employees who ran the stadium to book other events to provide a revenue stream to help pay for ongoing maintenance and improvements to the facilities demanded by these tenants and their fans.[58] After several management changes and declining revenues, the city created the Rose Bowl Operating Company (RBOC) in 1993.[59] The RBOC was intended to provide professional management of the stadium and golf course while also seeking to insulate operating decisions from city council politics. As a member of the Pasadena City Council, William Paparian, stated at the time: "It's not realistic to expect the City Council to manage the stadium and conduct a political referendum about every performer that comes."[60] The city council created the RBOC after a public debate over whether the city should sign a deal with a concert promoter to have two heavy metal bands, Guns N' Roses and Metallica, play the Rose Bowl. City officials wanted the concerts in order to bring in revenue, while some area residents complained about noise and traffic problems.[61]

The RBOC is a nonprofit corporation established by Pasadena with the mission of returning "economic and civic value to the City of Pasadena by managing a world-class stadium and a professional quality golf course complex in a community-based environment."[62] The RBOC board has thirteen members who are required to be residents of Pasadena. Seven of the members are nominated by a member of the city council to represent the seven council districts. One member of the city council also serves on the RBOC board. In addition, the mayor nominates one member of the board, and the city manager (or representative) serves on the board. One member of the board is nominated by each of the major tenants, UCLA and the Tournament of Roses, and there is one at-large board member.[63]

While the RBOC has improved the professional management of the stadium as a venue, the city council and mayor have had to balance use of the stadium with the concerns of people living in the Arroyo Seco. Area residents, particularly those close to the stadium, have complained to their elected officials about the number, size, and disruption associated with events. While city ordinance limits the number of events to twelve per year, the city council can approve additional events over that limit.[64] The RBOC has sought to use the upgraded facility more and regularly requests additional events that, in turn, are often opposed by area residents. Members of the city council, however, have been willing to approve additional events that are lucrative enough to help pay for the debt incurred by the past renovations and provide funds for future changes. The city council reevaluated its relationship with the RBOC after the financial problems that emerged during the 2011–2014 renovations of the stadium.[65] As part of a deal that included long-term lease extensions with both UCLA for its home football games and the Tournament of Roses for the Rose Bowl game, a major upgrade was approved by the Pasadena City Council in 2010 to replace the existing press box with a premium seating pavilion, improve entrances and exits, add public restrooms, expand the concessions area, and install a new video board.[66] The renovations were purposely done on an accelerated schedule so that construction would not disrupt the UCLA football season and to complete the luxury seating as soon as possible so that it could begin generating revenue. But, when the construction encountered problems resulting from the age of the stadium and previous renovations, the total cost of the project increased from $151 million to $195 million. The city council, RBOC, and UCLA agreed to scale back the renovations to reduce the cost to $181 million, but the city council still had to vote for an additional $30 million in bonds to pay the increased costs.[67] The additional debt led Fitch Ratings to downgrade Pasadena's credit rating.[68] These problems led the city council to review their arrangements with the RBOC and require more extensive reporting to city officials on financial matters.

Assessing the Life Cycle of a Sports Venue

Civic infrastructure is characterized here as large-scale taxpayer investments with a public purpose, and we argue that sports facilities should be considered with other civic infrastructure projects that enhance a city's competitiveness. Both the LA Memorial Coliseum and the Rose Bowl were built for the purpose of attracting attention to their home cities. That is, these venues were conceived and constructed to enhance the images of Los Angeles and Pasadena, respectively, with the hope of realizing economic gains in the future. Our review of the life cycles of these two stadiums illustrates the point that these long-term investments in civic infrastructure are not easily subject to a simple cost-benefit calculation because they have become a part of the promotional image of the city, its leaders, and its residents. Although in slightly different ways, these stadiums also illustrate the difficulties of public ownership and operation of these facilities as both the nature of sports facilities and the expectation for government activities have changed over the lives of these stadiums. Balancing demands raises two questions: Can these iconic sports venues be renovated and repurposed for the future? Should public investments help underwrite the costs of building private facilities?

Our analysis suggests that there are at least three dimensions in response to these questions. The first dimension concerns the economic and technical capacity for delivering the contemporary fan experience. As the entertainment value of spectator sports becomes increasingly important, the costs of investment for any venue whether new or repurposed go up. In large part this is due to the requirements for delivering the capacity for large-scale use of technologically mediated entertainment. For example, in 2011 only six NFL teams had Wi-Fi in their stadiums, but this number increased to twenty out of thirty-one stadiums in 2013.[69] In 2013, the NFL set new cellular and Wi-Fi standards for improving the fan experience while at an NFL venue. Even though most stadiums now have Wi-Fi, they need enough capacity to allow all the fifty thousand or more fans using different wireless services to upload, download, browse the Internet, and make phone calls from inside the venue. The goal is to permit the same connectivity a fan would enjoy at home. When stadiums are municipally owned and especially when there are other tenants, the costs and benefits of providing these additional services are more challenging.

The second dimension of analyzing the life cycle of sports venues raises the question: how do the politics of sports infrastructure policy making change over time? In their 1991 review of Rose Bowl financial operations, for example, the CPA firm of McGladrey & Pullen noted that twenty-two events annually were the breakeven point for the Rose Bowl, and double that number would be needed to provide funds for refurbishing and maintenance.[70] The analysis also noted that hosting mega-events such as the 1984 Olympics or Super Bowls resulted in spikes in revenues, but overall, the cost-volume-revenues relationship shifted in the late 1980s and costs increased faster than revenues being generated by venue activities.[71] In today's mobile sports entertainment environment, it is safe to say that the shift is continuing.

From the perspective of local governments, especially as owners of municipal stadiums, the facility must do no worse than break even on an annual basis, including the demands for maintenance. But if cities are to have the resources to update and refurbish their properties, they need to be able to generate additional revenues. The need for additional local government resources, however, often conflicts directly with the demands of tenants whether they are professional or university sports teams. For eight to twelve football games a year, this type of investment needs to be carefully considered. As has been the case in cities like San Diego and Oakland, whose NFL team owners want to move the teams to LA, the interests of the city (the public interest in infrastructure investment) may diverge substantially from the interests of franchise owners. In response to an NFL request to be a temporary host stadium in Los Angeles, the RBOC president, who also is a Pasadena City Council member, stated that the Rose Bowl was pursuing an annual Arroyo Seco Music and Arts Festival that was more in line "with Pasadena's brand and with the future of the stadium" and would not pursue temporarily being an NFL stadium.[72]

The third dimension of our analysis is consideration of the need to continue to examine the public purposes of civic infrastructure as these, too, change over time. Both the LA Memorial Coliseum and the Rose Bowl were built during a time when the priorities of many local governments in the region were to promote economic growth and attract attention to the opportunities in the West. These stadiums have been used to host image-building events such as Super Bowls, Olympic competitions, and concerts even as the surrounding communities have changed. Since the 1960s, the neighborhoods in and surrounding Exposition Park where the Coliseum and Sports Arena are located have fought for their community interests through university expansions, the 1984 Olympic Games, and the forces of gentrification. While there were some forty stakeholder meetings and four public meetings held over a two-year period to discuss the impact of USC managing the Coliseum on the neighborhoods around Exposition Park, these meetings had little impact on the terms of the new lease deal, which were determined almost entirely by the needs of the USC football program and desire of the LA Memorial Coliseum Commission to end the story of its financial mismanagement. The Arroyo Seco neighborhoods around the Rose Bowl have become more residential and many of these residents prefer peace and quiet. These generally well-off residents and their community associations have been vocal in expressing their concerns about how and how often the stadium is used. While these sorts of land-use conflicts may be expected during periods of infrastructure development, local governments must continue to attempt to balance the value of large-scale facilities to the public with interests of area residents who are most directly impacted by these periodic events.

The development of new sports facilities in Los Angeles is ongoing, and there will be continued demands for public resources to help finance new stadiums or to refurbish existing ones. While current city officials intuitively understand the appeal of landing a professional sports team or undertaking a big new project, the stories of the Rose Bowl and Memorial Coliseum should encourage city leaders and residents to think carefully before committing to such projects. As the brief recounting of the histories of these sports venues makes clear, large stadiums can have a long life cycle and the demands for public funding for renewal and operations will continue to be made as the role of sports, and sports venues, evolves alongside the local processes of urban restructuring.

CHAPTER TWO

On Los Chorizeros, the Classic, and El Tri

Sports and Community in Mexican Los Angeles

LUIS ALVAREZ

In September 2015 Barack Obama appointed legendary Los Angeles Dodgers pitcher Fernando Valenzuela as a presidential ambassador for citizenship and naturalization. The move was part of the White House's "Stand Stronger" campaign to assist eligible immigrants and refugees to become US citizens. Program supporters hoped Valenzuela would help inspire the nearly nine million lawful, permanent residents in the United States who qualified to consider naturalizing. In the team's official statement on Valenzeula's appointment, Dodgers president and CEO Stan Kasten congratulated him, recognized him as one of the greatest Dodger icons, and remembered that "Fernandomania was a special time in Los Angeles and all across Major League Baseball. He is a great American and will serve our country well as an ambassador."[1]

Valenzuela's appointment signaled his iconic status in the sporting history of Mexican Los Angeles.[2] Originally from Sonora, Mexico, Valenzuela was National League Rookie of the Year and Cy Young award winner as a twenty-year-old rookie in 1981. In that strike-shortened season, he led the Dodgers to World Series victory over the New York Yankees and sparked what came to be known as Fernandomania across the city and Major League Baseball. LA's most widely read Spanish-language newspaper, *La Opinión*, and the Dodgers Spanish-language radio voice, Jamie Jarrín, helped lead the charge in hailing Valenzuela a hero for all of Mexican LA. He was superstar pitcher, pop cultural sensation, and symbol of ethnic pride rolled into one.[3]

Valenzuela's appointment also recalled the longer history of sport in Mexican LA. When over a million Mexicans migrated to the United States during the Mexican Revolution between 1910 and 1920, sport emerged as an arena where new arrivals adapted to life north of the border. Athletics helped many immigrants and their US-born children forge an ethnic identity in the face of discriminatory conditions.[4] Success on the field or court helped dispel negative stereotypes of Mexicans as athletically and intellectually inferior.[5] Sport fostered community, ethnic pride, robust masculinities, working-class unity, and, at times, politicization beyond the game.[6] At the same time, sport fueled Americanization programs by local authorities, social control by employers with large numbers of Mexican workers who often played for company teams, and incorporation of Mexicans into US culture through the consumption of sport-related goods.[7] Sport, in other words, was a way for Mexicans to make sense of the city around them and the rest of the city to make sense of Mexicans.

In the largely favorable response to Valenzuela's ambassadorial appointment most observers failed to note that he had long lived in LA as a Mexican citizen. Despite having arrived in Los Angeles in 1980, Valenzuela did not become a US citizen until July 2015, a mere two months before being named ambassador. His naturalization followed that of his wife, Linda, also from Mexico, who naturalized earlier in 2015.[8] For nearly thirty-five years he remained a Mexican citizen, including through the entirety of his playing career, well into retirement, and after being hired as the color commentator for the Dodgers' Spanish-language radio broadcasts. For Valenzuela, his baseball career reflected neither a simple embrace of the United States or rejection of his Mexican roots, but revealed his multiple communities, attachments to place, and modes of belonging.

Following Valenzuela's lead, this chapter examines how Mexicans in Los Angeles built community and claimed belonging in the sports world.[9] I argue the history of sport in Mexican LA is less an example of community-based sports enthusiasts than sports-based community building. Sport was a site where boundaries of the civic polity were drawn and redrawn, and where people gave meaning to the places they lived. Whether athlete or spectator, professional or amateur, to borrow from historian Natalia Molina, Mexicans and Mexican Americans in sports were place-makers who established community "in ways that empower[ed] those who inhabit[ed] the surrounding area."[10] Their sporting history generated new and cemented existing intra-ethnic, multiracial, and transnational relationships. It showed how ordinary folk found common ground with others and stood their ground against powerful forces. At the same

Dodger pitcher Fernando Valenzuela signing autographs for fans. Photo courtesy of Los Angeles Dodgers. Photo Courtesy of Jon SooHoo/Dodgers.

time, sport helped envelope Mexican LA in the city's consumer markets, reinforced patriarchy and hypermasculinity, and, in some cases, was used to mark them as unworthy of full and equal citizenship. Ultimately, sport in Mexican LA is explained less by a binary between Americanization and ethnic pride, than a spectrum of reasons that explain why they mattered so deeply to so many. The rest of this chapter explores amateur baseball before the Dodgers, high school football in East LA, and the popularity of Mexico's national soccer team in the city. Far from a comprehensive history of sport in Mexican LA, what follows are three riffs on how the histories of Mexican Americans, sports, and Los Angeles may help explain one another.

Before the Dodgers

Long before Fernandomania took the city by storm, baseball helped stitch together the social fabric of Mexican Los Angeles. The sport's prominence in the city's barrios dated to the 1920s, when migrants fleeing the economic instability and political violence of the Mexican Revolution trekked north across the border and, by the hundreds of thousands, settled across the US Southwest.[11] The ethnic Mexican population in Los Angeles tripled during the 1920s and, by the eve of World War II, the number of American-born children of Mexican descent rose dramatically. Areas to the east of downtown, including close-knit neighborhoods like Boyle Heights, were home to much of this population growth. In the tradition of Mexican mutualistas, or mutual aid societies, baseball brought folks together and afforded them a forum to make sense of the world around them. In the face of economic catastrophe and repatriation campaigns during the Depression, xenophobia and the Zoot Suit Riots during the war years, and police violence and renewed deportation drives evidenced by the LAPD's so-called Bloody Christmas of 1951 and Operation Wetback in 1954, baseball mattered for social reasons as much as what happened on the diamond. As historian Jose Alamillo argued, Mexicans and Mexican Americans used baseball "to proclaim equality through athletic competition" and build community in the face of challenging economic and political conditions.[12]

In recent years, historians have shed light on the storied past of Mexican American baseball in Los Angeles by launching recovery efforts like the Baseball Reliquary–sponsored "Neighborhoods of Baseball" program on multiethnic baseball in LA and Latino Baseball History Project at Cal State San Bernardino.[13] Among the more remarkable narratives unearthed are those of squads like Los Chorizeros, Los Angeles Forty-Sixty, and El Paso Shoe Club. These were among the dozens of local teams affiliated with clubs, churches, and local businesses that played against one another in municipal leagues across the city and Southern California. Many even routinely traveled south across the border to play in Mexico. Prior to the arrival of the Dodgers in 1958 the professional ranks were headlined by the Los Angeles Angels and Hollywood Stars of the Pacific Coast League. For many Mexican Americans the real stars were those that played for neighborhood teams.

Los Chorizeros, known as the New York Yankees of East LA, are a case in point. Their story begins with Mario Lopez. Lopez was born in Chihuahua, Mexico, and immigrated to LA in the 1920s. After trying his hand as gas station owner and meatpacker, Lopez opened Carmelita Provision Company in 1948. Looking for a new business venture after World War II, he recalled that few stores catered to the ethnic food needs of the growing Mexican population when he arrived in the 1920s and decided his entrepreneurial calling was to market Mexican pork products. Longtime family friend Saul Toledo noted that "You couldn't find chorizo (spicy pork sausage) anywhere. So Mario started making that and pickled pigs feet and chicharrones."[14] Lopez put more than his Depression-era experience as a meatpacker to work. He was also a shortstop, played for a number of Eastside teams over the years, and organized a team when he owned Mario's Service Station. When he opened Carmelita's, it seemed only natural to begin a company-sponsored baseball team. If the Carmelita Provision Company found great success—its 2015 website touts "The Original Chorizo Since 1934," markets Carmelita apparel, and advertises that its products are widely available in major grocery stores—Los Chorizeros, as the company team was called, was equally prosperous.[15] Between 1948 and 1973, the team was said to have won nineteen city championships and was an Eastside institution.[16]

In the barrio, the *Los Angeles Times* noted years later, Chorizero "baseball wasn't just a game, it was an event."[17] Games were usually played on Sundays after church and involved the entire community. Baseball brought people together, but they also picnicked, gambled, played music, and danced. Lopez ensured that packages of chorizo were given away in the stands, young boys shagged fly balls and worked the scoreboard, and the club sponsored fundraisers for local schools and churches. Whole neighborhoods congregated as part of the festivities. Mexican American women were also part of game days, aided in preparing food, and socialized with family members, other wives, and friends. If the on-field play was an exercise in masculine performance and bonding, however, so, too, was pre- and post-game activity. Men often bought beers and tacos for one another after games, for example, and some women recall being asked to wait in the car with the children while their husbands drank. Most of the games were played at public parks like Evergreen in Boyle Heights under the auspices of the LA Department of Recreation and Parks. Al Padilla, who rooted for Carmelita as a young boy and later played for teams like the Evergreen Rangers and Ornelas Food Market, recalled that home runs at Evergreen Park often landed in the community pool beyond a chain-link fence. There was usually someone designated to dive in to retrieve the ball. Los Chorizeros was an amateur team and players were not paid, but that did not stop Lopez and longtime manager Manuel "Shorty" Perez from constantly recruiting fresh talent, including many who played stints in the minor leagues or starred for local high school teams. The lore of playing for the team enhanced its community profile and vice versa.

There was a wide range of people involved in the Chorizeros scene. Carmelita played mostly other Mexican American teams, but, because parts of

East LA were so diverse, they also played African American, Japanese American, white, and some racially mixed teams. Mario's son, Frank Lopez, remembered playing non-Mexican teams sparked an especially hypermasculine dynamic. "If we were playing the Watts Giants or one of the Caucasian teams from the other side of town," he claimed, "it was a machismo game. It was hard baseball."[18] Spectators at Chorizero games also included local political and labor leaders. Representatives from the Community Service Organization (CSO) and G.I. Forum were regulars, as was Congressman Ed Roybal and musician Lalo Guerrero. In fact, a number of Chorizero players assumed an active role in Roybal's campaign efforts, including his successful bid for Congress that saw him represent the Eastside district from 1949 to 1963.

Before the Dodgers came to town, teams like Los Chorizeros were the center of the baseball universe in Mexican Los Angeles and illumined an alternative LA, one that deviated from the city's white racial and spatial imaginary in the decades after World War II. Their intra-ethnic, cross-racial, and transnational sensibilities imbued the Eastside and the public facilities players and fans frequented with meaning. In an era when the Dodgers took possession of a stadium erected upon the foundations of one of the city's oldest Mexican American neighborhoods and freeway construction allowed increasingly suburbanized white populations to pass between points of interest with less direct interpersonal contact with nonwhite people, LA was resegregated instead of desegregated. Los Chorizeros, their opponents, and supporters reclaimed and marked public space in the city as Mexican and multiracial. Frank Lopez further noted, "there was a lot of prejudice in those days. This was a way to do something. Something for us."[19]

If Los Chorizeros showed how baseball rooted Mexicans and Mexican Americans in LA, Dodgers owner Walter O'Malley's decision to leave Brooklyn for LA and the well-recited narrative of the construction of their new stadium at Chavez Ravine just north of downtown underscored their displacement. Chavez Ravine was one of LA's longest-standing Mexican barrios. It was identified by some city authorities as blighted and in need of rehabilitation in the early 1950s, several years before O'Malley considered leaving New York. In 1952 and 1953, the community composed almost entirely of Mexican Americans and Mexicans was cleared from the area as part of a planned project to build more than three thousand units of public housing on an eight-hundred-acre parcel of land. The subsequent mayoral race made the future of Chavez Ravine a hot topic and, despite promises to former residents that new housing tracts would be made available, the public housing project was scrapped. Chavez Ravine was soon a key site in efforts to rehabilitate downtown and boost tourism. When the Dodgers announced intentions to move west, LA elites wanted to make Chavez Ravine available to O'Malley and razed the vestiges of the original neighborhood through the power of eminent domain. The last of the Mexican residents were excised in publicly recorded evictions in May 1959 and Dodger Stadium was ready for opening day in April 1962. Historian Eric Avila summed up the construction of Dodger Stadium as a critical moment in the "whitening" of LA's city center as part of a privatized corporate vision of downtown redevelopment.[20] This was a far cry from the community-based vision of Los Chorizeros and underscored how baseball proffered competing spatial and racial imaginaries in postwar Los Angeles.[21]

The East LA Classic

As the Eastside became increasingly Mexican in the decades after World War II, it continued to be a hotbed for much of the city's Mexican athletics. When the Chicano movement gained intensity in the late 1960s and early 1970s, sport-based community building in the spirit of Los Chorizeros remained a pillar of Mexican Los Angeles. El movimiento politicized Chicanas/os across the city to reject whiteness and assimilation at the same time they reclaimed their Mexican and indigenous heritage. Young folk across the city expressed feminist, cultural nationalist, and internationalist strains of antiracist, anti-imperial, and anticapitalist politics as part of groups like the Brown Berets, El Centro de Accion Social y Autonomo (CASA), and Movimiento Estudiantil Chicana/o de Aztlan (MEChA). East LA was home to one of the biggest anti-Vietnam war rallies, the Chicano Moratorium, in May 1970 and, just a few years prior in March 1968, students at Eastside high schools walked out of classes in protest against poor conditions in their schools, dropout rates of more than 50 percent, and a lack of resources. More than fifteen thousand students participated in the blowouts, including those from Garfield, Roosevelt, Lincoln, Wilson, and Belmont Highs. Amid such political upheaval, sports emerged yet again as an important site for Mexican LA to make sense of and change the city.

The football rivalry between Roosevelt and Garfield High Schools is evidence of how the politics of the day intertwined with sport. Ted Davis, who was a teacher at Garfield in the early 1970s, recalled the story of how the annual Roosevelt-Garfield game came to be known as the East LA Classic. "In 1972,"

Davis remembered, "Garfield coach Vic Loya, Roosevelt coach Al Chavez and I got together at Club Fujiyama—a hangout that teachers and friends from both schools would meet at before and after the game. We decided to call the game The East Los Angeles Classic. Before that it didn't have a name. The first Classic was in the fall of 1972."[22] While Davis is correct that the game did not have an official name prior to 1972, it was known around the city, especially by white observers beyond the Eastside, as the "Taco Bowl," "Tamale Bowl," or the "Chili Bowl."[23] In the spirit of the walkouts at their schools just a few years earlier, students and staff at Roosevelt and Garfield campaigned to give their rivalry a name that rejected negative stereotypes and reflected their school and community pride.

The game, which is still widely known as the East LA Classic, had a long and storied history. Roosevelt opened its doors to students in Boyle Heights in 1923, and Garfield did the same just three miles away in East Los Angeles in 1925. There was a rivalry from the beginning, in part because Roosevelt was on the west side of Indiana Street in the city of Los Angeles and Garfield on the east side in unincorporated Belvedere. In their initial decades, the ethnic makeup of the two schools was different, too. Roosevelt was more racially mixed in the 1930s and 1940s, drawing its student body from the diversity of Boyle Heights, which was a center of Jewish life in LA mixed with Mexican American, African American, Japanese American, Russian, and Turkish families. Garfield was more Mexican American than not in the 1930s and 1940s. The first gridiron meeting between Roosevelt's Roughriders and Garfield's Bulldogs was in 1926, a clash won by Roosevelt 26–3.[24] The game has been played annually since, save for 1939–1948, when a combination of the Great Depression, World War II, and the schools being in different athletic leagues saw the rivalry take a hiatus. When Roosevelt returned to the Eastern League in 1949, the rivalry resumed. Soon after in 1951, the game was moved to East Los Angeles College's (ELAC) Weingart Stadium because of its growing popularity. Weingart had a seating capacity of just over twenty-two thousand, and in years to come it was routine for the game to sell out and patrons to be turned away at the gates. School officials argue that the Classic is the biggest high school football game west of the Mississippi River. This may be the case, both in terms of attendance and the importance of the game to its surrounding community.

The Classic, according to 1948 Roosevelt graduate Al Padilla—the same Al Padilla who grew up watching Los Chorizeros—was "more than just a game." It was a "sociological happening!"[25] Padilla knew the rivalry as well as anyone.

Not only was he a student at Roosevelt, but he also coached and taught at both schools and East LA College. After leaving his alma mater to coach its rival, he claimed he was known as "the Benedict Arnold of East L.A." and "people would say I'm a traitor."[26] Despite the intensity of the rivalry, or perhaps because of it, the theme most commonly associated with it by Padilla and many others was community. Not unlike the Sunday afternoons when Los Chorizeros took to the diamond, the Roosevelt-Garfield game and associated events were bound up in the neighborhood and surrounding area. The game has long been a double homecoming for both schools and game week is chock-full of reunions, alumni parties, and fundraisers at nearby Eastside restaurants and bars. Area food markets traditionally posted the football schedules for both teams, the main discussion topic at Kiwanis Club breakfast meetings come football season was the Classic, and alumni from across Southern California returned for the matchup.[27] No matter one's role, whether as spectator, marching band member, or cheerleader, as Padilla argued, it was "important you participated in the game with honor."[28]

Former star Roosevelt running back Mike Garrett, who went on to win a Heisman Trophy at the University of Southern California (USC), remembered his five-touchdown game in 1961's 36–6 victory over Garfield as one of the greatest of his life. It was his senior year and the season following a 7–7 tie between the schools. In *Symbol of Heart*, the 2003 documentary on the East LA Classic, Garrett, one of the African American superstars of his era, was visibly emotional as he remembered the game. He later recalled, "Roosevelt-Garfield was *the* game. It was exactly like USC versus Notre Dame in East L.A. It's a rare treat that not many people have a chance to experience."[29] Garrett explained what the game meant to him. "All I really wanted to do in football was play in the Garfield-Roosevelt game. Later in life, I played in the Coliseum, I played in the pros, but I watched the Garfield-Roosevelt game at East L.A. College [as a kid] and I said, 'I want to play in that game someday.'"[30]

Others involved in the rivalry shared similar sentiments. Henry Ronquillo, alumnus and former principal of Roosevelt, noted in the 1990s, "It knits the community together with even more pride. It is definitely the biggest community event in East L.A. for the entire year."[31] His Garfield counterpart, former principal Maria Tostado, elaborated,

> The proximity of the schools adds to the rivalry, because the junior high schools—Robert Louis Stevenson, Hollenbeck and Griffith—feed into

Garfield and Roosevelt. Many of the kids who attend Garfield and Roosevelt went to the same junior high schools. In East Los Angeles, everyone knows one another. It is like a little Midwest town in a big city. Everyone knows everyone's family.[32]

Al Padilla also underscored the family and community dynamics of the Classic. "There's so much intermarriage between the alumni from each school. That's why on the night of the game there are the husbands and wives sitting on opposite sides, instead of together. Meanwhile, the kids are playing down on the field."[33] In his assessment of the rivalry, former Roosevelt coach David Endow similarly stressed that "Lots of the players (on both teams) grew up together and shared childhood experiences. There is a lot of intermarriage between the schools. You have cousins versus cousins and brothers versus brothers." Former Garfield coach John Aguirre simply stated: "It is a community event. It is as big as it gets on the Eastside." Armando Figueroa, ex-Roosevelt running back, agreed. "It is a real community game . . . To grow up watching the game and now get the chance to play in it is the greatest feeling in the world."[34] George Ramos, writing for the *Los Angeles Times* in 1995, summed up the rivalry by arguing: "very few events in the fall evoke more pride in the Eastside than the annual football game between Garfield and Roosevelt."[35]

Like those played by Los Chorizeros, the Roosevelt-Garfield game was rooted in Mexican Los Angeles and helped build community in East LA, in particular. In the face of political upheaval and less than ideal economic conditions, football provided deep attachment to place and a powerful claim to calling the city home. At the same time, as Mike Garrett and so many others demonstrated, the Classic reminds us that the history of Mexican LA was multiracial and intra-ethnic. Boyle Heights's diverse history and East Los Angeles's increasingly Mexican and Latino demographics were evident on the field and in the stands at Weingart Stadium. The Classic not only showed the attachment to place by Mexicans and other Eastsiders, but helped *make* East LA. The Classic brought Boyle Heights and East Los Angeles together, helping fuel the community bonds across and between neighborhoods and families. As the ethnic and racial composition of areas east of downtown shifted in the postwar years, "East LA" came to be viewed as inclusive of Mexican LA east of the Los Angeles River. Boyle Heights and Belvedere, Roosevelt and Garfield came to share a common association as East LA, as a single community. The Classic, perhaps as much as any other community institution, helped usher in and solidify this sense of place in East Los Angeles. If, as George Lipsitz argued, racism is grounded in material struggles over place, the longer history of the Classic showed the same is true of ethnic identity and multiracialism. In the case of Roosevelt v. Garfield, what it meant to be Mexican in East LA unfolded on and around the gridiron when the Roughriders and Bulldogs faced off.

Since the early 1990s, several proposals to move the Classic from ELAC threatened and further revealed the rivalry's deep-seated links on the Eastside. Amid concerns by school officials that the Classic had outgrown ELAC's Weingart Stadium and ELAC charged too much for use of their facilities, surveys were distributed to fans at the 1991 game. They asked, "The East L.A. Classic Rose Bowl Bound 1993? Would you go? Yes or no?" Out of thirty-five hundred returned surveys, 85 percent favored the move. Many believed that Roosevelt and Garfield would see more profits if they played in a bigger venue, despite ELAC only charging $11,000 compared to the $75,000–$100,000 the Rose Bowl would cost. Some believed playing in the Rose Bowl would bring "more clout" to the Classic. Others claimed leaving the Eastside for Pasadena would be a mistake. Plans by school administrators to secure a corporate sponsorship in order to afford the Rose Bowl and raise money for a scholarship trust fund did not come to fruition. The Classic stayed at ELAC, for the moment.[36] Rumors of a Rose Bowl move surfaced again in 1995. Supporters argued it was a natural sign of growth, the move would generate more revenue, and no one would be turned away for lack of seats. The *Los Angeles Times* noted, "On the other hand, traditionalists say the strong emotional ties to the Eastside will be lost if the game is moved out of East L.A."[37] Robert Carrillo, a Roosevelt grad, argued, "Moving the game defeats the whole purpose of the rivalry . . . It's a familia thing. We all come together for the game. You take it out of East L.A. and you take away something from it. Hell, I'm not from Pasadena. I'm from East L.A.!"[38]

Whether seduced by the prospect of heftier revenues or the lure of playing in a venue that had hosted two Olympic Games, Super Bowls, and the Rams, Raiders, and USC, the rivalry did move to the LA Coliseum in 2000. The *Los Angeles Times* queried, "Can the East L.A. Classic remain an Eastside community event if it is played in South Central Los Angeles?"[39] Feelings were mixed. Roosevelt coach Jose Casagran opined, "I'd say the response has been 50–50." He continued, "for as many people who are saying that it's great the game is growing, there are others who say you're abandoning the community."[40] Ruben Burgueno, a linebacker for the Roughriders at the time, exclaimed, "When I first heard it was going to be at the Coliseum, I was angry. I wanted it to be at ELAC because that's the community that always fills the stadium and you can feel the excitement from everybody once you walk in. I'm hoping I'm still going to feel that excitement, but it saddens me a little that it's not at ELAC."[41] Although thirty-three thousand filed into the Coliseum for the 2000 Classic, the cavernous one-hundred-thousand-seat stadium made the crowd appear smaller. When attendance dwindled over the next few years, school officials took a page from the game's own history book and remembered that place matters. The East LA Classic moved back to ELAC in 2004. Still, as recently as 2011, rumors of another proposed move to the Rose Bowl emerged. Increased revenues from parking, food, and beverage sales were again a driving force and a powerful reminder that sport-based community building in Mexican Los Angeles was contingent on the local economy and consumer markets.

The Most Popular Team in LA?

If Los Chorizeros and the East LA Classic showed the power of sport in Mexican LA, so too did the popularity of Mexico's national soccer team. El Tri, as it is known, may very well be the most popular sports franchise in Los Angeles, more so than the Trojans, Bruins, Dodgers, Kings, Raiders, Clippers, or even Lakers. After important victories by El Tri it is not unusual for Mexican fans throughout LA to take to the streets in raucous celebration, waving Mexican flags, stopping traffic, setting off fireworks, and prompting tactical responses by the LAPD riot squad. When Mexico defeated Croatia 3–1 in the 2014 World Cup to advance to the knockout stage, for example, crowds gathered across the Eastside and Southeast Los Angeles. In Huntington Park, police prepared for confrontations because of what they noted as the longer history of rowdy behavior by El Tri supporters dating back to 1994. In the 2014 version in Huntington Park, fans were arrested, police taunted, and a police horse was struck. The latter incident was widely reported by news outlets, effectively criminalizing the partiers and marking them as foreign.[42] When El Tri has played the US Men's National Team (USMNT) in LA, the scene has been particularly intense and their rivalry has been a site for fans, players, and media that cover the game to renegotiate and build new practices of citizenship, belonging, and race.[43]

Why has El Tri's fan base in the United States been so large and so often associated with Los Angeles since the early 1990s? The short answer is globalization and the emergence of El Tri as a hemispheric marketing brand worth millions to the Federación Mexicana de Fútbol Associación (FMF), the US Soccer Federation (US Soccer), television media conglomerates like Televisa and Univision, and the companies that sponsor them, including Coca Cola, Anheuser Busch, and Home Depot. The rapidly growing market for Mexican national team soccer reflects the dramatic rise of the ethnic Mexican population in the United States and Southern California since the 1980s. There were roughly 4.4 million Mexican immigrants and 15 million total Mexican-origin folks in the United States in 1990. Those numbers grew to 11.7 million and nearly 35 million, respectively by 2011.[44] One advertising executive argued, "put your latest advert inside a Mexico versus 'anyone' world cup match and you are guaranteed to reach a prime advertising market and lots of them."[45] The US-Mexico soccer rivalry is a literal product of neoliberal fueled migration and Los Angeles is a poster child for the resulting demographic revolution.

Results on the pitch and politics off it have made the US-Mexico soccer rivalry a flashpoint for vitriolic debate. Whether at the Rose Bowl, where the two sides have routinely played each other, the streets of Huntington Park, or elsewhere across the city, the fervor over El Tri in LA has illuminated different modes of belonging and citizenship. The 1998 and 2011 Gold Cup finals in Los Angeles (both won by Mexico), for example, sparked heated debate over whether immigrants should root against the USMNT. *Soccer America*'s report of the 1998 final noted, "Any remaining doubts about the identity of the home team were dispelled when the two teams took the field. The fans came, saw, booed and threw things—at the United States. Whistles greeted the US national team when it took the field and during its national anthem."[46] Opinion letters submitted to the *Los Angeles Times* after the 1998 match were printed under the headline, "What's Needed Is Some Civility." Letters included charges of "anti-Americanism," the "sub-human" character of Mexican fans and immigrants, and not so subtle calls to "go back to Mexico."[47] A letter from USMNT supporter Frank Rodriguez underscored the complex perspective of many Mexican Americans, in particular. Rodriguez wrote, "Never had I been so ashamed to be a Mexican-American. My son and I were pelted with beer, soda, and God knows what else for having had the temerity to display an American flag and cheer for our team. I watched with dread as I saw my son's eyes filled with confusion at the disrespect displayed while our national anthem was played." Such views were echoed following the 2011 final at the Rose Bowl, including by CNN's Ruben Navarrette Jr., who labeled Mexican fans booing the US spectacles of "misplaced" loyalty and "ugly nationalism" that "turn my stomach."⁴⁸ As online comments in response to Navarrette Jr. indicated, much of this debate was shrouded in hypermasculine terms. In the stands and on anonymous message boards, gender was often the terrain for casting and experiencing class, national, or racial insults.

Response to US-Mexico matches also included backlash from conservative political pundits like Pat Buchanan and Samuel Huntington. Buchanan summed up his view of the 1998 Gold Cup final by stating, "what took place in the LA Coliseum was a two-hour orgy of anti-Americanism, an explosion of hatred against the United States."⁴⁹ Conservative websites and blogs like Libertarian Today and the Southern Nationalist Network also got in on the action. In its coverage of the 2011 Gold Cup final, for instance, the latter argued,

> As events surrounding a recent soccer match in Los Angeles show, much of the Southwest is already ethnically and culturally Mexican. And the people living there for the most part have no desire and no incentive to assimilate into the lifestyle of the U.S. Anglo minority. As their numbers continue to explode, Mexicans living in California will expect to impose their politics, their language, their religion, etc. on the State. And the next generation of them, which will include many millions who were born in the States and therefore are entitled to vote, hold office and receive government benefits, will not sit idly by as a disenfranchised majority—they will expect *and insist on* running the show. And the US Federal Government will be unable to deal harshly with these Mexican nationalists because Hispanics will make up a huge percentage of the population in many states, tying the hands of the politicians. This could be how the US Empire dies—if the dollar hasn't been completely destroyed by that time.⁵⁰

Such racially tinged commentary about El Tri and Mexican-origin communities in LA and elsewhere in the United States was inextricable from the broader context and debate over immigration reform, border security, and related economic concerns north of the border. The backdrop to El Tri's popularity in LA and rivalry with the USMNT included what George Lipsitz described as "a brand of economic fundamentalism favoring free markets," the intensification of deregulation and global flow of capital, ideas, and labor, along with the growth of mass technology and communications, that has resulted in "low wages, high unemployment, slow growth, high interest rates, and devastating social spending on health, housing, and education."⁵¹

Combined with the 1986 Immigration Reform and Control Act (IRCA) that provided a path to citizenship for millions of undocumented immigrants, such conditions prompted a rash of policies targeting immigrants and Latinos in LA and elsewhere. Following IRCA and the 1994 North American Free Trade Agreement (NAFTA) the US-Mexico border was increasingly militarized, including Mexican and US authorities deploying low-intensity warfare to control human traffic across the border. Government initiatives like Operation Blockade in El Paso (1993), Operation Gatekeeper in San Diego (1994), Operation Safeguard in Nogales, Arizona (1994), and Operation Rio Grande in south Texas (1997) followed, each accompanied by increased border patrol, Immigration and Naturalization Service (INS), or, more recently, Immigration and Customs Enforcement (ICE) presence. The angry outcry over illegal immigration and shifting demographics toward "majority-minority" status and "Latinoization" led to a number of anti-immigrant legislations and campaigns in California including Proposition 187 in 1994 that limited access to health care and education for undocumented immigrants. The late 1990s and early 2000s also saw anti-affirmative action, anti-bilingual education, and anti-gang campaigns that targeted Latino communities. Beyond California, House Resolution 4437 passed by Congress in 2005 imposed stiff legal sanctions for "aiding" undocumented immigrants and Arizona passed Senate bill 1070 criminalizing undocumented immigrants in 2010. These combined with similar bills in several other states all served to stir an anti-immigrant, racially tense political climate.

In this high-stakes political context, it is no wonder that players with the option to compete for both the United States and Mexico have often been at the center of debate. Neither is it coincidence that many of their backgrounds have an LA storyline. Since its inception, the USMNT included players with immigrant backgrounds, in part because immigrant communities fueled the popularity of soccer in Los Angeles and the United States more broadly. Hugo Salcedo, for instance, was born in Jalisco, Mexico, but grew up in East LA and attended UC Riverside. He was part of the US Olympic team in the 1972 Munich Games and played in the Pan American Games in 1971. Hercules Gomez, a more recent example, played routinely for the United States in the 2000s. Gomez, born in LA of immigrant parents and raised in Las Vegas, summarized the relationship between the United States and Mexico by saying, "Sometimes you do feel like you're stuck in the middle."[52] A number of other players for the USMNT and the Mexican women's national team have similar stories.[53] Many of them, like the fans who cheered them on, challenged the borders of us versus them on and off the pitch and showed how the civic imaginary in LA might be re-bordered to include a broader range of citizenship and belonging.

The story of Michael Orozco Fiscal, the Mexican American center back born in Orange, California, not far from Los Angeles, illustrates the point. Orozco Fiscal scored the lone goal in the US's 1–0 victory over Mexico in a friendly at Estadio Azteca in Mexico City in 2012. It was the first ever win for the United States on Mexican soil, despite twenty-four previous tries, and was viewed as a major breakthrough for the USMNT because it broke the vaunted Azteca curse. Orozco's goal came late in the match and earned him persona non grata in Mexico, even though he had played professionally in Liga MX. Just a year later in October 2013 he scored a goal for the United States that tied Panama in a World Cup qualifier and kept Mexico's hopes of qualification alive. In an interview with Univision, he said he thought he had redeemed himself in the eyes of Mexican fans. "Not even a year ago I was one of the most hated players because of 'El Aztecazo' (as his 2012 goal was known) but I think the tides have turned and now I am one of the most loved for the goal for the tie (against Panama). It is close to my heart because Mexico has to get to the World Cup ... I wish them luck and I will continue to support them." He continued, "Here (in Mexico) the doors were opened for me to start my career and I enjoyed it very much. My parents are Mexican, I am Mexican. I ended up defending another jersey but I continue to be Mexican."[54]

The next time the United States and Mexico square off at the Rose Bowl there will surely be nearly one hundred thousand flag-waving fans, many of them Mexicans in support of El Tri. Just as the match will showcase the soccer talent of both nations, so too will it again give form to the transnational citizenships, competing visions of belonging, and meanings of place in Los Angeles. Like Los Chorizeros and the East LA Classic, the US-Mexico soccer rivalry has much to teach us about the intertwined histories of ethnic Mexicans, sport, and Los Angeles.

Conclusion

There are any number of topics, athletes, and stories to be included in an essay on Mexican sport in Los Angeles. One could point to the long history of Mexican and Chicano boxing in LA, including Oscar De La Hoya's remarkable journey to the Olympic gold medal and subsequent professional career; the

Los Angeles Raiders' magical run to the 1983 Super Bowl championship under the helm of Mexican American head coach Tom Flores and Mexican American quarterback Jim Plunkett, followed by a legion of Mexican American fans from LA; the history of the failed Chivas USA experiment in Major League Soccer to bring the iconic Chivas brand from Mexican professional soccer to Los Angeles; the shifting terrain of interscholastic athletics in LA as a result of the growing number of Mexicans and other Latinos in the city; the grassroots and municipal soccer leagues that Latino immigrants play in by the thousands; or the response in LA to the National Basketball Association's attempt to attract Latino fans by marketing "Los Lakers" and "Los Clippers." In all of these instances and many more, the history of sport reveals a complicated relationship between Mexican LA and the rest of the city, resulting in multiple and contested meanings of place, belonging, and citizenship.

A more extensive history of sport in Mexican LA might also recall the uproar in response to USC quarterback Mark Sanchez wearing a mouth guard decorated in the green, white, and red tricolors of the Mexican flag when USC played at Notre Dame in 2007. Despite leading the Trojans to a 38–0 victory over their rival, Sanchez caught a lot of heat for being "un-American" and worse on radio call-in shows and Internet chat rooms. The USC football program even reported receiving streams of hate mail, e-mails, and phone calls after the game.[55] For his part, Sanchez, who later went on to play in the NFL and generate a sizable following among Latino NFL fans, explained his mouth guard this way. "It's my heritage," he said. He described the mouthpiece as "sweet" and "cool" and "a portrayal of my love for my race."[56] Sanchez also said he hoped that his choice to represent the colors of the Mexican flag would inspire other young Latinos to follow in his footsteps. Sanchez, for the record, is third-generation US born. He was born in Long Beach and went to high school in Mission Viejo, a well-to-do area in Orange County just south of Los Angeles. His paternal great-grandparents migrated from Mexico to California to work as fruit pickers. On his mother's side, his great-grandparents left Jalisco for Arizona before settling in Los Angeles. Upon arriving in LA, his grandfather Nicholas settled in Chavez Ravine, only to be displaced in the 1950s by the unfulfilled plans for low-income housing and the eventual construction of Dodger Stadium discussed above. In an interview with journalist David Davis, Nick Sanchez Sr., Mark's father, said, "Second base, that's where they used to live, right where second base is now." Mark Sanchez added, "My grandfather was a little bitter about Dodger Stadium. He rooted for the Giants."[57]

Mark Sanchez's story is not unlike the longer histories of Los Chorizeros, the East LA Classic, and the US-Mexico soccer rivalry in LA. Taken together, these seemingly disparate moments offer several observations about the history of sports, Mexicans and Mexican Americans, and Los Angeles. First, and perhaps most importantly, is that all of these histories inform the others. The history of Mexican LA is sport history and vice versa. Second, much of sport history in Mexican LA cannot be explained by the moniker community-based sports. It is, rather, much more often a story of sports-based community building where athletes, spectators, and others actively constructed new racial imaginaries and practiced new forms of belonging and citizenship. Whether at Evergreen Park in Boyle Heights (which was also the site of massive immigrant rights marches in May 2006 and 2007), Weingart Stadium at ELAC (which continues to host the East LA Classic), or the Rose Bowl in Pasadena (where El Tri faced off against the United States as recently as October 2015) sport was the vehicle to build community and give new meaning to places across LA. Third, viewing sport in LA as only a site where Mexicans and Mexican Americans made themselves would be a mistake. It was also where they shaped and were shaped by the city at large, its political economy, their fellow Angelenos, and the power of consumer markets. Fourth, sports in Mexican LA shows that the longer history of Mexicans and Mexican Americans in the city radiates in at least three directions, including the "intra" (as in intra-ethnic relations of citizenship, gender, and class), the "cross" (as in cross-ethnically and cross-racially), and the "trans" (as in trans-US-Mexico border). Fifth, and finally, these snippets of sports in Mexican LA are a reminder that we should continue to pay attention to Mexican and Mexican American athletes, fans, broadcasters, and sports executives in the city. They might just teach us something about the meaning of place, community, and citizenship in the City of Angels.

CHAPTER THREE

Pitches Less Than Perfect

Notes on the Landscape of Soccer in Los Angeles

JENNIFER DOYLE

Between December 2007 and September 2013, I wrote a sports blog called *From a Left Wing*. *From a Left Wing* began as a chronicle of my participation in "pick-up" soccer games in Los Angeles—mostly in Westlake/Pico Union (a neighborhood just east of downtown) and on the margins of Ferraro Fields, a network of soccer pitches on the eastern edge of Griffith Park. During this period, I also joined women's teams playing in municipal leagues in the region, and cofounded and ran a men's league on a Pico/Union field, just east of MacArthur Park.[1] I played in loosely regulated, easy-to-access public spaces. If a field was fenced off, either its fence was not hard to climb or we knew someone who had been trusted with a key. Although much economic activity frames these fields, they are not centers of commercial sports. My perspective on soccer in Los Angeles is limited, in other words, to my experiences playing in the long shadow of the global sports spectacle, just outside the reach of the sport's official cultures and economies.

Nationally, Los Angeles is an important center for the sport.[2] The American Youth Soccer Organization (AYSO) was founded in Los Angeles in 1964; this massive volunteer organization is still headquartered in Los Angeles. For a while, the city hosted two Major League Soccer (MLS) teams, the now-defunct Chivas USA (2004–2014) and the LA Galaxy (1996–present). Plans are afoot for another expansion team and entrepreneurs in this sporting community are dreaming of a new, dedicated stadium.[3] Fox Sports, one of the English-language networks most committed to soccer, is produced in Los Angeles. Los Angeles is, furthermore, a major center for Spanish-language media in the United States (the television station KMEX, for example, has been broadcasting since 1962;

La Opinion is the nation's biggest daily Spanish-language newspaper). Spanish-language networks (local and national) have long provided the backbone for television coverage of this sport. When one includes Spanish-language broadcasts, television audiences for soccer matches can outstrip basketball and baseball, depending on the match. Cable TV subscription services are bundled differently for English-language and Spanish-language customers. The most significant difference between these bundles is that Spanish-language packages include soccer-dedicated networks from around the world instead of American football and other sports.

In the summer, European clubs train in Los Angles (UCLA is a summer home for Real Madrid). The region has a reputation, in the game, as an excellent host.[4] In 2007, David Beckham, the sport's biggest celebrity, made an infamous but very successful move to the LA Galaxy. Since then, the city has drawn others who made their name playing in England and Europe, including former Tottenham Hotspur Robbie Keane (Ireland), Liverpool's Steven Gerrard (England), and Giovanni Dos Santos (Mexico), who has played for Barcelona, Tottenham, and Villareal. World Cup and Olympic matches have been played in Los Angeles. One of the most well-known matches in the history of the women's game (the 1999 Women's World Cup final, in which USWNT beat China, in a penalty kick shoot-out) was played in Pasadena's Rose Bowl, before nearly one hundred thousand people. In 2015, Mexico and the USMNT met at the Rose Bowl for the final for the CONCACAF Cup. Just over ninety-three thousand people watched that insane match (which was won by Mexico in extra-time). In the off-season, Angelenos pack the biggest stadiums in the region to watch the biggest clubs in the world play pointless off-season friendly matches. The city is mad for the international game. During the 2010 men's World Cup, for example, Radio Korea USA used the large square in front of their Koreatown headquarters to host midnight outdoor broadcasts of all of South Korea's matches. Thousands of people filled the square every night, no matter the hour. Mexican restaurants opened at 6 a.m. to host breakfast broadcasts from South Africa—fans were caught in mad scrambles all around town for the restaurant with the best combination of viewing+menu options. One can't say that the World Cup arrives in Los Angeles on a monolithic wave of nationalism. Instead, the World Cup draws out a panoply of nationalisms—nationalisms, furthermore, often mixed or split by personal and family histories of immigration. Mexican American fans, in particular, straddle one of the world's most intense rivalries.[5]

These large stories frame my access to the sport. Here, I share anecdotes that describe the everyday life of soccer in Los Angeles. These fragments center on problems of field access and contestations of space and place. Woven in between material that originated on my blog is an overview of those aspects of the national context for soccer relevant to thinking about this sport, as it is practiced by ordinary Angelenos, for whom this game is not work, but play.[6]

Boulders and Boundaries

Years ago, my neighborhood park (Bellevue Park) hosted rolling nighttime pick-up soccer games. It was also home to a fair amount of criminal activity—drug dealing, mostly, with the periodic shoot-out. Two men were shot, one killed, in 2003. At that time, gang-related gun violence stood in sharp contrast with the deep gentrification that had already redefined Silverlake.[7] Park officials decided it was time to do something. Bellevue Park was closed, and redesigned. Two large, fenced-off baseball fields were placed squarely over the section of the park that used to host these pick-up games. Each field has a set of bleachers and a covered area where players can sit while waiting for their turn at bat. Neither baseball nor softball are played there much. In all my years of using the park I've only seen a handful of teams using the diamonds. Most hours of the day, they sit empty. They take up more than half of Bellevue's open space. The rest of the park consists of picnic areas, a basketball court, two jungle gyms for kids, and a set of rings and pull-up bars. There is not much open space left—and what is there, is not flat and is broken up by large, old trees. Any grassy expanse that might have invited play is broken up by boulders that were placed to make such a thing impossible.

For those park users who have not gotten the landscaped message, signs ring the park and declare "No Fútbol" and "No Se Puede Jugar Soccer." Most of those signs show a stick figure kicking a ball, crossed out. There are a lot of other signs in the park ("No Scooters," "No Bikes," "No Skateboards," "No Golf") but the "No Soccer" signs are one of only two sets of edicts in Spanish. The other is "No Bebidas Alcoholicas." In Bellevue, in spite of all that fútbol-phobic design, some players initiate a small game of five or six a side in the early evening—they play on a little mound (using the curve to curl passes around each other). They use two garbage cans to make one goal, and two gorgeous fir trees as the other. The trees could not be more perfectly spaced, and, in fact, even when there are not enough people to make a full game, you see one or two kids practicing shots with a friend tending goal between the trunks. There is no grass there. It has been worn away by criminal keepers, stealing this space between "the sticks."

Soccer as a Countercultural Sport

Just about every attempt to describe soccer in the United States requires painting a picture like the following: In the United States, soccer never quite rises the level of a national sport, even though (according to FIFA) the United States boasts the second-largest population of soccer players in the world.[8] On this score, the United States places below China (by fewer than two million) and above India (by about three million). The general population for those two countries is about three times that of the United States. The United States has more registered players than does Brazil, a country for whom the sport is not just a national pastime; it is a national identity.[9] FIFA's statistics (which are best approached in terms of a reasonable, if somewhat self-serving guess) indicate, at the very least, that there is no necessary relationship between the numbers of people who play soccer and discourse identifying a sport as a "national" one. In the United States, soccer is more countercultural than dominant even if it is played by huge numbers of people.[10] Commercial and national structures like ESPN, USSF (the US Soccer Federation), and MLS (the men's professional league) are intensely ambivalent about the sport's shifting identity as foreign, Latino, and female.[11] Ideological baggage codes each identity marker as "not mainstream" or "not commercial."[12] Although we tend to want to fold soccer's embattled relationship to national sports culture into a narrative of US exceptionalism, we find that the sport is associated with immigrant communities around the world, and that it functions, globally, as a platform for debates about local, national, and global identities. If, in the United States, pundits declare "Why soccer is un-American," in France they ask if football is still French. The game's distinctly international character makes it a powerful medium through which questions of national identity are contested.[13]

In the United States in general, and in the Southwest in particular, discourse about identity and soccer bodies bring forth major conflicts in narratives about US history and national identity. Fans and sports officials are invested in the sense that English soccer is more serious, more professional, more admirable than soccer practiced anywhere else in the world; it's often said that broadcasts of English Premiership matches are the enemy of the development of the sport everywhere, including England (as fans flock to TV sets, for the best broadcast product, instead of supporting local teams). In the United States, the consumption of broadcasts of international matches and a popular romance of the history and legacies of international sides eclipse awareness of the sport at home. Discourse about the sport is also haunted by the colonial history of the West. Before it became a part of the United States in 1848, California was a part of Mexico. Before that, California was a part of New Spain. Our roots are also Mexico's. Nationally, official structures of the sport struggle to reconcile themselves to the scale and diversity and significance of the US Latino population. Conversations among fans of especially the men's game will toggle between the question of whether soccer will ever be as big or as good as it is in England and what the role of US Latinos could or should be within the sport's future.[14]

The above is just a sketch of some of the broad historical forces that shape the contemporary landscape of the soccer in Los Angeles, especially within the neighborhood in which I played. Pico-Union is, according to statistics provided by the LA Department of City Planning (based on the 2000 Census), 85.4 percent Latino. Its median household income is $26,424; only 6.7 percent of residents over twenty-five have a four-year degree. Sixty-four percent of the neighborhood was born outside the United States.[15] The social landscape of this neighborhood is shaped by NAFTA, the militarization of the Mexico-US border, radical defunding of public education in the state, and decades of war and violence across Central America (much of which is itself the consequence of US foreign policy in the region). The story that perhaps most defines the soccer in this neighborhood is the estrangement of Latinos from the sport's official development, nationally and locally, even as a certain fantasy about the "Latin" game shapes marketing and popular culture depictions of the sport in the United States. US Latino fans and players find themselves both courted by national structures as consumers and disavowed as athletes and as agentic subjects. Although Latinos in this region form the bedrock of the grassroots game and have long constituted a sizable, reliable audience for broadcasts of professional matches, it is only recently that the sport's institutions (USSF, MLS, and sports media like Univision, Fox Sports, and ESPN) have reconsidered the marginalization of Latino audiences and players.[16] Today, MLS clubs do seek out Latino players (in part to appeal to Latino audiences), and the latter are more actively sought out by the United States development program—although there is still a long way to go on that score (for both men and women). The significant differences among

Mexican, Mexican American, and US Latino soccer communities from the Caribbean, Central America, and South America are slowly becoming more legible to Anglo structures, which have suffered from a tendency to collapse "Latino" and "Mexican." The boundaries between Anglo and Latino spaces and institutions have not, however, been happily bridged by the appeal (and commercial pull) of the "global game."

Midnight Fantasy

Los Angeles cups Lafayette Park in its palm. This scrappy patch of grass, dust, magnolia and palm trees nests among stucco-covered California bungalows that squeeze up against cottages and squat apartment buildings. The corporate signatures of the middle class have not yet made their inroads here: storefronts are mom-and-pop operations—Filipino and Cuban bakeries, Oaxacan restaurants, travel agencies that also send money and packages to family back home. Small Pentacostal churches are everywhere, pumping music out onto the sidewalks. There are members-only Korean clubs, art galleries that come and go. There are *fútbol* shops stacked with knock-off shirts, shoes, and sun-bleached posters of Messi, "Los Galacticos," various World Cup champions (men, always and only the men). A block away, you'll find one of the oldest gay bars in the city welcoming transwomen, Latinas mostly from Central America, with boisterous and loving drag shows. You can see the soccer field at Lafayette Park from the sidewalk in front of that bar, and, inside, you can sometimes find people who have played there. It is often said that Los Angeles has no center, but it is more the case that it has many centers. Living inside one of these centers, one might be forgiven for not knowing that the others exist.

Lafayette Park takes its name from the Frenchman who renounced his aristocratic title to fight in both the French and American revolutions. There is a statue to General Lafayette at the southwestern entrance to the park. He grips the handle of his sword, lifting it slightly from its scabbard. "VOICI MON ÉPÉE" is etched into the statue's base. The statement is usually associated with a military assertion of loyalty—"I am here, and I am ready to fight." In relation to the Americas, however, Lafayette's most famous statement about his sword is one of regret: "I would never have drawn my sword in the cause of America if I could have conceived thereby that I was founding a land of slavery." He wrote this in a letter to George Washington, urging the first president to free those he held in bondage. (Washington would only do so in his will, and even then, these people were only freed on the death of his wife, Martha.) Which Lafayette do we honor? The one who fought in the American Revolution? Or the one who expressed his regret about having done so? I linger over his ambivalent figure, because it speaks to the difficult place of nationalism in this neighborhood. Lafayette's battles were fought in Maryland and Virginia. The equivalent for California might be the "Mexican Robin Hood," Joaquín Murrieta, who was hunted by California State Rangers in the 1850s as an enemy of the state.

Lafayette Park loves *fútbol*. You can play it on the basketball courts, in between the park tables and benches, around the palm trees. The parks department tried to keep players off the grass. One year they covered some of the ground with netting to protect seedlings, only to have it torn to shreds by those of us who just played over it. For weeks we were all picking the plastic threads out of our cleats. Rather than push us out with baseball fields and boulders, the park gave up on the grass and put down sand—for beach soccer.

The real game at Lafayette is played on a fenced-in futsal-sized turf field. Leagues play there day and night. The field's lights seem to never go off, so when teams are done, pick-up games take off and continue until the wee hours of the morning. Games at Lafayette are recorded by no newspaper; they are played for no camera by teams with no budget. They are no less epic for being off the record.

Words

The vocabulary of soccer in Los Angeles is helpful for understanding who constitutes the city's playing public: "Anglo" is used to describe white, native English-speaking players. (I am, for example, an Anglo player.) This term generally excludes recent European immigrants, unless they are from England. In scholarship, independent leagues grounded in specific ethnic communities are usually described as "ethnic leagues." Korean evangelical churches in Los Angeles, for example, organize a league of church-based teams. Most "ethnic" teams/leagues are not so precisely organized, however, and relatively few are exclusive where race and ethnicity are concerned. Locally, people often describe teams and leagues with a Latino majority "Latin" (when speaking of them in English). I've seen this word used in a range of ways: this lumping together of Latin American, Central American, Mexican, and US Latino players can read as ignorant, but it also, sometimes, functions as a relaxed shorthand for the way that, in soccer, these communities are actually linked. The designation

Youth soccer in LA takes many forms. Here a middle school girl plays in an after-school program of the Los Angeles Unified School District. Photo courtesy of LA84 Foundation.

"Latin" partly acknowledges the history of those leagues as social and cultural spaces as quite distinct from the "Anglo" scene, which is grounded at the youth level in organizations like the all-volunteer/"everybody plays" AYSO, and its opposite: expensive, competitive "traveling clubs." In the densest parts of Los Angeles, public high schools are not reliable spaces for youth sports, as many are poorly funded; the coaching and development of talented Latino players from under-resourced communities is largely staged via ethnic/Latin leagues, which the USSF has only recently begun to integrate into its own development strategies. National team programs from Mexico and Central America scout from ethnic/independent/"Latin" leagues.

This, however, can also be the site for graft, as families pay to register their kids for such camps, with little chance that those kids are actually under serious consideration—national team programs more serious about recruiting eligible international players from the United States will exploit the NCAA's player pool.

We romance the idea that this sport transcends material difference, but in point of fact, at the grassroots level, one runs up against the simple truth that the sport's association with Latino men marks it as something to be policed rather than nurtured. ("No se puede jugar soccer.") That is one of the most important things I learned from my years playing in the sport's unincorporated zones, "kickabouts," and "independent"/"ethnic" leagues. These spaces can be utopian and transformative. But these spaces also mark out the racialized frontline of class warfare, and the city's deeply conflicted identity.

Synthetic Meadows

Thanks to Donna Summer's disco cover of a Jimmy Webb love song, MacArthur Park is one of Los Angeles's most famous. Built in the 1880s, the park enjoyed a few decades as a vacation spot surrounded by luxury hotels. One hundred years later, it had become notorious as one of the most dangerous places in LA. Famously, when the lake was drained in the 1970s, workers found hundreds of discarded firearms.

In the new century, however, things turned around. City officials attributed the drop in crime to the Los Angeles Police Department's patrols and security cameras. Gradually, the park seemed to open its arms to its neighbors. During the day, the park is carpeted with picnicking families, teenagers, workers eating lunch, loafers taking naps, and street vendors selling everything from toys to roasted corn and ice cream. On the weekend, streets around the park are taken over by carnivals. The park's social fabric reminds people of hometowns in Mexico, Honduras, El Salvador, and Guatemala even as the park's design and geography (open, exposed to the sun, framed and sliced in half by wide boulevards) couldn't feel more different from an Oaxacan or Honduran village square.[17] But people feel recognized and welcome in a city that often does not acknowledge them as Angelenos. It is no accident that marches on behalf of the immigrant and migrant communities in Los Angeles have ended here—peaceful marches that the LAPD met with batons, rubber bullets, and tear gas. Video footage of the LAPD's 2007 May Day assault on the neighborhood shows them advancing with their weapons across, as it happens, a dirt soccer field.

There are no official fields in MacArthur Park. But until October 2008, two were chalked out on packed dirt in its northern half. Daniel Morales, a community center employee, had claimed this section of the park and organized leagues from the abundant informal games that animated almost every spot they could. Urban studies scholar Kelly Main speculates that the park's renaissance owed less to the LAPD security cameras, which they don't have the funds to maintain, than to the presence of these squatting leagues that brought scores of the same people to the park every day and gave them a reason to care about what was happening there. The community center employee's scheme was in fact so successful that the games played here came to *represent* Los Angeles soccer culture. For more than a decade, when the media has needed to invoke images of local *fútbol* culture, it has turned to this pirate *cancha*. The 2005 international hit movie *Goal* opens with a young Mexican migrant worker being scouted for the English Premiership while playing in an independent, "Latin" league. The *Los Angeles Times* mines this part of the park for soccer stories when it wants to paint a quaint picture of the communities that define the city, as in a 2008 feel-good profile of a Guatemalan women's team in which squad members describe feeling most like "American women" when they step onto the dusty ground in their uniforms.[18] In 2006, when Adidas mounted a series of television spots (Adidas+10) in which two players from rival national teams meet up and recruit people off the street to play improvised showdowns, the USA v. Mexico game was staged in this dusty bowl. The ad implicitly reproduced the racial geographies of the city: the USA squad was recruited from Venice Beach, the Mexico side was recruited from the neighborhood around MacArthur Park itself. They might have easily recruited from within the park, but had they done this, both teams would likely have been entirely Latino, and posed problems for viewers who imagine Americans otherwise. In any case, the fact that the neighborhood around MacArthur Park is largely Salvadoran, and that Los Angeles's most-celebrated Mexican/Chicano neighborhoods are farther to the east, was perhaps not relevant to the Adidas folks, who were more after a Mexican "look" than a Mexican, or Chicano, reality. USA won, on penalty kicks. MacArthur Park, apparently, is not the Estadio Azteca.

As this part of the park became a favored cinematic location, and even as crime in the park nosedived thanks to its popularity, neighborhood "stakeholders" organized to try to force the squatting leagues out. In the same month that the *Times* ran its profile of the Guatemalan women players, the city broke ground on the "MacArthur Park Improvement Project." The Department of Parks and Recreation promised to add a new, flood-lit artificial turf field to the half dozen they manage across Los Angeles. A local city councilman hosted a "soccerfest" carnival, celebrating the *fútbol* community of MacArthur Park and heralding the park's future playing space. The *Times* ran a story about the temporary displacement of the leagues and how much everyone was looking forward to returning to the new and improved field.[19]

This section of MacArthur Park was fenced off, and the city relocated the informal leagues to Vista Hermosa, which is a short bus ride from MacArthur Park. Vista Hermosa is tucked into a forgotten corner of Los Angeles in a former oil field near the Hollywood Freeway. It was the first new park opened in this part of Los Angeles in nearly one hundred years. The location was the site of public scandal in the 1990s when the city had to abandon the construction of a high school over the toxic, methane-pocketed land. The field sits at the base of a terraced hillside, populated now by native plants. The field is a little tight, probably more suited for nine-a-side, if such a thing existed. One edge of the field faces a broad street, and some design regulation has prevented the building of a high fence. So balls fly off the field and bounce into the neighborhood.

People around MacArthur Park were excited about the new field being built there. People were excited by the vision described in a press release from the Los Angeles Department of Recreation and Parks: "A 37,000 square-foot synthetic field will replace the existing dirt field. When completed the new field will be added to the half dozen synthetic turf playing fields managed by the Department."[20] The artificial surface would be easier to play on, and, given its central location, it would have become a marquee ground—a great place to play before a crowd. It is hard to overstate what such a thing would have meant for the neighborhood—to have this pastime, so fundamental to social life, embraced and even showcased. As the contractor put down the turf and the improvements began to take shape, however, a complex reality emerged.

A gently sloped and curved patch of green plastic replaced the dirt field. It is barely half the length of a field and far too narrow. The field is ringed not by floodlights, but by fake gas lamps. Such changes are symptomatic of the investment of Los Angeles property owners and city officials in pastoral fantasies of green "passive use" parks—fantasies rooted in the geography and climate of cities like New York or London. For many, park improvement means green grass, romantic couples in paddleboats, and other pretty pictures. The huge parks that ring Los Angeles (like Griffith Park, one of the largest municipal parks in the United States) certainly invite such ambitions, but they are also home to mountain lions, rattlesnakes, and wildfires, hardly the stuff of bourgeois daydreams. Some Angelenos long to have their own Central Park—a tasteful urban oasis. MacArthur Park has, traditionally, been the staging ground for that fantasy.

Set between an ocean and a desert, hot and dry most of the year, Los Angeles is the most densely populated urban area west of the Mississippi River; a park here will never be green unless it is fenced off and the grass continuously nursed. MacArthur Park isn't big like Central Park or the Bois de Boulogne; it will never be a "quiet" space unless you push out the noisy people who use it. Roughly the size of six large city blocks, it is a bit of rare open space in a neighborhood where buildings swell and eat up every inch of grass.

When the mayor broke ground on the project, the city said it was building a soccer field. A few months later, they started calling it a "synthetic children's meadow."[21] As a spokesperson for the contractor (Parkwest Landscape, Inc.) explained to me, "It is definitely not a soccer field." A walkway of packed dirt rings this bean-shaped playground. Where there should be corners, there are curves. The surface slopes so much that with a little momentum, a kid can roll on her side across it. Given the appalling shape of the "field," we thought *fútbol* here was done. But leagues came back. Small games are played up- and downhill, with portable goals and a serpentine touchline like no other I've ever seen. It is still the best place in Los Angeles to watch a game.

Meanwhile, rents in this part of town more than doubled, aggravating overcrowding for some, as people pack even hallways to make the rent, and pushing others out as they give up on the neighborhood altogether. Two aspiring journalists (Kara Mears and Devin Browne), both white women, set up camp in an apartment near the park and published a blog that approached the neighborhood as if it were Los Angeles's own Dark Continent. Evidencing the problem of white, liberal approaches of this and other Latino neighborhoods, the two documented their time in the neighborhood with the depth of an enthusiastic, sentimental poverty tourist. Journalist Daniel Hernandez published a sharp critique of the project, in which he shared the following observation, from fellow reporter Eileen Truax:

> Latinos are half the population of L.A. but they [Anglos] still see us as an uncomfortable appendage, as if we were a tumor that grows on and invades half the body; it is occupying the space but it is not the body itself.[22]

Truax's language captures the situation of the grassroots game in Los Angeles: in a very real way, Latino fans and players are narrated as aliens in their home. The players who insist on staging games on the bean-shaped synthetic meadow of MacArthur Park appear from one angle as an occupying force, and from another, as indigenous. Either way, the story is one that moves toward removal. Where once MacArthur Park's *fútbolistas* played under the surveillance of LADP cameras, they now play under the watchful eyes of neighborhood developers.[23]

Police Playing the Police

I was a founding officer for the Union Football League, an AYSO-affiliated adult men's league that played its matches from 2009 to 2011 on a pitch just east of MacArthur Park, at the corner of 7th Street and Union Avenue. When we heard that the Los Angeles Police Department would field a team during our first season we were a bit wary.

The field is smack in the middle of Pico-Union and right down the street from a new police station. This neighborhood is the home of the infamous 1990s Ramparts Scandal (a terrible case of police corruption and abuse of power within a unit specializing in policing gangs). It is also the neighborhood of the May Day "Melee" in which the LAPD used violence to break up a peaceful march and demonstration calling for reform in immigration policies in the United States, and for recognition of the rights of the migrant communities that define the region. The cops in this neighborhood have long been working under a self-generated cloud of fear, anger, and mistrust.

The whole experience was something of a nightmare. The LAPD squad that signed up for our league was muscle bound and incredibly fit. They were a tough team. They could run you into next year, and they did not shy away from using their size advantage to win the ball. There was nothing wrong with that. But they also had a coach who shouted from the sidelines: "Take him out!" "Take him down!" and "Get him!"—while wearing a dark blue jacket with the letters "LAPD" across his back. Guys from several teams reported more disturbing remarks made on and off the field by LAPD players. The cops had a tendency for what I came to think of as existentialist trash talk; for example, "This [the game] is all you have, you have nothing to go home to. You *are* nothing."

As fit as they were, their ball handling was just OK. When confronted with the better teams in our league—who played a fast passing game dependent on footwork, bursts of speed, and an ability to change direction and turn in a blink—the cops were sometimes undone by the very thing they normally relied on: their size and their physicality. It's an old story: the confrontation between a militaristic defensive game and the flash, bob, and weave of joga bonito.

In general, when things didn't go their way, they got visibly and audibly frustrated, and played not better but meaner and harder. They played with a win-at-all-costs attitude and were convinced every whistle made in their direction was misplaced. They complained endlessly about the referees—so much so that I suspect the referees dreaded working their matches. As I was the league treasurer, I may have spoken with the team the most. They were the last team to pay its dues. Every week I checked in about the outstanding dues, made small talk, and tried to get to know them.

I had a series of conversations with their manager about the problems that were growing from their presence in our league. He was genuinely upset by the tone of the games and remarkably open in sharing his perspective and experience. It seemed to them that neither their opponents nor the referees could forget that they were the "cop team." He said that they never had this problem playing in more Anglo settings on the west side or in the south bay area (both whiter areas of the city and wealthier). Although a majority of the men on the LAPD team were Latino, according to the team manager, they seemed only to have problems playing in parts of the city like ours.

It all comes to a head toward the end of the season. It was a big game between the LAPD team and Niky's Sports. Niky's was an unbeatable squad sponsored by the soccer shop across from our field. Niky's had everything: skill, knowledge, experience, strength, and speed. They, in fact, played some of the best, most entertaining football I'd ever seen. I didn't get to see that side of their game, however, the night they took on the LAPD. The LAPD team committed a series of violent and illegal tackles. They were relentless in antagonizing their opponent and the referees. The center referee lost control of the match after thirty minutes, and, fearing that a player would be seriously hurt, or that the game would descend into a melee, he rightly called it off.

All of the referees and the spectators with whom I spoke held the LAPD team responsible for the disintegration of the match. Their game was marked that night by verbal abuse, dangerous play, and free-floating anger. The men from Niky's, normally the more "emotional" of the teams in our league (one of the many reasons they were entertaining to watch), were remarkably calm (and went on to finish the season with an almost perfect record).

The day after that disastrous match, the manager withdrew the LAPD from the league. Their departure was inevitable and we were glad they knew this. We talked on the phone, and I learned this wasn't the first time this had happened. The manager (who had spent the weekend assisting with wildfires and wasn't at the match) sounded exhausted and depressed. It had been years since they'd tried playing in a league like ours, because previous attempts had ended exactly this way. He told me, in fact, that Internal Affairs advised them to withdraw from our league (fearing that if they injured an opposing player, the LAPD might be sued). In that conversation, I caught a glimpse of the complexity of his position—and the seductive lure of the fantasy we had all indulged in imagining things could unfold any other way than they did.

People wax romantic about the utopic possibilities generated through football but realities of power and authority and significant histories of abuses of both can't be wished away. It is not possible for a cop team to play in one of the most policed neighborhoods in the region and imagine that we can all forget who they are. The cops don't forget it. The player stopped and searched as he pulled into his own driveway ("lots of Toyotas in this neighborhood are stolen") and then issued a citation for making a dangerous turn (again, into his own driveway) won't forget. Nor will the guy with a brother in jail. Nor the guy harassed because of his immigration status. Nor will the guy arrested last week for doing what people do at parties in the Hollywood Hills sans repercussion.

Forgetting is a form of entitlement. Forgetting who and where we are is a luxury. If Anglo teams in middle-class swaths of beachside communities "forget" they are playing the cops, it's because they do not experience themselves as "policed." And if the cops can forget that they are cops when they play those teams, it's because those players were not the ones they were policing.

CHAPTER FOUR

Figure Skating in Southern California

From Frontier to Epicenter

SUSAN BROWNELL

The year 2016 marks the centennial anniversary of the introduction of ice skating in Southern California, a development that depended on the arrival of artificial ice-making technology. In January 1916, after a Saturday on which three thousand skaters and spectators had spent the day at the newly opened Broadway Ice Palace, the rink manager predicted to a reporter, "Ice skating promises to become as popular in Southern California as tennis or golf." The reporter was dubious: "A broad assertion, but one can never tell."[1] The reporter would clearly have been surprised that in five decades sunny Southern California would become a world center for figure skating, and would host the World Championships in 2009. A main reason for this unlikely relationship was the uneasy position of ice skating between sport and entertainment. Hollywood was a natural incubator for show skating, and show skating and amateur competitive skating mutually benefited each other. In the early skating centers on the eastern seaboard and Chicago, competitive skating was controlled by clubs that were also social clubs for elites of European and American backgrounds who could afford the expensive sport and who strictly enforced an "amateur" ideal to keep out those who could not. By contrast, in Southern California the economic opportunities in show skating enabled coaches and skaters from diverse backgrounds to prosper. Therefore, the rise of Southern Californians in the sport over the course of the twentieth century was one facet reflecting the emergence of a more equitable American society.

The 1916–1917 Tank Show Craze

As early as 1868, a huge artificial ice rink opened in New York City under an arched, cast-iron ceiling that covered an ice surface the size of a football field; but the West Coast lagged far behind.[2] The outbreak of World War I in Europe sent history's first "ice ballet" star, Charlotte Oelschlagel, from Berlin to New York in 1915. She and her chorus line were the climactic act for the wildly popular music and dance extravaganza "Hip-Hip Hurray" at the Hippodrome, the premier theater in New York. The show went on the road, utilizing a recently invented technology—small portable ice surfaces known as "tanks." The "tank show" craze arrived in Los Angeles in March 1916 when the Bristol Café at 4th and Spring, one of the most popular eating places in Los Angeles, installed the first permanent tank ice rink in Southern California in order to stage ice shows to complement its cabaret shows.[3] The *Los Angeles Evening Herald* declared, "Ice skating has broken the ice in Los Angeles. The latest craze of society in the east has caught on here like wildfire and the Angeleno smart set is preparing to give it a warm welcome." The first amateur ice skating racing tournament in Southern California was held there on March 31, overseen by the president of the International Skating Union of America.[4]

The rink that opened in April 1916 at the head of the amusement zone at the Panama-California Exposition in Balboa Park, San Diego, was said to be twice as large as any artificial rink in California at that time. "Thousands of native sons and daughters are enjoying their first skating at this amusement place, and it has proven one of the most popular amusement enterprises ever opened in the West."[5] While it is not clear how long that rink lasted, Balboa Park has housed ice rinks off and on since that time and does so today. George Marston, the park's developer and a major figure in the development of San Diego, had learned "fancy skating" as a boy in Wisconsin before his father moved to San Diego. He was such a lover of ice skating that in the 1940s, when he was in his nineties, he would sneak away to Los Angeles to skate since his doctors in San Diego had forbidden it.[6]

Ice skating was one of the few sports considered acceptable for women because it conformed with the ideals of femininity. When the "skating queen" Lora Jean came to the Bristol Café for an engagement, she promoted skating for women by arguing that "ice is an aid to beauty": "skating on ice makes the feet graceful and the lower limbs shapely. It reduces the size of the hips, thus making for a good figure." She asserted that skating was more beneficial than dancing and walking and that California girls lacked the ruddy glow on their cheeks, for which eastern girls were famous, because they did not ice skate.[7]

In 1917 the Bristol Café and the nearby Harlow Café were the two rinks in Los Angeles available for entertainment engagements, according to the *Billboard* magazine, which covered the entertainment industry nationwide then as now. Actually, at that time roller skating was far more popular than ice skating, with the list of roller rinks across the country numbering around 575, while the ice rinks only numbered 27. California had 10 roller rinks and 5 ice rinks—with the 2 café rinks and the Ice Rink in Balboa Park bringing the total of rinks in Southern California to 3.[8]

The *Billboard* missed the third rink in Los Angeles, the Broadway Ice Skating Palace located at 1041 South Broadway, five blocks due east of today's Staples Center. Shortly after opening, it had to eliminate all formal entertainment "in answer to an insistent demand that nothing be allowed to obtrude upon the three hours of public skating at each session." The Southern California Hockey League was formed in February 1917. Games were played on Monday and Thursday evenings. Perhaps not surprisingly, the "Canadian team" composed of Canadian ex-patriots beat out the other four teams to win the first championship.[9]

Tank ice was short lived in Los Angeles because of the escalation of World War I: key male employees left for military service, a more frugal clientele led the Bristol to lower its meal prices, and at the end of 1917 it changed its name to the American Café, hoping that its patriotic rebranding would attract more customers. It was remodeled at the start of 1918, after which there was no more mention of the Ice Palace. Both the Bristol and the Harlow closed when an ordinance prohibiting saloons went into effect on April 1, 1918.

The East v. the West

The International Skating Union (ISU) of America, which had been founded in 1907 to represent American and Canadian members, was primarily interested in speed skating. In part due to the absence of a responsible organization, it does not appear that figure skating competitions were organized in California until decades after that first speed skating competition. In 1921, the ISU-America agreed to hand over control of figure skating to an association dedicated to the discipline, and the United States Figure Skating Association (USFS) was founded.[10]

In 1928 the Glacier Palace opened at 613 North Van Ness Avenue, a huge wooden structure like most of the rinks being built in that era. In 1934 it changed its name to the Polar Palace and the Los Angeles Figure Skating Club moved there, turning it into an anchor of figure skating in the city until, like many of the wooden rinks, it burned to the ground in 1963. The Ice Follies performed there for the first time in Los Angeles in 1939 and the US Championships were held there in 1954.[11]

Figure skating had been contested in the London 1908 Olympics and the Antwerp 1920 Olympics. The first separate winter Games were in 1924. When Los Angeles was bidding for the 1932 summer Olympic Games, it was the first bid contest after the International Olympic Committee decided that one country should host both the summer and winter Games. Yosemite Park in central California had built a new skating rink, and to support its Olympic bid it began organizing competitions under the auspices of the California Skating Association (CSA). The CSA had been organizing roller skating road races and speed skating races on ice in Los Angeles since the mid-1920s. In 1929 the Yosemite Winter Club was organized at the request of the California Chamber of Commerce and the San Joaquin Valley Tourist and Travel Association, and requested affiliation with the CSA.

Felix Locher was the one who presented the request to the CSA for recognition of the Yosemite Club. Originally from Berne, Switzerland, he had won the Swiss amateur figure skating championships in St. Moritz in 1911, and in the same year emigrated to Fresno. His request to the CSA was not as simple as it might seem today, since it was apparently the first organization to seek an affiliation.[12] He became a member of the board of the CSA, a competition judge, and an officer of the Los Angeles Figure Skating Club.[13] The First Outdoor California Figure Skating Championships were held in Yosemite in February 1933; Los Angelenos won six of the seven gold medals contested in freestyle, figures, and dance. In September Locher moved to Los Angeles.[14] The close link between Hollywood, elite Angeleno society, and skating was seen in the fact that a number of "society and movie people" attended the contests in Yosemite as spectators.[15] The Los Angeles Figure Skating Club became the first USFS member club in Southern California in October 1933. It is likely that Locher's expertise and connections were crucial to the early success of the club, since it appears that the main qualification of the first president, J. M. LeRoy, was that he moved in the leading Los Angeles social circles and was married to a "Hollywood clubwoman" (i.e., socialite).[16] Locher was also quickly snapped up by the USFS and named the Amateur Committee representative in Southern California, giving him the all-important power to approve the amateur status of skaters, which was necessary to compete in USFS-sanctioned competitions.[17]

Locher later became known as the father of the actor Jon Hall (whose given name was Charles Felix Locher), who starred in the 1937 smash hit *The Hurricane* opposite Dorothy Lamour and has two stars on the Hollywood Walk of Fame—one for film and one for television. After his son retired, Locher himself began acting at the age of seventy-three and appeared in numerous television shows and movies, including an episode in the original *Star Trek*, before he died in 1969.[18]

In its annual meeting in 1933, the Executive Committee of the USFS considered the situation in California "to be most complicated involving considerable danger to the U.S.F.S. if district associations were given permanent power to control figure skating."[19] Given the domination of figure skating by the Northeast, it was not surprising that Lake Placid won the 1932 Olympic bid, but the USFS realized that it must extend its influence west of the Mississippi River in order to neutralize the threat posed by an organization—the CSA—that claimed control over an entire region. On the one hand, the founder and president of the CSA was the formidable Donald Tresidder, who was president of the Yosemite Park and Curry Co. (the main concessioner at the park, at that time building a hotel inside Yosemite) and later became the fourth president of Stanford University.[20] Tresidder had staked his claim in a letter to the USFS stating that "the only way figure skating can be developed in California was through the California Skating Association and its Figure Skating Board."[21]

On the other hand, skating in California did not conform to the amateur rules required by the IOC and promulgated by the ISU and the USFS. Exhibitions were not sanctioned and amateur skaters were appearing in motion pictures. The Amateur Committee of the USFS had ruled that amateur skaters should not appear in such productions, whether paid or not. The Executive Committee decided that the USFS would send a delegate to California to negotiate an agreement with the CSA and the local clubs. The visit of USFS secretary Richard Hapgood in December "was the first occasion that an Eastern figure skating representative had ever, as far as is known, established official contact with the figure skating enthusiasts of the Pacific Coast."[22] Although the initial agreement allowed the CSA to act as an intermediary organization between the local clubs and the USFS, the CSA's raison d'être was undermined and it soon disappeared.[23]

In short, in 1933 American figure skating was thoroughly dominated by the eastern seaboard. Out of the total of fifty-six competitors in the 1933 National Championships, there were only four competitors from west of the Mississippi—and even then just barely, since three were from the Twin Cities and one from Detroit.[24] By 1934, four California clubs had become members of the USFS, with a total of 280 members: Oakland's St. Moritz Ice Skating Club (150 members), San Francisco's The Skate and Ski Club (45), Yosemite Winter Club (65), and Los Angeles Figure Skating Club (20).[25]

But in only a few years, the fledgling sport would receive a big boost with Sonja Henie's grand entry into Hollywood.

Sonja Henie

Sonja Henie grew up in Norway, and won ten Ladies' Figure Skating World Championships from 1927 to 1936 and three Olympic gold medals in 1928, 1932, and 1936. After her final Olympics, she traveled to the United States accompanied by her mother, father, and World silver medalist Jack Dunn from Britain, and appeared in shows from the East Coast to Minneapolis. She finally reached the West Coast when her promoter rented the Polar Palace, the only rink in Hollywood, and put on a spectacular show to which film executives and stars were invited. She was signed by Twentieth Century Fox, resulting in nine motion pictures over seven years. In 1937, "Miss Sonja Henie with her Hollywood Ice Review," a cast of sixty skaters, rehearsed at the Polar Palace and toured the country to sold-out performances.[26]

Henie and her retinue either practiced or performed at all of the area ice rinks, where her costumes, jewelry, makeup, and regal carriage—not to mention her skating—left a lasting impression on the local skaters and coaches. Most of the area champions of the following two decades listed seeing one of her movies or shows as one of the reasons they became involved in the sport. Henie's shows employed large numbers of local skaters, and although their skating levels were at first low, they no doubt improved while taking part in the shows and watching her. Many of the skaters went on to coach, manage, and perform elsewhere. The success of Henie's shows encouraged other shows to stop over in Los Angeles and stimulated the establishment of more shows. When the Pan-Pacific Auditorium at 7600 West Beverly Boulevard was enlarged in 1939, the credit was given to her: "Sonja Henie has shown how much influence a pretty young lady on skates can exert by making ice skating one of the fastest-growing sports in America."[27]

Perhaps Henie's most important contribution was to make skating economically viable—she was, after all, one of the highest-paid stars in Hollywood in her heyday.

The First National Champions from Southern California

Henie might have made Los Angeles the epicenter of show skating, but Californians had not yet made their mark in national competitions. Los Angeles skaters were lured into turning professional for movies and shows, and the Los Angeles Skating Club lost many promising skaters to the entertainment industry. After a visit to the West Coast in 1939, a USFS leader predicted that amateur skating would only develop if "the amateur life becomes sufficiently attractive to bridle the alluring and glamorous appeal portrayed by professional promoters."[28]

At the end of 1936, Maribel Vinson traveled to several cities on the West Coast. She had eight of her eventual nine US ladies' championships under her belt, a record that would only be equaled by one skater in the following seventy years—Southern California's Michelle Kwan. Vinson observed that the Los Angeles Figure Skating Club's fifty members skated under difficult conditions because "The Polar Palace management is not overly friendly to figure skating." It only rented an hour and a half weekly to the club, and provided "a victrola that could play pieces at only one tempo and that so fast no one could skate to it." Nevertheless, "It was great fun, all of it, and now it's up to the Western skaters to come East. That's the next move."[29]

California was coming on. The 1937 National Championships in Chicago were the first to be held away from the eastern seaboard; *Skating* magazine observed that "the outstanding feature of the meet was undoubtedly the participation of a contingent of skaters from the Pacific coast."[30] The following year Eugene Turner, who was from the Los Angeles Figure Skating Club and coached by Henie's skating partner Jack Dunn, became the first National Champion from the West Coast when he won the Men's Junior Championship.[31] After a bronze in the Senior Championship in 1939, he became the first skater from west of the Mississippi to win a National Senior Men's title in 1940; ironically, he beat out another non–East Coast skater, his rival Ollie Haupt Jr., from St. Louis.[32] Neither had a chance to compete in the Olympic Games, which were canceled due to the war. Turner repeated the title in 1941, receiving a perfect score from one judge. He also won the pairs title with Donna Atwood of the Mercury Figure Skating Club and was second in dance with Elizabeth

Kennedy, becoming the first and only skater to win national medals in all three disciplines.

When the 1941 World Championships were canceled due to the war, Atwood turned pro and joined the Ice Capades, and Turner spent a year with Sonja Henie's touring show as her primary skating partner.[33] He then joined the US Army Air Corps and completed sixty-nine missions over Germany.[34] He eventually became an influential coach at the Polar Palace where, among other accomplishments, he choreographed Tenley Albright's freestyle program for her 1956 Olympic gold medal. He also wrote the "Turner's Turn" column for *Skating* magazine for many years.[35]

In the days of the mandatory draft, wars dealt a blow to sports. As had happened during World War I, the exodus of young men into the military took its toll on the sport, and eventually the National Men's Singles Championships were canceled in 1944 and 1945. This temporarily stymied the growth spurt that had just begun in the Midwest and Pacific Coast: eighteen of twenty-three new USFS clubs formed from 1939 to 1941 were located in those sections of the country.[36] In 1939 the San Diego Figure Skating Club was established as well as another club in Los Angeles that was to become a powerhouse in figure skating—All Year Figure Skating Club, which made its home in the recently opened Tropical Ice Gardens, a huge outdoor, all-year ice rink at the edge of the UCLA campus, which was the home to Bruins ice hockey.[37] In 1941 there were ninety-one USFS clubs in the United States, of which six were in Southern California. The Los Angeles Figure Skating Club was the tenth biggest in the country, with its 119 subscribers to *Skating* magazine slightly outnumbering those of the oldest club in the United States, the Philadelphia Skating Club and Humane Society.[38]

Innovative Technology: The Zamboni Machine

In the 1920s, Frank Zamboni and his brother Lawrence built refrigeration units for dairies to keep their milk cool and also produced ice blocks in Hynes and Clearwater (later unified as the city of Paramount in 1948). As refrigeration technology began to make the ice-making business obsolete, in 1939 they applied their skills in a new direction and opened the Iceland rink (later known as the Paramount Iceland) across the street from the ice plant, which sent refrigerant under the street to the rink.[39] The Arctic Blades Figure Skating Club, founded in 1942, made Iceland its home, and became another takeoff point for future champions.⁴⁰ The club hosted the 1963 US Championships, which were held at the Long Beach Arena.

The process of maintaining smooth ice in the early rinks was very time-consuming. As many as five workers spent an hour or more following a tractor-pulled scraper, scooping up the trail of shavings, spraying water, and smoothing the ice. When a pulley cable broke on the machine used to make the ice at the Broadway Ice Skating Palace in 1917, it made the news because the afternoon and evening sessions were canceled, hundreds of people were turned away, and the Palace lost several hundred dollars in revenue.⁴¹ For seven years Frank Zamboni experimented before finally coming up with a better solution in 1949. The contraption could make smooth ice in just fifteen minutes.⁴² The Zamboni machine became not only a fixture at ice rinks around the world, it also made its way into popular culture. The *Peanuts* cartoon character Charlie Brown once said, "there are three things in life that people like to stare at: a flowing stream, a crackling fire, and a Zamboni clearing the ice."⁴³

Southern California's Rise and the World Team's Plane Crash

It was fifteen years until Southern California produced its next national champions. Joan Zamboni and Roland Junso won the Senior Dance Championship in 1956. Zamboni, "an attractive 22-year-old, with shoulder length auburn hair and chameleon eyes," was the only child of Frank Zamboni, skated at the Iceland rink that he owned, and was employed at his company.⁴⁴ The dance pair retired and become pros at the Iceland rink. They were succeeded as national champions the following year by Sharon McKenzie and Bert Wright, members of the Los Angeles Figure Skating Club, who won the bronze medal at the World Championships. This was the first American medal in dance, which had not been included in the World Championships until 1952. Southern Californians dominated US ice dance until 1966, winning seven of the eleven championships. Kristin Fortune and Dennis Sveum, members of the Los Angeles Figure Skating Club, became the second Americans to win a silver medal at the World Championships in 1966. For the next forty-five years, no American couple would do better than silver until Meryl Davis and Charlie White finally seized the top spot in 2011.

In 1960, Squaw Valley, California, hosted the second US winter Olympics, establishing the resort area as the mecca for figure skating that it has remained since then. The ebullience about the bright future of the sport after the gold medal performances by Carol Heiss and David Jenkins was shattered one year later, when the airplane carrying the US team crashed on its approach to the Brussels airport on route to the World Championships in Prague. Eighteen members of the US team along with sixteen of their friends, family, and coaches died in the disaster. The brightest young stars and some of the most talented coaches were snuffed out before fulfilling their potential. Gone were Maribel Vinson, by then an extremely influential coach, and her two skating daughters. As a measure of how Southern California was beginning to emerge as a center for the sport, it suffered a disproportionately heavy loss. Eight of the thirty-four deceased were from Southern California: national dance champions Diane Sherbloom and Larry Pierce; silver medalists Dona Lee Carrier and Roger Campbell, Roger's mother, and their coach William Kipp (who had been largely responsible for the area's rise in ice dance); Ladies' Singles bronze medalist Rhode Lee Michelson; and World team manager Dean McMinn, a 1960 Olympic judge and one of the founding members of the Arctic Blades club. Sylvia Stoddard, a skater at the time, recalled that leading up to the memorial ceremony held at the Lafayette Hotel Ballroom in Long Beach, "first we trooped to funeral after funeral, a grim task heightened by the youth of so many of the dead."[45]

As severe a blow as the tragedy was, it was also the ashes out of which arose the heyday of Southern California skating. The Arctic Blades Figure Skating Club, which had claimed four of the deceased as members, came back for redemption. The following year, Barbara Roles-Pursley was persuaded to come out of retirement after her bronze medal-winning performance in the 1960 Olympics and the birth of her son. She won the first National Singles title for a Southern Californian in the twenty-two years since Eugene Turner's victory. An Arctic Blades couple also won the National Dance Championship.

Peggy Fleming

Peggy Fleming was born on a farm outside of San Jose and moved to Los Angeles to train with William Kipp. Following the airplane disaster, she won a silver medal in the Novice Ladies division in 1962 and was pushed into the limelight before her turn. It was customary that skaters moved in an orderly succession up through the ranks from Novice to Junior to Senior, based on consensus among the USFS-credentialed judges, who held a great deal of power over the sport. Normally, Fleming would have had to wait until the previous champions retired before being allowed into the top spot. However, the cohort above her had been wiped out. In addition, her family did not belong to the social stratum that controlled the sport. "We were often made to feel that we were crashing the party. We just weren't from the same world as the more well-off families whose sons and daughters were part of the country club set known as 'the skating world,'" she wrote in her biography.[46] Representing the Arctic Blades, she won the 1964 Senior Ladies title at the age of fifteen.

After working with John Nicks and choreographer Robert Paul through 1965, she moved to Colorado Springs to train with Carlo Fassi and proceeded to win five consecutive US championships through 1968. At that time, compulsory exercises in figures—figure-eight shapes that had to be retraced several times in a tedious process demanding tremendous concentration—accounted for 60 percent of the total score compared to 40 percent for the freestyle program. Fleming's figures improved due both to Fassi's coaching and to better training conditions: the Broadmoor had the special gray-tinted ice that skaters needed to see the tracings of their figures clearly, which she did not have in California.[47] Her improvement in figures took her to the top of the podium at the 1966 World Championships, and she repeated in 1967 and 1968.

Fleming's rise coincided with the arrival of a new era in sports television. ABC's *Wide World of Sports* was begun in 1961; it covered the World Figure Skating Championships the next year, and broadcast the first coverage of a US figure skating championship in 1964, followed by the Innsbruck winter Games.[48] Figure skating was one of the marquee sports for ABC, and television made figure skating champions into some of the most famous athletes in the United States. When Fleming capped off her career with a gold medal at the Grenoble 1968 Olympics wearing a chartreuse dress sewn by her mother, and with a pile of brown hair atop her head, she became one of the most iconic female athletes of the twentieth century. Of course, there was a lot of pent-up heroine worship among the female fans, because those were the days before Title IX opened up opportunities in other sports, and rigid ideas of femininity meant that figure skaters and tennis players were the only female athletes whom the media held up for that kind of adulation. In the same era, tennis player Billie Jean King was the other national sports idol. Nevertheless, as E. M. Swift later wrote in a retrospective for *Sports Illustrated*,

> When 19-year-old Peggy Fleming glided into the adoring embrace of the American public by winning the gold medal at the 1968 Olympics in Grenoble,

she launched figure skating's modern era. Pretty and balletic, elegant and stylish, Fleming took a staid sport that was shackled by its inscrutable compulsory figures and arcane scoring system and, with television as her ally, made it marvelously glamorous.[49]

The sport began to be remade for television: in 1968, figures were devalued to 50 percent of the total score to give more weight to the television-friendly freestyle program. After the Olympics she signed a five-year television contract reported to be worth $500,000, and her five television specials proved to be surprisingly popular.[50] In addition to being one of the best-known athletes of the last half century, Fleming advanced the development of the sport through her professional shows and thirty years of skating commentary for ABC with Dick Button starting in 1981.

John Nicks and Frank Carroll

Meanwhile, two of history's greatest figure skating coaches were setting up shop in Southern California. John Nicks came from Great Britain to replace William Kipp at Frank Zamboni's Paramount Iceland after the plane crash. As a pairs skater with his sister, he had won four World Championship medals (including gold in 1953) and competed at the 1948 and 1952 Olympic Winter Games. By 1968 he had guided the pairs team of JoJo Starbuck and Ken Shelley to the Olympic Games. They were followed by Tai Babilonia and Randy Gardner, Natasha Kuchiki and Todd Sand, and then Jenni Meno and Todd Sand. In the 1990s, Nicks discovered Sasha Cohen in a Costa Mesa skating class. In 2006 she won both the National Championships and the Olympic silver medal in Torino, the last American woman to reach an Olympic medal podium after a half-century run of dominance. She changed the sport with her excellent flexibility and popularized the "pole spin," an upright spin with the free leg held close to the torso in a vertical split.[51]

Frank Carroll had been coached by the great Maribel Vinson. After skating for the Ice Follies from 1960 to 1964, he was persuaded by friends in the movie business to move to Hollywood. Realizing that he could not compete with the good-looking, New York–trained male actors, he began teaching skating at Paramount Iceland. He recalled,

Olympic silver medalist and two-time World Champion Linda Fratianne training in Southern California. Photo courtesy of LA84 Foundation.

I quickly grasped the fact that most of the people teaching skating didn't have a very good background and didn't have a formidable teacher like I did in Maribel. And in just a few lessons I could get kids to do things that they had been struggling months to do. And so my teaching sort of snowballed from one month to the other and I developed quite a little league of very fine developing skaters.[52]

His first standout was Linda Fratianne, a four-time National Champion (1977–1980) and two-time World Champion (1977 and 1979). As the reigning World Champion going into the 1980 Olympics, she was favored to win, and her second place behind East German Annett Pötzsch incited accusations of Eastern Bloc judging. In addition to being the first woman to land two different triple jumps in one program, Fratianne made another contribution to figure skating: she introduced some Hollywood glamour by wearing costumes designed by Hollywood designer Bob Mackie, in a sport in which mothers had traditionally sewn their daughters' dresses.[53] Frank Carroll's first National Men's Champion was Christopher Bowman, who won the title in 1989 and 1992.

For a time, another star coach, Richard Callaghan, was located in San Diego, and his pupil Todd Eldredge represented the Los Angeles Figure Skating Club for three of his six men's national titles between 1990 and 2002. Nicks, Carroll, and Los Angeles emerged as an epicenter in a new phenomenon in the skating world: increasingly, skaters moved across the country and even around the world in search of the right coaching guru, and Nicks and Carroll became two of the most sought-after coaches.

Mabel Fairbanks

Actually, Frank Carroll was not the first student of Maribel Vinson to arrive in Los Angeles. The first protégé had arrived sixteen years earlier, and behind the scenes her work had quietly laid the foundation that opened the door for many future stars and made possible much of the success of John Nicks and Frank Carroll.

Mabel Fairbanks was born in the Florida Everglades, the child of an African American father and a mother who was half Seminole Indian and half English. She moved to New York at a young age, where she fell in love with the figure skating that she observed in Central Park. African Americans were usually prohibited from entering the rinks, but she managed to get onto the ice through persistence, and after she began to master tricks she was enough of a novelty that she attracted gawkers and was tolerated by the rink management. All doors were officially closed to her: blacks were not admitted into skating clubs; without club membership they could not enter competitions; they were banned from rinks; they were not hired by ice shows. However, Fairbanks came to the attention of two people who were top international coaches in their day: Sonja Henie's coach Howard Nicholson and Maribel Vinson. Nicholson was the head coach at a local New York rink, and Vinson gave Fairbanks lessons when she came to New York to perform in Sonja Henie's shows. Vinson was the one to tell Fairbanks that since she was never going to be allowed into competitions or shows, she would have to start her own show. The African American promoter (itself a rarity) Wallace Hunter, whom Fairbanks called "Uncle Wally," took her under his wing, and she began performing before black and mixed audiences on her own 6×6-foot portable skating rink.

Irene West, a member of the African American community in Los Angeles, brought Fairbanks to the West Coast in January 1946. The publicity in the African American–run *Los Angeles Sentinel* gushed, "Miss Fairbanks is pioneering in this field of sport in which Negroes have no star. She is the first and only ice skating star—the greatest in the Negro world."[54] It was claimed that she was nineteen, but actually she was already thirty when she moved to Los Angeles "in the hope of obtaining the help in furthering her career which the prejudices in the East had denied her."[55] While she did find work with ice shows, most of it involved touring outside the United States in Cuba, Mexico, and the West Indies.[56] In 1951 she gained a role in *Frosty Frolics* on KTLA television, an ice skating show broadcast each week from the Polar Ice Palace. Surprisingly, it became one of the most popular television shows in Los Angeles in the early 1950s.[57] When it folded after four years, Fairbanks found a new calling: in 1955 she felt that God called her to the task of helping minority skaters to achieve that which had been denied to her: "Since I could not get in then I had to train other Black skaters to get in." She was an excellent teacher; in New York she had, after all, been taught by some of the top coaches in the world and trained next to some of the top skaters. In addition, she was popular with celebrities, who asked her to coach them and their children, including the likes of Ricardo Montalban, Heddie LaMarr, Betty Hutton, Natalie Cole, Tab Hunter, Dean Martin, and Eartha Kitt.[58]

Roller skating was popular in the black community in Los Angeles even though they were turned away from rinks. As early as 1934, the NAACP had filed a discrimination lawsuit against a roller skating rink that refused to admit a black high school student when he went to a school event, and in the late 1940s, roller rinks were still turning away African American children.⁵⁹ However, there were few black ice skaters. White producers apparently believed that audiences expected black performers to stumble and take pratfalls on the ice, because that is how black performers were often presented. In 1933, the annual carnival at the Winter Ice Gardens featured a one-lap "novelty novice" race for "colored boys" who had never worn skates before; one has to imagine that the intention of the race was *not* to develop future champions.⁶⁰ Fairbanks was reportedly offered only one role in a Sonja Henie review, the role of a clown with a bandana on her head, falling all over the rink—she turned it down.⁶¹ At the end of her life, Fairbanks stated that her only regret was agreeing to perform a pratfall instead of a proper pose at the end of a routine on *Frosty Frolics*.⁶²

Hispanic skaters encountered considerably fewer barriers than African Americans. In the late 1940s, Catherine Machado was accepted into the Los Angeles Figure Skating Club. In 1954 she won the National Junior Championship, the first Hispanic national champion at any level. In 1956, after placing third in Senior Ladies for the second year in a row, she became the first Hispanic to represent the United States in the Olympic Winter Games.⁶³ Two years later Fairbanks's student Billy Chapel started competing. He placed third in Senior Men at the 1966 US Nationals and made the World team. In the oral history on file at the LA84 Foundation, Fairbanks stated that he was "Mexican," but this was not recorded in any of the skating annals. This is not surprising, given the tenor of the times: it was not until decades later that these skaters would be publicly lauded as pioneers.

However, into the 1960s there was no black member of the USFS. Since its inception, the USFS had allowed individuals to apply for "individual membership," requiring only two letters of recommendation from USFS club members. Fairbanks did not realize this until the 1950s, when she had skaters who wanted to take tests and compete. In 1956, Zenobia Holloway passed the preliminary test as an individual member and three years later so did Atoy Wilson. It is not clear whether the USFS knew they were black when it accepted their membership, although it is possible that it did since Fairbanks stated that an editor at *Skating* magazine was the one who had pointed out to her the possibility of an individual membership. When the clubs told her, "We don't test Negroes," she pointed out that her skaters were individual members, and the USFS Rulebook said that individual members were eligible to take tests. "Oh, boy, they were mad," she recalled.⁶⁴

Fairbanks began coaching another talented African American, Richard Ewell, in 1963. In 1964 the Civil Rights Act outlawed discrimination on the basis of race. Fairbanks, who had attended Law School for some years, would hint to recalcitrant rinks and clubs that she had connections with the NAACP and the Black Panthers; in addition, she was also unafraid to go to the media, which was generally willing to give her coverage. Sometime between April and August 1965, Fairbanks finally succeeded after two decades of trying: Ewell was admitted into the All Year Figure Skating Club, and in the same week, Wilson was admitted into the Los Angeles Figure Skating Club. In 1966 Wilson won the Novice Men's Championship, and in 1969 became the first African American to pass the eighth (most difficult) figure test.[65] This required much behind-the-scenes politicking, since passing the eighth test was as much a test of a skater's network as of his skills, and Wilson failed it several times before the judges finally gave him the nod.[66] In 1970 Ewell won the Junior Men's title, and in 1972 the Junior Pairs title with Michelle McCladdie, who was also African American. These three became the first African American National Champions, although not yet at the Senior level. Wilson became the first black principal in a major ice show in 1972 and was followed by his training pal Leslie Robinson in 1973.

With her red hair and a different color of skates for each day of the week, Fairbanks made skating fun for children and was one of the most influential developmental coaches in Los Angeles. However, when her skaters began to compete at higher levels, parents were advised by insiders that a respected white coach should be seen standing with their child at the boards. Richard Ewell was officially coached by John Nicks when he won his championship, as were he and McCladdie. Many of Fairbanks's skaters were handed over to Nicks when they entered the competitive track, and Fairbanks was relegated to a role behind the stage curtain. Her reaction was ambivalent. Of course, she had never competed herself. She regarded Nicks as a friend, and their skaters were joint projects up to a point. At the same time, in her oral history she said that Nicks "wanted all the glory."[67]

Still, the proof of her coaching expertise was in the performance of her skaters. Figure skating—like ballet, gymnastics, or violin—is an activity that must not only be learned at an early age, but also must be learned correctly because poor technique learned early is very difficult to correct later. The fact that Fairbanks coached so many skaters who ended up at the top of the sport is proof that she taught excellent technique. Just as importantly, she was known for instilling a positive mental attitude. Her mentorship was particularly important for minority skaters, to whom she would give practical advice about how to respond to insults and, in the case of Debi Thomas, even an intentional gash in the leg by a rival.[68] Fairbanks also worked with other minority skaters, including Japanese American Kristi Yamaguchi (later a singles Olympic gold medalist), and her Hispanic pairs partner Rudy Galindo (later 1996 National Champion).[69] Whenever talented minority skaters emerged anywhere in California, it was common to take them to Fairbanks for lessons. She made them believe that anything was possible.

In the late 1960s, Randy Gardner started taking her group classes, followed by Tai Babilonia, who was of mixed African American, Indian, and Filipino descent. Fairbanks became a second mother to them as she was to all of her young skaters. Babilonia recalled, "Mabel knew what she was doing with respect to technique, but there was more to her success. We connected with her on a personal level."[70] When Fairbanks paired them for a number in a club exhibition, their talent was immediately evident. As soon as they had success in lower-level pairs competitions, John Nicks took over. When they won their first National Championship in 1976, Babilonia became the first African American National Champion at the Senior level. They won five consecutive National Pairs Championships and in 1979 became the first American pair to win the World Championship, also a first for a skater of African descent. When they were unable to compete in the 1980 Olympics in Lake Placid due to Gardner's groin injury, they became the heartbreak kids of the Games and emerged as two of the biggest stars from those Olympics.

Tai and Randy were just the beginning of the coming wave in figure skating. Tiffany Chin had also taken lessons from Fairbanks before Nicks took over. Representing the San Diego Figure Skating Club, she became the first person of color and first Asian American to win a Singles National Championship at the Senior level in 1985, and earned a bronze medal in the World Championships then and in the next year. In 1986, representing the Los Angeles Figure Skating Club, Debi Thomas became the first African American Singles National Champion at the Senior level, and she continued on to win the World Championships in the same year and a silver Olympic medal behind the legendary Katarina Witt in 1988. In those same Olympics, another John Nicks pair earned the bronze medal, three-time national champions Jill Watson and Peter Oppegard, marking the emergence of Los Angeles as a world leader in the sport.

On the World Championships scene, Midori Ito's gold medal for Japan marked the start of a period when eighteen of twenty-seven World Champions in Ladies' Singles were won by skaters from Japan, China, or Korea, or Americans of Japanese or Chinese descent (1989–2015). A change in the sport facilitated this. Figures were eliminated from competitions starting in 1991, leaving only freestyle performances. Most of Southern California's previous minority skaters would have benefited from this, because they were known as artists who had to come from behind after the compulsory figures. Then again, who knows how good their figures were, because figures were notoriously open to biased judging since they were not performed before a public audience.

In any case, by the mid-1990s, in large part due to the efforts of Mabel Fairbanks, the foundation had been laid for the emergence of one of the all-time greatest skaters—Michelle Kwan, a daughter of Hong Kong immigrants. Kwan was coached by Frank Carroll throughout most of her career and represented the Los Angeles Figure Skating Club. She tied Maribel Vinson's record of nine US Championships with her victories between 1996 and 2005, and she also won five World Championships, two Olympic silver medals (1994 and 1998), and one Olympic bronze (2002). When Yamaguchi won Olympic gold in 1992, some observers had questioned whether her endorsements were less lucrative because she was Asian American. In 1998, Kwan gained more endorsements than Tara Lipinski, who beat her for Olympic gold. Kwan was one of the most sought-after American athletes: a survey that asked one thousand advertising agencies and marketing executives to list the most appealing athletic endorsers in 2000 ranked her ninth, behind Michael Jordan, Wayne Gretzky, and Tiger Woods, but ahead of Magic Johnson and Muhammad Ali.[71]

When Kwan was named to the 2006 Olympic team but was unable to compete due to an injury, one reporter remembered,

> During her 12 years in the Games, figure skating has been a controversy-riddled, tabloid-worthy travesty, rife with scandals and cheating. When Kwan began her career, skating was on the verge of becoming Olympic professional wrestling.
>
> But Kwan offered us another image, a counterbalance to the scandals. Always, she was a classy competitor, a good sport, a role model, a gracious ambassador.[72]

When Mabel Fairbanks was inducted into the US Figure Skating Hall of Fame in 1997, those who knew her marveled at the fact that she had never seemed bitter. Nevertheless, she did tell a story that hinted at the emotions she must have sometimes felt. It took place at a competition when the judging was absurdly biased against a Jewish skater. Fairbanks pushed her way into the judges' room, which is normally off limits to skaters and coaches. She said to the judges, "Guess what? God tried to tell you people to be fair and unbiased. You had a plane crash to teach you, and there wasn't one black kid on that plane and I doubt whether there was a Jewish kid on there. So since you didn't learn anything from that, he'll get each one of you sitting here, individually."[73]

If the 1961 plane crash had been an expression of God's wrath over the elitism and unfairness in American figure skating, then taking away Maribel Vinson would seem counterproductive. Still, in the bigger picture, the crash was a turning point when the sport started to become more egalitarian and fair.

In the beginning, the economic opportunities afforded by the entertainment industry had lured people to Southern California. They included Europeans such as Felix Locher, Sonja Henie, and John Nicks; East Coasters such as Mabel Fairbanks and Frank Carroll; and parents such as the Kwans and Marjorie Chin. Exactly one hundred years after the introduction of the sport in San Diego and Los Angeles, there were thirteen figure skating clubs registered with the USFS in Southern California, and skaters from around the United States and the world moved to Southern California to train with the top coaches.

Certainly, a major reason that the center of gravity in American skating shifted toward Southern California was the presence of John Nicks and Frank Carroll. Heading into his eighties, John Nicks revived Ashley Wagner's career by taking her to the first two of her three national championships (2012, 2013, 2015). When he retired at the age of eighty-four, he had coached skaters on twelve US Olympic teams and given lessons to more than twelve hundred local skaters in more than half a century.[74] In his seventies, Frank Carroll guided Gracie Gold to her first national championship (2014). Among the skaters who had journeyed to California to train with him were Timothy Goebel, 2002 Olympic bronze medalist; Evan Lysacek, Olympic gold medalist in 2010; and Denis Ten, the 2010 Olympic bronze medalist from Kazakhstan.

Southern California was a leader, albeit a somewhat reluctant one, in providing opportunities to minority skaters, and from their numbers it produced a large proportion of its champions and some of the brightest stars in the sport. The champions attracted more champions, who retired and became coaches in the area who trained more champions. The region created a more diverse social world for skaters than the hierarchical and tradition-bound East Coast. That diversity helped push forward the evolution of the sport; perhaps it should have been a *revolution,* but eventually the sport was transformed to better reflect the society around it.

CHAPTER FIVE

Sports Car Paradise

Racing in Los Angeles

JEREMY R. KINNEY

On the weekend of September 21–22, 1957, the California Sports Car Club held the first running of the International Road Races at Riverside International Motor Raceway. Almost two hundred drivers, predominantly from towns and cities across Southern California, competed against one another over the course of thirteen races in European and American sports cars in front of twenty-seven thousand spectators. Sports columnist Bob Hunter of the *Los Angeles Examiner* lauded Riverside as the "newest spoke" in the region's "major league wheel" that included football, boxing, golf, and tennis. Southern California sports car racers finally had a "home" that was "worthy of their skills" so they would not have to venture out to "foreign" tracks to win trophies and thrill crowds.[1] The US Grand Prix for Sports Cars at Riverside the following year in October 1958 drew in seventy-two thousand fans, an impressive number for a sport that was barely ten years old. That same year witnessed one hundred thousand in attendance at the Los Angeles Rams-Chicago Bears football game, a major league baseball record crowd of seventy-eight thousand at the Dodger's opening day, and sixty-one thousand horse racing fans at Santa Anita on Derby Day. The popularity of sports car racing supported the *Los Angeles Times*'s claim that Southern California was the "sports capital of the world."[2]

Beginning in the late 1940s, a community of motoring enthusiasts centered in Los Angeles embraced the amateur racing of two-seat European and American performance cars. They drove the sport to the forefront of activity and popularity over the course of the 1950s and early 1960s. In the process, they tested the strengths of the organizations that emerged to control it. One was a staunchly independent regional club and the other part of a far-reaching

British, German, and Italian sports cars at the start of the 215-mile Invitational 3-Hour Enduro Race held as part of the *Times-Mirror* Grand Prix at Riverside International Raceway on October 14, 1961. From the collections of the Henry Ford.

national group, as they clashed over differing ideas of the nature of their chosen motorsport. The period 1947–1963 witnessed the emergence, chaotic growth, and stabilization of racing in the sports car paradise of Southern California, which had ramifications for the larger motorsports community in the United States.

The Automobile and Motorsports in Southern California

A study of sports car racing in Southern California from the late 1940s to the early 1960s illustrates how deeply motorsports and leisure were interwoven with the automobile and American culture. Southern California, specifically Los Angeles, was predisposed toward the automobile. The widespread rejection of railways, trolleys, and busses as the primary means of transportation before World War II ensured that Los Angeles was well on its way to becoming a decentralized metropolis of suburban, business, and industrial districts by the 1950s.[3] The city and the automobile were inseparable, which resulted in Los Angeles becoming a center of American car culture.

Along with making the car a part of everyday life, the people of Los Angeles fostered a vibrant motorsports community. The subtropical Mediterranean climate allowed for virtually year-round racing and driving. The first competition, called the Fiesta Bicycle, Motorcycle, and Automobile Meet, occurred at what is now Exposition Park in May 1903. Road races in Santa Monica and Corona witnessed upward of one hundred thousand spectators lining the streets beginning in 1909 before spectator fatalities ended them. The Los Angeles Motordrome at Playa del Rey was the world's first wooden board track built for automobile and motorcycle racing in 1910. Dedicated long and short oval tracks, including Beverly Hills Speedway, Legion Ascot, and Gilmore Stadium, hosted thousands of fans through the 1930s. Famous American drivers, including Barney Oldfield, Ralph De Palma, and Eddie Rickenbacker, raced, won, and broke speed records at those events.

Besides racing on city streets and oval tracks, race car builders and drivers from Los Angeles were dominant players in America's premiere race, the Indianapolis 500, from the early 1920s to the early 1980s. Cars and engines built by Harry Miller, Fred Offenhauser, Louis Meyer and Dale Drake, and Dan Gurney's All American Racers set the standard for racing technology. Numerous Southern Californian drivers, including Louie Meyer, Rodger Ward, and Rick Mears won at Indianapolis.

Area motorsports enthusiasts pioneered other forms of competition. The Southern California Timing Association, the oldest racing organization in the United States, sponsored land speed racing events on California's dry lakes and the salt flats of Bonneville, Utah, beginning in November 1937. After World War II, hot rod enthusiasts invented drag racing in Los Angeles in 1950 and created a nationwide sensation governed by Wally Parks's National Hot Rod Association. Legendary drag racing strips included Santa Ana and Lions near Long Beach.[4]

Historians have addressed some of the Southern California motorsport communities that emerged after World War II. Robert Post's important study of drag racing revealed the cultural value of analyzing a dramatic "theater of machines" that had "no practical purpose" other than going very fast in a straight line over a one-quarter-mile track.[5] The "participatory phenomenon" of hot-rodding, according to David Lucsko, was a significant example of how end-user agency opened up the black box of the automobile to millions of Americans as they sought more speed, power, and individuality.[6] These expressions of enthusiasm for automotive technology reveal much about the American infatuation with cars as the people of Los Angeles and Southern California built communities based on the ownership, use, and strong identification with specific types of automobiles.[7]

Intertwined with these enthusiastic automotive communities was the growth of leisure in post–World War II America. The style of "conspicuous" leisure and consumption that emanated from the wealthy classes of the late nineteenth century took hold on a larger scale for a growing and more affluent segment of the population.[8] Historian Lawrence Culver placed Southern California at the forefront of this "democratization of American leisure" where the middle and lower classes aspired to experience the same forms of play as the wealthier classes.[9] With communal enthusiasm and the growth of leisure came the creation of automotive lifestyle sports where active participants worked to cultivate their respective movements through their social organization of clubs and activities on regional and national scales.[10]

The story of sports cars in the greater Los Angeles area reflects those themes as individuals bought and used them in spectacular, competitive, and communal ways to exercise their enthusiasm for the automobile. Historian John Heitmann recognized the influence of European sports cars and racing in 1950s America at the recreational level.[11] Witnesses, participants, and their descendants have written about Los Angeles and Southern California within the context of its centrality to the history of sports car racing in the United States.[12]

Origins of Sports Car Racing in the United States

The modern sports car movement emerged before World War II. Affluent Easterners, like Briggs Cunningham, embraced the first generation of sports cars from Great Britain, Italy, Germany, and France and strove to emulate the spectacles they saw on European racing circuits such as Brooklands, Monza, Nürburgring, and Le Mans in the 1930s. A group of motoring enthusiasts in Boston formed the Sports Car Club of America (SCCA) on February 26, 1944.[13] The SCCA defined a "sports car" to be "any quality car which was built primarily for sports motoring as opposed to mere transportation."[14]

In response to the availability of sports cars from Europe in the immediate postwar period, sports car clubs "sprang up like daffodils in March" according to automotive writer Ken Purdy.[15] The most popular and prolific activity for clubs was racing on courses laid out on public roads just as they were in Europe.

The SCCA sanctioned the first postwar road race in October 1948 with the inauguration of the first International Sports Car Grand Prix at Watkins Glen, New York.[16] The club grew exponentially as its members established regional chapters, or "regions," across the country and numbered approximately five thousand members by 1952. Above all else, the SCCA wanted to frame racing as a genteel activity that should be strictly amateur in nature.[17]

Sports Car Racing in Southern California

The first sports cars, fifty red MG TCs from England, arrived in Los Angeles in 1947.[18] By the early 1950s, other British car makers introduced their own designs while European and American manufacturers produced new sports car designs that gained a market share in the United States. Jaguar, Austin-Healey, and Triumph in Great Britain; Mercedes and Porsche in Germany; Alfa Romeo, Ferrari, and Osca in Italy; and Chevrolet, Cunningham, Glasspar, and Kurtis in the United States ensured there were a variety of cars available to a willing consumer base that ranged from the lower middle class to millionaires and Hollywood stars.[19]

Southern Californians embraced the competitive nature of sports cars and welcomed them into the myriad layers of automotive enthusiasm in the area. Three enthusiasts in Los Angeles, Roger Barlow, John von Neumann, and Taylor Lucas, formed the California Sports Car Club, or Cal Club, in 1947. Barlow was a documentary filmmaker-turned-import car dealer. His International Motors was one of the first foreign car dealerships on the West Coast and was responsible for that first delivery of MG TCs to Los Angeles. An Austrian émigré, von Neumann worked for Barlow as a salesman before building his own foreign car empire. Lucas was a mechanic with an interest in sports cars.[20] Barlow remembered that he and his compatriots were dissatisfied with the lack of activity in the only existing club at the time and decided to create their own with a focus on driving and competition.[21]

The Cal Club quickly set about organizing sporting events on public roads for its members whether they had the blessing of local authorities or not. The first event was a legal hill climb at Palos Verdes in August and December 1947. Von Neumann followed up with a one-hundred-mile road race through the canyon and mountain roads of Santa Clarita called the Cento Miglio. The club ran the illegal event several times during the 1947 to 1948 period under the cover of night to avoid the California Highway Patrol. There were only six to eight participants in each race, but their presence could be felt as the MGs and other sports cars zoomed by unsuspecting motorists.[22]

After that brief period of lawless racing, the Cal Club incorporated in March 1950 and established its offices on Hollywood Boulevard.[23] The club quickly rose to prominence as the only major independent amateur sports car racing group in the United States with approximately fifteen hundred members by 1958.[24] One thing was certain; the Cal Club leadership wanted it to be the primary racing organization in Southern California.

Despite the prominence of the Cal Club in Southern California, some of its members wanted to affiliate with the SCCA to benefit from belonging to a national organization. They broke away and formed the Los Angeles (LA) Region in July 1949. John R. Bond, a writer and editor at *Road & Track* magazine, was the first regional executive, or president. They held their first event, a hill climb at Sandberg northwest of Los Angeles, on April 2, 1950. Like the Cento Miglio, these initial events were held on public roads, which were under the threat of cancellation with the unwelcome appearance of local law enforcement.[25]

The Cal Club, LA Region, and other clubs needed places to race. They first competed at Carrell Speedway in Gardena, a one-half-mile banked oval that hosted stock car, hot rod, and motorcycle races. The track's promoters sponsored "Foreign Car Races" beginning in July 1949. The Cal Club took over responsibility for the races two years later and attracted six thousand spectators at their first event. Carrell Speedway was not ideal because the oval track did not permit drivers to handle their cars in a way consistent with European-style road racing. Nevertheless, it was a legal venue that attracted both drivers and spectators.[26]

Public roads were the traditional venue for sports car racing. They provided the twists, turns, and changes in elevation that required the skillful and efficient operation of the cars, which made driving a sports car fun. They were also in the proximity of buildings, streetlights, road signs, trees, and spectators that served as hazards for the racers. Only hay bales, sand-filled containers, and snow fencing stood between the cars and the public. An alternative was to use the runways and connecting taxiways of local municipal airports or military airfields, which were closed to air traffic for the day or no longer in use, as a course. The long, wide, flat, and smooth circuits facilitated high speeds approaching 150 mph, challenged the drivers with hairpin turns, and reduced the probability of crashing. The open spaces of airport courses facilitated purpose-built grandstands and well-protected viewings areas that made crowd control easier and safer.[27] Both types persisted over the course of the 1950s and 1960s in regard to the specific locale that a race took place.

Cal Club members organized the first legally sanctioned sports car road race in Southern California at Palm Springs on April 16, 1950. The 2.6-mile course consisted of the roads found at a local airfield and an unfinished housing development. The 6,000-foot straight enabled speeds of up to two miles a minute.[28] The short-lived Sports Car Racing Association held what is considered the second race in the region at the decommissioned Naval Lighter-Than-Air Station Santa Ana on June 25, 1950.[29]

The Cal Club, LA Region, and a small number of other racing-oriented clubs sponsored races at a myriad of venues throughout the 1950s. Southern California races began at Torrey Pines in December 1951, Santa Barbara in September 1953, Bakersfield in March 1954, Willow Springs and March Air Force Base in November 1953, Hansen Dam in June 1955, Pomona in June 1956, Paramount Ranch in August 1956, and Hourglass Field in May 1957.[30] Each course had its strengths, weaknesses, and idiosyncrasies. With the exception of Willow Springs, these courses were temporary, which involved a lot of work on the part of the clubs regarding designing a course on preexisting roads, liaison with the communities that owned them, and planning and coordinating the actual execution of the races.

Drivers, Sports Cars, and Spectators

Hundreds of sports car racers emerged to compete at the Southern California tracks. They and the motorsports press referred to themselves as "pilots" in an aviation analogy that echoed the glamour, skill, and danger of operating sophisticated machinery in a high-pressure environment. A few worked in motorsports as a result of their skill as drivers, mechanics, and managers. Others found the challenge of racing a distraction from more ordinary jobs in business and industry. On the track, they were all technically amateurs under the auspices of their membership in either the Cal Club or the LA Region.

Emulating the earlier success found in other forms of racing, Southern California produced a new class of celebrity drivers that fueled the popularity of sports car racing and European-style motorsports in general. Their meteoric paths also served as stepping-stones into professional racing careers. Phil Hill of Santa Monica was the best known of all. He started racing a variety of cars ranging from MGs to Ferraris in 1949. He quickly catapulted to national and international fame, which included multiple wins in the Sebring and Le Mans endurance races. Hill's greatness culminated when he became the world's first and only American-born Formula 1 champion in 1961 as a member of the Ferrari factory team.[31]

Another outstanding Southern California sports car racer was Ken Miles. He started racing in England at Silverstone and Prescott before immigrating to Los Angeles in 1952. Miles made his racing debut that year and quickly made a name for himself as both a driver and builder of cars, including his famous MG and Porsche specials.[32] During his three terms as president of the Cal Club from 1954 to 1957, the membership grew from three hundred fifty to fifteen hundred.[33]

Other Southern Californians realized sports car racing fame and fortune as well. Richie Ginther, Dan Gurney, Jack McAfee, Chuck Daigh, Lance Reventlow, and Max Balchowsky followed Hill and Miles into national and international racing notoriety in various forms. Mainstays of the Cal Club racing scene included founders John von Neumann and Roger Barlow and leading members like Bill Pollack.[34] While these racers were either born in California or made their home in the state, another racer, Texan Carroll Shelby, became a fixture on the local scene after a spectacular win at Torrey Pines in a Ferrari in July 1955. His quick rise to international prominence included an SCCA national championship and designation as "Sports Car Driver of the Year" by both *Sports Illustrated* and the *New York Times*.[35]

Southern California women were also enthusiastic for sports car racing. The Cal Club was quick to include them, but in a controlled way. It incorporated a "Ladies Handicap Race" into the schedule at the December 1951 Torrey Pines event. John von Neumann's nineteen-year-old stepdaughter, Josie, won the race in her MG.[36] Shortly thereafter, fourteen female enthusiasts in Los Angeles created the Women's Sports Car Club (WSCC) in 1952 to bring together like-minded women who did not want to watch from the side lines or serve on their husband or boyfriend's pit crew. They pushed for increased participation for women in sports car racing when there was no presence at all. Their efforts resulted in the "Ladies Race" becoming a standard part of race schedules.[37] Besides von Neumann, leading women drivers included Mary Davis, Maxine Elmer, Ruth Levy, Marion Lowe, and Pat Sawyer.

The majority of WSCC members served in a nonracing capacity behind the scenes at events in support of the Cal Club and LA Region. They conducted lap scoring, registration and check-in, and technical inspections; ran mimeograph copies; prepared lunches for volunteer race workers; and organized glamorous award banquets to conclude each race. These "Gal Fridays," as one of their own called them, did the work that was required for the races to take place.[38]

There were two general classifications of cars in which drivers competed. Modified "sports racing cars" were purpose-built race cars designed for competition at the highest levels in terms of speed and endurance. They were the most popular with racing fans and spectators due to their unique nature and higher performance. The category included Aston Martin, Ferrari, Maserati, and Porsche racers straight from the factory that cost upward of $10,000. There was also a variety of "specials" that featured original workmanship and clever combinations of American and European engines, chassis, and bodies. Multimillionaire Lance Reventlow invested $75,000 in the development of three Scarab racers that dominated the 1958 racing season. In contrast, builders like Max and Ina Balchowsky had as little as $1,000 in their garage-built and junkyard-sourced racer *Old Yeller II* that had its share of racing success.[39]

The exorbitant cost of modified sports racing cars created a new owner/driver relationship. A review of entry lists in race programs reveal that drivers did not have to be the owners of the cars they raced. Multimillionaire sportsmen and successful entrepreneurs like John Edgar, Tony Parravano, John and Eleanor von Neumann, and Frank Arciero provided Ferrari, Maserati, and Porsche cars for successful drivers like Phil Hill, Bill Pollack, Richie Ginther, Ken Miles, Dan Gurney, Jack McAfee, Chuck Daigh, and Carroll Shelby to drive at high-profile races in Southern California and across the nation.[40] These team owners were the only individuals capable of affording the factory-trained mechanics for expert maintenance; the specialized transports that carried the tools, parts, and cars to races; the repairs needed if the drivers crashed them on the track; and expenses and salary for the drivers so they could race in amateur events.

Production, or stock, sports cars required cars to be as they left the factory without any major changes to their design. One of the key appeals of sports car racing was the fact that enthusiasts could drive the same car for daily transportation during the week. On the weekend, they donned helmets, used tape to cover their headlights and add numbers to their cars, and enlisted friends to support them in the pits. An enthusiast had a wide range of cars and prices from which to choose for competition in the production category. A used MG TC could be bought for as little as $850. A brand-new MG, Triumph, or Austin-Healey cost under $3,000. For more performance and money, a prospective racer could buy a Jaguar or Corvette for around $4,000.[41]

To determine the winner of a race weekend, the Cal Club and the SCCA adopted similar methods of organization. They developed a two-day weekend race schedule that divided the entrants' cars into the production and modified categories and, in turn, broke each down into distinct classes based on engine displacement and overall performance and represented by a letter of the alphabet.[42] The cars with the largest displacement engines were in Class A while those with the smallest were in Class H or J. On Saturday, class groupings raced at the same time so there would be several "races within a race" to maximize time on the track for all entrants. On Sunday, the Saturday winners competed against one another in two "main events" where both production and modified cars faced each other in "over" and "under" events based again on engine displacement.[43] The main event and class winners received trophies to reflect their amateur status.

Beginning in the mid-1950s, the trend in the greater American sports car community was to establish permanent closed road tracks. They offered increased revenue for local communities, spectator safety, a "home" course for local racers, and a consistent driving experience that, when combined with other permanent tracks, provided a regional and national circuit for racers to compete. Tracks opened at Lime Rock in Connecticut and Elkhart Lake in Wisconsin in 1955, Watkins Glen in 1956, Laguna Seca in Northern California, Bridgehampton on Long Island, and the Virginia International Raceway in Danville in 1957. Willow Springs had opened earlier in 1953, but its largely undeveloped state hindered its widespread use. Southern California's answer for a permanent road racing track was the Riverside International Raceway, which opened officially on September 21, 1957. Located near March Air Force Base west of Los Angeles, the original 3.3-mile, thirteen-turn course included a 1.1-mile back straight that would permit lap averages above 100 mph. Sportswriter Art Lauring of the *Los Angeles Times* asserted that the racing would be "fast and furious."[44]

Since Riverside was a commercial enterprise, the Cal Club and the LA Region alternated sponsorship of follow-on races in November 1957 and June 1958, respectively. The next event, the US Grand Prix for Sports Cars held on October 11–12, 1958, was a turning point in the history of Southern California sports car racing. The marquee event was a 200-mile race with a purse of $14,500 for an international roster of professional competitors. The Times-Mirror Company, operator of the *Los Angeles Times* and *Los Angeles Mirror*, sponsored the race to raise proceeds for charity. The organizing body was the

Cal Club, which granted permission to its members to participate in the race. The sanctioning bodies were the Federation Internationale de L'Automobile, the world governing body for sports car racing, and the United States Auto Club (USAC), the largest American professional racing organization and organizer of the Indianapolis 500. With top European professionals like Jean Behra, Joakim Bonnier, and Roy Salvadori competing, the *Los Angeles Times* heralded the race as the "biggest of its kind in U.S. history."[45] To Bill Pollack, president of the Cal Club, the running of the Grand Prix marked the "real coming of age of sports car racing" in the United States where years of hard work and amateur sportsmanship provided the foundation for mainstream success.[46] An unprecedented crowd of seventy-two thousand spectators watched Chuck Daigh win the feature race.[47] Fellow Southern Californians and Cal Club members, Phil Hill and Bill Krause, won the next two years in a row.

Attending a Southern California sports car race was a major event for spectators. Fans congregated to see the rare and exotic modified racers or the production cars they drove themselves being raced by both well-known and relatively anonymous drivers. They came from all walks of life in terms of education and employment with the core being professionals in their late twenties and thirties, but many of them were college students.[48] The number-one goal of a true sports car spectator was to analyze the driver's skill in maneuvering the car, especially how they "set up" for a turn.[49] There was not one crowd as there was at a baseball or football game. There were several crowds as spectators positioned themselves at the various turns and straightaways.[50] For those who could not make the journey, they could watch races on their television at home via local stations like KTTV Channel 11.[51]

Trouble in Paradise: The Cal Club v. the SCCA

By the mid-1950s, sports car racing was a major activity in Southern California. For drivers and fans, there were a variety of events to attend almost every weekend of the year. Unfortunately, there was trouble in sports car paradise. The Cal Club and the LA Region were two different groups. The Cal Club formed specifically to provide the organizational structure for racing. The LA Region incorporated racing into a broader-based program of activities that, according to Cal Club members, was predominately social in nature at the expense of serious competition.[52] Regardless of their motivations, tensions emerged between the two clubs centered on which group would secure the precious few calendar dates and venues for racing. Southern California also became a battleground in the national debate over whether sports car racers should be strictly amateurs or could they take money for racing. The two clubs became bitter foes or friendly rivals depending on the opinion of individual members, but a Cal Club-LA Region feud was in full bloom by 1957.

The scheduling of concurrent races was the first major issue. The primary responsibility of the Southern California Council of Sports Car Clubs was to rationalize the regional events calendar for its member clubs, which included the Cal Club and the LA Region. Nevertheless, there were so many conflicts over dates and venues that it was difficult to alleviate the situation and the calls for order went unheeded.[53] There were over twenty races planned on the West Coast with many on the same date in 1958 alone.[54] It was obvious that the scheduling problem would dilute driver and spectator attendance.

The Cal Club and the LA Region also competed against each other in securing venues in local communities. The Cal Club, by far, utilized the largest number of venues and exclusively used Paramount Ranch, Santa Barbara, and Torrey Pines. Both the Cal Club and the LA Region alternated and even shared use of the commercial Riverside raceway for high-profile events like the Grand Prix for Sports Cars. The Cal Club lost Palm Springs to the LA Region after a dispute with the local promoter. In reaction, the Cal Club coordinated with the Pomona Elks Lodge to use the Los Angeles County Fairgrounds in June 1956.[55]

The two clubs were also "bickering" over whether the two organizations should recognize each other's competition licenses and car preparation rules at their respective sanctioned races.[56] The SCCA national leadership advocated that its members retain a purely amateur status and established strict license and car requirements. By the late 1950s, the Cal Club welcomed both amateurs and professionals and was critical of the SCCA's position.[57] The two groups continued to coexist in a tense environment where members like the outspoken president of the Cal Club, Ken Miles, were absent from high-profile races like the November 1956 Palm Springs event due to their criticism of the SCCA.[58]

The SCCA had over 10,000 members nationwide in 1958 with the overwhelming majority of regions and membership located east of the Mississippi River.[59] There was an east-west divide in the club centered on the amateur versus professional debate, which John Bond of *Road & Track* equated to a "a civil war," and the independent nature of the western regions. The SCCA leadership in Connecticut, known as the "Westport Pharaohs" due to their direct rule of the national club, demanded staunch adherence to amateurism and accountability on the part of its regions.[60] The independent nature of the 554 members of the LA Region was not unnoticed by the SCCA leadership in the early 1960s. They charged the region with allowing members to participate in professional racing at Riverside, nonadherence to SCCA car classifications, failing to submit proper documentation of a fatal accident at Pomona in July 1961, and maintaining improper liaison with the SCCA national office overall. For the region's continuous disregard of the national club's rules and regulations and overall noncooperation, the SCCA summarily revoked the charter of the LA Region on November 25, 1961.[61]

In a surprising turn of events, the SCCA immediately awarded the Cal Club a regional charter making it the club's representative in Southern California. D. D. Michelmore, president of the Cal Club, welcomed the opportunity to merge with the SCCA.[62] The advantage for the club was that it gained the resources of the SCCA national organization in regard to securing the requisite insurance for its racing program.[63] At a meeting of the Cal Club Board of Governors in Hollywood on November 25, the members decided by a vote of 88 to 7 to become the California Sports Car Club Region of the SCCA, or the Cal Club Region, effective December 6.[64] The club's first event was the Pacific Coast Championship races at Riverside on March 3–4, 1962. Josh Hogue, sports car columnist for the *San Francisco Chronicle*, remarked, "The change in Smogville is a good one. If we may use an old expression, 'it should clean the air.'"[65]

It did not clean the air. James E. Peterson, president of the LA Region, wrote to the SCCA executive director threatening legal action that could effectively stop sports car racing in Southern California if not resolved.[66] Disaffected LA Region members formed an alliance with the USAC, which earlier in May 1958 had announced the creation of a professional sports car road racing category, or "go-for-dough" racing as sports columnist Art Lauring called it, under the aegis of the United States Sports Car Club (USSCC) division.[67] In an immediate act of defiance, the newly created LA Chapter of the USSCC announced that its first race would be at the Los Angeles County Fairgrounds at Pomona in March 1962.[68] The LA Chapter had beaten out the Cal Club Region to get the exclusive contract with the Elks Lodge for the Pomona event, which up to that point had been a Cal Club race.

The Cal Club Region went on the offensive. It ordered its members to avoid the Pomona race or face banishment from club events for the rest of the year.[69] In the end, the LA Chapter canceled the Pomona race. The reasons given were due to the lack of entries and the inability to acquire insurance for the event. Either way, a lawsuit resulted blaming the SCCA.[70] The Cal Club Region continued to ban drivers that acted counter to SCCA rulings. Rising star Bob Bondurant was "uninvited" from the May 1962 Santa Barbara races due to his participation at an USSCC-affiliated race in Las Vegas.[71]

The LA Chapter initiated its own campaign to win the hearts and minds of Southern California sports car racers. Its "Open Letter to Sports Car Drivers" that appeared in *Motoracing* in April 1962 emphasized democratic elections, rules reflecting the California experience and not "eastern customs," scheduling of both amateur and professional events, and the freedom to secure advertising and sponsors for cars and racers. Most important, the LA Chapter urged participation in "other events" while guaranteeing to all drivers that "we don't ban you; we'll support you."[72]

In the interest of the sport, the Cal Club Region and the LA Chapter agreed to a merger in June 1962.[73] The merger stalled for the remainder of the year due to a disagreement on how to actually go about the process among the leadership of the two clubs. In hopes of finding a solution, a general meeting for members in good standing of the Cal Club Region and LA Chapter was held in Hollywood in December 1962. The members agreed to a merger of the two clubs after a vote of 172 to 95. It took two rounds to settle on retaining the Cal Club name. The group elected an eleven-member board, which included a new executive, Otto Zipper, a Ferrari and Porsche dealer and race team owner. The Cal Club Region announced a full slate of races for 1963, which included events at Dodger Stadium in Chavez Ravine and Riverside.[74]

The Cal Club Region went on to be one of the most successful and active SCCA regions in the United States through the early twenty-first century. It hosted numerous semiprivate amateur events that primarily catered to drivers that did not require spectator participation. The Region also benefited from the SCCA's incorporation of professional racing as it hosted the highly popular United States Road Racing Championship (1963–1968) and the Can-Am (1966–1987) and Trans-Am (1966–present) series at Southern California circuits.

Sports car racing, however, faced a dilemma. An expanding regional population, rising property values, and the need for more housing and commercial infrastructure ensured that urban development in the paradise of Southern California forced the closure of many racing venues serving motorsports. Riverside and Willow Springs remained as the only two viable road race courses by the 1980s. A developer bought Riverside, which had risen in prominence as a venue for West Coast NASCAR competition, in 1983 with the intention of turning it into a shopping mall and housing subdivision. During the first weekend of July 1988, the Cal Club Region organized the last amateur races to be held at Riverside with more than seven hundred cars entered. Part of the festivities included one last lap around the course by the now legendary drivers from the early years, including Phil Hill, Carroll Shelby, and Dan Gurney.[75] The Cal Club Region opened its own motorsports complex, Buttonwillow Raceway Park, located two hours north of Los Angeles in Kern County in 1995.[76]

Conclusion

The importance of Los Angeles and Southern California to sports car racing can be viewed from two perspectives. The struggle for control of racing between the Cal Club and the SCCA reveals that not all sports car enthusiasts agreed on what was the correct path for their sport. The democratization of this particular automotive lifestyle sport in the 1950s was not a singularly objective process, but subjective as Southern Californians agreed and disagreed with each other, and with other parts of the country, over their perceptions of how sports car racing fit within their motorsports culture. Tensions emanating from differences in club operations, rules, and style, competition for dates and venues, and the explosive amateur v. professional debate illustrated that Southern California was not big enough for both an independent Cal Club and the SCCA.

Overall, Los Angeles was an epicenter of American motorsports and car culture in the decades following World War II. The success and style of Southern California sports car racing introduced a new pastime to more Americans who looked to the region for motorsports inspiration. As the popularity of drivers and their cars grew, European manufacturers and American importers found a growing market for their products as new enthusiasts joined the larger community to go racing themselves. This new strain of automotive enthusiasm rooted in Europe had arrived in the United States, which in a large way was only possible by entering through the sports car paradise of Southern California.

CHAPTER SIX

Professional Football in the City of Angels
The Game Moves West

RAYMOND SCHMIDT

American football has a long history in California, especially in greater Los Angeles. Major league professional football, as represented by the National Football League (NFL), chose to not place a regular franchise in Los Angeles or elsewhere on the West Coast for the first quarter-century of its existence. Despite the continuing growth in population and commerce, beautiful weather, and the glamour of the area enhanced by the Hollywood movie industry, the conservative owners of the NFL considered the realities of commercial travel by railroad to be an overwhelming reason not to locate a franchise in Los Angeles during the 1920s and 1930s.

Immediately after World War II, with commercial air travel a reality, the conservative owners of the NFL suddenly found themselves confronted by a young and relatively new NFL team owner, Dan Reeves, and a new rival professional football league, the All-American Football Conference (AAFC). Both the NFL and AAFC saw the benefits of relocating to the West Coast. When the two leagues launched their Los Angeles franchises in 1946 they were opening the West and its potential financial bounty to all of professional sport, leading the way for Major League Baseball and professional basketball to begin their own successful expansions just over a decade later.

Considering the success of professional football in Los Angeles over the next forty-nine years, as the NFL capitalized on the city's growing economic engine, the league's departure from the City of Angels after 1994 is difficult to understand from either a business or sporting perspective. The second-leading media center in America, and a city with an impressive professional football past, was left without an NFL franchise for over two decades.

Origins of the Game

Beginning in the 1890s, football was played among the colleges in and around the city, including the University of Southern California (USC). The rough-and-tumble sport generated considerable enthusiasm, with the result that many town and club teams in the area began playing the sport by the early 1900s.

While some of these noncollegiate gridiron teams may have been semiprofessional outfits that paid some of its players, the fact remains that full-time professional football teams did not spring up in the Los Angeles area for several decades. Legitimate professional football teams in the Midwest and East had played since early in the century, yet pro football everywhere struggled to gain acceptance because of the opposition from advocates of Victorian principles of amateurism.

Despite the continuing growth in college football's popularity, the general attitudes toward professional football began to improve rapidly, along with a rise in its popularity, beginning in the mid-1920s. The impetus for this move began in late 1925 when one of the greatest halfbacks in college football history—Harold "Red" Grange of the University of Illinois—signed a contract to play professional football with the Chicago Bears of the NFL immediately after his final game for the Illini.

Recognizing the money to be made with Grange as the centerpiece, owner George Halas of the Bears immediately put together a barnstorming tour in late 1925 and early 1926. The flood of national newspaper publicity covering the tour was overwhelming from the very beginning. On January 16, 1926, Grange and the Bears landed in Los Angeles amid overwhelming pregame publicity and played an exhibition game at the Los Angeles Coliseum against a pick-up team called the Los Angeles Tigers with an official attendance of 61,923.[1]

For the 1926 season, the owners of the NFL and the new American Football League (AFL) each recognized the mystique of the California city's name and so decided to add franchises called the Los Angeles Buccaneers (NFL) and the Los Angeles Wildcats (AFL). Aware of the prohibitive travel time and expense to the West Coast, both leagues set their new members up as traveling teams operating out of Chicago. After the 1926 season, both Los Angeles professional teams went on barnstorming tours that carried them to the West Coast for the first time. There in late January, the AFL's Wildcats defeated the NFL's Buccaneers, 17–0, in their only meeting. Both teams then went out of business, ending any ideas of professional football in Los Angeles at the time.[2]

Arrival of the Bulldogs

By the mid-1930s, officials of the Los Angeles American Legion viewed professional football as a vehicle to publicize their rapidly growing West Coast city. Having heard that the NFL was intending to soon add a new franchise, the local American Legion and a trio of Los Angeles newspapers raised the $10,000 required to enter the league. They then sent a Los Angeles man named Harry Myers to the NFL's 1936 meeting to present their case.

At the meeting of the NFL owners, Myers presented the case for placing a regular franchise in Los Angeles; a team that would play its six home games in the city rather than being just a traveling squad. Myers stated that in addition to the usual guarantee for visiting teams, the Los Angeles club would pay transportation costs from and back to Chicago. He also noted that when the Los Angeles team played its six road games against the eastern teams it expected only the usual visitor's guarantee, with the provision that all six games would be scheduled in consecutive weeks.

The Los Angeles bid for an NFL franchise interested a number of owners, so adding a new team to the league was held off for one year and Los Angeles was granted a "temporary" place in the NFL for the 1936 season. The Bulldogs—as the Los Angeles pro team would be nicknamed—would host games against several NFL teams, most of them to be played after the league's regular season schedule. At the 1937 NFL meeting the owners would review the experiences of the teams that had made the trip west and make a final decision on the Los Angeles application.[3]

Therefore, Los Angeles had its first fully professional football team in the Bulldogs. Leon V. McCardle was named team president, while Myers was retained as the general manager, and the club set up its headquarters in the Hayward Hotel, located at Sixth and Spring Streets in downtown Los Angeles. The relatively new Gilmore Stadium, with a seating capacity of eighteen thousand and located between Beverly Boulevard and Third Street at approximately Fairfax Avenue (now the site of CBS Television City), was leased to serve as the team's home field.

Elmer "Gus" Henderson, no stranger to Los Angeles football fans since he served as the head coach at USC from 1919 to 1924, was signed as the Bulldogs' first head coach. Myers and Henderson began recruiting as many quality players as they could afford, managing to sign several with previous experience in the NFL. The Bulldogs had been organized to take on visiting NFL teams in 1936 and hopefully earn a spot in the league. Yet a couple of semiprofessional teams had also been organized for 1936 and would be the Bulldogs major in-state rivals for the balance of the 1930s—the Hollywood Stars and the Salinas Packers. The Bulldogs played their first game ever on October 25 at Gilmore Stadium where they handed the Stars a 36–0 defeat before about seven thousand fans.

Two weeks later the games against visiting NFL teams began, and the Bulldogs upset the Philadelphia Eagles, the Pittsburgh Pirates, and the Chicago Cardinals. The outpouring of excitement from Los Angeles newspapers seemed unending in the aftermath of the unexpected victories. After a hard-fought tie with the Brooklyn Dodgers, the last two games of the 1936 "trial" brought losses to the tough Chicago Bears and the champion Green Bay Packers.

The Bulldogs finished with a 3–2–1 record against the NFL visitors, as part of an overall 6–3–1 1936 season. Attendance averaged 10,250 per contest at Gilmore Stadium for the six games against the NFL clubs, and the "trial" for the Los Angeles Bulldogs seemingly demonstrated that the West Coast team would be able to compete successfully against NFL clubs and local fans would support them. Yet, at the 1937 NFL meeting, owners decided that the lengthy travel to and from Los Angeles would outweigh any potential benefits, and so the franchise opening was awarded to the Cleveland Rams.[4]

The American Legion backers of the Bulldogs believed there would be another chance at joining the NFL in the near future, so the group decided to maintain its team through the 1937 and 1938 seasons. After going through the 1937 season unbeaten and winning the title of an eastern minor league, the Bulldogs put together an interesting schedule for the 1938 season that saw them playing five games against NFL teams. Also, Paul Schissler—a recent head coach of the Brooklyn Dodgers and the Chicago Cardinals of the NFL—reorganized the Hollywood Stars team for 1938. Early in the season the Bulldogs headed to Charleston, West Virginia, where they spent two weeks and played both the Chicago Bears and the Chicago Cardinals, and then played their way back to Los Angeles. On the first Sunday of November the Bulldogs trounced the Hollywood Stars at Gilmore Stadium. Over the next seven days the Bulldogs

Team program covers illustrate half a century of pro football in LA, from 1939 to 1989. Photo courtesy of LA84 Foundation.

played the NFL's Pittsburgh Pirates twice—winning the first game 17–6 at Colorado Springs, followed by a 14–14 tie at Gilmore.

One week later in a highly publicized showdown, the Bulldogs played host to the despised Cleveland Rams, the team that had taken the spot in the NFL the Bulldogs believed they deserved. The Rams stunned the crowd of fourteen thousand fans on the first play of the game when they returned a Bulldog fumble for a touchdown and a 7–0 lead. Bouncing right back though, the rest of the way it was all Los Angeles as the Bulldogs pulled out everything in their playbook in the best game in the team's history, totally dominating the NFL team and rolling to a convincing 28–7 victory. The Bulldogs by then were widely considered to be the best non-NFL professional team in the country after their first three seasons, and the teams of 1936 and 1938 were the best in franchise history.[5]

Myers, the Bulldogs' general manager, in early 1939 again presented a bid for membership in the NFL. Despite the Bulldogs' success on the playing field during the previous three seasons, the application for a franchise in Los Angeles was again rejected. This convinced the Los Angeles American Legion to sell the Bulldogs' franchise to a new owner named Jerry Corcoran, who also took over as general manager when Myers left the team. Meanwhile, Gus Henderson left Los Angeles—taking along several of the best Bulldog players—to serve as head coach of the NFL's Detroit Lions for 1939, where he lasted only one season. By the start of the 1939 season Corcoran signed players to replace those departed for Detroit and elsewhere, yet by November it became noticeable that the Bulldogs were no longer as talented as they had been during their first three seasons, despite compiling a record of 11–2–0.[6]

The 1940 season got off to an interesting start with the announcement that a new minor league called the Pacific Coast Professional Football League (PCL), which included the Los Angeles Bulldogs, would begin play that year. The new league would offer plenty of local excitement as Paul Schissler had organized a new team called the Hollywood Bears, with a talent level capable of seriously challenging the Bulldogs. The Hollywood Bears featured Kenny Washington, a very talented triple-threat tailback and two-time All-American at UCLA. As one of the top stars of college football in 1939, Washington easily should have been playing in the NFL, but as an African American athlete he was prohibited by the league's "color barrier." He was teamed in the backfield with Elvin "Kink" Richards, a standout halfback who had played seven seasons with the New York Giants. Also on the Bears was another standout black player at end from UCLA named Woody Strode. African American players were not uncommon on Los Angeles gridirons; several played in the PCL over the years.[7]

For the 1940 season the Bulldogs and Bears split their four meetings, with the Bulldogs' 16–14 victory on the final day giving them the league title. In 1941, the Hollywood Bears rolled to an 8-0-0 record that included winning all three games against the Bulldogs, who during the season had added ex-UCLA halfback Jackie Robinson, who would integrate Major League Baseball in 1947 with the Brooklyn Dodgers.[8]

During World War II, with many of the players in the military, the PCL struggled along with shortened schedules. The Bears had to suspend operations until after the war. In 1945, the Hollywood Bears were back with Coach Paul Schissler and Kenny Washington, while the Bulldogs were bolstered in the second half of the season by future Pro Hall of Fame quarterback, Frankie Albert. With Washington having another outstanding season, the Bears narrowly won the league title for 1945.[9]

The Rams and Dons Take Over

With the ending of World War II, the steady growth of Southern California quickly began to turn into a rapid expansion of population, commerce, and urban sprawl. Despite ignoring the Bulldogs for admission to the NFL, it soon became clear that there were some who recognized the importance of expanding professional football to the West Coast.

In late 1944 an organizational meeting was held in Chicago for a new professional football major league, with Arch Ward—sports editor of the *Chicago Tribune*—being the driving force in pulling together the potential owners. The new league, the AAFC, initially sought a peaceful coexistence with the NFL, which the older league arrogantly rejected. By January 1946, the AAFC had its teams assembled and ready to begin play that season. One of the eight teams would play in Los Angeles and was nicknamed the "Dons."

The owner of the Los Angeles Dons was a wealthy racetrack proprietor named Ben Lindheimer. Actor Don Ameche, one of the major investors, was named team president. Other principal stockholders included movie producer Louis B. Mayer, along with entertainers Bing Crosby, Bob Hope, and Pat O'Brien. The club set up its offices at 607 South Hill Street, Suite 331, in downtown, and named Dud DeGroot as its first head coach.[10]

Meanwhile, in 1941 a wealthy young heir to a grocery chain fortune, named Dan Reeves, had purchased the NFL's Cleveland Rams for $125,000 with the intention of eventually relocating the franchise to Los Angeles. The team continued to struggle financially in Cleveland, and despite winning the 1945 NFL championship Reeves lost $50,000 that year. By this time Reeves believed he had the necessary votes to obtain approval for relocating to the West Coast, so at the NFL owners meeting in January 1946 he presented his request. To ensure success, Reeves offered to pay $5,000 over the existing guarantee when NFL teams traveled to Los Angeles for games. Yet his bid was strongly opposed by owners George Halas of the Chicago Bears and George Marshall of the Washington Redskins, and voted down by the group, prompting Reeves to threaten to withdraw the Rams from the league.

The NFL had dropped the last of the small-time community teams in 1934, with the exception of Green Bay, and it now considered itself to be truly major league. With the exception of Reeves, the ten-team league had been directed by basically the same close-knit corps of owners since the early 1930s. With a couple exceptions, none of the owners were particularly wealthy and all had faced continual financial difficulties while in the league. The result was an old-school, unimaginative group of owners who were overly conservative, frugal, and basically opposed to change of any consequence in "their" league.

After voting down the relocation bid from Reeves, owners cited the cost and difficulties of traveling to the West Coast for their opposition. Back in 1937 when the NFL had rejected the bid of the Los Angeles Bulldogs with this same explanation these were valid concerns, but by 1946 the technical advancements in commercial aviation had wiped out the travel time excuse. The Los Angeles area was clearly a growing market with plenty of upside potential, as its population had increased by nearly 650,000 just since 1930. Also, in Dan Reeves the old-school owners were dealing with a fellow owner far different from their previous experiences. He had plenty of financing at his disposal, was a very capable businessman, and was not afraid to act on his convictions.

The NFL owners were fully aware of the launching of the new AAFC and the problems they would face if Reeves did withdraw the Rams from "their" league. After years of relative stability, the NFL did not want a return to an odd number of teams with the resulting schedule and expansion problems, and there was the fear that Reeves would transfer his NFL champion Rams into the AAFC. But most of all was the fear that if the Rams headed west as members of the AAFC, along with the two franchises the new league was already placing in California, the AAFC would have a solid foothold on the West Coast. The NFL would then be quickly forced into some undesired major expansion or face not being able to establish a significant West Coast presence for years. Reconsidering the possibilities, the NFL owners recast their votes and approved the relocation of the Rams to Los Angeles, effective with the 1946 season.[11]

A major obstacle to be overcome was where the professional games would be played in Los Angeles in 1946. The only appropriate venue was the gigantic Coliseum, yet the Los Angeles Coliseum Commission had considered it to be an arena for the college football teams of USC and UCLA. While the prospect of at least thirteen more rental dates in the fall was appealing, some of the commission members were also sympathetic to pressure from local black sportswriters demanding that Kenny Washington be given a serious tryout by the Rams before any lease discussions.

Here was the first real challenge to the "color barrier" that the NFL had followed since 1934. But to Reeves, a new breed of team owner who did not buy into the prejudices of the older owners, signing an African American represented no problem. Washington was well known after his All-American days at UCLA and several seasons with the Hollywood Bears. After the tryout, Reeves signed Washington and former Hollywood teammate Woody Strode to contracts, shattering the NFL's "color barrier." At the time this major event in football made little impact with the public. Yet, the signing of four African American players by the Browns and Rams in 1946 was a milestone in professional team sports.

Washington's talent pointed Reeves to a major new source of capable players that had been ignored for years, and so the Rams immediately became the leading pursuer in the NFL of African American football players. This tied in perfectly with the player scouting system Reeves had been enhancing significantly, and here also the Rams would move ahead of the other teams for well over a decade.

Using his business acumen, Reeves had organized a scouting department and procedures for the Rams that would soon be producing a steady flow of playing talent, and not just the All-American names, and soon led to their top era of 1949–1955. Other NFL officials later called the Rams' scouting network far ahead of its time in producing draft prospects, and said Reeves had even developed a precursor to the modern scouting combines used by many NFL teams today. With the end of the color barrier, Reeves expanded the scope of his scouting network to include evaluating African American players at the mainly white schools and, most important, added scouting of all historically black colleges to his network. By the early 1950s all the other teams were attempting to emulate Reeves's scouting success, yet the Rams continued to lead in signing outstanding young players into the 1960s.

Despite the additional football talent now available, no other NFL teams joined the Rams in adding black players until 1948. Meanwhile, the AAFC was more aggressive, and in 1947 the first three players from the historically black colleges had signed with the new league—including two joining the Los Angeles Dons. That season six teams of the AAFC had at least one African American player. In 1949 the Dons signed a sensational black halfback named George Taliaferro of Indiana, while the Rams found a great running back in Paul "Tank" Younger from Grambling. The Rams continued to lead the way in 1950 by drafting four black players from predominantly white colleges; each played at least five seasons with the team.

The American Football League that began play in 1960 with the Los Angeles Chargers a prominent member, was much more open to adding excellent black players to their rosters, and this contributed greatly to the revolution in the professional game's offensive styles of play. The evolution into today's modern NFL was facilitated in great part over the years by Reeves's innovative scouting network, along with the shattering of the color barrier.[12]

The Rams struggled on the field through their first three seasons (1946–48) in Los Angeles, and fans began staying away from the Coliseum in large numbers, causing Reeves to lose over $600,000 in that period. Unable to sustain those financial losses, Reeves sold 30 percent of the team's stock in late 1947 to a wealthy oilman named Edwin Pauley for the sum of just one dollar. With the losses continuing, Reeves then sold another 36 2/3 percent of the stock among three more investors—each of whom also paid one dollar apiece for their shares—with all four of the partners prepared to share in any of the club's profits or losses.

By the 1949 season the Rams bolstered their roster with a number of outstanding players joining star quarterback Bob Waterfield, including Tom Fears, Elroy Hirsch, Paul Younger, and Norm Van Brocklin. With this infusion of talent, the Rams won the western division title, although incurring further financial losses, and advanced to the NFL championship game at the Coliseum against the Philadelphia Eagles. Unfortunately, a heavy rain that began early and continued through most of the game left the Coliseum field a sea of mud.

Only 22,245 fans showed up in the rain as the powerful Philadelphia team dominated the game, defeating the Rams, 14–0.[13]

Meanwhile, back in 1946 the Los Angeles Dons of the AAFC had put together a talented team of former college stars such as Charley O'Rourke, John Kimbrough, and Angelo Bertelli. The Dons played their first regular season game on September 13, 1946, at the Coliseum and defeated the Brooklyn Dodgers. The overall quality of play in the AAFC was excellent with the Cleveland Browns of that era regarded as one of pro football's greatest teams. Two of the high points of 1946 for the Dons came against the Browns—the first when the teams staged a hard-fought battle in Cleveland before 71,134 fans, and the other at the Coliseum when the Dons handed the eventual league champions a stunning 17–16 defeat.

After Los Angeles fans had seen the high quality of football in the AAFC, it was no surprise when 82,675 fans turned up at the Coliseum for the Dons' 1947 home opener against the tough New York Yankees. The high point of the season for the Dons was another upset victory over the rugged Browns; this time in Cleveland. When the season ended the Dons had posted a 7–7–0 record, with an impressive average attendance of 43,452 at the Coliseum. Despite having a very good football team the Dons again finished 7–7–0 in the rugged league in 1948. The top crowds of the season came in the final two contests at the Coliseum when the Dons drew 60,031 for the Cleveland game and 51,460 when the 49ers came to town. For the season, the Dons average home attendance was 40,049, while the Rams reported an average home attendance of 33,796.

The 1949 season proved to be the most momentous in professional football history until the mid-1960s NFL/AFL merger.[14] Before the season, the owners of both professional football leagues decided that everyone had enough of the escalating player salaries and other costs resulting from their "war," and so a merger of the NFL and the AAFC was soon agreed upon. The NFL took in the Cleveland Browns, San Francisco 49ers, and Baltimore Colts for 1950, while the rest of the AAFC teams (including the Dons) were disbanded and their players placed in a draft for selection by one of the surviving teams.

The Dons had played an exciting brand of football and Los Angeles fans at the Coliseum turnstiles in effect voted them as their favorite team. But the NFL carried more influence so the Rams were the survivors. The last victory for the Dons at the Coliseum came on October 9, 1949, against the Buffalo Bills, while the team's final win ever came on November 20 at Baltimore over the Colts by a score of 21–10. The Dons last game was at the Coliseum on November 24, 1949, against the New York Yankees before 20,096 fans.[15]

To the Top and Back Again

As the 1950s dawned, the Rams were about to field a few of their best teams in franchise history, yet Dan Reeves was still looking for more income sources. For the 1950 season he arranged for television broadcasts in Los Angeles of all Rams games—both home and away. Reeves convinced the sponsor of the telecasts—Admiral Television—to contractually agree that the dollar amount of any decrease in Coliseum attendance for 1950 below the 1949 ticket sales would be repaid to the Rams by Admiral. Despite fielding a terrific team, home game season attendance plummeted to only 110,000 and Admiral had to pay $307,000 to fulfill the agreement. In early 1951, NFL commissioner Bert Bell ruled that in the future teams would be required to blackout the telecasting of their home games within a seventy-five-mile radius of their stadium.[16]

In 1950, head coach Joe Stydahar led one of the top teams in professional football history as the Rams scored 466 points in just twelve games while finishing in a tie with the Chicago Bears for the division title. When they met in the playoff game at the Coliseum, the Rams posted a 24–14 win before nearly eighty-four thousand fans. Taking on the host Cleveland Browns a week later for the NFL championship, the Rams nearly hung on for the win but gave up a field goal with twenty-eight seconds to play and lost 30–28. Three weeks later the NFL resumed its prewar Pro Bowl series in Los Angeles, the games now between all-star teams representing each of the league's conferences.

The Rams were also loaded with talent in 1951 with a high-powered passing attack as they again won the division title to set up a rematch with the Browns for the league crown. Played at the Coliseum before 59,475 fans, Norm Van Brocklin connected with a pass to end Tom Fears for a 73-yard touchdown midway in the fourth quarter that held up to give the Rams a 24–17 victory and the NFL championship.[17]

In 1952 the Rams edged Pittsburgh at the Coliseum on the final day of the season to finish in a tie with the Detroit Lions for the division title. In their playoff at Detroit, the Lions had too much firepower and handed the Rams a 31–21 defeat. Despite the retirement of Bob Waterfield after the 1952 season, the

Rams still posted winning records in the 1953–1954 seasons. In 1955, the Rams were locked in a tight division race all season and only a win in their final game got them into the NFL title game. There, on a gloomy day in the Coliseum before 85,693 fans, the Cleveland Browns intercepted six of Van Brocklin's passes and ran all over the Rams for a 38–14 win and the NFL championship. Beginning with the 1956 season, the Rams went into a decline on the playing field that saw them post just one winning record over the next ten seasons as a number of key players left the team early in this period.[18]

There were some notable developments during the early stages of this down period, one coming in 1957 when the Rams drafted an acrobatic halfback from USC named Jon Arnett, who went on to seven brilliant seasons for the Rams. Also, fans continued coming out to the Coliseum for a time before the inevitable decline in attendance, highlighted by attendance figures of 102,368 for a 1957 game with the 49ers and 100,470 for a 1958 matchup with the Bears. In 1957 an average of 74,296 attended the six home games. Then, a few weeks after the 1959 draft, Rams' general manager Pete Rozelle completed a trade that brought explosive halfback Ollie Matson to Los Angeles from the Chicago Cardinals in exchange for nine players. Matson—a future Pro Football Hall of Famer—was still a standout running back and in 1959 he rushed for 863 yards for the Rams, who were terrible that season. Yet many of the players made clear their resentment of Matson's salary and the fact that many of their friends had been traded for him.

Complicating matters for the Rams were ongoing serious problems in the front office. As early as 1957, there had been the start of a dispute among the club's ownership—specifically Reeves, Pauley, and Fred Levy—and it became very difficult to make any significant changes in the organization. Things finally came to a head in 1962 as Reeves and the four other owners each sought to buy a majority of the club's stock. There was so much animosity that the sale ended up being decided by sealed bids, with now-commissioner Rozelle conducting the auction. In the end Reeves purchased the Rams for a staggering $7.1 million, which included buying out his four current partners—who each had purchased their shares for just one dollar—for $4.8 million. Reeves himself purchased 51 percent of the stock for just over $1 million, and the remaining 49 percent went to a seven-man ownership group Reeves had incorporated as the Los Angeles Rams Football Company, Inc. It was a popular outcome within the organization.[19]

Another New Team in Town

As though the Rams did not have enough problems, in late 1959 they learned that Los Angeles would have a second professional football team competing for attention beginning with the 1960 season. The name of the team was the Los Angeles Chargers of the new eight-team AFL—a league that began with a national television contract with ABC—who were owned by thirty-two-year-old Barron Hilton, son of the wealthy Conrad Hilton.

The Chargers opened their preseason training camp at Chapman College in Orange, California, and it quickly became obvious that they were putting together a very good football team that included such excellent players as Jack Kemp, Paul Lowe, Charlie Flowers, and Ron Mix. The high level of play across the AFL was brought about in part because its teams actively signed African American players from historically black colleges and other schools, who despite earlier signings by the NFL and the AAFC still remained a relatively underutilized source of football talent.[20]

In the Chargers first exhibition game Paul Lowe returned the opening kickoff 105 yards for a touchdown. In the regular season opener at the Coliseum the Chargers defeated the Dallas Texans before 17,724 fans. Some of the offensive concepts displayed by the two teams were typical of the wide-open style of play that would characterize the AFL and that would eventually revolutionize all of professional football. The high points of the season, along with winning the Dallas game, came at the Coliseum when the Chargers defeated the rugged Houston Oilers and the New York Titans, yet home game attendance was a serious problem. With the 21,805 fans for the Houston game easily the highest Coliseum crowd, the Chargers drew a total of only 110,376 for seven home games for an average attendance of 15,768—the actual paid attendance much lower.

The Chargers won eight of their last nine games to finish with a 10–4–0 record and the western division title. With Los Angeles scheduled to host Houston in the AFL championship game on ABC nationally, neither Commissioner Joe Foss nor the network wanted to televise the game with acres of empty seats visible in the Coliseum. The game, therefore, was moved to the much smaller Jeppesen Field in Houston, where on New Year's Day 1961 the Oilers defeated the Chargers before 32,183 fans to win the first AFL title.

Although Barron Hilton had publicly predicted success for the Chargers, by October there were already rumors that he was extremely unhappy in Los Angeles. When Hilton learned that the club had lost about $910,000 for the

1960 season, he began talking openly about moving the team. Sportswriters from San Diego quickly brought in their local officials and business leaders, and soon a deal was offered to Hilton to move the club to that city. On February 10, 1961, the AFL owners gave Hilton permission to move the Chargers to San Diego and quickly they were gone from Los Angeles.[21]

Back on Top Amid Tragedy

After only one winning season since 1956, the Rams struggled to an 8–6–0 record in 1966 to begin an era of relative prosperity for the team. Yet the 1966 season was of much greater significance to professional football in general as the AFL and NFL agreed to a merger after the owners had tired of the escalating player salaries and demands. Unlike 1949 when the NFL had forced the AAFC to abandon most of its franchises, this time the AFL had proved itself an equal and therefore all its teams were included in the merger, which would be completed in 1970. At the close of the 1966 season, the champions of the two leagues began meeting in a postseason game, which eventually, in 1969, would be called the "Super Bowl." The first AFL/NFL championship game was played on January 15, 1967, between Green Bay and Kansas City at the Los Angeles Coliseum before 61,946 fans. The Coliseum would also host the 1973 Super Bowl, with several other Super Bowls played at Pasadena's Rose Bowl.[22]

The Rams finally won a division title in 1967 for the first time since 1955, and then repeated in 1969. Yet the Los Angeles club and all of the NFL were stunned when Dan Reeves passed away on April 15, 1971, after battling a serious illness since 1968. Business partner William Barnes replaced him as team president for a time.

In retrospect, Dan Reeves proved to be one of the most influential and indispensable owners during the first fifty years of the NFL. Arguably his most significant accomplishment was in overcoming the resistance of the old-school owners to move his team to Los Angeles and open the West to the NFL. This was followed quickly by his role in shattering the NFL's color barrier in 1946, and then the aggressive search every season for more outstanding collegiate African American playing talent through his sophisticated scouting network—superior to the methods of other clubs and years ahead of its time.

By 1960 Reeves was considered among the most powerful owners in the NFL, and so his agreement with Commissioner Pete Rozelle's plan for all the teams to equally share the revenues from the first league-wide national television contract was critical to its adoption. Also, when the talks began in early 1966 for the merger of the NFL and the AFL, Reeves was heavily involved in the discussions of potential franchise changes and other issues among the two leagues. Clearly, without his involvement as a team owner for over two decades the history of the NFL would have been far different.

The Rams were sold in July 1972 by Reeves's estate to Robert Irsay and Bud Kelend for a record $19 million. Then in a bizarre deal, Carroll Rosenbloom—owner of the Baltimore Colts—traded his franchise to Irsay and Kelend in exchange for the Los Angeles franchise, throwing in nearly $4 million to balance the value of the Baltimore team. Thus Rosenbloom—with twenty years' experience in professional football—was the new owner of the Rams. For 1973 Rosenbloom hired Chuck Knox as the new head coach, and then began rebuilding the team with young talent. The Rams went on to win the western division title for the next five seasons (1973–1977) under Knox before he resigned, although losing each year in an early round of the playoffs.[23]

The Rams organization had high hopes for 1979, but tragedy struck when Rosenbloom died in a swimming accident off Florida on April 2 of that year. His widow, Georgia Frontiere, inherited majority ownership of the club and took over operation of the franchise. It had previously been decided that the Rams were going to move their home games to Anaheim Stadium beginning in 1980 because of declining attendance and population growth in Orange County.

On the field, 1979 proved to be a landmark season in Rams' history as they returned to the NFL's championship game (the Super Bowl) for the first time in twenty-four years. The Rams just barely won the western division—despite losing their last game ever in the Coliseum as the home team—and then surprisingly won playoff games on the road over Dallas and Tampa Bay to advance to Super Bowl XIV. Before a crowd of 103,985 in the Rose Bowl, the Rams gave up a pair of fourth-quarter touchdowns and lost to the Pittsburgh Steelers 31–19.[24]

More Teams Come to Town

When the 1980 season opened, the Rams home stadium and team headquarters had both been switched to Anaheim. The Rams lost their regular season opening game to Detroit at Anaheim Stadium before posting their first-ever win in their new facility over Green Bay in week three. The Rams ended up finishing second in their division, yet they struggled through the next couple seasons.

Then, to compound their problems another NFL team took up residence at the Coliseum.

The new team in town was the Raiders—formerly of Oakland—who moved to Los Angeles for the 1982 season. As early as 1979, Raiders owner Al Davis had been negotiating with the Coliseum Commission to relocate his team, but in 1980 the city of Oakland had filed an eminent-domain lawsuit to keep the Raiders from leaving. The NFL also indicated it would not approve such a move so the Coliseum Commission and the Raiders joined in an antitrust suit against the league. After the city of Oakland's attempt to retain the Raiders failed in court, a decision against the NFL in the Davis-Coliseum antitrust suit was issued on May 7, 1982, and so Davis was immediately free to move the Raiders to Los Angeles for the 1982 season.

After attracting a disappointing crowd to the Coliseum for the 1983 home opener, Coach Tom Flores rallied the Raiders and they ended up capturing the AFC western division title. In the playoffs the Raiders defeated Pittsburgh and Seattle, the latter game before a crowd of nearly ninety-three thousand at the Coliseum, and advanced to Super Bowl XVIII against the Washington Redskins. The Raiders easily won the game by a score of 38–9. It was the first NFL championship for the city of Los Angeles since 1951.[25]

The Raiders' Super Bowl win was a perfect finish to a year that also brought Los Angeles yet another professional football team early in 1983. A new pro league called the United States Football League (USFL) had been formed to begin play in 1983 with an ABC national television contract. The league scheduled games to run from early spring through midsummer so as not to compete directly with the NFL. Yet the USFL teams tried to sign the best possible NFL players as their contracts expired, along with drafting and attempting to sign top college players.

The new team calling the Coliseum home was the Los Angeles Express. The franchise's first owners were Bill Daniels and Alan Harmon, a pair of cable company operators from San Diego. They hired Hugh Campbell as head coach, opened the club's offices in Manhattan Beach, and set about putting together a roster that initially had a relatively large number of rookies and others who had played at Southern California colleges.

In their 1983 season opener, the Express played at the Coliseum before a national television audience and a crowd of 34,002, which would prove to be the largest home crowd in franchise history. The big attraction was the New Jersey Generals, an excellent team that featured halfback Herschel Walker, who had won college football's Heisman Trophy in 1982. With quarterback Tom Ramsey coming on in relief to throw a pair of touchdown passes, the Express pulled out a thrilling 20–15 upset victory. The Express had a roller-coaster season that ended with an 8–10–0 record, as they attracted only two more home crowds over 20,000; reporting an average attendance figure of 18,780.[26]

At the end of the season Daniels and Harmon put the Express up for sale, and late in the year they had a potential new owner. His name was J. William Oldenburg, a wealthy investment mortgage banker who also owned a large savings and loan. The USFL approved the sale of the Express to him on December 22, 1983. Oldenburg named a longtime football man, Don Klosterman, as team president and general manager, and by late January the Express was putting together a good young team as it had signed seventeen of its college draft choices. After the second game of the season, the club also signed quarterback Steve Young to a $40 million, ten-year contract, which shocked everyone.

The Express dropped their 1984 opening game to Denver at the Coliseum before 32,082, and struggled until midseason before winning eight of their last eleven games to finish 10–8–0 and in a deadlock for the division title. Yet trouble was brewing. In June, Oldenburg's representatives notified the league that he would not be able to pay for operating the team through the end of the 1984 season. The USFL quickly moved in and collected on the Express owner's $1.5 million letter of credit to the league in order to cover the team's remaining expenses.

This was unfortunate since in the 1984 playoffs the Express played one of the most exciting games in professional football history in their first round matchup. Taking on the Michigan Panthers at the Coliseum, an embarrassing crowd of just 8,753 turned up to watch a classic struggle. With fifty-two seconds left to play in the fourth quarter, the Express scored a touchdown and then added a two-point conversion to send the game into overtime tied at 21–21. The two teams fought through two scoreless quarters of extra-time, until finally Mel Gray dashed 24 yards to a touchdown after 3:33 of the third overtime to give the Express a historic 27–21 victory. It seemed anticlimactic when the Express lost in the next round.[27]

Shortly after the 1984 season the USFL announced that the league would be financing the club until a new owner could be found. In September a potential new owner emerged, a Denver real estate man named Jay Roulier. He soon purchased the Express for $3.5 million, yet in January 1985 the USFL reacquired the team after Roulier had already projected a loss of over $6 million for 1985.

On the field, the 1985 season was a disaster. The Express lost their season opener at the Coliseum before 18,828 fans when they blew a 19-point lead in the last nine minutes to Houston. Things got worse and the team finished with a 3–15–0 record as home attendance continued to plummet. The Express captured their last win ever at midseason with a 17–12 triumph over the Portland Breakers and played their last game at the Coliseum on May 30, 1985, against Denver before just 3,059 fans. The Express played their final home game at Pierce Junior College before an estimated crowd of 8,200 fans. The Los Angeles Express lost in Orlando in the last game they ever played, and within a few months the USFL and the Express were out of business.[28]

The Inevitable Ending and Rebirth

In 1984 Al Davis signed a ten-year lease, retroactive to 1982, for the Raiders to continue playing at the Coliseum. Yet, by the late 1980s Raiders' home attendance began declining and, with no progress in getting improvements such as luxury boxes added to the Coliseum, discussions circulated about the team moving back to Oakland. Then Davis signed a proposal in August 1987 for a new stadium in the town of Irwindale, but in March 1990 he announced that the Raiders would be moving back to Oakland after that city completed the installation of luxury boxes and other improvements. After a good deal of further wrangling, the Los Angeles Raiders lost their last game of the 1994 season to Kansas City at the Coliseum before 64,130 fans, and then moved back to Oakland.[29]

The Rams captured one division title (1985) and qualified for the playoffs six times between 1983 and 1991, yet struggled on the field in the early 1990s with the inevitable declining attendance. The club's owner, Georgia Frontiere, now dissatisfied with Anaheim Stadium, had attempted to get either Orange County or the city of Los Angeles to build a new taxpayer-financed stadium with no success. She then turned to St. Louis, which was building a new stadium and eager to attract an NFL team. After overcoming attempts by the league to block her efforts to relocate, with numerous financial incentives available to the team, Frontiere soon agreed to move the Rams to St. Louis for the 1995 season.

The Los Angeles Rams played their final game on Christmas eve, 1994, as they lost to Washington at Anaheim Stadium before 25,705 angry fans.[30] While the final approval of the transfer was still pending on that last day of the 1994 season, everyone knew that the reign of the fabled Rams in Los Angeles was over after forty-nine seasons. The City of Angels was about to be without professional football for the first time in sixty years.[31]

Yet, over the next twenty-one years, as the business of professional football continued to generate substantially increasing revenue, the return of the NFL to Los Angeles seemed almost inevitable. Finally, after years of unsuccessful and often complicated efforts to establish an NFL franchise in the city, Commissioner Roger Goodell announced on January 12, 2016, that the league's owners had approved the return of the Rams from St. Louis to Los Angeles effective in the 2016 season. The Rams would play at the Los Angeles Memorial Coliseum while awaiting the completion, in 2020, of a new $2.6 billion stadium in nearby Inglewood. Further, the league gave the San Diego Chargers a one-year option to relocate to Los Angeles. Exactly one year after the Rams announced their move to the city, the Chargers exercised their option and relocated to Los Angeles. The Chargers announced that they would play their first three seasons at StubHub Center, the home stadium of Major League Soccer's Los Angeles Galaxy, before moving, in 2020, to the Inglewood stadium, which they would share with the Rams. Pro football had at last come back to the City of Angels with not one, but two NFL teams.

CHAPTER SEVEN

The 1932 Olympics

Spectacle and Growth in Interwar Los Angeles

SEAN DINCES

Social scientists make liberal use of tags like "entrepreneurial city," "tourist city," and "city of leisure" to describe economic development in American cities today. These labels are scholarly shorthand for the relatively recent embrace by many urban powerbrokers of the entertainment and leisure industries as a cure for deindustrialization and fiscal crisis. Over the last forty years, so the story goes, private capitalists and municipal officials have reached a consensus that cities with unique recreational opportunities compete better for investment and tax revenues by appealing to potential employers, residents, and tourists. To be sure, such an approach has proliferated in recent decades; even economically established metropolises like Chicago and New York City have made the growth of fun, diversion, and spectacle a top economic development priority.[1]

In fact, this approach to marketing cities has a long history. Urban boosterism aimed at enticing pleasure seekers goes back well over a century in the United States. Yet experts insist that after 1970 the phenomenon underwent two fundamental transformations. The first shift stemmed from the increasing globalization of communication and transport, which undercut traditional claims by boosters about the economic advantages offered by their cities' geographical location (e.g., the past promotion of Chicago as an unparalleled hub of rail and water transport). As a result, metropolitan boosters increasingly turned to touting distinct cultural and leisure amenities like sports teams and mega-events such as the Olympics and World Cup.[2]

The second shift entailed the transformation of urban boosterism, at the level of the individual city, from an uncoordinated hodgepodge of discrete efforts by promoters to a streamlined, joint effort between private capital and local governments. This latter iteration has typically coalesced around projecting what sociologist Miriam Greenberg describes as a "consistent" urban "brand," agreed upon by newly formed (and formal) public-private coalitions, that promises to improve the reputation of the city in question. In other words, the promotion of place has become far more systematized. The scholarly explanation for this change goes something like this: in the midst of slower growth of federal expenditures on cities and the spread of municipal fiscal crises during the 1970s and 1980s, local elites came to view spending on "urban branding" campaigns and tourist infrastructure as a quick fix for economic decline. In theory, this spending would encourage expanded private investment, and cost less than maintaining or expanding the relatively robust public works and social welfare programs that helped sustain consumer demand in the decades immediately following World War II.[3]

The enthusiasm of their supporters notwithstanding, these urban branding initiatives have typically projected very selective—some might say misleading—images of cities. That is, they have conveniently papered over the increasing inequality and impoverishment, as well as the ongoing racial tensions, that continue to rack urban America. Rather than offering meaningful solutions to these problems, elites in new tourist cities have simply tried to cover them up.

In what follows, I use the case of the 1932 Summer Olympics in Los Angeles to argue that, at least in Southern California, the sort of systematic, public-private urban branding efforts described above have a lineage stretching back much further than the 1970s. Well before the economic tumult of the last quarter of the twentieth century, the organization of the 1932 Games exemplified urban elites' turn to spectacles like international sporting events as tools for restoring growth and profitability in the face of economic instability. Notably, the organizational effort depended on tight, formalized alliances between private capitalists and municipal officials—alliances that, much like today, subverted local democratic processes and minimized the risk borne by private capital. And just like urban mega-events in the late twentieth and early twenty-first centuries, the 1932 Games distracted local and national attention from socioeconomic fissures in the host city.

So why take the time here to rehash this story? After all, the 1932 Games have been the subject of extensive scholarly treatment spanning from the early 1980s to the present. The bulk of this work, my own included, has approached the Games either in terms of their specific relevance to Olympic history or their import to the urban history of Los Angeles before World War II. In this chapter, I do my best to broaden the frame of reference to urban capitalism writ large during the twentieth century, drawing on the secondary literature to show how the first Los Angeles Olympics established an early model for using large-scale sporting events to promote urban growth—a model that, today, represents the status quo in the American city. In doing so, I approach a conclusion somewhat at odds with the recent social science literature: formalized urban economic development blueprints based on enhancing cities' reputations by way of mega-events like the Olympics—blueprints that almost invariably threaten local democratic processes, reduce public engagement with socioeconomic inequality, and impose regressive public costs—are not simply a late twentieth- or early twenty-first-century phenomenon. Rather, for the better part of the last hundred years, elites have used such strategies to respond to periods of unstable, boom-and-bust urban capitalism (i.e., more or less everything but the quarter century immediately following World War II).

The point of this chapter is not to suggest that the role of sporting events and sports infrastructure in urban growth in the United States was exactly the same in the 1920s and 1930s as it is today. The last three to four decades have undoubtedly witnessed the increasing—and increasingly controversial—embrace by urban elites of hosting events like the Olympics and World Cup in the name of enhancing the image of their cities. It is also clear that the expenditure of public subsidies on these efforts in place of more traditional spending on social welfare has gained significant traction as mainstream policy orthodoxy since 1980. But even with these qualifications in mind, the 1932 Games are best understood as a precursor to these more recent phenomena, but also as an indication of how the interwar period and the postindustrial, or "neoliberal," era encouraged similar models of sports-linked urban development.[4]

The 1932 Games, Urban Boosterism, and Economic Crisis

While conversations among local elites in Los Angeles about the possibility of hosting the summer Olympics began as early as 1915, it was not until after World War I that their efforts to secure a winning bid for the Games took on the character of a streamlined campaign. It was postwar demobilization and the accompanying recession that really pushed local boosters to move from idle conversation to proactive organization of the bid. The economic downturn resulted in a sharp drop in the number of tourists visiting Los Angeles, a development that local business interests viewed as a major threat to the city's economy. Since the 1880s, investors had gambled with some success on the ability of Southern California's climate and the dissemination of a romanticized version of the region's Spanish missionary history to support consistent growth in the local real estate and tourism industries.[5]

In 1919, in response to the recession, Los Angeles mayor Meredith Snyder appointed a group of one hundred local elites to the new California Fiesta Association and tasked them with combating the decline in tourism by boosting the city's appeal to outsiders. A year after the Fiesta Association's founding, twenty-two select members reorganized it as the Community Development Association (CDA). At its first meeting in 1920, *Los Angeles Examiner* publisher Max Ihmsen proposed that the group take the lead in seeking the privilege of hosting the Olympics in Los Angeles. According to historian Steven Riess, Ihmsen "argued that holding such a spectacle would direct a lot of attention to the city, improve its prestige, and bring a great deal of free publicity." His colleagues embraced the idea. In May 1923, after extensive lobbying of the International Olympic Committee (IOC) by CDA president and local real estate mogul William May Garland, Los Angeles secured the Games of the Xth Olympiad in 1932.[6]

As historians Mark Dyreson and Matthew Llewellyn note, the CDA membership's vision of the event as a "centrepiece for advertising their climate, culture and cachet in the global marketplace" marked a break from the history of the modern Olympic movement up to that point. IOC president Pierre de Coubertin, who helped found the modern Olympics at the end of the nineteenth century, understood the Games as many things—for example, as an occasion for fostering internationalism—but he was not particularly invested in their potential as a business opportunity.[7] In fact, much of the funding for the Games before 1932 came from philanthropic contributions from de Coubertin's personal fortune. Garland and the rest of the CDA, which in 1927 formed the offshoot Xth Olympiad Committee to promote and administer the Games, were different.[8] According to historian Jeremy White, "From the very beginning the Los Angeles committee looked to the games as an advertising opportunity."[9]

Official promotional materials created in anticipation of the Games make it patently clear that local Olympic boosters were concerned much less with the sporting aspect of the event than with the occasion it provided to sell Los Angeles as a nice place to visit. For example, Olympic maps and pamphlets printed by the Los Angeles Chamber of Commerce, an organization whose membership overlapped extensively with that of the CDA and Xth Olympiad

Promotional photo for 1932 summer Olympic Games. Photo courtesy of LA84 Foundation.

Committee, hardly mentioned specific athletic events. They did, however, gush over "the crumbling ruins and interesting old [mission] landmarks scattered" throughout the region. The pamphlets also touted potential tours of the Pacific Fleet and visits to Hollywood movie studios.[10] As portrayed by the promotional photo above, boosters were more concerned with using the Games as a vehicle for selling warm weather, pristine beaches, and (non-Olympian) women in swimsuits than with promoting specific sporting events or athletes.[11]

This was one of the first times—if not *the* first time—in the United States that a coalition of pro-growth advocates used a sporting mega-event to showcase their city to the outside world in the hopes of attracting tourists, moneyed migrants, and investors. Putting the dated production quality of the promotional materials aside, they seem to draw from a playbook still used by local Olympic boosters today—one that involves using the Games as a jumping-off point, to borrow from Llewellyn and Dyreson, for "manufacturing" a larger-than-life reputation for the host city.[12] Olympic organizers in 1932 envisioned this enhanced local profile as, above all else, a tool for quickly attracting consumer demand from visitors and new residents, as well as new private investment. Moreover, the effects of the post-WWI recession made competing for this investment all the more urgent and heightened the appeal of the Olympics to members of the CDA.

The CDA's perception of the 1932 Games as a local cure for the crisis tendencies of urban capitalism merits further exploration, as it tightly links the efforts of the group with those of Olympic organizers of today. In 1920, as the negative economic effects of postwar demobilization lingered, CDA executive committee member Henry McKee wrote to a colleague, "In order to avoid a period of business depression in the future, we must plan in advance ... The thing we must plan is the intelligent development of our one most productive natural resource. This resource is the attractiveness of this locality to travelers and home-seekers."[13] The message was clear: the systematic enhancement of the city's international reputation offered the possibility of ongoing and expanded growth in spite of the boom-and-bust instability of American capitalism. Proponents of this strategy believed that it would bolster existing industries like real estate and international transportation (i.e., port services), and by extension reinforce existing economic hierarchies within the city.

Not surprisingly, the onset of the Great Depression at the end of the 1920s added to the sense of urgency among Los Angeles's elite regarding the need to find a quick fix for the economy. Local pro-growth advocates increasingly latched on to the 1932 Games as a solution. In March 1932, a few months before the opening ceremonies, Los Angeles Chamber of Commerce executive Harry Harper described the Games as "a most necessary contribution to aid a revival of business conditions here."[14] The following month, he added, "We need all the visitors possible this year ... both to make a success of the Games from the attendance standpoint and to keep the flow of new money into the Southwest up to the volume of more prosperous times."[15] In July, with just weeks to go before the start of the festivities, the *Los Angeles Times* rejoiced, "Instead of the depression discouraging the Tenth Olympiad, the Tenth Olympiad is discouraging the depression."[16]

In the wake of the Games, which actually produced a surplus (more on this below) and which the media widely heralded as an unprecedented success, CDA president William May Garland pegged the local economic activity sparked by Olympic-related marketing at $10 million.[17] The reliability of this figure is beside the point; "economic impact" statements of this sort, particularly those offered by event organizers, are typically unreliable. More important is that it indicates an emerging belief among local boosters and businessmen that *the* key to robust growth in the face of macroeconomic instability was flashy spectacle that would enhance the reputation and global visibility of their home city.

Today there is a justifiable tendency to view this approach to urban economic development as an outgrowth of economic restructuring and fiscal crises since the 1970s. However, the history of the 1932 Olympics suggests that it had much earlier precedents. One reading of all this is that Los Angeles was ahead of the historical curve in terms of spectacle-driven growth because of the distinctive structure of its economy in the early twentieth century. In the City of Angels of the 1920s, industries especially sensitive to local image and reputation—for example, real estate and global trade—played outsized roles, and likely encouraged aggressive urban marketing relatively early on.[18] This is part of the story, but it is also helpful to think about how the emergence of the 1932 Games as a purported economic savior for Los Angeles suggests continuities in urban capitalism *in general* as it existed on either side of the post-WWII boom.

Increasingly, historians view the two to three decades of economic stability and relatively equal distribution of growth after the Second World War as an aberration, or "long exception," within the much longer history of American capitalism.[19] This is not to say that the American economy today is indistinguishable from that of the 1920s, but rather that it has a similar tendency toward periodic, profound crises. In this broader context, it makes sense that the organizers of the 1932 Olympics, who were clearly consumed with using the mega-event as a catalyst for growth during postwar recession and later the Great Depression, behaved in much the same way as pro-growth coalitions in American cities at the end of the century. In both periods, economic instability and unpredictable growth trends represented central challenges faced by urban elites throughout the United States. And in both periods, flashy mega-events appealed to those elites as a relatively cheap and politically uncontroversial means of increasing local consumer demand, since they did not require any significant redistribution of wealth within cities.

"Public-Private Partnership" and the First Los Angeles Olympics

Urbanists like Miriam Greenberg suggest that boosterism in American cities before World War II was poorly coordinated across industries and institutions in contrast to the well-oiled "urban branding" campaigns of the present day. In fact, the organizational efforts behind the 1932 Games indicate that "urban branding" has a lengthier history than sociologists like Greenberg let on.[20] The CDA and Xth Olympiad Committee designed a sweeping promotional offensive that drew the support and active participation of a wide array of local business interests and associations. Much of this no doubt had to do with the original makeup of the CDA, which from the outset consisted of major players in the local banking, real estate, contracting, retail, publishing, legal, and automotive industries.[21]

The list of private companies and trade associations that produced promotional materials, the vast majority of which peddled the same general imagery of Southern California as an idyllic coastal refuge scattered with picturesque Spanish and Native American artifacts, underscores the breadth of the coordination. The Los Angeles Chamber of Commerce, Shell Gasoline, Texaco Gasoline, the California State Chamber of Commerce, and the California Newspaper Publishers' Association were just some of those who got in on the act. And, as several scholars have detailed, Hollywood's movie industry also played a key role. For example, the Xth Olympiad Committee successfully recruited noted film producer Louis B. Mayer as a member, and the committee collaborated with the Motion Pictures Producers Association to create two promotional radio shows in the months leading up to the Games.[22]

Even more than the widespread support lent by the local private sector to this cohesive promotional campaign, it was Los Angeles capitalists' close collaboration with local government in the planning and execution of the 1932 Games that makes this story sound so similar to more contemporary urban branding campaigns described by Greenberg. Using the "I ♥ New York" initiative from the late 1970s as her primary case study, Greenberg argues that, during the last two to three decades of the twentieth century, "erratic" booster efforts gave way to "urban branding campaigns . . . highly coordinated by public-private partnerships."[23] In the nearly decade and a half of planning that went into the 1932 Olympics, the CDA and Xth Olympiad Committee would successfully press for the formation of several such partnerships. None of these proved more important than the one that facilitated public funding for the new Los Angeles Coliseum—an asset that allegedly played a key role in William May Garland's success in convincing the IOC to award Southern California the Games.[24]

In 1920 the public funding of large-scale sports facilities was virtually unheard of. Indeed, according to stadium finance expert Judith Grant Long, there is no record of government subsidies for any major league sports facility completed between 1876 and 1922.[25] In Los Angeles, CDA membership broke with this trend, promoting a new Olympic stadium as a public good while they sought out local taxpayer money to underwrite the project. But Los Angelenos proved skeptical of digging into their own pockets to fund the facility. In August 1920, Los Angeles voters rejected the CDA-supported plan to finance the new stadium through a municipal bond issue.[26]

The CDA managed to work around—some would say "subvert"—the democratic process in order to achieve its aims. It convinced the city and county of Los Angeles to lease the CDA seventeen acres of land in Exposition Park (adjacent to the University of Southern California), and proceeded to secure a private loan to construct a stadium there. But it was ultimately the public who paid off the loan. In November 1921 the city and county agreed to make "rent" payments to the CDA to retire the debt incurred to construct the stadium. Construction crews put the finishing touches on the new seventy-five-thousand-seat Los Angeles Coliseum in 1923, and together Los Angeles City and Los Angeles County transferred nearly $1 million back to the CDA during the first half decade of the facility's operation. According to historian Steven Riess, this made Los Angeles "the first major metropolitan area to complete its [publicly funded] municipal stadium."[27]

This history of the Coliseum suggests a close resemblance between the CDA's interaction with municipal bodies like the Los Angeles City Council and the intricate public-private partnerships typically described by scholars as a hallmark of sports-linked economic development—and urban growth more generally—since the 1970s.[28] In interwar Los Angeles, as in the postindustrial or "neoliberal" American city, complex dealings between businessmen and municipal officials became the basis for funneling public dollars into sports spectacle and infrastructure dreamed up entirely by the private sector. In short, the CDA's aggressive pursuit of public support in constructing the Coliseum yielded the first major example in US urban history of local taxpayers assuming the bulk of the risk for a stadium-linked urban branding campaign.

There is a temptation to situate this part of the 1932 Olympics story as the first step in a gradual, linear expansion of these types of sports infrastructure financing deals. Indeed, Long's data indicate that, by the 1930s, public funding of large-scale stadium projects had become more or less the norm across the United States. Between the New Deal and 1980, much of the public funding for stadiums came from municipal governments, often in rapidly growing suburbs, eager to partner with major-league teams to develop new sports facilities as "civic infrastructure." In this period, municipalities typically executed these deals by way of publicly approved bond issues (the financing mechanism previously rejected by Los Angeles voters).[29]

The public-private partnership struck between the CDA and municipal officials in Los Angeles shared much more in common with the types of stadium deals designed after 1980 than with those of the immediate post-WWII period. For example, Olympic boosters secured taxpayer subsidization of the Coliseum by *working around* the democratic process instead of successfully winning popular approval from voters. This approach to building public-private partnerships in support of sports mega-events and stadium infrastructure proliferated considerably at the end of the twentieth century, as economists and taxpayers became increasingly wary of the fiscal prudence of bankrolling sports facilities and the spectacles staged inside of them. While the mechanisms for averting democratic approval have varied from case to case—one popular approach has been the establishment of "quasi-state" agencies that can issue bonds without public approval—the end result has been the same as in Los Angeles in the 1920s: a unilateral decision made by the private sector (and sanctioned by local policy makers) to funnel public subsidies into their pet sports projects.[30]

Interestingly, the rationale invoked by local boosters to justify the unpopular use of taxpayer money to build the Coliseum appears, in some cases, nearly identical to that of contemporary advocates of publicly funded stadiums, who are eager to deflect scholarly and public skepticism about who actually benefits from such projects. After hearing an address from William May Garland just weeks ahead of the opening ceremonies, the president of the Los Angeles Chamber of Commerce opined gleefully, "I know when you try to think of the value of this [Olympic] thing for years to come in the way of favorable advertising for California . . . it is just beyond our ability to measure from the standpoint of affirmative results."[31] The rhetoric of "immeasurable," "intangible," or "unquantifiable" benefits linked to urban branding or "big-league" status has grown increasingly aggressive among pro-stadium boosters in recent decades as a way to neutralize mounting academic evidence that taxpayer subsidies are little more than corporate welfare veiled under the banner of "economic development."[32]

Another aspect of the public-private partnership behind the Coliseum that resembles contemporary stadium financing much more than the immediate post-WWII variant is the degree of control over stadium administration and revenues secured by the private "partners." As Riess explains, good-government organizations active in Los Angeles during the 1920s reported that the arrangement struck between the CDA and local officials granted the former "nearly complete control over what was in reality a public facility." Despite covering the entire cost of the new stadium by way of rental payments, under the agreement the city and county only enjoyed the right to schedule public events at the Coliseum for fifteen days every other month during its first decade of operation. In the meantime, the CDA received more or less free reign to operate the stadium at the whim of its membership. The nominally "nonprofit" entity even controlled the title to the facility. Not surprisingly, given the close connection between CDA members and the (private) University of Southern California, hosting the school's football games emerged as the Coliseum's primary function in the years leading up to the 1932 Games.[33]

Local watchdogs reported that the ceding of administrative authority to the CDA encouraged the latter to engage in questionable financial practices. For example, critics alleged that the CDA was using revenues generated by the facility to pay exorbitant salaries to those members involved in its administration, and available data back up this claim. Moreover, many outsiders scoffed at the failure of the CDA to make its accounting records public.[34] This would spark a much broader controversy at the end of 1929 when, despite the fact that the CDA had amassed more than $300,000 in surplus funds from operating the Coliseum during its first eight years, it solicited money from the city and county to complete an expansion of the stadium in preparation for the Xth Olympiad.[35]

By this point, even some local officials had begun to criticize the CDA's management of the stadium, but CDA membership successfully used the specter of the impending Games to pressure the city and county to contribute nearly half a million dollars (combined) to pay for the expansion. All of this escaped the scrutiny of the democratic process, as municipal officials unilaterally transferred the funds to the Coliseum from a previously canceled public works project. After the closing ceremonies for the 1932 Games, the public had not only picked up the tab for the construction and expansion of the Coliseum, but also $1 million in operational funding for the event. Unlike the capital costs for the stadium, voters throughout the state approved the latter amount.[36]

The CDA's formula for running the Coliseum—privatizing facility revenues while socializing facility expenses—has, in recent decades, become the norm in stadium finance. Public subsidization of these sorts of structures in the twenty to thirty years after World War II was typically contingent on municipalities retaining a relatively high degree of fiscal and operational control over them; often teams or other occupants channeled event revenues back to the public in the form of significant rent payments. But since the end of the 1970s, public-private stadium partnerships have increasingly operated according to the principle that, regardless of the amount of taxpayer money involved in construction and operation, all revenues belong to private partners.[37]

The seeming symmetry between the public-private partnership behind the 1932 Olympics and those behind contemporary stadium schemes should not necessarily come as a surprise. A strong tendency toward periodic crisis is not the only similarity between American capitalism of the interwar period and that of the late twentieth and early twenty-first centuries; the two eras also bear a striking resemblance in terms of prevailing economic dogma and the relationship between capital and the state. As economic historian David Kotz explains, the successful peddling by economic elites of "free market" ideology—in other words, the notion that the government should not intervene in the economy—characterizes both periods. But so does the *practice* by those elites of effectively lobbying for and exploiting government resources and actions ultimately intended to minimize risk and maximize private profits.[38]

In spite of the lack of transparency, the dismissal of citizen input, and the heavy public costs incurred at the whim of a handful of local boosters, the fiscal history of the Los Angeles Coliseum and the 1932 Games had some silver linings. Increasing public pressure not only forced the CDA to finally fulfill its long-running promise to hand over control of the stadium, but also to give the "surplus" from the Games themselves—a sum that the most generous estimate pegs at $1.5 million—to the city and county after the event.[39]

But even adhering to the most liberal numbers, the money from the Games recycled back into the public purse fell far short of the total expended by taxpayers.[40] These silver linings were, in other words, relatively thin consolation for what was ultimately the pet project of Los Angeles's "power elite"—one that took place despite widespread public opposition, and that unilaterally prioritized private profits above all else.[41]

Olympic "Community" as Urban Façade

Over the last decade, scholars have made much of what they describe as recent efforts by Olympic host cities/nations to use the Games to conceal the persistence of local socioeconomic inequality. In one of several recent academic articles tackling the issue, Mark Falcous and Michael Silk argue that the official rhetoric of "multiculturalism" propagated by organizers of the 2012 London Olympics "mask[ed], if not further reinforce[d], the complexities of regional and national interplays, assemblages, and juxtapositions of diversity in everyday life."[42] Translated into plain English: by peddling images of unity and social harmony, the event distracted from, and in so doing helped perpetuate, persistent economic and social divisions.

According to these scholars, the proliferation of such images in the context of the Olympics is a decidedly "neoliberal" phenomenon. More specifically, they group them under a "neoliberal urban politics that stresses the aesthetics of place" in order to shield tourists, affluent residents, and prospective investors from the harsh realities of urban life.[43] This is consistent with critiques by scholars like Henry Giroux, who argues in the context of the United States that the end of the twentieth century witnessed "a drying up of images" of poverty and racism within the corporate-controlled media—a process that has served the interests of established elites wary of a public informed about the injustices inherent in contemporary capitalism.[44]

While it is fair to argue that mass media has increasingly whitewashed its depictions of American society relative to the 1960s and 1970s, such whitewashing was a fixture of urban capitalism before the Second World War. The official promotion of the 1932 Games clarifies the implication of the Olympics in this earlier history. Even if organizers of the 1932 Olympics felt they had successfully identified and harnessed the power of sports spectacle to resuscitate healthy economic growth, the type of growth they coveted proved far from inclusive. And the Olympics themselves became a façade behind which to hide this less than flattering truth.

Before and during the 1932 Games, local officials and boosters stressed the region's alleged reputation as a progressive melting pot perfectly suited for hosting athletes and tourists from across the globe. In an "official" appeal to those outside Los Angeles in the lead up to the Games, California governor James Rolph offered his assurances that all would be welcomed "regardless of race, color, or creed."[45] The local press played along, celebrating the allegedly harmonious interaction between white locals and nonwhite foreigners. The *Los Angeles Times*, for example, noted how Los Angeles mayor John Porter commended the Japanese Olympians on their exemplary sportsmanship.[46]

Much more than these incidents, it was the 1932 Olympic village, built in Baldwin Hills in order to provide housing for male Olympians, that became the focus of booster rhetoric about the international, interracial, and interclass unity fostered by the Games *and* the host city. Architectural historian Jeremy White argues that the village, the first ever erected by a host city, "was articulated by organizers and their allies in the local press as a utopian space, a space that was at once a tangible manifestation of an otherwise abstract Olympic ideology, and most interestingly . . . a representation of Los Angeles itself."[47] As the *Los Angeles Times* explained:

> Thirty six flags of thirty six peoples, created equal in opportunity, will float above the city of Los Angeles in the democratic free-for-all struggle . . . No makeshift camp of tents thrown hastily together are the training quarters provided for its 2000 athletic contestants by its sponsors of the Tenth Olympiad . . . Its temporary occupants are filled with amazement and delight and are telling the world about the Los Angeles way of doing things.[48]

As White explains, these odes to diversity were accompanied by discussions of how the village's design precluded social hierarchy. For example, organizers and the press focused on the alleged effects of the close quarters in the village, suggesting that "the two beds in each room forced together rich and poor, aristocrat and worker in a democratizing confrontation."[49] Even if, on the whole, the United States remained a starkly segregated society along lines of class and race, so the story went, the Olympic village—and Los Angeles more broadly—offered a forward-thinking, egalitarian refuge.

Perhaps there was something to all of this chatter about Los Angeles as a unique bastion of multicultural and multiracial unity. Members of the Japanese delegation, for example, offered largely positive reviews of their reception in Los Angeles. Local mainstream papers even went so far as to cease using the racial slur "Jap" when covering Japanese athletes.[50]

Moreover, nonwhite press outlets in the city corroborated boosters' claims of social harmony, at least in the context of the Olympics. An editorial from *Rafu Shimpo*, Los Angeles's main Japanese American news outlet, posited that the Games transcended racism. "When [African American Eddie] Tolan won the sprints for the United States, what Southerner did not get up and cheer," it asked. "When [Shoichiro] Takenaka stepped over two lanes [in the 5000-meter race] to let Hill and Lehtinen fight it out, the crowd that cheered him was not made up only of Nipponese."[51] The *California Eagle*, the city's leading African American paper, offered its own endorsement of the Xth Olympiad Committee's approach to fostering a truly harmonious Games, asserting that the group acted "with the bright star of fairness, tolerance, and impartiality."[52]

These anecdotes, however, represented a selective rendering of social relations in Los Angeles and at the Games. The *Japan Times*, an English-language daily from Japan, reported on swanky restaurants in Southern California refusing to serve Japanese athletes because of their race. And black entertainers slated to perform at the allegedly utopian Olympic village were ultimately banned—an occurrence that the *California Eagle* chalked up to an individual bad apple working in the village administration.[53]

But the bad-apple thesis offered a wanting explanation for something that went unsaid in the local press coverage and booster literature: in 1932 Los Angeles remained a bastion of racism, segregation, anti-immigrant sentiment, and violent antagonism between labor and capital. One indication of the hollowness of the official rhetoric was that John Porter, the aforementioned mayor of the city who offered his praise to Japanese athletes, formerly belonged to the Ku Klux Klan.[54] In fact, as noted by Mike Davis, the Klan maintained a strong presence in Los Angeles during the 1920s and 1930s, engaging in "vigilantism" intended to support white homeowner groups like the Anti-African Housing Association, which organized and maintained restrictive racial covenants intended to keep blacks and Asians out of their neighborhoods.[55]

It should come as no surprise that a city in which ordinary residents *and* municipal leadership had strong links to the Klan incubated intense racial segregation across space. As the census data in table 1 shows, a full 70 percent of Los Angeles's African Americans were crowded in to *one* of the city's sixteen state assembly districts. Moreover, in only three of the sixteen districts did the percentage of the population made up of African Americans reach at least 3.14 percent—the percentage of the total population made up of blacks.

While the hope among many nonwhite residents and athletes that, to borrow from historian Eriko Yamamoto, the Games "would help dispel American prejudices" was understandable, it failed to square with the post-Olympic reality in Los Angeles (or anywhere else in the United States for that matter).[56] The color line in the city's housing market and various cultural institutions

Table 1. Selected Population Statistics by State Assembly District, Los Angeles, 1930

Assembly District	Total	African Americans	Percent African American
51	51,636	64	0.12
54	74,398	38	0.05
55	109,955	450	0.41
56	33,522	275	0.82
57	123,752	590	0.48
58	91,340	849	0.93
59	73,538	2,880	3.92
60	110,875	913	0.82
61	81,672	830	1.02
62	76,503	27,227	35.59
63	64,843	114	0.18
64	80,443	1,092	1.36
65	20,506	6	0.03
66	67,283	39	0.06
67	72,884	27	0.04
72	104,898	3,500	3.34
TOTALS=	1,238,048	38,894	3.14

Source: Bureau of the Census, *Census of Population and Housing*, Vol. 3, Part 1 (Washington, DC: Government Printing Office, 1932), Table 23, 287.

Note: "African American" corresponds to the category "Negro" in the 1930 census.

would, in practice, remain entrenched well into the postwar period, and in many ways endures even today. By 1980, just before the Olympics came to Southern California for a second time, Los Angeles ranked among the most intensely segregated metropolitan areas in the country, on par with cities like Newark and St. Louis according to a quantitative measure known as the "dissimilarity index." The 1980 measure indicated that more than 80 percent of African Americans would have to relocate to a different census tract in order to achieve perfectly proportional black-white integration.[57]

Another manifestation of interracial tension masked by promotion and press coverage of the Games was the Depression-era "repatriation" campaigns targeting Mexican Los Angelenos. Despite the fact that Olympic organizers readily appealed to potential tourists by touting the region's "Spanish fantasy past"—a sanitized and romanticized version of Southern California's Spanish colonial history—during the 1930s local authorities used a combination of incentives and coercion to ensure that as many Mexican immigrants as possible boarded one-way trains back to Mexico. Justification for the deportations typically had to do with implicitly or explicitly racist claims, exacerbated by the economic context of the Great Depression, that Mexican immigrants were "stealing" jobs from whites, relying too much on public assistance, and bringing disease and deviance to the United States.[58]

While such campaigns existed beyond Southern California, Los Angeles witnessed particularly intense repatriation efforts. Historians Francisco Balderrama and Raymond Rodriguez cite reports estimating that between February 10 and March 23, 1931, Los Angeles authorities repatriated fifty thousand Mexican nationals and their children. Ironically enough, many of the repatriation "roundups" occurred at Olvera Street, a purported Spanish and Mexican heritage site near downtown with shops and restaurants that local boosters invented a few years prior to the 1932 Olympics and used liberally in promotional materials for the Games.[59] In other words, local elites embraced Mexican identity only insofar as it appealed to tourists planning their next trip to Southern California.

Beyond the issue of race, the notion that the Olympic village encapsulated some sort of utopia of good will between the classes simply did not gel with what was, by the 1930s, a protracted history of intense conflict between capital and labor in California's Southland. Under the political and economic influence of the virulently antilabor *Los Angeles Times* and equally hostile trade associations like the Merchant and Manufacturers Association, local police and municipal officials used whatever means necessary to maintain the "Open Shop" (i.e., keep the city union-free). Jeremy White notes that as Olympic boosters touted economic democracy at the village, "The Los Angeles Police Department, the same organization that supported the Games by offering its shooting range to the Organizing Committee for the Rifle and Pistol Shooting competitions, was also busy arresting picketing 'reds.'" At the same time, muckrakers like Louis Adamic and Carey McWilliams chronicled what Mike Davis describes as a local "ruling-class brutality" during the first half of the twentieth century that "had driven labor to desperation" and the reciprocation of violence.[60]

Under the open shop, the economic crises of the 1930s took a devastating toll on workers. Two years before the Games, the number of unemployed Californians reached seven hundred thousand, with the Los Angeles metropolitan area containing nearly 50 percent of the total. Social services for ordinary Angelenos suffered as a result of severe municipal budget cuts; in 1930 Mayor Porter slashed $5.3 million in municipal spending (more than $82 million in 2015 dollars).[61] No wonder, then, that vulnerable workers looked to collective action and occasional violence to remedy the situation. Several major strikes in Los Angeles would follow on the heels of the feel-good Olympics, including the 1933 work stoppage by the International Ladies' Garment Workers Union and a 1934 waterfront strike that saw clashes between San Pedro longshoremen on one side and local police and private company security forces on the other.[62]

Describing the 1932 Games as a smokescreen that obscured the profound socioeconomic fissures in pre–New Deal Los Angeles might strike some as excessively cynical, but there was precedent among the city's boosters for using touristic spectacle to distract from local controversy. As Mike Davis explains, local elites organized the first "Los Angeles Fiesta," a public celebration of the city's cultural heritage, as a "public distraction" from the labor conflict that spread to Los Angeles as a result of the 1894 Pullman strike.[63] This was, in other words, nothing new in the City of Angels. In the end, the Games offered local boosters a solution to urban economic crisis only insofar as they promised to restore growth for the benefit of established elites. As far as the rest of the city was concerned, the event offered empty platitudes about social harmony in place of more meaningful attempts to incorporate nonwhites and the working class as genuine beneficiaries of Olympic capitalism.

* * *

As this chapter goes to press, a handful of urban elites in Boston are reeling after being forced by a broad coalition of local residents to abandon their bid for the 2024 Olympics (coincidentally Los Angeles is now on the verge of a third successful bid for the Games, with Paris the only extant competitor). Ordinary Bostonians, some organized under the banner of a group dubbed No Boston Olympics, pushed back against familiar promises by boosters that the Games would prove an economic and cultural boon to the city with a range of arguments that academics and critical journalists have been making for decades. The group claimed that a full accounting of prospective costs showed that taxpayers would end up expending more than the Games would bring in, that the US Olympic Committee and International Olympic Committee consistently resisted transparency in terms of disclosing the details of the bid process, and that hosting the Olympics would involve serious opportunity costs, such as the diversion of attention and scarce public resources away from basic infrastructure and affordable housing.[64]

The swiftness and efficacy with which No Boston Olympics organized their resistance to the Games is a seeming aberration when viewed as part of the longer history of sports-linked urban capitalism in the United States. Much more often, residents of America's cities have been forced to watch as local politicians bend over backward to accommodate the whims of team owners or organizing committees. At this point, it is too early to tell if the Boston case portends a tectonic shift in the politics of constructing stadia and staging sports mega-events. It remains unclear whether or not other cities can incubate the sort of sweeping alliances between working- and middle-class urbanites fostered by opposition leaders in Boston.

Either way, the criticisms articulated by Bostonians who opposed hosting the Games—most of them backed up by empirical evidence—highlight the continuities between interwar Los Angeles and urban America in the twenty-first century in terms of the political economy of sport in the city. It was during the 1920s and 1930s that urban elites in Los Angeles established the template for staging the Olympics most often associated with the neoliberal era, and which has by now generated widespread cynicism among the public. The key elements of this model included the transfer of as much financial risk as possible onto the backs of local taxpayers, the subversion of the democratic process in order to neutralize public opposition, and the use of glitzy spectacle to distract from ongoing socioeconomic turmoil. In other words, today the urban underside of the Olympics looks very much like it did nearly a century ago.

Revisiting the 1932 Games reminds us that the threats posed by the Olympics to fiscal health, good governance, and socioeconomic progress in the host city are not unique to today's neoliberal capitalism. Rather, for much of the twentieth century these hazards have proven a recurring theme in cities where urban elites have viewed sport and large-scale entertainment spectacle as a quick fix for the economic and social crises that are part and parcel of urban capitalism.

CHAPTER EIGHT

"Never Go Back"

Pasadena Racial Politics and the Robinson Brothers

GREGORY KALISS

In November 1997, the city of Pasadena unveiled a $250,000 memorial across the street from city hall. Featuring two 10-foot bronze heads, the memorial commemorated the remarkable Robinson brothers: Matthew "Mack" Robinson (1914–2000), who had won Olympic silver as a sprinter in the famous 1936 Berlin Games, and Jack "Jackie" Robinson (1919–1972), the first black baseball player in Major League Baseball (MLB) history when he debuted with the Brooklyn Dodgers in 1947. The sporting achievements of these two men, and the international acclaim afforded them, made them likely candidates to be memorialized in their hometown of Pasadena, where they grew up on Pepper Street. And yet the monument's subtle details reflect complexities in the Robinson brothers' story. Mack Robinson's bust faces across the street toward city hall, a reflection of his involvement with the city, and his unapologetic criticisms of it, throughout his life—first as a street sweeper and laborer, and later as an activist and youth counselor. Jackie's bust, meanwhile, looks east, a recognition of his move to Brooklyn in the 1940s and his abandonment of his hometown in later years. In turning away from city hall, Jackie's bust showcases his disgust for the racial discrimination he and his family faced during their many years living in the city.

The memorial's discontinuities reflect the tangled history of athletic accomplishments and Southern California racial politics at the heart of the Robinsons' story. Internationally acclaimed stars in their respective sports, the Robinson brothers received almost no celebration in their hometown; although the city of Los Angeles proved slightly more accommodating, ongoing racial prejudice dominated the brothers' stories. After all, the memorial to the brothers came more than sixty years after Mack's Olympic feat, fifty years after Jackie's debut with the Dodgers, and twenty-five years after Jackie's death. The long delay in commemorating these sports stars, two of Pasadena's most celebrated residents, highlighted the persistent racism of the wealthy town on the outskirts of Los Angeles. Exploring the stories of the Robinson family, most notably the trials and triumphs of the Robinson brothers, showcases the opportunities for black athletic accomplishments in Southern California in the pre–World War II years, but also the numerous ways in which white civic culture sought to minimize the significance of those athletic achievements and to perpetuate the systemic racism that kept African Americans in an inferior place. These racial barriers accentuated sibling rivalry and created tensions between the two brothers over the unequal access to public recognition and financial rewards.

Pasadena and the Realities of Race

The Robinson family arrived in Southern California in 1920, part of the Great Migration of African Americans out of the rural South to urban centers north and west. Mack was the third and Jackie the youngest of five children born to Jerry and Mallie Robinson in Cairo, Georgia. Impoverished sharecroppers, the family managed to eke out a living, largely due to the persistence and strength of Mallie, the family's matriarch. By 1920, however, their fortunes had turned. Jerry Robinson had tired of the harsh life of fieldwork and had grown romantically attached to a neighbor's wife and left the family. After hearing of better conditions in Southern California from her half-brother Burton Thomas, Mallie made the decision to move her five children, all under the age of eleven, west. Arriving in Pasadena in June 1920, the family quickly established roots, with Mallie purchasing a home on Pepper Street within two years. Here, in Pasadena, the Robinson family flourished and became one of the most notable families in the city's history.[1]

The Robinsons were certainly not the only black family to be drawn to the Los Angeles area in the pre–World War II years. Los Angeles had long been considered a place of opportunity for black Americans, with W. E. B. Du Bois writing of Los Angeles in the *Crisis* in 1913, that "nowhere in the United States is the Negro so well and beautifully housed, nor the average efficiency and intelligence in the colored population so high." Homeownership for African Americans in the region bore out Du Bois's optimistic appraisal: in 1910, "almost 40 percent of African Americans in Los Angeles County owned their homes, compared to only 2.4 percent in New York and 8 percent in Chicago."[2] The "Western Ideal" promoted by many white leaders emphasized California as a place of expansive democracy, a place "where opportunity was open to all citizens, regardless of background, lineage, or wealth."[3] Still, significant barriers remained. African Americans in Los Angeles County faced both unofficial and official discrimination in public accommodations, and restrictive covenants isolated blacks and other minorities in certain sections of the county's cities and towns.[4]

Pasadena proved especially bigoted. As Mack Robinson observed in later years, "Pasadena was as prejudiced as any town in the South. They let us in all right, but they wouldn't let us live."[5] The city's wealthy white residents—many of them Hollywood moguls who worked in Los Angeles, located only ten miles to the southwest, disdained the city's minority population. When the city's first pool opened in 1914, the city restricted its use to whites only. After protests, the city announced a weekly "International Day" when anyone could swim at the pool, but officials promised to empty and clean the pool before the next day. In addition, black people faced severe (if unofficial) restrictions on where they could live in the city and found employment opportunities severely limited. The local government hired almost no African Americans, and when it did, it was only as laborers, never as professionals. When the NAACP tried to contest the segregation of the community swimming pool in Pasadena, Mack Robinson as well as all other black workers who had been hired recently by the town, were fired by the town manager in apparent retaliation for the NAACP's agitation. That same summer, 1939, also featured the founding of the Pasadena Improvement Association, which, with the endorsement of "every important business and real-estate organization in Pasadena," vowed to "restrict the 'use and occupancy of property'" in the city "to members of the White or Caucasian Race only."[6]

The Robinson family's experiences reflected this bitter racial climate. One of Jackie Robinson's first recollections was of a scuffle with a young white girl from the neighborhood when he was eight years old after she called him a "nigger." Robinson and the girl's father had a rock fight until the man's wife called her husband into the house.[7] Robinson also noted that the neighbors complained to the police that his brother Edgar "made too much noise on their sidewalks with his skates," and that they "signed petitions to try to get rid of us."[8] Robinson's sister Willa Mae recalled that one neighbor across the street "was actually afraid of black people" and "would slam her door" whenever the

Robinson children appeared outside to play. On one occasion, unknown white neighbors burned a cross on the Robinson family's lawn.[9]

The arrest of the eldest Robinson boy, Edgar, in January 1939, illustrated the brutality and arbitrary bigotry that black residents often encountered. When asked about some chairs he had rented for the Tournament of Roses Parade, Edgar reached in to pull out his license and was knocked down by one of the police officers. He then scuffled with the officers, receiving a black eye and bruises, before being taken to jail. There, given neither medical treatment nor an opportunity to call home, Edgar pleaded guilty to the charges and paid a ten-dollar fine. He discovered that the police had stolen money from his clothing and he was not allowed to file a complaint with the chief. According to Jackie Robinson biographer Arnold Rampersad, "this incident, and other episodes like it, eventually made Jack loathe Pasadena." He later said that if his family didn't live there, he would "never go back."[10]

The Robinson Brothers Ascendant

Even as the Robinson family faced these unrelenting signs of racial prejudice, Mack and Jackie began to carve out places of esteem as a result of their athletic prowess. As Jackie observed in his first autobiography, published in 1948, sports came "nearer to offering an American Negro equality of opportunity than does any other field of social and economic activity." Thus, he and Mack found "the going much easier than for our Negro schoolmates who were not athletically inclined."[11] In his high school and junior college years, Mack earned significant esteem for his accomplishments in track.[12] As Jackie began to star in football, basketball, track, and baseball, he also became celebrated by the local media and fans. As his sister Willa Mae recalled, poor treatment from the family's white neighbors "changed, of course, after Mack became a famous athlete around here, and then Jack. Then they all started bragging how they knew the famous player from Pasadena Junior College, Jackie Robinson, and you would think they were great buddies."[13]

Even so, the barriers to black success remained. Jackie was arrested on two occasions by local police under dubious circumstances—first, in January 1938 as the result of singing a song that a white police officer did not like, and for not backing down when the officer challenged him. Such was the tenuous position of blacks in Pasadena. Although Robinson's ten-day sentence was suspended on the condition that he was not arrested for two years, the incident became well known in the town. That incident was followed by another encounter with local police, one that showed that athletic stardom did not protect black youths from encountering harsh bigotry. On September 5, 1939, as Jackie prepared to enter the University of California at Los Angeles (UCLA), he was driving home from a softball game with some friends when some white men from a passing crowd called Robinson and his friends "niggers." When an argument ensued and a large crowd gathered, Robinson was the only one arrested, even though he had not instigated the confrontation and had thrown no punches. The arresting officers almost certainly targeted him because of his celebrity as a star athlete.[14]

Mack Robinson knew all too well the barriers imposed by race in Los Angeles in the pre–World War II and post–World War II years, and his experiences following his triumphant Olympic performance in 1936 caused him to view the area, and American culture in general, with a great deal of bitterness. Mack's athletic success almost never occurred: though he enjoyed playing a variety of sports as a youth, he was diagnosed with a heart murmur in junior high school. School officials wanted to ban him from all athletics, but his mother's persistence enabled him to participate in noncontact sports. As a result, he turned his attention to track and field.[15] Earning success first at Washington Junior High School, then Muir Tech High School, then Pasadena Junior College (PJC), Mack "became a local legend" in track and field. He excelled at the 100-, 220-, and 440-yard dashes, and was a national junior college record holder in the broad jump.[16] Although Mack did not have the Olympics in mind when he enrolled at PJC, he found that his performances there earned him placement in the western Olympic trials in Los Angeles.[17] National newspapers noted his strong performances there on June 27, 1936, and local Pasadena businessmen raised money for him and a teammate to travel to New York for the national trials.[18] Although Robinson's performance in the 100-meter dash earned him a disappointing seventh place, he excelled at the 200-meter race, placing second behind Jesse Owens, and earning one of the national team's starting roles for that event.[19]

The 1936 Berlin Olympics would mark the highlight of Mack Robinson's athletic career, but also served as the cause of much personal distress in later years. Traveling to Berlin with the Olympic team, Robinson cut a solitary figure. Track teammate Marty Glickman recalled that Mack was "surly and private" during the Olympics.[20] Nonetheless, he performed well on the field, helping the US track team dominate the Games. The 1936 Olympics were, of course, freighted with symbolic meaning. Taking place in Berlin during Adolf Hitler's ascension to power in Germany, Hitler hoped the Games would validate his ideals of Aryan supremacy. The regime's increasingly repressive policies toward Jews and other minorities made some Americans hesitant to participate in the Games, and a possible boycott gained currency. However, the US Olympic Committee eventually decided to participate and most black athletes leaped at the chance to prove their worth on the world stage. Although the US squad faired poorly on the whole, the track team, led by black athletes such as Jesse Owens, Ralph Metcalfe, Mack Robinson, John Woodruff, and Fritz Pollard Jr., dominated their portion of the Games and proved inspirational to many in the United States. Owens's four gold-medal-winning performance made him an international star and countless publications celebrated his accomplishments as an invalidation of Hitler's racist ideals.[21]

As the Olympics unfolded, Mack Robinson did his part in regards to the US team's success. Breezing through the preliminary heats, Mack faced off against his teammate Owens for supremacy in the 200-meters. In front of tens of thousands of fans, the two sprinters delivered. Although Owens won convincingly, Robinson finished only .4 seconds behind the winner, despite wearing worn-out spikes that put him at a disadvantage. The silver medal was an impressive accomplishment, and US newspapers celebrated the 1–2 finish in the event.[22] Back home, his family gathered around the radio to hear the broadcast of the race and celebrated joyously when he earned the silver medal.[23]

Mack hoped he had one more race to run—the 4×100 relay. Although his seventh-place finish at the trials had denied him the opportunity to run the 100-meter dash in the Games, the relay team had been traditionally stocked with the sprinters who hadn't run the 100-meter race. In this case, since Owens, Ralph Metcalfe, and Frank Wykoff had earned the top three spots in the 100-meter event, the next four finishers would occupy the relay team: white runners Foy Draper, Marty Glickman, and Sam Stoller, along with Robinson.[24] And yet the track coaches changed their usual strategy, putting Wykoff on the relay team in addition to his role in the individual race, leaving Mack out of the relay.[25] For Robinson, then, his silver medal performance in the 200 would be his only prize, an honor that he hoped would open up professional opportunities.

Mack's hopes for a hero's welcome on his return to the United States, however, did not materialize. "There was no ticker-tape parades, no plaques, no nothing.... The first night home we were segregated by color in different hotels." After racing against fascism in Germany, the American racism he encountered in New York hurt him: "I just said to myself 'the hell with it' and went home. But it wasn't any different in Pasadena."[26] On his arrival in Southern California, Mack found little celebration of his achievements: "There was no basic celebrations of any sort.... There was no major program put on to honor me." His achievements led to no jobs or financial rewards: "Nothing was offered to me, job-wise or any other recognition."[27] Mack's memory may have been slightly flawed: the historians Mark Dyreson and John Gleaves have noted that Los Angeles hosted a parade for returning American Olympians; a story in the *Pasadena Post* indicates that Pasadena Junior College held an event to honor the track star; and the UCLA student newspaper the *Daily Bruin* reported a gathering sponsored by the black community to celebrate Mack and two other black Olympians—and to raise money to help with their education.[28]

But Robinson's larger complaint about the lack of opportunities afforded black men—even star athletes—rings true. After his Olympic performance, Mack found himself sweeping the streets of Pasadena in the dead of night, wearing his Olympic jacket ostensibly to keep himself warm, but also reminding the town of its poor treatment of its black citizens. Even that job proved temporary: Mack and other black city workers lost their jobs when the NAACP protested the city's segregated swimming pools.[29] In the spring of 1938, Mack left Pasadena for the University of Oregon, where he performed on the track team and earned a degree in physical education in 1941.[30] The cancellation of the 1940 Olympics with the outbreak of World War II prevented Mack from continuing his track career at the international level. When his college career ended, he returned home to Pasadena and took up menial work once again, apparently unable to use his degree to land a position in physical education or coaching. In ensuing decades, he worked primarily as a laborer in construction, raising a growing family in one of the homes owned by Mallie Robinson on Pepper Street.[31] The lack of employment opportunities, according to his younger brother Jackie, "broke his spirit."[32]

As Mack faded out of the athletic spotlight, however, Jackie began to earn considerable acclaim for his remarkable talents. As a child, Jackie had been drawn to sports, and he showed a prodigious competitive desire to win at any sport he played.[33] Mack believed that Jackie developed his quickness in part as a way to deal with playing with the older kids in the neighborhood—he wasn't as big, so he used his speed and agility to his advantage. By junior high, Jackie was attracting attention as a result of his athletic ability; as Mack recalled, Jackie "took up a sport and he was the best in the neighborhood before anybody knew it."[34] Mack provided a model for Jackie; as biographer Arnold Rampersad notes, "Mack was Jack's intimate introduction to the glory and glamour of sports."[35] At Muir Tech High School, Jackie followed in his older brother's footsteps as an athletic star, but he branched out into a greater variety of sports, lettering in football, baseball, basketball, and track. Mack's perseverance through his health issues motivated Jackie. In his autobiography *I Never Had It Made*, Jackie wrote: "I had the greatest respect for Mack because of his achievements in track. Even though doctors warned him that his participation in sports could be fatal because he had a heart ailment, he couldn't give up. . . . The heart condition never defeated Mack."[36]

Following his successful athletic career in high school, Robinson attended PJC, enrolling in January 1937. Although Jackie had been recruited by major colleges and universities, he preferred staying closer to home to be near his mother. As a result, the two brothers were briefly enrolled at PJC together. Although Mack was the bigger star because of his track accomplishments, Jackie began to make his own name, dominating a wide range of sports and earning considerable media acclaim. When Mack left for the University of Oregon, Jackie took his brother's place as the school's star athlete. In fact, the two were set to square off at a track meet in the broad jump in the summer of 1938, but Mack withdrew from the event after winning the 200-meter sprint.[37]

Jackie did much more than run track. Excelling at football, basketball, baseball, and tennis as well, Robinson earned the most plaudits for his performance with the PJC football squad. Although an injury derailed the first half of his freshman year, he performed well in the second half of the season. In the fall of 1938, his second and final year with the team, he was simply extraordinary, scoring more points than any football player in the country, leading his team to an undefeated season, a mythical junior college championship, and earning praise from local black and white newspaper writers alike.[38] Jackie's skills drew out record-setting crowds, and at the conclusion of his second season on the PJC squad, he was named the team's most valuable player, earned a place on a national junior college all-star team, and was feted with a "Jack Robinson Day" by the Scott M. E. Church of Pasadena.[39]

As a celebrated junior college athlete, Jackie could have attended nearly any major college and university that accepted black athletes, and a wide range of people took interest in his choice. Mack urged him to attend the University of Oregon with him.[40] One "devoted Stanford alumnus" offered Robinson money to attend school in the East so that he did not play against Stanford in football.[41] But Robinson, wanting to stay close to home and to his mother, and aware of the University of Southern California's (USC) poor reputation when it came to black athletes, chose hometown UCLA, an up-and-coming school with a record of admitting—and playing—black athletes on its sports teams.[42] With two successful and popular black athletes already on the football team in running back Kenny Washington and end Woody Strode, Jackie would join a competitive team and one that featured more black athletes than nearly any predominantly white institution in the country to that point in time. He enrolled in the school in February 1939.[43]

Jackie Robinson's career at UCLA only added to his reputation as one of the best athletes in the history of Los Angeles. As a Bruin, Jackie became the first student to letter in four different sports: football, basketball, baseball, and track. Although he would go on to great fame in baseball, it was the sport in which he was least successful at UCLA; he only played one year and did not perform particularly well. Instead, Robinson earned the most attention for his exploits on the gridiron. In his first season, the fall of 1939, Robinson, Washington, and Strode led the Bruins to an undefeated record of 5 wins, 4 draws, and 0 losses. The team earned national press coverage for its exploits, especially in the black press, as black sportswriters delighted in the team's three black stars (Robinson's friend Ray Bartlett, another black player, was also a key reserve). Although the team came up just short in its attempt to earn a bid to the Rose Bowl—at the time, the most prestigious postseason bowl game—Jackie earned plaudits for his sensational open-field running.[44]

The celebration of the team—Robinson included—came from more than just the black press. In the *Los Angeles Examiner*, Bob Hunter gave Robinson and Washington credit for "almost single handedly" leading the team to an early season upset victory over Texas Christian University.[45] Paul Zimmerman, writing in the *Los Angeles Times*, noted that "you have to throw racial prejudice out the window when a couple of gentlemen like Jackie Robinson and Kenny Washington do the things they do."[46] As various local groups feted Robinson and his UCLA teammates, both blacks and whites expressed optimism that this successful integrated squad was providing a model of an egalitarian society. As fan Michael Joseph Hart observed, in a letter to University of California president Robert Sproul, "the remarkable colored players on the U.C.L.A. team" showcased "U.C.L.A.'s consistency with Old Glory's principles and our beloved Democracy." The black and white players on the team, "sincere patriots" and "decent citizens," modeled an egalitarian democracy as they were worked together to achieve a common goal.⁴⁷

The acclaim generated by Robinson and his black teammates came with bitter reminders of prejudice and bigotry. Although UCLA may have been more open-minded about fielding black athletes, many whites still dismissed, or minimized, the achievements of Jackie and others. Nicknames such as the "Gold Dust Trio," used in the mainstream Los Angeles media to refer to Washington, Robinson, and Strode, came from a brand of soap called Franklin's Gold Dust Soap Powder that, in Strode's words, "used a picture of two coal-black kids on the cover." Similarly, one of the major nicknames employed for Washington was "Kingfish," a reference to one of the main black characters on the infamous *Amos 'n' Andy* radio show.⁴⁸ Rival fans at USC created a homecoming display in which the black players of UCLA were hung in effigy while a USC Trojan captained a "slave ship."⁴⁹ Even Robinson's white teammates apparently resented his success and his refusal to be cowed by white authority figures. Early in the 1939 season, two white reserves deliberately injured Robinson in practice, apparently in response to his growing reputation as an athlete and his refusal to take any racial abuse.⁵⁰

Despite these brutal reminders of the racial climate—in addition to the biased treatment he received at the hands of the local police—Jackie continued to excel at UCLA, and he spoke admiringly in later years of his time at the school. Robinson described his time at UCLA as being "happy days," and he delighted in being "a college star, a campus hero."⁵¹ At UCLA, Robinson won the 1940 national championship in the long jump in track, led the conference in scoring in basketball, and, in the midst of a miserable season for the UCLA football team in fall 1940, continued to put up dazzling individual numbers. In one game against Washington State University, he accounted for 339 yards of total offense, ran for two touchdowns, passed for one other score, intercepted three of the opposing team's passes, and kicked all four of UCLA's extra points.⁵² These wide-ranging athletic accomplishments earned him significant attention locally and nationally and made him a local celebrity.

But Jackie Robinson's career at UCLA marked the end of his time in Los Angeles. Early in 1941, Jackie made the decision to leave school, even before he earned the credits necessary to graduate. In his autobiography *I Never Had It Made*, he explained that he left the school because he "was convinced that no amount of education would help a black man get a job" and he wanted to help his mother financially instead of playing sports for fun.⁵³ Given the significant employment barriers that Mack faced despite his college degree, Robinson was probably correct. After leaving UCLA, Robinson apparently helped to put together the Pasadena Community Athletic club in February 1941, an event the black newspaper the *California Eagle* reported briefly. Jackie was listed as the president of the organization, which also included Mack and other Pasadena athletes.[54]

After dabbling in coaching, and in semiprofessional football in Hawaii and Los Angeles in 1941, Jackie Robinson was drafted into the military in 1942 and assigned to a base in Kansas.[55] Although he made one more foray into semi-professional football in the Los Angeles area in late 1944, he left soon after for a job in Texas and never returned to Los Angeles for any substantive period of time. An invitation from the Kansas City Monarchs to play professional baseball—arriving to his family's Pasadena home, where it was dutifully read by his sister and by Mack—set him on a course for professional baseball stardom. It was Mack who encouraged him to take the job offer with the Monarchs, a job that ultimately paved the way for his breakthrough role in Major League Baseball with the Brooklyn Dodgers. But that career took him far away from Los Angeles, leaving his family behind. Indeed, when Jackie made his debut for Brooklyn in 1947, his family piled into a 1936 Ford and drove across country to watch Jackie play in Brooklyn.[56] Jackie had left Los Angeles for good.

Beyond Pasadena and the Memory of the Robinson Brothers

After World War II, the paths for Jackie and Mack Robinson diverged dramatically. While both had been athletic stars in the pre–World War II years, Jackie's enormous success eclipsed Mack's, and left his brother a mostly forgotten man. Jackie played one year with the Monarchs before signing with the Brooklyn Dodgers' farm team in Montreal. After one year with the Montreal Royals, Jackie took the field for the Dodgers at the start of the 1947 season. He quickly became a star, earning honors as the National League Rookie of the Year in his debut season, landing on the All-Star team six times, winning the National League Most Valuable Player award in 1949, and eventually leading the Dodgers to six pennants and one World Series title. As Jackie plied his trade in professional baseball on the East Coast, however, Mack continued to live in Pasadena, scrounging out a living in the same difficult circumstances that Los Angeles–area African Americans had faced for decades. Inevitably, these divergent stories caused tension between the two. The lack of recognition afforded both brothers from their hometown of Pasadena, meanwhile, showcased the persistence of racial bigotry.

Jackie Robinson's role as a pioneer in Major League Baseball came with a host of pressures, threats, and opportunities—a story that has been chronicled in texts such as historian Jules Tygiel's *Baseball's Great Experiment: Jackie Robinson and His Legacy* and in a plethora of scholarly articles and popular publications. As Robinson faced the pressures of being the first black player in the major leagues, his family nervously monitored his success from a distance, worried that someone would follow through on the numerous death threats that Jackie received.[57] As Jackie's footing with the Dodgers became more secure, he and his family became more comfortable and more settled on the East Coast. Robinson and his family lived in St. Albans on Long Island for a time and, as his family expanded, they eventually moved to North Stamford, Connecticut. Following his playing career, Robinson accepted a job with the New York–based Chock Full o' Nuts company as vice president of personnel. His later ventures, including his work in fundraising for the NAACP and his involvement in the founding of the Freedom Bank, kept him closely tied to the New York metropolitan area. In *I Never Had It Made*, Robinson makes no mention of returning to Pasadena in later years, except on the occasion of his mother's death in 1968.[58] In the media spotlight for his sports accomplishments and his political activism, Jackie instead remained a visible presence in the New York metropolitan area until his untimely death from a heart attack in 1972.[59]

But if Jackie earned notoriety and wealth from his playing career and the opportunities it afforded him in his retirement, his older brother Mack saw nothing of the kind. Remaining in Pasadena until his death in 2000, Mack Robinson continued to resent the limited opportunities available to black men—even those who had earned national fame and honor. After his job as a street sweeper was eliminated, Mack worked primarily as a laborer, helping in the construction of area highways. In later years, he worked as a security guard for parks in Los Angeles where he "was shot at a couple of times."[60] Despite graduating from the University of Oregon with a degree in physical education, Mack Robinson found no employment in the city schools, except in later years when he was offered security work. As early as 1940, the area's black newspapers lamented his fate, with black sportswriter J. Cullen Fentress using the case of Mack to critique "a system wherein an athlete is the toast of a race, a nation and the world one year and a few years later, a 'forgotten' man." Fentress expressed displeasure that "the medals, trophies," and other acclaim from athletics did not "carry over into his present extremity—that of feeding and clothing a family and providing it some measure of security."[61] That reality dominated Mack's life throughout his time in Pasadena.

Inevitably, the different trajectories of the brothers' lives and careers must have caused jealousy and tension, particularly from Mack toward his younger brother. According to Rampersad, "a friend guessed" that Mack was a bit envious of Jackie's success, believing that his younger brother "got some breaks that he should have had." But Mack denied those claims, saying that he and the rest of the family were "right there pushing for" Jackie's success and "rooting" for him to succeed.[62] In a 1957 *Ebony* story that Mack cowrote with noted black sportswriter A. S. "Doc" Young, Mack opened the article by saying how "proud" he was of Jackie for his success in baseball and in his new career with Chock Full o' Nuts. He insisted that he did not "begrudge Jackie a thing" and that he "exulted in all of his triumphs." Later in the story, he defended Jackie against complaints that he ought to have told the Dodgers of his intention to retire before it was announced in *Look* magazine. And he celebrated Jackie as "the greatest all-around athlete that ever lived."[63]

However, enough anecdotal evidence exists to suggest that the limited opportunities afforded to Mack in Pasadena caused him to view his brother's situation enviously. Even Mack's 1957 story for *Ebony* betrays some animosity, with Mack speculating that Jackie earned his success instead of the other Robinson children because he was "the luckiest kid I ever ran across."[64] A 1968 story by Young, meanwhile, depicted Mack Robinson as an ungrateful and bitter has-been. After Jackie "became an international hero," wrote Young, "Mack, having fallen back into obscurity, became a nobody whose memories became, with the passage of the years, increasingly bitter." According to Young, during the filming of Robinson's autobiographical movie, "Mack stood on the edge of the set, when he wasn't working, complaining about 'how lucky' Jackie has always been."[65] Olympic teammate Marty Glickman observed that when Mack "went back to California he had a tough time. He wasn't just in Owens' shadow, he was also in Jackie's."[66] It is little wonder that Mack reportedly said, "I am getting awfully tired . . . of being referred to just as Jackie Robinson's brother"—a sentiment that also made its way into his 1957 story when he noted that Jackie used to be called Mack Robinson's brother.[67]

But if Mack resented the attention that his younger brother received, he also campaigned throughout his life for more recognition, especially in Pasadena, of both his and Jackie's accomplishments. He wrote in 1957 that "Pasadena never did anything officially to make Jackie feel" celebrated. "He has received an absolute minimum of official recognition," Mack noted, and city officials had "yet to endorse Jackie as an outstanding citizen." Ten years after his groundbreaking role in MLB, there had "been no Jackie Robinson Day" and Jackie had not "been invited to be an honored guest at a Pasadena Homecoming."[68] After Jackie's death in 1972, a three-hundred-person tribute took place at Pasadena's City Hall, with representatives from Muir High School and PJC in attendance.[69] But as Mack campaigned for a memorial in Pasadena to honor his brother, his pleas apparently fell on deaf ears.[70] Even as Jackie continued to be celebrated nationally, with President Ronald Reagan posthumously awarding him the Medal of Freedom, the nation's highest civilian award, in March 1984, officials in his hometown refrained from official proclamations and memorials.[71]

The same year Jackie earned the Medal of Freedom, Mack returned to the spotlight briefly when he was honored as one of the flag bearers for the Opening Ceremonies of the 1984 summer Olympics in Los Angeles. Carrying the Olympic flag with seven former gold medalists and the grandchildren of Jesse Owens and Olympic legend Jim Thorpe, Mack was in esteemed company.[72] Mentioned in local and national news coverage of the Games, the increased attention led to other honors. That same year, Mack was also inducted into the Oregon Sports Hall of Fame, and his alma mater, the University of Oregon, awarded Robinson their "Webfoot" award, which "recognizes a graduate who exemplifies the best the university has to offer."[73]

Nonetheless, Mack felt frustrated by the failure of Pasadena to officially commemorate his and his brother's accomplishments. In a September 1984 interview, just months after the Olympics, Mack observed: "Here in my own hometown ... I am basically looked down upon because I did achieve something ... it's more of a jealous thing." Noting that Jackie had received no formal recognition from the town either, Mack believed that people in Pasadena did not want to acknowledge the racial barriers that had to be broken down, and he pleaded for more celebration of Jackie's career and life: "I firmly believe that Jack should be placed at the top of the structure of blacks ... in this society. ... The society has advanced because we became more aware of what our possibilities were."[74] In a 1986 interview, he still lamented the lack of commemoration for him and Jackie, and the fate of black Americans in Pasadena more generally: "Blacks are better off in some ways today than they were when we were kids," he mused, "but in a lot of ways we aren't. There's no adequate housing, there are no good jobs, there is still prejudice in a lot of ways."[75] Feeling neglected,

Sculptures of Mack and Jackie Robinson near Pasadena City Hall. Courtesy of Karen Borter (http://flic.kr/p/rVAueK).

Mack reportedly told a friend, "I have lost my identity. People don't know that I ran in the Olympics, that the only two times I raced Jesse, he broke world records to beat me."[76]

The 1990s, however, proved to be a time of resurgent interest in the Robinson brothers—even in their apparently begrudging hometown. The release of the popular Ken Burns–directed documentary *Baseball* in 1994—which gave considerable importance to Jackie Robinson's life and career—undoubtedly helped call more attention to his life. The fiftieth anniversary of his first game with the Dodgers in April 1997 also occasioned a number of tributes, most notably the league-wide retirement of Jackie Robinson's number 42 by Major League Baseball. These and other events also generated more discussion of the importance of his career in baseball and afterward.[77] While UCLA had honored Jackie earlier—naming its baseball stadium after him in 1981 and placing a statue of him there in 1985—Pasadena had still failed to offer any substantial memorial to either of the Robinson brothers. Although Robinson Park was named in honor of the brothers, and a community center was named for Jackie Robinson, there was no explicit celebration of the two brothers' lives.[78] But in April 1997, the city of Pasadena announced the building of the Robinson Memorial. Designed by sculptors Ralph Helmick, Stuart Schecter, and John Outterbridge, the memorial cost approximately $250,000 to make and install, with the city footing $100,000 and private sources providing the rest.[79] Dedicated in November 1997, the sculpture's large size and central location across the street from city hall place the Robinson brothers in a prominent and visible place in the town.[80]

Others would follow suit. Pasadena City College completed Robinson Stadium in 1999 with fifty-four hundred seats, featuring track facilities and a field meant for both soccer and football.[81] The following year, the United States Postal Service named a new post office building in Mack Robinson's honor.[82] As recently as July 2014, Pasadena celebrated "Robinson Family Weekend," meant to commemorate the accomplishments of Mack and Jackie. Timed to coincide with what would have been the one hundredth birthday of Mack, the celebration featured receptions at city hall and at Pasadena City College and concluded with Rachel Isum Robinson's induction into the Baseball Reliquary's Shrine of the Eternals in Pasadena. Pasadena mayor Bill Bogaard declared July 18 "Mack Robinson Day."[83] At long last, the Robinson brothers' hometown was fully embracing and celebrating the duo's lives and careers.

Conclusion: The Robinson Brothers, Race, and Pasadena

The reluctance to embrace the Robinson brothers' lives and careers speaks to the long-simmering racial tensions in Pasadena and the Los Angeles area in general. Initially unwelcome and subjected to harassment, poor treatment, and police brutality, the Robinsons were like most of the black families trying to make a life in the supposed paradise of Southern California in the pre–World War II years. As Mack and Jackie pursued their athletic careers with great success, they were only grudgingly appreciated for the fame they brought their city, with few public celebrations and financial opportunities made available. The barriers to black advancement and the denigration of black achievement were all too familiar to African Americans in greater Los Angeles. They were the reality of a region that promised enlightenment and opportunity but often treated its people of color with disdain.[84]

But the long fight for success and recognition by Mack and Jackie Robinson—especially Mack in his long life in Pasadena—also show the tenacity with which black Americans fought for acceptance and opportunity.

Although Mack Robinson found only menial jobs in his post-sports career, he took up a mantle as a community leader, getting involved in the local chapter of the NAACP, aiding youth organizations, and fighting for the revitalization of black neighborhoods in his hometown.[85] Although frustrated by ongoing prejudice and inequality, Mack never lost the courage of his convictions and continued to press for more recognition of black achievements—including, of course, his own. As he and his brother became more celebrated, the animosities and envy of the past dissipated. By the early 1990s, according to former teammate Marty Glickman, "Mack was at peace with himself." Visiting New York, Mack enjoyed talking about old times with his teammate. "That surly side was gone," Glickman said. Although disabled by strokes and seizures prior to the dedication of the Robinson Memorial in 1997, Mack would have surely been gratified by the event.[86] The gesture, long overdue, finally gave proper recognition to one of the most remarkable families in Southern Californian—and American—history.

CHAPTER NINE

Reel Sports

Hollywood Stars at Play in LA

DANIEL A. NATHAN

Few images in Southern California are as iconic as the Hollywood sign. Built in 1923 on the southern slope of Mount Lee, which is part of the Santa Monica Mountains, it looms over Los Angeles and in millions of imaginations. The big white, nine-letter sign (which originally read Hollywoodland and promoted a local real estate development) signifies all kinds of things: dreams of success, of fame and fortune, on the one hand, and superficiality and crass materialism on the other. For some, the Hollywood sign symbolizes a site of great artistry, creativity, and masterful storytelling; for others, it is a stand-in for formulaic, soul-deadening movies and TV shows rife with stereotypes and visual clichés.

Either way, for many people Los Angeles, Hollywood, and the film industry have become synonymous. According to the cultural historian Thomas Doherty, "Chicago means gangsters, Texas means cowboys, and Hollywood—well, Hollywood means the movies."[1] Doherty is right, of course. So, too, is journalist Adam Nagourney, who writes that Hollywood is a "cultural touchstone for anyone who grew up on movies, for those people for whom Los Angeles really means Hollywood, with its celebrities, mansions, swimming pools, palm tree-lined boulevard and movie studios."[2]

At the same time, Los Angeles is much bigger and more complex than Hollywood (which, after all, is a neighborhood) or the industry for which it is a metonym. Indeed, Los Angeles is not one thing or a mere place, no matter how large—and it is gigantic, an amazing megalopolis.[3] It is also an ideal, for some people a sun-drenched dream. Obviously the social reality of Los Angeles is a different matter. This chapter is not about that reality, although it is important and fascinating.

Rather, this chapter briefly chronicles the history of Hollywood-made sports films, considers some of the ways in which Hollywood filmmakers have thought about and represented sports, and critiques selected sports films made and set in Los Angeles, defined broadly, such as *The Bad News Bears* (1976), *White Men Can't Jump* (1992), and *Lords of Dogtown* (2005), among others. The idea is to think critically about Hollywood's multifaceted relationship to the games people play and cheer, and to consider how Hollywood filmmakers depict their own local sports landscape.

A Brief History of Hollywood Sports Films

Thirty years ago, journalist David T. Friendly declared, "Hollywood has long had a love-hate relationship with sports films."[4] It may have seemed that way at the time, but Friendly (who is now a film producer) was being hyperbolic. It is true that for many years powerful Hollywood filmmakers and respected critics did not think much of sports films. Hate is too strong a word, but certainly some Hollywood insiders derided sports films as juvenile and thought of them as "box-office poison."[5] Yet we have to ask: how financially poisonous could they have been when so many were produced over so many years? Since the earliest days of the silent movie era in the United States (and elsewhere), filmmakers have been drawn to sports, which often provided them with compelling, action-packed narratives rife with conflict, tension, and triumph.[6]

In *Sports Films: A Complete Reference* (1987), Harvey Marc Zucker and Lawrence J. Babich catalog over two thousand films about sports produced from the late nineteenth century—among the earliest is Thomas Edison's *Ball Game* (1896), which is less than a minute long—through the mid-1980s. Some are well known and widely regarded as classics, such as *The Pride of the Yankees* (1942) and *Rocky* (1976). Many more are obscure and justifiably forgotten, such as *One-Round Hogan* (1927) and *Out of It* (1969).

In the thirty-plus years since Zucker and Babich published their book, filmmakers from all over the world have made hundreds of sports films. If anything, declares Bruce Babington in *The Sports Film* (2014), "the genre's output has accelerated tremendously, until in the last few decades more sports-based features have been made, especially in the US, than ever before."[7] As is the case with all genres, sports films vary a great deal in terms of quality. Unsurprisingly, most of them are mediocre at best, with formulaic narrative structures and tired tropes (e.g., the hard-working underdog athlete or team overcoming adversity to achieve success). At the same time, many of the sports films—feature films and documentaries—made in the last thirty years are creative and engaging, original, and dramatic and sometimes comedic. A few are superb, truly brilliant. Martin Scorsese's *Raging Bull* (1980) immediately comes to mind.

Obviously some Hollywood filmmakers have embraced the idea that sports films are worthy endeavors, artistically and commercially. In Hollywood, as one would expect, the latter almost always trumps the former. Speaking from experience and years of study, Martin Scorsese asserts that in Hollywood "one iron rule remains true: every decision is shaped by the money men's perception of what the audience wants."[8] The "money men" are not always right about what people want from sports films, but they often are; it is their job, after all, to understand the market.

So, there are millions of reasons (close to a billion of them) Sylvester Stallone's Rocky Balboa saga and franchise is going strong, almost forty years after *Rocky* won the Academy Award for Best Picture. The same goes for many of the annually produced a-season-in-the-life-of-a-bunch-of-misfits-or-underdogs films. People pay good money to see these movies. *Friday Night Lights* (2004) made $62 million, *Glory Road* (2006) made $43 million, and *Moneyball* (2011) made $110 million and was nominated for six Academy Awards.

Considering the national and global proliferation and popularity of actual sports, one might think that cinematic sports would not be able to find or sustain audiences. That is not the case. If it were, fewer sports films would be produced. And yet they keep coming. When produced with intelligence, creativity, and nuance, when they push against conventions or stretch the boundaries of the genre, or when they are simply extremely well crafted, as is the case with, say, *Hoosiers* (1986), they resonate with millions of people. Furthermore, they can impact how moviegoers think about sport as an institution and practice, about history and culture, as well as a host of social identities (race, class, gender, etc.) and relationships.[9]

LA at Play

Thom Andersen's excellent documentary *Los Angeles Plays Itself* (2003) critiques how feature films have represented his hometown. Early on, Andersen dryly notes that "movies are not about places, they're about stories. If we notice the location, we're not really watching the movie. It's what's up front that counts."[10] Even if Andersen is being ironic, I suspect that he is correct. For most moviegoers, plot and character development and relationships usually trump setting (unless it is especially "exotic"). Actually, though, plot, character, and setting are interrelated and interdependent. Characters exist in time and space. They are someplace—which is Andersen's point. Place matters. How it is represented matters, too. "Like dramatic license," Andersen argues, "geographic license [in films] is usually an alibi for laziness. Silly geography makes for silly movies." Obviously the geography, the place, he and we are concerned with is Los Angeles. More specifically, we are interested in Los Angeles at play. Well, Hollywood's representations of Angelenos at play.[11]

One way to begin is with a stranger coming to town.

Five minutes into *The Karate Kid* (1984), it is clear that the Newark, New Jersey, native Daniel LaRusso (played by Ralph Macchio) does not yearn to go west. But his persistently upbeat single mother, Lucille (Randee Heller), does. So mother and son embark on a cross-country road trip in their decrepit station wagon to Southern California, where Lucille has a new job waiting for her and which (as Woody Guthrie sang) she imagines is "a garden of Eden, a paradise to live in or see." Like many films set in Southern California, there are palm trees, but the LaRusso's new home in Reseda, which is in the San Fernando Valley, is no Eden. The apartment building's pool is less than half-full, with algae-laden water, and the LaRusso's apartment needs repairs.

Socially, there are also problems. A scrawny smart aleck, Daniel has a hard time making friends and is harassed by motorbike-riding bullies, in part because he quickly finds a love interest in the blonde, affluent Ali (Elisabeth Shue). To defend himself from the arrogant, hyperaggressive Johnny (William Zabka), who is Ali's former boyfriend, and his fellow Cobra Kai karate disciples, Daniel turns to his lone friend, the wise handyman at his apartment complex, Mr. Miyagi (Noriyuki "Pat" Morita), a quietly charming, thoughtful man from Okinawa who trims bonsai trees and is a karate master. Thanks to Mr. Miyagi's unorthodox training methods and his sagacious tutelage, Daniel excels at the Valley karate tournament, where he (somehow) bests his Cobra Kai tormentors (despite having no competitive karate experience and an injured leg) and earns their respect, thus completing the improbable yet predictable zero to hero narrative arc, à la another underdog Italian American fighter, Rocky Balboa.[12]

Directed by John G. Avildsen, who won an Academy Award for *Rocky* in 1977, *The Karate Kid* is "essentially a fairy tale," observes film critic Janet Maslin.[13] The ninety-eight-pound weakling from New Jersey not only proves his mettle against the big, bad Cobra Kai, but he also finds an admirable father figure in Mr. Miyagi and resolves his social class-driven conflicts with the beautiful and supportive Ali, who is from wealthy Encino, rather than rundown Reseda. More to the point, it is a Los Angeles fairy tale. "*The Karate Kid* is an L.A. film to its core," journalist Jared Cowan writes, "it was shot almost entirely on location in the San Fernando Valley and other L.A.-area sites" and effectively "conveys a strong sense of place" and verisimilitude.[14] The Valley is huge, suburban, and often unfairly characterized as homogenous. "It's not like the kids were from Beverly Hills or Santa Monica. The Valley is a real place," Shue declares. "Where you live becomes who you are. That was a really important theme of the movie."[15] Perhaps a more important theme in *The Karate Kid* is that Southern California is a land of fresh starts, a place where dreams can come true (at least on the big screen).

One might assume that *The Bad News Bears* (1976), directed by veteran filmmaker Michael Ritchie and written by Angeleno Bill Lancaster (Burt's son), would be as formulaic and predictable as *The Karate Kid*, since it has most of the trappings of the popular band-of-misfits sports film. But *The Bad News Bears* is more original and trenchant than it appears. Drenched in California sunshine, *The Bad News Bears* was mostly filmed in Chatsworth—which is in the Valley, northwest of Reseda—at Mason Park, with the scenic Santa Susana Mountains often in the background. Despite the idyllic Southern California setting and its comedic pleasures, *The Bad News Bears* "skewers that most American of youth activities [little league baseball] by turning . . . pipsqueak players into a potty-mouthed roster of anarchists," observe former sportswriters Ray Didinger and Glen Macnow. "On one level, it's stinging satire. On another, it's downright funny."[16]

The movie begins with Morris Buttermaker (played brilliantly by Walter Matthau), who is hired to coach a youth baseball team, the Bears, because none of the boys' fathers are willing to do it. An alcoholic, former minor-leaguer-turned-pool-cleaner who drives a beat-up yellow Cadillac convertible, the irritable Buttermaker inherits a racially and ethnically diverse crew of boys without much, if any, athletic talent. Rather than teach them how to play the game, he sits in the dugout and drinks beer as they get pounded, 26–0, in the first half inning of their first game before forfeiting it. To improve the team, Buttermaker bribes an ex-girlfriend's daughter, the hard-throwing Amanda Whurlitzer (Academy Award-winner Tatum O'Neal), to join the Bears. We first meet the fast-talking, hard-throwing eleven-year old when she is selling maps to the homes of the stars off of Sunset Boulevard. Soon thereafter, Buttermaker and Amanda recruit the dirt-bike-riding juvenile delinquent, Kelly Leak (Jackie Earle Haley), who is a terrific athlete, to join the Bears. With the infusion of new talent and the improved play of some Bears, the team improbably reaches the league championship game, which it loses in dramatic fashion to the obnoxiously arrogant Yankees. After the loss, Buttermaker, who realizes that he had, like many adults in the community, started to care too much about winning, gives bottles of beer to all of his players. At the trophy ceremony, one of the smug Yankees semi-apologizes for disrespecting the Bears, whom the Yankees then give a cheer. In response the diminutive, pugnacious, and profane Tanner (Chris Barnes) yells, "Hey, Yankees! You can take your apology and your trophy and shove it straight up your ass!" When the ultra-shy, "booger-eating moron" Timmy Lupus (Quinn Smith) throws the Bears' runner-up trophy at the Yankees and declares, "And another thing, just wait 'til next year!" jubilant, beer-soaked chaos ensues, to the rousing music from Georges Bizet's *Carmen*.

A huge commercial success, *The Bad News Bears* is also one of the most critical and derisive Hollywood sports films of its or any era. Indeed, historian David W. Zang calls *The Bad News Bears* "the most subversive sports film ever made."[17] Besides not being good at baseball, many of the Bears are foulmouthed, dysfunctional, and disrespectful to the point of anti-authoritarian (one of them even looks like Harpo Marx). Unfortunately, the film's real reprobates are the win-at-all-cost little league coaches, administrators, and parents, some of whom are verbally and even physically abusive. "*The Bad News Bears* is a brilliant, relentless attack on the world of frustrated adults who play out their fantasies through their children, then punish those children either physically or mentally because the kids can't fulfill their parents' dreams," writes media historian Hal Erickson. "And when confronted, these adults will insist that they're doing all this for their kids' benefit and that the youngsters love what they're doing."[18] The film does not show a lot of that love. If anything, the Bears sometimes seem like the Little Rascals on acid. In most ways, it is an uncomplicated film set in Southern California middle-class suburbia, but all these years later it is still satisfying and scathing.

Southern California dreams often include the beach, which is where the (deliberately) goofy-looking Billy Hoyle (Woody Harrelson) goes to hustle unsuspecting hoop chumps in *White Men Can't Jump* (1992). Written and directed by Ron Shelton, a former college basketball player best known for his critically acclaimed film *Bull Durham* (1988), *White Men Can't Jump* opens early in the morning with locals stirring on Venice Beach's Ocean Front Walk.

(Rip Cronk's famous mural *Venice Reconstituted* is briefly featured in the background.) Billy patiently waits to be included in a pickup game at the Venice Beach courts, a mecca of street basketball. Eventually, the fast-talking, boastful Sidney Deane (Wesley Snipes) needs a replacement player and asks the white, seemingly nonathletic Billy to run in the game. Despite his appearance, Billy is a talented player who twice bests the brash African American Sidney—thus setting in motion an ebony-and-ivory rivalry turned partnership and then friendship. For most of the film, Billy and Sidney are about as mature as the Bad News Bears. They constantly squabble, play the dozens, and appear to be "a couple of Peter Pans trying to make a living at a kids' game on the playgrounds."[19]

The film's plot is unremarkable. Janet Maslin of the *New York Times* calls it "cheerfully lackadaisical."[20] It focuses on Billy and his girlfriend Gloria (Rosie Perez), a former disco queen studying to be a *Jeopardy!* game show contestant, who are being chased by two-bit gangsters trying to collect a $6,000 debt, and on Sidney's struggles to provide financially for his family. The former is silly and the latter is mundane. *White Men Can't Jump* is at its best when Billy and Sidney are performing what film critic Hal Hinson calls "verbal jazz," which is most artfully enacted on outdoor basketball courts in Venice Beach, Compton near the Watts Towers, and Lafayette Park in downtown Los Angeles.[21] Shelton's characters, Hinson argues, "talk for the sheer pleasure of talking. It's their jive art form, their way of inventing and expressing themselves."[22] Their incessant trash talk is emblematic of how many men—black and white—use sport and language to construct their identity and relationships with other men. Sometimes Billy and Sidney's banter is funny and sometimes it is tiresomely repetitive.

More interesting is how *White Men Can't Jump* represents Los Angeles. Apparently, one of Shelton's goals was to "show the real Los Angeles, the places where people live, not the exotic postcard images."[23] Quirky Venice Beach, with its turban-wearing and bikini-clad roller skaters, its bodybuilders and sizable homeless population is certainly gritty. The same can be said of the chain-link fence encircled basketball courts around the city where Billy and Sidney play. Additionally, Billy and Gloria stay in cheap, probably flea-infested motels. Sidney's apartment building, which is in Crenshaw, one of the city's largest African American communities, is rough, too. His apartment complex is called Vista View, but as Sidney's disgruntled wife puts it, "there ain't no vista, there ain't no views, and there sure as hell ain't no vista of no views." Ultimately, in terms of verisimilitude, the film more effectively represents some unglamorous sections of Los Angeles than it does high-caliber street basketball. This despite the fact that "Shelton recruited some NBA and former college stars, including Marques Johnson, Nigel Miguel, Duane Martin and Freeman Williams as supporting players."[24] They all give fine performances and remind us that the relatively diminutive Woody Harrelson and Wesley Snipes (both of whom are sub-six-footers) were wise not to quit their day jobs.[25]

The basketball in writer-director Gina Prince-Bythewood's *Love and Basketball* (2000) is less cartoonish than in *White Men Can't Jump* and takes several forms: playground, interscholastic, intercollegiate, and professional. Divided into four quarters, the film begins in 1981 with pickup ball, played by children on a well-paved driveway. The kids include eleven-year-old Quincy McCall (Glenndon Chatman), two of his buddies, and the brand-new next-door neighbor Monica Wright (Kyla Pratt). She is just as talented, confident, and competitive as Q, whose father Zeke (Dennis Haysbert) plays for the Los Angeles Clippers.[26] Q also aspires to be an NBA player. Monica hopes to be the first woman to play in the NBA. Frustrated by being beaten by a girl, Q pushes and bloodies Monica, apologizes, and the next day asks her if she wants to be his girl. Their childhood romance lasts about two minutes before they resort to fisticuffs. Flashing forward to 1988, the film's second quarter is set at Crenshaw High School, where Q (Omar Epps) and Monica (Sanaa Lathan) are stars of their respective teams, although he is the more popular, celebrated, and highly recruited athlete. Longtime friends who often squabble, Q and Monica eventually become lovers, after Monica's sister (Regina Hall) and mother (Alfre Woodard) transform her from a tomboyish jock into a beautiful woman for the school dance.

The Cinderella story continues in the film's third quarter, which is set at the University of Southern California (USC), where Q is a frosh phenom on the basketball team and Monica struggles for playing time. Their relationship is challenged by a series of twists and turns, including revelations that Zeke McCall has been cheating on his wife. Frustrated that Monica is unable to give him the emotional support he needs when he needs it—because of her own commitment to basketball—Q ends their relationship and simultaneously his college career by declaring for the NBA draft. The film's final quarter is set in 1993. Monica is playing professionally in Barcelona. She is successful but personally unfulfilled and lonely. Q has a lackluster NBA career as a journeyman, ends up on the bench for the hometown Lakers, and suffers a career-threatening knee injury. Estranged from his father, Q is engaged (the wedding is two weeks away) when Monica visits him in Los Angeles. Her love for basketball on the wane, Monica realizes she wants to be with Q and challenges him to a game of one-on-one. She is playing for his heart. He wins. But then, realizing that he loves her, says, "Double or nothing." Cinderella in high tops wins, after all. A brief coda shows Monica playing at the Great Western Forum, Lakers jerseys hanging from the rafters and Magic Johnson sitting courtside, for the WNBA's Los Angeles Sparks, with Q on the sideline, proudly bouncing their daughter on his knee. The film's poised, determined, beautiful, thoughtful, feminist heroine has it all.

A well-made if conventional girl-meets-boy, loses boy, gets-boy-back narrative, *Love and Basketball* "follows all the rules yet still emerges as fresh and original," asserts film critic Stephanie Zacharek.[27] That is partly because it represents upper-middle-class black life and partly because it is a sports romance told from a "woman's point of view," notes the late great Roger Ebert. "And here's the most amazing thing: It considers sports in terms of career, training, motivation and strategy. The big game scenes involve behavior and attitude, not scoring. The movie sees basketball as something the characters do as a skill and a living, not as an excuse for audience-pleasing jump shots at the buzzer."[28] Truth be told, there is more love than basketball in *Love and Basketball*. Prince-Bythewood admitted as much, years later, when reminiscing about the casting process. Who should play Monica: the veteran actress Sanaa Lathan or former college-baller-turned-aspiring-actress Niesha Butler? According to Prince-Bythewood, "finally my husband said, 'Is this a basketball movie, or is it a love story?' And at the end of the day, I realized it was a love story and you can fake a jump shot, but you can't fake a close-up."[29] The film does not fake the city, either. Set in Crenshaw and Baldwin Hills—an affluent African American neighborhood in Los Angeles—and on USC's campus, *Love and Basketball* may be another sports fairy tale, "a universal love story with black characters in the lead," as Prince-Bythewood puts it, but it is enhanced by how it represents parts of the city that most moviegoers rarely see.[30]

Hollywood of course loves romance more than sports. Yet as we have just seen, bringing them together can be productive. *Jerry Maguire* (1996) is probably the best example of this. A critically acclaimed romantic comedy, nominated for five Academy Awards, including Best Picture, *Jerry Maguire* was written and directed by Cameron Crowe and stars Tom Cruise as the eponymously named protagonist.[31] Jerry Maguire is a handsome, talkative, successful sports agent who has a crisis of conscience and, in the middle of the night, impetuously writes an idealistic mission statement that advocates for a less avaricious, more humane business model. He distributes *The Things We Think and Do Not Say: The Future of Our Business* to his colleagues, who publically applaud him, but actually think he is being foolish. Maguire promptly loses just about everything: his job at Sports Management International (SMI), almost all of his athlete clients, his beautiful, if hyperaggressive fiancée, his money, his confidence, and a big chunk of his identity. About the only thing he does not lose is his Newport Beach condo with an ocean view and easy access to the beach, neither of which seem to interest the self-absorbed Maguire.

Jerry also retains two of his seventy-two clients. The more high profile of them is hotshot Texas quarterback Frank "Cush" Cushman (Jerry O'Connell), who is projected to be the No. 1 pick in the upcoming National Football League (NFL) draft. The other client is Rod Tidwell (Cuba Gooding Jr.), an undersized, dynamic, and loquacious Arizona Cardinals wide receiver who perpetually feels underappreciated and underpaid and wants Jerry to "show me the money!" Fortunately for Jerry, who fears being alone, he also has Dorothy Boyd (Renée Zellweger), an accountant and young single mother, the lone SMI employee who joins him when he leaves the agency. She does so because his mission statement inspires her—and because she has a crush on him. Jerry is blindsided when he loses Cush to his duplicitous protégé-turned-nemesis Bob Sugar (Jay Mohr), but his relationships with Rod and Dorothy, and especially Dorothy's adorable six-year-old bespectacled son Ray (Jonathan Lipnicki), deepen. There are many bumps and laughs along the way as Jerry experiences emotional growth and maturity. Rewards ensue. A devoted family man, Rod Tidwell earns, with Jerry's help, the multimillion-dollar contract he covets. Jerry wins back Dorothy, whom he married, largely because he loves Ray, thus completing himself and the American dream.

A skillfully written and performed film, for which Gooding won the Oscar for Best Supporting Actor, *Jerry Maguire* represents "the venal, high-stakes world of pro sports with deadly wit."[32] It is also littered with amusing cameos by real-life sports figures, including super agent Leigh Steinberg, who some people think was the inspiration for Maguire. Structurally, the film creatively melds two popular formulas: the odd couple buddy narrative and the love triangle. Jerry and Rod constitute a bickering, interracial odd couple. Their interactions are often witty and rewarding, full of energy, humor, and sometimes tension. It is the proud and passionate Rod, more so than anyone else, who helps Jerry become an emotionally honest and better man. Theirs is a beautiful bromance. The love triangle features Jerry, Dorothy, and the scene-stealing Ray. It is Ray, not Dorothy, who first captures Jerry's heart. Moreover, Ray's affection for Jerry contributes to Dorothy's feelings for him. Late at night, sitting together on the couch in Dorothy's sister's small house, which is in the "Tree Section" of Manhattan Beach, Jerry and Ray have a touching, funny moment. Jerry is talking about himself (as usual) and Ray wants to go to the zoo. "The fuckin zoo is closed, Ray," Jerry says. Startled by the profanity, Ray says, "You said fuck," and then quietly confides, "I won't tell." A bond is forged. For Jerry, Los Angeles is initially a place of commerce and a jumping-off point to airports and hotels all across the country in order to serve and sign more clients. But once he falls for Ray and then Dorothy, Los Angeles becomes a place of domestic fulfillment, as the film's final scene, with the newly constituted nuclear family walking hand-in-hand in a lovely public park, attests.

There is nothing similarly idyllic about *Lords of Dogtown* (2005), which is mostly set in south Santa Monica, Ocean Park, and Venice in the mid-1970s, when these places were grittier than they are today, and is a fictional version of the story told in Stacy Perlata's outstanding documentary *Dogtown & Z-Boys* (2001). Written by Perlata, a former world-champion skateboarder, and directed by Catherine Hardwicke, who lives in Venice and is a surfer, *Lords of Dogtown* is about a small group of scruffy, mischievous, mostly working-class teenagers and their pot-smoking, ne'er-do-well mentors who together revolutionized skateboarding. The mentors are the shaggy Skip Engblom (Heath Ledger, who is terrific) and the camera-toting Craig Stecyk (Pablo Schreiber), whose photos and later magazine articles successfully promoted the Dogtown movement and aesthetic. Skip and Craig own and work in the Zephyr surfboard shop, now legendary and long gone. They and their buddies live to surf and work when they want. They especially love to surf among the detritus of the dilapidated Pacific Ocean Park pier, about which they are proprietary. They were, explains the narrator in *Dogtown & Z-Boys*, "infamous for their aggressive localism and outcast behavior." Engblom and Stecyk's protégés are young surfers who unexpectedly metamorphosed into world-class skateboarders due to a fortuitous confluence of events and their remarkable skills and daring.

One day, Skip is given some urethane skateboard wheels, which firmly grip the road and thus allow for hard, sharp turns. Almost immediately, the teenagers who hang out at the Zephyr shop put them on their skateboards and try them out at local school playgrounds, which have long stretches of asphalt, some of it banked. It does not take long for Tony Alva (Victor Rasuk), Jay Adams (Emile Hirsch), Stacy Perlata (John Robinson), and some of the

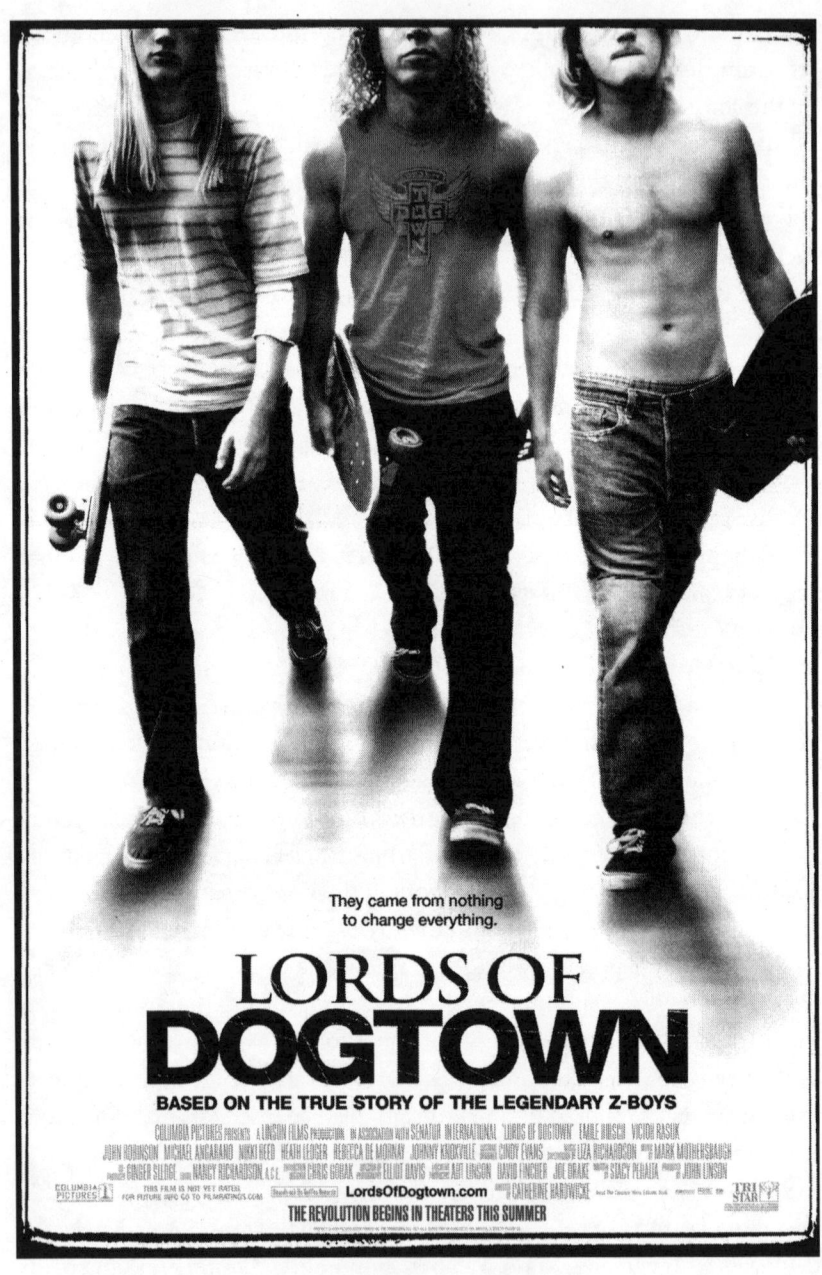

Movie poster of director Catherine Hardwicke's *Lords of Dogtown* (2005). Courtesy of Photofest.

others to become proficient and increasingly creative and audacious on the new and much improved skateboards. Almost as quickly, Skip and Craig form a Zephyr skateboard team to represent the shop in local competitions and to help sell skateboards. The Z-Boys are born.

The timing was fortuitous, because California was experiencing one of the worst droughts in its history. This led to intense water restrictions, which led to myriad empty backyard swimming pools all over Los Angeles. The resourceful, stealthy Z-Boys use the smooth walls of the empty pools as cement waves to be ridden and carved. Innovative and increasingly popular skateboarders, Alva, Adams, and Perlata find that their relationships with each other and with Skip change as they all experience success at competitions in places such as Del Mar and Huntington Beach. Always concerned with being stylish and distinctive, the young men become rivals, which strains their friendship. For many reasons—ambition, ego, financial need and desire—the Z-Boys leave Skip and go their own ways. The curly haired Alva, an "alpha dog showboat," becomes a skateboarding rock star.[33] Likewise, the blond Perlata competes all over the world for his corporate sponsor and even has a cameo on the popular TV show *Charlie's Angels*. Adams, however, a brooding, "self-destructive renegade," stays close to home, in part to support his struggling, trippy middle-age mother Philaine (Rebecca De Mornay).[34] Ultimately, the former Z-Boys reunite because one of their skating compadres, the loyal sidekick Sid (Michael Angarano), has brain cancer. From an extremely wealthy family in north Santa Monica, the wheelchair-stricken Sid is given permission to drain his pool and invites Alva, Adams, and Perlata to skate it. They do so with abandon and genuine admiration for one another. The film ends here—with the famous Dogbowl sessions and a crane shot of the skateboarders gracefully skating the pool to the melancholy strains of Pink Floyd's "Wish You Were Here." The film concludes with a postscript that explains what happened to the Z-Boys, including their friend Sid, who died shortly after the Dogbowl sessions.

Lords of Dogtown is impressive: it is an engaging collective bildungsroman and a cinematic social history deeply committed to authenticity, place, and local culture. There is, writes Rachel Abramowitz of the *Los Angeles Times*, a "kind of hallucinogenic lyricism" to the film, which is sometimes frenetic, thanks to its splendid cinematography and fast-paced, deliberately rough editing when the surfers and skateboarders are in action.[35] The film has "an appropriately scruffy, unpolished look consistent with the resourceful, do-it-yourself aesthetic of the place and time it depicts," film critic A. O. Scott asserts.[36] He correctly adds that the filmmakers were primarily "interested in evoking a milieu" and admires many of the scenes that have "the loose, stop-and-start rhythms of a long summer day and the restless, competitive energy of young men in the heat of adolescence."[37] The Z-Boys, simultaneously reckless and committed to their craft, which Alva elevated to an art form, are complicated, flawed young men who personify a "perhaps typically Southern California blend of hedonism and striving."[38] The film's tremendous attention to detail and attempts at verisimilitude (some of it due to the use of computer-generated imagery, some of it because almost all of the original Z-Boys have cameos) are effective, for as Scott notes, "there is something about it that feels right—the looseness of its construction, the eclectic welter of its soundtrack, the faces of its cast."[39] The real-life Peralta put it well when he quipped: "This is where *Endless Summer* meets *Mean Streets*."[40] *Lords of Dogtown* is also, despite some understandable nostalgia for its subjects and many modifications to the historical record, an exceptional Los Angeles sports film, one of the best.

Leaps of Poetic Faith

Set in and about Los Angeles, Lawrence Kasdan's *Grand Canyon* (1991) is not a sports film, but it does begin with a pickup playground basketball game (the kind where Billy Hoyle and Sidney Deane trash talk and hustle). The game is played by African American men and shot in black and white and balletic slow motion to a haunting score. The music's tempo gradually increases as the scene segues to the colorful, crowded Great Western Forum and a Los Angeles Lakers game featuring the iconic Magic Johnson and his Showtime teammates. In a few brief minutes, *Grand Canyon*—which depicts numerous urban social anxieties, divisions, and tensions—effectively represents different Angelenos at play, on and off the court. Soon thereafter, these worlds collide. The point is that Los Angeles's social terrain is sprawling, diverse, and sometimes dangerous.

In *Grand Canyon* and, taken collectively, the sports films examined here, Los Angeles is a huge, heterogeneous, complicated place. People come together (not always harmoniously) and play different sports in different communities for different reasons. The games they play mean different things and are contested. It is a long way from the Valley to Venice Beach, from community-based youth sport and asphalt playgrounds to big-time intercollegiate basketball and professional football to skateboarding illicitly in empty pools. And yet it is all here, in Hollywood's backyard.

There are also various forms of romance in these films. Lovers meet and are frequently reunited. Friendships develop, are fraught with tension, and yet are sustained. These are Hollywood films, after all, works of art *and* commerce, so these developments are to be expected. The same is true of the sentimentalism and the romance of sport in these movies. Jack McCallum of *Sports Illustrated* correctly notes that Hollywood sports film "are, for the most part, fractured fairy tales with soft, gooey centers."[41] There is plenty of evidence to support that in this chapter. Exceptions like *The Bad News Bears* just accentuate the tendency.

Yet clearly Americans have an appetite for syrupy sweet sporting fairy tales, such as *The Karate Kid, Love and Basketball*, and *Jerry Maguire*. "It was never reality that audiences asked of Hollywood," the late film scholar William F. Van Wert reminds us, "a fact not lost in Hollywood's love-hate relationship with verisimilitude and occasional flights of excess."[42] We see some glimmers of verisimilitude and more frequently flights of excess in the sports films assessed in this chapter. That's show business. It is what Hollywood filmmakers do. It is also what their audiences expect and seemingly want.

In a city where the relationship between reality and representation is sometimes hard to determine, it is unsurprising that Hollywood sports films tend to depict athletic dreams realized. In *Hollywood Jock* (2006), writer and basketball consultant Rob Ryder wonders about the scene in *White Men Can't Jump* where the vertically challenged Billy Hoyle finally dunks: "Exactly how high was that rim??? Ah, barely over nine feet. But it looked real, right? It looked real."[43] Well, close enough, if we suspend our disbelief. Doing so is a leap of poetic faith many are willing to make.

CHAPTER TEN

Behind the Curtain

Leadership, Ingenuity, and Culture in the Making of Earvin "Magic" Johnson, Showtime, and the Laker Dynasty

SCOTT N. BROOKS

I learned to respect Magic Johnson and the Showtime Lakers at the age of nine or ten. My uncle moved into my family's home in Oakland, circa 1981, and decorated one wall with two 7Up posters; one of Magic Johnson in his purple-and-gold Los Angeles Lakers uniform, and the other of Larry Bird in his green-with-white-trim Boston Celtic jersey. I asked my uncle who the men were and why he liked them. He told me that Magic and Larry were the best young players in the NBA. I pushed further, "Which one do you like best?" He struggled to answer, telling me more about their backgrounds. Magic played at Michigan State and won the national championship in college. Larry played at Indiana and then Indiana State and got to the national championship in college but lost to Magic. Uncle Kevin could not answer who was best or choose one over the other, and yet, I felt I had to. The tie went to the player with the closest family connection and my preferred color wave—my mother was born and raised in Indiana and I liked green and white far better than purple and gold. This decision was not an easy one to stand by and I often faced ridicule from family members because I am a Californian and the Lakers' dominated the NBA in the 1980s. Everyone in my family was a Lakers fan; my father grew up in South Central and attended Manual Arts High School and Cal State LA, and most of my mother's family had moved from Indiana to Los Angeles. I heard it when the Showtime Lakers won; it was loudest when they beat my beloved Celtics for the championship in 1985 and 1987. Thirty years later, the

Lakers have captured five more championships (to just one additional ring for my team) and sit only one championship shy of the Celtics.

In the final analysis, the Magic-led Showtime Lakers were much more than their championships. Showtime has been a culture tour de force that moved the Lakers, basketball, and Los Angeles ahead. Going behind the curtain, Showtime attracted the biggest stars, created new nontraditional ones, and taught the sportsworld how to do business at a grand scale, surpassing baseball, America's favorite pastime. And this all started with an unexpected visionary, Dr. Jerry Buss, a white, rags-to-riches, chemist-turned-real-estate-mogul from Wyoming, who banked on Earvin "Magic" Johnson, a young black, wide-eyed, toothy-grin prom king from Lansing, Michigan. Although they carried the bulk load, it was a collective action and effort guided by a specific attainable goal, to entertain by providing the greatest product. This chapter will highlight the leadership of Dr. Buss and the collective action needed to create the dynasty, push the NBA and basketball forward, and help make Magic a global icon.

Making Showtime

The Lakers did not simply change from bridesmaids to brides overnight and Magic's greatness cannot be seen as a foregone conclusion. Instead, the environment matters; central components were assembled that promoted a championship culture and Buss's leadership withstood change and nurtured the evolution of key players and coaches: he created a championship culture—a way of doing things that reflected the value he placed on entertainment, friendship and commitment, and success. Culture is the primary force in the Lakers' dominance since 1979. Esteemed sport sociologist Dr. Harry Edwards has compared the tremendous gravitational pull of space to culture. Paraphrasing him:

> When Hubble looked through his telescope and observed stars and galaxies moving at speeds close to the speed of light, Hubble marveled at the speed in which these celestial masses moved, carrying space and matter with them. But, in time, with more observations and understanding, scientists discovered that the stars and galaxies weren't moving and carrying space and matter along. Rather, space was moving, pulling galaxies, stars and matter. Culture does the same, operating like space, it is the pulling force, gathering people, ideas, and behavior.[1]

It is clear that great players make their teammates better and contribute significantly to championships. But, no one does it alone. The rest of the team's cast of players, coaches, management, and owner all play a part in the cooperative action needed to win championships. Culture is the connective tissue binding personalities, getting them to behave in accord, unison, and toward a single goal, even if only fleetingly, just long enough to win five championships in a single ten-year span. The Lakers' transition from being a good team in the 1970s to a dynasty in the 1980s and basketball's version of "America's team" is a story of a cultural shift from top-down. Dr. Jerry Buss planted and nurtured a culture starting with a vision that transcended basketball and ultimately, business—the Lakers are part of America's influence on the world.

When Dr. Jerry Buss purchased the Lakers, Kings, and Forum for $67 million in 1979, he set out to create something special in sports and he saw both the physical skills and intangibles of Magic that could make his dream a reality.[2] The Showtime Lakers started with an overriding goal—to be a show—and a commitment to promote Magic. This was not an unrealistic vision. Buss loved living in Los Angeles, the city of movie stars, playboy playmates, and big dreams. The importance of the show was local, a part of Los Angeles culture, it was fun and intoxicating. He was creative in his business planning, seeking new ways to attract the audience's attention. Importantly, he decided that Magic would be the face of the organization. Buss's commitment to Magic was evident in the consistent lines of action and decisions that filtered down to team management, coaches, and players. Buss believed that keeping Magic happy was in the organization's best interest.

The Showtime Lakers became the city's team. Buss understood and wanted to take advantage of being in Los Angeles, a home for celebrities. Celebrities would bring more attention to the event; everyone wants to rub shoulders with the rich and famous. This approach had been attempted by Buss's predecessors Bob Short and Jack Kent Cooke, but they did not know how to approximate cool nightlife like he did. Buss strove to create a world-class product/show to maintain interest, draw more fans, and ensure the financial stability of his organization. The phrase "Showtime" came from a local nightclub that Buss frequented.[3] It was a hip place, attracting an upscale clientele, and the nightly show opened with a trio singing "It's Showtime." He sought to replicate the ambience, crowd, and energy. Buss replaced the downhome, trite amateur feel of professional sporting events at that time with dramatic flair in player introductions, lively announcing, sexy dancers, soul and disco tunes, and a marching band. Before Buss, VIPs had been given free tickets to the games, but the then owner, Jack Kent Cooke, stopped giving away free tickets because he only wanted paying customers and believed that he was not getting enough in return simply by having movie stars in attendance. The Forum became a place where he could hang out and mingle with top-dollar customers. Buss ensured that he got a hefty return for having movie stars and VIPS. He instituted a guest list and made room for celebrities to buy season tickets—like avid Laker fans Jack Nicholson and Dyan Cannon—and renovated his skybox to accommodate as many out-of-town "A-listers" as possible.[4] Buss envisioned a new function of the press—spotting celebrities—so he moved the press down to the court for a closer view. Additionally, he capitalized on celebrities being in awe of athletes; he took famous persons like Michael Jackson and Stevie Wonder into the locker room where his athletes felt at home and could be the stars.[5] Buss paid his top players well and reasoned that paying million-dollar salaries increased celebrity worship and therefore, was good for business; it made everyone pay attention, especially wealthy and famous individuals who wanted to catch a glimpse of the million-dollar men. Most importantly, Buss wanted a winning team; style without substance would not suffice. He was an avid sports fan, choosing USC for his graduate work over other schools because of the football team's history and achievement. People paid to see history—a once in a lifetime player or team—and success. Winning championships, drafting champions, and signing All-Stars would keep the Lakers in the news and create extraordinary excitement. The Showtime Lakers were never without at least three players who had won NCAA championships—Jamal Wilkes and Kareem from UCLA; Magic from Michigan State; and James Worthy from North Carolina. Buss assessed what he created: "I really tried to create a Laker image, a distinct identity. I think we've been successful. I mean, the Lakers are pretty damn Hollywood."[6]

While working on the image Buss became a marketing and financial pioneer in the business of sports in small and large ways.[7] There were few revenue streams in the late 1970s, with ticket sales making up the bulk of a team's revenue. Thus, Buss focused early attention on what he thought drove sales—fan base. Buss wanted a loyal, mixed crowd at games, so he set new variable ticket pricing that accommodated people of all socioeconomic classes, breaking with the tradition of uniform ticket pricing. Trying to free up courtside seats for celebrities, Buss increased the courtside prices dramatically in his first few years, hoping that courtside ticket holders would relinquish their seats.[8] This did not work exactly as he planned and many top-dollar season ticket holders held on to their seats. It was perfect for wooing business clients who did not want to miss the new show that Buss was putting together. Courtside seats cost $15 when he purchased the team in 1979—but now cost more than $2,700 per seat. He tapped into local pride and appealed to the average Los Angeles fan by keeping Southern California natives and local college superstars on the roster—Wilkes (UCLA), Kareem (UCLA), Brad Holland (UCLA), Swen Nater (UCLA), Michael Cooper (Pasadena High School alum), and Byron Scott (Morningside High School alum in Inglewood). Buss pushed for greater television coverage and began his own network to draw even more attention and fan loyalty. To take advantage of the television boom and the selective regional programming, he helped launch Prime Ticket Network (now FS West/Prime Ticket) in 1985. Key NBA playoff games, including some championship games, had been shown on three-hour tape delay so as not to disrupt NBC's normal programming. The 1979–80 season held much promise after the dramatically high ratings captured by Magic and Larry Bird's college championship game, which helped the NBA to secure a four-year, $91.9 million TV deal with CBS 1982–1986—the NBA's latest television contract is worth around $23 billion over nine years.[9] Live and full coverage of the finals did not occur until the 1984–85 season when the Lakers met the Boston Celtics in the championship.[10] This series created media fireworks as a follow-up to the Magic-Bird college rivalry. Buss also made breakthroughs in advertising and sales. Great Western Bank purchased rights to Buss's Forum in 1987, something only two franchises had done going into the 1990 season.[11] Many of Buss's initiatives have become standard procedures across the league and sports generally. Basketball Hall of Famer and former Laker executive Jerry West spoke about the genius of Buss after his death:

> He knew what he wanted with the team. "Here's what I want to see, I want people to come and see a winning basketball team," he said, "but I want entertainment, very much like a Broadway show." I said, "my gosh." Here we were in the stone ages as far as the development of the league and the promoting of the league. Here's a man who changed not only basketball, he changed them all, he left a shadow over the entire sports world.[12]

Buss threw his full support behind Magic, an early commitment that superseded any other team decisions. With Magic at the helm, Buss and the Lakers had a winner and a showman. Magic's rookie year championship set the stage for his amazing playing career. He missed only one All-Star game in his career (in 1981) and earned three league MVPs and three championship MVPs. Altogether, Magic's court brilliance, iconic status, and personal friendship positioned him to earn even more money and one day assume a management role with the Lakers. After only his second season, Buss gave Magic a $25-million contract extension, the longest contract in sports history. Buss's "lifetime contract," as it would be called, raised a lot of questions: "Is this a joke?" "He can not believe that Magic could play for twenty-five years, can he?" Buss responded with joy.

> He may even be my coach or general manager. Or maybe he'll run the team and I'll just sit back and watch. Magic is a bright kid and I plan to make him my protege, teach him the business aspect of sports. I realize this is a very unusual contract because we're talking about a kid whose college class just graduated. But what it comes down to is that Magic is part of the family.[13]

This was the ultimate statement of Buss's commitment. Not only did it put Magic in the same category of Kareem and Moses Malone after only his second year—Kareem and Moses were the two highest paid and most dominant players at that time and now are Hall of Famers—but it said to the world that Buss wanted Magic for life.

Becoming Hollywood

Los Angeles was the perfect setting for Magic's celebrity and the Lakers Showtime; it has been a global city that captures the world's attention because of Hollywood and its famous residents. The Hollywood vision, business innovation, and commitment to building a star were necessary parts to the Lakers' metamorphosis into Showtime. Still, many people, events, and things had to come together. The state of the NBA and Showtime came about in a specific time and Magic's growth was as much social as it was physical. His status and role, handed to him by ownership, was akin to a birthright and it had great impact on how he was treated, and he was able to push the boundaries for what was possible for black male athletes at that time. Magic benefited greatly from timing, opportunity, and a friendship.

The national context and perception of black athletes and sports posed a challenge and opportunity. The NBA in the 1970s was a public image nightmare and revenues were spiraling downward as it became known as the blackest professional sports league.[14] The Lakers epitomized the potential and reality of the league; they were talked about with a mix of praise and ridicule. Their win-loss record was very good since moving from Minneapolis (where they were perennial giants due to their dominant center George Mikan) to Los Angeles in 1960 (they had won 60 percent of their games, 485 out of 820 total games, between 1969 and 1979). Some fans felt that the Los Angeles Lakers were underachievers since they had only one championship in twenty years despite having Hall of Fame worthy players such as Wilt Chamberlain, Jerry West, Kareem Abdul-Jabbar, and Gail Goodrich. They were clearly second best in the league behind the dynastic Celtics, celebrating their lone championship in 1972 over the 76ers, but losing eight times in the championships to Bill Russell's Boston Celtics. The Lakers acquired Kareem entering the 1975 season. He was the league's unstoppable star and had won a championship in Milwaukee, but with few other standouts on the new Lakers, the team was unable to get over the hump. They hit rock bottom during the 1977–78 season. Kareem missed twenty games with a hand injury suffered when he retaliated with a punch after being elbowed by an opponent. The biggest event in the Lakers slide came when Kermit Washington, already engaged in a skirmish with one Houston Rocket, turned and threw a devastating straight right-hand blow that hospitalized Rudy Tomjanovich for two weeks. The public reacted, led by a media searching for answers. The Lakers became the "black eye" of the NBA and sports for these incidents of violence. Fan enthusiasm and support for the team waned and the giant spectacle and excellence of Kareem could not rescue the team; a private and sensitive man, he was largely misunderstood and often portrayed as distant, even rude. Lakers owner Cooke had managed to field very competitive teams that should have been able to win championships, at least on paper, but this was not enough. The NBA's problems with violence, race relations, and drugs were brought to light by a *Saturday Night Live* skit, a *New York Times* editorial, and a Walter Cronkite investigation of the league.[15] However, the public reaction hid other dangers. The league's leadership had not adjusted to changes in the game, which put players and the league at risk. Kareem defended his actions and those of his teammate:

> As long as this league continues to view the game as a "contact" sport, a philosophy which in my view is highly questionable, violent fouls will continue to go undetected. This philosophy maximizes rather than minimizes the potential for

violent reaction, I've had to learn to play the game as a contact sport—really at the expense of playing basketball.[16]

Players were seen as big, overpaid monsters and the image would have to change for the Lakers and the NBA to rise out of the open grave.

The 1979 NCAA championship game foreshadowed hope in the form of a media-driven rivalry that excited the country and created a surge in television ratings. Michigan State versus Indiana State was not a battle between perennial powerhouse programs, like Indiana, Kentucky, or UCLA. The marketing and hype was centered around a clash of cultures, or so it seemed. Larry Bird was 6'8", a small town farm boy. Earvin "Magic" Johnson, was 6'9", an inner-city kid. Both came from large families, had strong parental figures, worked hard, preferred sharing the ball with teammates, and played basketball with flare. But, Larry was an introvert and Magic an extrovert, Larry was white and Magic was black, and so the sports media machine ran with a storyline of opposites. The NCAA championship game did not live up to expectations; Magic's Michigan State Spartans easily handled Larry's toothless Indiana State. NBA commissioner Larry O'Brien and league owners smartly prepared to take advantage of the individual talents of Magic and Larry and television fueled the rivalry. The question was whether it would be enough to save the league.

A gregarious and fun-loving guy, Magic was well liked by everyone and his enthusiasm was contagious. He was a prized asset for the Lakers and the league. His stardom crossed over racial, ethnic, and class differences and he became an icon of popular culture. Julius Erving, popularly known as Dr. J, was the first black basketball player to have mainstream appeal: he was Dr. Chapstick, the spokesperson for Chapstick lip balm, and a spokesperson for Coca-Cola where he partnered with Bill Cosby in a commercial spot that had the punchline "Two doctors agree . . ." Magic took over where Dr. J left off and set the stage for Michael Jordan as a black athlete whom whites could/would love. He was the image bearer of the league during this time as an aging Dr. J's stardom faded and Larry Bird showed indifference to publicity and the media. Magic endorsed 7Up and Converse among others and had his own video game, the first of its kind in basketball. In 1988, Magic confronted Commissioner David Stern regarding the NBA's licensing rights. As a burgeoning businessperson, he was looking for opportunities and realized that there was money to be made in NBA merchandising. Stern originally rejected the idea of giving licensing permission, but gave in when Magic threatened to sit out for the season. He became a licensee of the NBA, the first active player with their own licensing NBA deal, and sold 150,000 t-shirts in four days after the Lakers won back-to-back championships in 1989.[17]

Buss took Magic under his wing, promoted and advised him, ensured that he felt appreciated, and the two built a genuine friendship. Through Buss and Showtime, Magic's network multiplied and he learned how to be a star and a businessman, among other roles. Buss took Magic to lunch after practices, to his first boxing and tennis matches, and introduced him to horse racing and hockey. Very few places offered all of these social activities. And a much older Buss and Magic were two of LA's most eligible bachelors and running buddies; they double-dated and Buss introduced Magic to Hugh Heffner's Playboy mansion. Time and time again, Buss made personnel and management choices that were favorable to Magic.

Built for Magic

From 1979 to 1989, the Lakers could hardly be thought of as a static franchise: they had an ownership change, four different head coaches, drafted players who never panned out, and Hall of Famers and all-stars who flopped, incurred serious injuries, or did not like their roles. Buss and his coaches had to be careful in their management of superstars and their egos ... a different decision here and there could have hijacked Showtime at any time.

Ownership

Lakers owner (1964–1979) Jack Kent Cooke sold the Lakers to Buss in the spring of 1979 just prior to drafting Magic. Cooke was battling a very expensive divorce and believed the sale was necessary to protect himself from having to give the team over to his wife.[18] Cooke was a serious sports franchise owner, he owned a professional hockey and football team, and without the divorce, Cooke probably holds on to the Lakers. Buss's ownership brought significant change, but purchasing a professional sports team was not easy; he had failed on five prior attempts to purchase professional football and baseball teams and his ability to purchase an NBA franchise had to be ratified by the owners.[19] The sixth time proved to be the charm for Buss, but he still needed a coach because Jerry West had stepped down to serve as general manager.

Coaches

Jack McKinney became the Lakers head coach and a first-time NBA coach in July 1970. He was not the first or obvious choice; Buss offered the job to Jerry Tarkanian, who had wanted the job but rethought the possibility after his agent was murdered while trying to deliver the Laker contract. Also, there were several others available with head coaching experience and some of the best college coaches could have been pursued, including John Wooden (the legendary UCLA coach who had coached the Lakers' Kareem, Jamal Wilkes, and Brad Holland) and Jud Heathcote (Magic's college coach). Ultimately, Buss loved McKinney's Philly grit and determination, his heart and love for coaching, and the style of play he would implement. Buss wanted a show, a lot of scoring, fast-paced play that went up and down the court, and McKinney's offensive minded "run and gun" style came well recommended from his former head coaches, Dr. Jack Ramsay and Hubie Brown. McKinney promised to bring an up-tempo, entertaining style that would not simply rely on passing the ball to Kareem.[20] Magic was key to his plans and the new Lakers would "run every chance and under every possible situation."[21] McKinney's attitude and energy mirrored the pace; he regularly jumped off the bench after exciting plays to give high-fives to players. The team began the 1979–80 season with ten wins and only four losses when tragedy struck. In a freak bicycle accident, McKinney suffered a severe concussion, fractured cheekbone and an elbow, and was hospitalized for more than three months before beginning the long road to physical and cognitive recovery. His assistant coach, Paul Westhead, was asked to take over as the interim head coach and he did so with a heavy heart. The Lakers got to the finals and upset the Philadelphia 76ers in dramatic fashion, without Kareem, who had badly sprained his ankle in game 5; Magic gave an exceptional performance to beat the 76ers in Philadelphia and was named the championship MVP. During the championship press conference, Westhead shared the title with McKinney, whom he credited for creating the vision of "showtime." The big question that off-season was who would be the coach next season. Buss answered in short time, figuring that McKinney would never fully recover. Westhead was given the full-time job.

Players respected the way Westhead stepped up and took charge after McKinney's accident and for his handling of some difficult players.[22] However, he mastered his own destruction when his desire to make "improvements" to the offensive system changed the roles of certain key players and the feel of the game.[23] What this led to was predictability and a stagnant, slow, unbalanced attack. Westhead was not the head coach for long and his termination was possibly the first time that a coach was fired to suit a single player... at least this is how many saw it.[24] He was terminated eleven games into the 1981–82 season following a standoff with Magic. He yelled at Magic for not paying attention during a timeout and then asked to speak with him after the game where he revisited Magic's failure to pay attention. Magic responded, "Hey, you might as well sit me down because I ain't being used anyway. Just sit me down."[25] Magic raised the stakes when he got to the locker room and spoke to the media:

> I can't play here anymore, I've got to leave. I want to be traded. I haven't been happy all season. It's nothing towards the guys. I love them and everybody. But I'm not happy. I'm just showing up. I play as hard as I can, but I'm not having any fun. I can't deal with it no more... I've got to go in and ask him [Buss] to trade me.[26]

Magic felt that he was not alone in his disappointment with the team's direction and accepted the role of making it public.[27] Of all of the players, Kareem was Westhead's strongest supporter and yet he understood that there were problems with the way that the team was playing.[28] Westhead had to go. It took a week, but his fate had been determined by Magic's implicit ultimatum—it was either him or Westhead. The pressure to win was great and the dissension hurt fan appeal and revenue. Buss felt he needed to respond quickly and he sided with Magic.

Next up was Pat Riley. Like Westhead, Riley had never been a head coach but got the interim job because of timing and proximity—it was still early in the season and he was the assistant coach, an insider. Riley believed that Westhead's downfall had been his poor relations with the players and Magic's power with Buss. This was his focus early on and he won over Kareem and Magic. The Lakers won their second championship of the decade in Riley's first season, again defeating Dr. J and the 76ers. Riley proved that he was more than just a substitute coach—he dressed the Hollywood part and he won. He was good-looking and his trademark slicked-back, dark hair, and fine Italian, tailored suits fit well with the Hollywood image—he looked like a movie star. Riley would lead the team to four more championships in seven years on his way to becoming a Hall of Fame coach.

Lakers coach Pat Riley between stars Kareem Abdul-Jabbar (33) and Magic Johnson (32). Photo © by Jon SooHoo

The interim placements of both Westhead and Riley were convenient, thought to provide continuity and lessen disruption, and they also highlighted the belief by Buss and Jerry West (general manager) that the championship core was in place and the team did not need a complete overhaul, only some tinkering.

Co-Stars

> Showtime was . . . that's what it was [chuckling loud]. Showtime was coming down on a fast break, looking left . . . [smacking hands] throwing right. Showtime was, ya know, coming down kicking it to somebody, then they say, "naw, I don't have the shot," then kicking it to somebody else, "naw, I don't have it." Then kicking it to somebody else, "naw, I don't have it." And finally somebody cut . . . BAM! dunk.[29]

The Showtime Lakers were just that—a show—7–8 grown men playing a game like kids, having fun, sharing the ball, high-fiving, slam dunking, and running up and down the court with grace, wonderful athleticism, flare, and excellence. Every great show has a leading actor and Showtime had Magic. However, as described above by Magic, Showtime wasn't a solo act: he needed competent others with whom to perform. Magic lived up to the hype from the start, which provoked jealousy among some of his teammates and awe from others. The business of acquiring players was not easy; some players did not want to share the spotlight and/or make changes to how they played, or may have been able to demand more money from lesser teams looking to invest in a marquee player. The collection of players over the ten-year span took a lot of coordination, brainstorming, and trial-and-error. Norm Nixon was the most notable personnel move for Showtime.

Magic joined a winning team with several great players already on the roster. The year before Magic's arrival the Lakers had won 47 games (out of 82) and reached the playoffs in the 1978–79 season behind three standout players, Jamaal Wilkes, Kareem, and Norm Nixon. But these stars were as cool, ineffectual, and alienating as they were good. Nixon, understandably, was threatened by Magic on the court from day one because they played the same position. Nixon felt slighted by Buss, Jerry West, and his coaches. He was the Lakers' 1977 first-round draft pick, arriving in Los Angeles two years before Magic. He was one of the best in the league at his position; a solid, scoring point guard averaging 17.1 points per game and 9 assists per game during the 1978–79 season. And yet, the Lakers drafted a new point guard. In addition, Nixon was a ladies' man and Magic cut into his action off the court too. Nixon had a good friendship with Buss and even partied with him—as did most of the Lakers (Buss installed a nightclub at the arena to host celebrities before the game and act as a players' lounge after the game), but no one's relationship approximated what Buss had with Magic. Nixon had cause for concern. He was appreciated for his talent, but not well liked by the team's leadership.[30] As described by Westhead: "Norm was difficult. Talented, quick, fast—but feisty and stubborn."[31] Ultimately, Nixon's talking was his undoing. His first misstep took place during a postgame interview the night of Magic's return from an injury during the 1980–81 season. Nixon was asked how it felt to relinquish control back to Magic. "'It's not my preference,' he said. '... Even if there was resentment within myself, the guy [Magic] plays as hard as he can, so he can do anything he wants to do.'"[32] Nixon compounded this error in a *Los Angeles Times* feature story—"The Lakers' Other Guard."[33] The article initially cast him as an underrated, if not, underappreciated star. Nixon discussed how Magic was given the keys to the kingdom from the moment he joined the team. "I thought Magic would have to come in and adjust to our game. But we had to adjust to him. The first thing they said in training camp that year was that Kareem and I had been handling the ball too much."[34] Nixon criticized his role on the team. "I'm a point guard, a ball handler. Playing with Magic, I'm the number two guard. I'm not a number two guard. It's not what I do best. This is not the best situation for me personally. If I can play point guard, I can be an All-Pro. I could be that on a lot of teams."[35] Nixon summarized his frustration and what he saw as the central issue. "I'm not one of the chosen people."[36] Nixon lasted one more season before he was traded to the lowly San Diego Clippers for the rights to Byron Scott.

Nixon was not the only Laker who questioned his value to the organization. From the beginning, Kareem and Magic found a way to work well together but their friendship off the floor developed much more slowly primarily due to the spotlight given to Magic by Buss (and the media). Magic shied away from Kareem early on as a sign of respect and he was also in awe of the living legend whom he encountered as an eleven-year-old.[37] One version of the story is that Magic attended a professional game (Kareem's Bucks versus the Detroit Pistons) and received an autograph after the game.[38] Another account, given by Magic, is that Kareem ignored his autograph request.[39] Regardless,

Magic generally showed deference and great appreciation for the "Big Fella" in public. And, Kareem understood that Magic was more than another great player. Kareem struggled to make sense of his own position with the Lakers when Magic, after only his second season, was handed the $25-million contract extension. Kareem did not feel that Magic had earned his money and status. It was not just the money, although that was significant; Buss's action stated clearly how he felt about Magic, and every other player in comparison. Former Laker and NBA icon Wilt Chamberlain weighed in on the possible deleterious effect on the team. "I don't know how Magic can be totally loved by his teammates now. He's getting all that money, and all the publicity."[40] Magic worried that Kareem might be offended and he worked to limit the damage.

> We got to have the Man. If the Man ain't right, the Lakers ain't right, the Lakers are in trouble. I can tear up my contract right now if it causes problems on the team. I just want to win ... We had enough problems last year. We definitely don't want any problems with The Big Fella.[41]

Kareem reached out to Buss right away and was reassured of his value verbally and financially—Buss increased Kareem's salary to $1.5 million per year.[42] Yet, Kareem said more than once that Magic was the "favorite child."[43]

In addition to veterans, the team experienced roster changes with draft picks and free agents. The Lakers had eight first-round and four second-round draft picks from 1980 to 1990. The most productive picks by far were A. C. Green and James Worthy. For all intents and purposes, Byron Scott was their 1983 first-round draft pick since he was drafted by the San Diego Clippers but traded (for Nixon) before starting his rookie season. Green, Worthy, and Scott developed into starters contributing to the back-to-back championships in 1987 and 1988 (Worthy and Scott were also around for the 1985 championship).[44] A case could also be made for the importance of two other first-round draft picks, Vlade Divac and Elden Campbell, two centers who "by committee" came to fill the void left by Kareem's retirement but never won championships. However, none of the Lakers' second-round picks lasted longer than a season with the team and only one first-rounder (besides those mentioned above) stuck past two seasons.

The Showtime Lakers' roster and team mix, like most teams, varied from year to year. On average, three to four new players were added each season and six or more new players were brought in twice between 1980 and 1990.

In the dynasty's first five seasons, the Lakers would add and subtract proven veterans, among them were two future Hall of Famers: Spencer Haywood, five-time All-Star and Rookie of the Year, who crashed and burned as a Laker due to his drug addiction; and the scoring machine Bob McAdoo, who had been a five-time All-Star, Rookie of the Year, and League MVP prior to playing for the Lakers. Mitch Kupchak, a power forward who could bang and score, came to the team and was injured in his first year and never fully recovered. And Mychal Thompson was a staunch defender, the secret weapon against the Celtics, dubbed "the Kevin McHale stopper." In addition, a young, hungry upstart Michael Cooper was in Los Angeles a couple of years before Magic and eventually became a mainstay and bedrock of the dynasty. Ultimately, players had to accept Magic's position as king and themselves as role players to fit with the Lakers.

Conclusion

It's the 1982 NBA Finals, Lakers v. Sixers, game one. Norm Nixon wheels down the right sideline, steps back, and shoots a jump shot over the long outstretched arms of a defender. The ball falls short. But Kareem, on the right block, bats the rebound to the left, where teammate Jamaal Wilkes corrals the loose ball, dribbles, and turns into two defenders. He spots and passes the ball to Kurt Rambis at the free throw line. Two defenders rush to meet Rambis, so he zips the ball to Kareem, who had moved two steps outside of the right block. Another defender slides to stop Kareem but he quickly bounces the ball to Magic standing under the basket, and he finishes with an easy layup before any defender can stop him. The Lakers finish the game with thirty-four assists and went on to win the championship in six games.

The style of the Magic-led Showtime Lakers transcended team loyalties—and has had a lasting cultural impact: it redefined how the pro game should be played, legitimated the contemporary black athlete, and inspired generations of players globally. Showtime, as a style, was not invented by the Lakers and had not been the preferred style of the NBA. The passing game was the modus operandi of black barnstorming teams like the Harlem Globetrotters, who entertained with their skill, synchronization, and pranks. They dribbled and fell to the ground, sliding while maintaining their dribble, passed the ball back and forth between teammates, controlling possession, and hid the ball under their shirts. They ran their opponents ragged and usually scored a lot of points, keeping games close with white home teams, while playing with a smile, to escape possible lynch mobs. The Globetrotters' passing game and panache was clearly recognizable in the Showtime Lakers, and to some fans, who might call themselves purists, the Lakers were not to be taken seriously because they played symbolically "black" basketball—improvisational, fast, athletic, seemingly disorganized and lacking in skill. However, the Lakers' dominance pushed the wide acceptance of black basketball style, legitimizing black culture and the historical black teams of the past at a time when the image of the black male athlete had reached a nadir.

Showtime has been a spark, an event and phenomenon, inspiring many young black Angelenos and others worldwide. Hall of Famers Lisa Leslie and Tina Thompson recognize the effect of the Showtime Lakers on their basketball passion, style, and dreams. "I was a Lakers fan," Leslie claimed proudly, "I watched the Lakers during the Showtime era with Magic Johnson, and anytime Magic needed a basket he would tell you himself that he's going to Big Game James [Worthy]. I wanted to be like him [Worthy], so I would get on the block and make that same kind of baseline spin move."[45] Thompson explained how basketball inspired her and served as an excuse for her to spend time with her brother. "I was a huge Lakers fan of the 80s teams and my older brother played. So more than anything I would say my basketball influence came from admiration of Earvin 'Magic' Johnson, 'Showtime' and wanting to hang out with my older brother."[46] Leslie and Thompson were not the only talented professionals positively affected. Andre Miller, now a sixteen-year veteran, grew up on the fast-paced style and was captured by the joy of team play. "It was fun. It was a fun experience. It was the Lakers era. Everybody wanted to be like the Lakers, just like run-and-gun and have fun when you're kids."[47] Black neighborhoods like Inglewood, where the Forum was located, experienced small changes as scores of kids were drawn away from the allure of gangs and to basketball leagues, recreation centers (like Rogers Park), and the YMCA. Another current player and future Hall of Famer, Paul Pierce, credits Showtime with being his introduction to basketball and his style of play. "That was the beginning for me, watching the Lakers and Celtics battle it out in the Finals . . . I enjoyed it at the time because the Lakers won . . . We played one on one and used to argue about who would be Magic, who would be [Larry] Bird. It would always end with one of us being Magic and the other would be Worthy or Scott."[48] Pierce is a versatile player, able to play guard and forward; his game evolved from imitating how Magic used his body while dribbling to ward off smaller players, James Worthy's fearless attacking on drives and fastbreak finishes, and the shooting touch of Byron Scott. Magic's influence is not limited to stateside; former Laker champion and probable Hall of Famer Pau Gasol has said that Magic was one of his heroes while growing up and playing basketball in Spain. So much so, that Gasol was devastated by Magic's "announcement" (contracting HIV) and planned on becoming a doctor to find a cure for AIDS and save Magic (the assumption at the time was that everyone with HIV would eventually have AIDS).

The influences of Magic and Showtime speak to the power of sport and athletes to inspire others, locally and globally, and to Buss's effective leadership and cross-industry, ingenious business practices. There has only been one Showtime Lakers, but Buss has put together other dynastic Laker teams, which is proof of the powerful, pulling force he helped set in motion. The Lakers have remained true to their culture since Showtime, winning five more championships in bunches and treating Shaquille O'Neal and Kobe Bryant as they did Magic Johnson. They continue to make player moves and coaching changes based on what was thought to be best for their featured star(s): to pay them handsomely—Kobe received an astronomical bonus (a $24.3 million balloon payment in November 2014), garnering mass attention—and have remained loyal to Kobe throughout his ups and downs, on and off the court. In Buss's Hall of Fame enshrinement speech, he expressed gratitude for his players and management and explained succinctly the pulling power of collective action and culture. "So you see, it's really not such a miracle I'm here [in the Hall of Fame]. These men put their hands together, their souls together and brought me with them. And I thank each and every one of you from the bottom of my heart."[49]

CHAPTER ELEVEN

The Golden Games
The 1984 Los Angeles Olympics

MATTHEW P. LLEWELLYN, TOBY C. RIDER,
AND JOHN GLEAVES

The 1984 Los Angeles summer Olympic Games took place at a time when staging the Olympics generated international controversy and condemnation.[1] The fear of debt, infrastructural "white elephants," political boycotts, and terrorist attacks had grown so strong that metropolitan cities around the globe abstained from even bidding to host the Olympic spectacle. The future of the near-hundred-year-old Olympic movement appeared to be in the balance. The rising politics of Third World nationalism, fueling a unified protest against South African and Rhodesian apartheid, precipitated a mass African and Caribbean boycott of the 1976 Montreal Olympics.[2] Amid political turmoil and a diminished roster of participant nations, the Montreal Games recorded substantial financial losses. Cold War nationalism, long a key ingredient in the post–World War II growth and popularity of the Olympic Games, also took a decidedly deleterious turn. In response to the Soviet invasion of Afghanistan, the United States refused to send its athletes to the 1980 Moscow Games to punish the Kremlin's belligerent actions.[3] In the face of these monumental challenges, the Olympics appeared to have lost their luster. Perhaps the clearest signal of the festival's declining image was the number of cities that bid for the 1984 Olympics. There was but one: Los Angeles.[4]

The city of Los Angeles, the capital of the world's popular culture industry, redesigned and revitalized the Olympic movement at a crucial time. Led by the dynamic and sagacious Peter Ueberroth, the Games set new standards in Olympic commercialism, boasting record-breaking television contracts and corporate sponsorship deals. Ueberroth cleverly negotiated licensing deals

More than ninety-two thousand spectators and a worldwide television audience estimated at 2.5 billion watched the Opening Ceremonies at the Los Angeles Memorial Coliseum on July 28. Photo courtesy of LA84 Foundation.

with a limited number of companies such as Coca-Cola, McDonalds, and IBM, granting them exclusive rights in their product categories to market their position as "official" Olympic sponsors.[5] International Olympic Committee (IOC) president Juan Antonio Samaranch would subsequently embrace this model for commercializing the Olympic Games with the "Olympic Partner (TOP) Programme."[6] Despite the absence of the Soviet Union and fourteen of its communist allies, an impressive 6,829 (1,566 women, 5,263 men) athletes from 140 nations, including the People's Republic of China and Romania, arrived in the Golden State to vie for Olympic glory. Millions of spectators attended. Billions watched on television.[7] The 1984 Olympic Games recorded unprecedented profits, establishing a new cultural template that would keep the Olympics relevant in the twenty-first century.[8]

Despite its financial and organizational success, the 1984 Los Angeles Olympics also proved to be both provocative and polarizing. Some scholarly critics have repudiated the Games as a manifestation of commercial excess and a platform for Western political and cultural propaganda.[9] Others have castigated the Games for encouraging a culture of greed and corruption within the

Olympic movement.[10] One cannot deny the wave of heightened commercialism that followed in the wake of the 1984 Los Angeles Olympics, and the fact that the festival further diverged from the idealistic vision of IOC presidents such as Pierre de Coubertin and Avery Brundage.

The Eternal Bid

The city of Los Angeles's connection with the Olympic movement is both rich and historical. The relationship began in the summer of 1932, when a team of local businessmen and civic boosters led by William May Garland (who also served as an IOC member from 1922 to 1948), succeeded in bringing the Olympic spectacle to Southern California. Garland, one of the state's biggest land speculators and two-term president of the National Association of Realtors, spearheaded Los Angeles's drive to host the Olympic Games. Highlighting the promise of a superior climate and scenery as well as the construction of a huge one-hundred-thousand-person capacity stadium, Garland and his colleagues convinced the European princes, counts, barons, generals, and wealthy businessmen that comprised the IOC membership to award the 1932 Olympics to Los Angeles, a city which at that time was a largely unknown outpost of America's western frontier.[11]

For Garland, hosting the Olympics seemed to be an ideal way to advertise Los Angeles to the rest of the world. Fueled by a boom in real estate and petroleum, as well as the birth of the movie and entertainment industries, the city had undergone rapid growth during the early decades of the twentieth century, climbing from thirty-sixth to fifth place on the nation's list of largest urban areas.[12] In Garland's estimations, the soil was fertile for further growth. When earlier efforts to win the bid to host the 1924 and 1928 Olympic Games failed, a resolute Garland successfully turned his attentions toward 1932. Along with his team of entrepreneurs, business moguls, and property developers, Garland calculated that the Olympic Games would bring international visibility, recognition, and trade to Los Angeles. They packaged the allure of Hollywood, along with the grand—albeit inaccurate—vision that Los Angeles was a dazzling democracy, unfettered by the stain of ethnic and racial division.[13]

Against the backdrop of the Wall Street Crash, a global economic crisis that mercilessly drove financial systems to their knees and sparked surging rates of inflation and unemployment, the 1932 Los Angeles Games proved a remarkable and unprecedented triumph. Connecting the Games with the glamour and stardom of Hollywood, as well as harnessing their full commercial potential as an attractive commodity, the Los Angeles organizers provided the blueprint for transforming the Olympics from "a relatively marginal and elitist event" into one of the world's most important entertainment extravaganzas.[14] Print, radio, and newsreel media chronicled Olympic feats, and silver screen celebrities and studio moguls flocked to Olympic events. Metro-Goldwyn Mayer's (MGM) Louis B. Mayer even agreed to serve on the Olympic Organizing Committee. As a sign of the inextricable bond that would grow to exist between the Olympic Games, commerce, and corporate marketing, US companies such as Coca-Cola, Kellogg's, and Helms Bakery avariciously engineered ways to exploit the Olympic brand.[15]

The 1932 Los Angeles organizers also set new standards in event management by perfecting the modern bid process, boasting an impressive array of sporting infrastructures, including the recently constructed Los Angeles Coliseum. The Games were the first to celebrate the achievements of Olympic medalists in a formal victory ceremony, while male athletes were housed for the first time in an Olympic village, located in Baldwin Hills at the end of West Vernon Place and west of Crenshaw Boulevard.[16] Drawing upon the organizational, salesmanship, and promotional skills that had made the United States the world leader in mass culture, and Los Angeles one of the world's fastest-growing cities, the 1932 Olympics overcame the gloom of a global depression to achieve economic solvency, recording a surplus of $1.5 million and, more importantly, ensuring the future stability of the Olympic movement.[17] Such was the scale of precision, organization, publicity, and spectacle that German Olympic officials used the 1932 Los Angeles Games as a template for staging the infamous "Nazi Olympics" four years later.[18]

The 1932 Olympics propelled Los Angeles to the forefront of the world's imagination. The Games created an image of Los Angeles as a vibrant, modern metropolis. In the years following the Olympics, the city became synonymous with sport and entertainment, fitness and fashion. Even the palm tree, an icon of California and Californian lifestyle, owes its iconic status to the Olympics. In the build-up to the 1932 Games, organizers persuaded the city to spend more than $100,000 of the Olympic budget to plant thirty thousand palms in an effort to spruce up the city's drab urban sprawl.[19] The Olympic Games helped to define both California and the Californian lifestyle for future generations of global visitors and consumers. Los Angeles became "*the* Olympic city."[20] To all but the most pessimistic observer, the Games were an unprecedented triumph. Local journalist Bill Wise waxed jubilant, labeling the 1932 Olympics as the "most successful—the most memorable—in the history of this honorable sports tradition reaching back, deep into the archives of mythology."[21]

Exhilarated by the success of the 1932 Olympics, city planners immediately embarked on a fifty-year "odyssey" to bring the Games back to Los Angeles.[22] Under the leadership of William May Garland, and later his son, John Jewett Garland, civic boosters formed the Southern California Committee for the Olympic Games (SCCOG) and tasked the nascent body with producing, promoting, and advancing "knowledge and appreciation of the noble, chivalric, patriotic, educational and social character of the International Olympic movement and ideals as practiced in the quadrennial Olympic Games."[23] More specifically, the SCCOG committed itself to returning the Games to Los Angeles. From its inception in 1939, the SCCOG bid for every single summer Olympic Games. In fact, no city has bid more frequently or more furiously for the right to host the Olympics.[24]

Year after year the SCCOG implored the IOC to return the festival to Southern California. Yet for over four decades their impassioned pleas went unanswered as the summer Olympics headed to Helsinki (1952), Melbourne (1956), Rome (1960), Tokyo (1964), Mexico City (1968), Munich (1972), Montreal (1976) and Moscow (1980). Winning was a two-step process. First, the SCCOG had to convince the United States Olympic Committee (USOC) to select Los Angeles as the country's candidate city. Second, Los Angeles had to make a successful presentation to the IOC. Throughout the bid wars of the '50s, '60s, and '70s, Los Angeles was not even the USOC's first choice; Detroit, the car manufacturing capital of the United States, consistently secured the vote over the Southern Californian metropolis.[25] Even when Los Angeles did finally vanquish Detroit to win the USOC's backing for the 1976 Games, the IOC opted for Montreal instead. Internal bickering between the SCCOG and the newly established "Los Angeles 1976 Olympic Committee," formed at the behest of then Los Angeles mayor Sam Yorty, scuttled the city's Olympic ambitions. This pattern of disappointment was again repeated in 1980 when, despite narrowly beating New York to secure the USOC's nomination, Los Angeles watched as the IOC awarded the Games to Moscow.[26]

Undaunted by losing bid after bid, the leaders of the SCCOG held steadfast to their dream of returning Pierre de Coubertin's Olympian festival back to Southern California. On May 18, 1978, the dream was finally realized. At its eightieth session in Athens, Greece, the IOC awarded the Games of the XXIII

Olympiad to Los Angeles.[27] The successful bid for the 1984 Olympics was a cooperative effort between the SCCOG (headed by Los Angeles attorney John Argue), Mayor Tom Bradley, and the city of Los Angeles, as well as a host of private financial backers. Despite fierce criticism of the SCCOG's proposed use of existing facilities and a heavy reliance on corporate sponsorships, the path to securing the IOC's vote proved easy: the Iranian capitol, Teheran, was the only other city to mount a bid effort, but withdrew from the race as the nation descended into revolution. The Olympic Games, swaddled by political and economic controversies, were finally returning back to the "City of Angels."

Building the Games

With the right to host confirmed, citizens of Los Angeles expressed nervousness over the cost of organizing the Games. The economic calamity of Montreal loomed large in the public consciousness. On November 15, 1977, Baxter Ward, a Los Angeles county supervisor, proposed that residents should "decide whether or not to ban the use of county funds" to finance the Games.[28] The Los Angeles City Council proposed a more far-reaching referendum: "whether the city should be prohibited from hosting the Olympics at all."[29] Against the backdrop of growing public cynicism, Los Angeles mayor Tom Bradley entered the fray. With the support of his fellow Angelenos, Bradley insisted that the city of Los Angeles would not assume any financial liability for the Games. Since the IOC stipulated in Rule 4 of the *Olympic Charter* that the host city must bear the full financial responsibility for hosting the Games, Mayor Bradley recommended that his city's bid be withdrawn.[30] SCCOG chief and Los Angeles attorney, John Argue, took an equally assertive tone, affirming that Los Angeles would "rather lose the Olympics than go forward on the wrong foot."[31] After fifty years of lobbying to return the Olympics to Los Angeles, the city's efforts to host the 1984 Games immediately looked in trouble.

Fearing that the Olympic Games would be thrown into even deeper turmoil should Los Angeles officially retract its bid, the IOC altered its sacred *Olympic Charter*. Without a viable alternative should Mayor Bradley and the city of Los Angeles withdraw, the IOC agreed to a plan whereby the privately financed Los Angeles Olympic Organizing Committee (LAOOC), along with the USOC, would assume full financial responsibility for the Games. "Under the contract that has now been drawn, the city is absolved of liability," the then president of the IOC Lord Killanin assured.[32] Rejecting the flurry of gloomy economic forecasts, William Simon, the treasurer of the USOC, declared that the 1984 Los Angeles Games would even turn a healthy profit. Simon revealed the blueprints to the city's thrifty organizational model, one that favored the refurbishment and use of preexisting facilities and venues. "It will not become another Montreal," he vowed.[33]

After taking on a significant financial risk, the newly created LAOOC made a surprising second step by appointing Peter Ueberroth, a relatively unknown but successful business mogul, to be its president. Ueberroth, a graduate of San Jose State University and former collegiate water polo player, had accumulated his fortune by developing his company, First Travel, into the nation's largest travel agency.[34] Through his entrepreneurial spirit, business acumen, and international negotiating ability, Ueberroth remained a central figure throughout the planning and organizing of the Games.[35] David Wolper, a member of the LAOOC search committee, believed Ueberroth's mixture of athletic talent (Ueberroth had tried out for the 1956 US Olympic water polo team) and experience with global commerce made him the right person for the task.[36]

Ueberroth, along with his right-hand man, the LAOOC vice president and executive director, Harry Usher, are widely credited with creating many strategies that limited costs and maximized revenue. Collectively, Ueberroth and Usher would leave an indelible mark on the planning and organization of the event. Under their skillful guidance, the LAOOC staff swelled from an initial eleven members to over twelve thousand paid employees.[37]

Many of the challenges Ueberroth and Usher faced stemmed from a lack of state and public funds. As a result, the LAOOC had to explore new ways to cut costs while creating revenue. To reduce expenditures, Ueberroth and the LAOOC board prioritized the use of existing sports facilities rather than building new ones from scratch. They refurbished the Los Angeles Memorial Coliseum, which was the host site for the 1932 Los Angeles Games. This would be the first time that a single stadium had ever hosted two Olympic Games. In fact, of the twenty-nine Olympic venues, only three new venues were built specifically for the Games, all of which received corporate sponsorship (the "7-Eleven" velodrome, the "McDonald's" swim stadium, and the "Fuji" shooting range). The LAOOC's usage of refurbished as opposed to new athletic facilities proved a financial masterstroke. Total construction costs for the 1984 Games were $92,973,000 compared to the staggering $1,708,596,472 spent by Soviet organizers for the 1980 Moscow Olympics.[38] The refurbished LA Olympic venues, decorated in an eye-popping collage of pastel colors and unusual geometric shapes (a design scheme known as "Festive Federalism," or the "Look"), gained widespread international applause.[39]

Relying on existing infrastructure helped spread the Olympic events to host communities throughout Los Angeles and its surrounding areas. The geographic scope of the 1984 Games was enormous. Cities such as Long Beach (volleyball and archery), Arcadia (equestrian), Fullerton (team handball), and Anaheim (wrestling) hosted multiple events. There were also three Olympic villages. Given Ueberroth's and the LAOOC's desire to eschew the construction of expensive accommodations for athletes, the University of California at Los Angeles, the University of Southern California, and the University of California, Santa Barbara, served as low-cost alternatives. In total, the Games encompassed approximately forty-five hundred square miles of Southern California.[40] The broad distribution of the Games helped immerse locals, some of whom were skeptical about using public funds for the events in the first place, in the Olympic experience.

Selling the Games

The 1984 Los Angeles Games have become widely remembered for the innovative (and some would say undesirable) developments in commercializing the Olympic Games.[41] The irony that the "unwanted" 1984 Games would appeal to commercial interests highlights international sport's changing landscape. It was no longer the "amateur" affair it had been when the Games first visited LA in 1932, but it was still far from the contemporary mega-event that Olympic festivals have become in the twenty-first century. In large part, Peter Ueberroth's ingenuity and financial savvy helped illustrate what the Olympics could become at a time when others failed to see its potential. Without state or public financial backing, Ueberroth had to effectively manage costs while finding new revenue streams. He identified the sale of television broadcasting rights to the Games as a source of considerable income. He entered into prolonged negotiations with rival US television networks, the American Broadcasting Company (ABC), the National Broadcasting Company (NBC), and the Colombia Broadcasting System (CBS), who each placed a $500,000 deposit just to negotiate. Being an astute businessman, he then shrewdly used the interest on the deposits to generate early capital to fund the fledgling venture. ABC ultimately won the broadcasting rights with an eye-popping $225 million bid, an amount that dwarfed the previous fee the company had paid for the 1976 Montreal Games.

After negotiating a far less lucrative deal with the European Broadcasting Union, the LAOOC's coffers were overflowing with $286.9 million in total television revenue. Though IOC president Samaranch was upset over Ueberroth's aggressive corporate tactics, his movement's $33 million share of the television revenue placated his dissent.[42]

This would not be the only time Ueberroth introduced new methods for increasing revenue. When it came to securing corporate sponsorship, he devised a "less is more" approach. His plan to limit the number of licensed corporate sponsors was a bold move. Previous Olympic Organizing Committees had offered licensing rights to as many parties as would pay, sometimes simply in exchange for free goods.[43] For example, the financially disastrous 1976 Montreal Games had over six hundred sponsors and netted only $5 million. With widespread licensing, sponsors received little return on investment and thus were willing to pay very little for the rights. Ueberroth realized that exclusivity could ultimately command more money from sponsors. His intuition proved accurate. Thirty-five commercial sponsors, sixty-four commercial suppliers, and sixty-five licenses paid a combined $157.2 million for exclusive rights to the 1984 Los Angeles Games.[44]

The IOC remained apprehensive over these tactics. Ueberroth, ironically, defended his approach as a way "to stop the proliferation of commercialization" at the Olympic Games.[45] Ueberroth's claim that his licensing plan would reduce commercialism appealed to the IOC members, many of whom had long felt that the wave of Olympic-branded trinkets and products diluted the Olympic movement's gravitas. However, what those sitting opposite Ueberroth failed to consider was what sponsors who were paying upward of $13 million for the licensing rights would do to receive a return on their investment.[46] By the Games' conclusion, the Coca-Cola and McDonald's-laden Olympic village would leave many feeling that the 1984 Summer Olympics had been by far the most corporate Games in Olympic history.[47]

Nevertheless, most of the exclusive sponsors reported positive benefits from their association with the Los Angeles Olympics. The Games provided global exposure and enhanced brand recognition. Some, like the official shoe supplier Converse, did not find their sponsorship paid off. In part, Converse was a victim of clever "ambush" marketing by Nike, the Oregon-based athletic shoe company. For their 1984 Olympic ad campaign, Nike turned to Chiat/Day, a Los Angeles–based advertising firm to launch a minute-long commercial that would make a big splash.[48] Set to Randy Newman's song "I Love

LA" the commercial featured Olympic athletes running and jumping around Los Angeles's landmarks. The advertisement ended with the vague tagline "Nike: This Summer." Nike's advertisement, along with its stable of medal-winning sponsored athletes, led most people to assume that Nike, as opposed to Converse, was the official shoe sponsor of the Olympic Games.[49]

Nike was not the only ones who found the 1984 Games massively profitable. The Olympics generated $768,644,000 in revenue for the LAOOC through corporate sponsorship, television broadcasting rights, tickets sales, as well as the sale of commemorative Olympic coins.[50] A 1986 report published by the Chicago-based firm, Economic Research Associates, estimated that the Olympics also brought $2.4 billion into the Southern Californian economy.[51] Ueberroth and the LAOOC's decision to use preexisting facilities, maximize revenue from television rights negotiations, and implement an exclusive corporate sponsorship program established the Olympic movement as not only economically viable, but financially lucrative. Though many decried the commercialism, Samaranch adopted Ueberroth's model of exclusive sponsors and created "The Olympic Partner (TOP) Programme." Instead of allowing organizing committees to negotiate on licensing, the IOC would now select the exclusive group of corporate sponsors and also receive a larger cut of the profits.

The Boycott Wars

While the 1984 Los Angeles Games were undeniably a commercial and financial triumph, Ueberroth and his colleagues had rather less success in the realm of international diplomacy. Indeed, one of the dominating historical narratives of the 1984 summer Olympics is the Soviet Union's decision not to attend them. The Soviet blow was struck on May 8, only three months before the opening ceremonies. "When the announcement came, it was sudden, unexpected, devastating," wrote journalist Kenneth Reich in *Sports Illustrated* magazine.[52] Why, then, had the Soviets reneged on their invitation to Los Angeles? At the time, most Americans had the same answer. They thought the Soviets were simply retaliating for the US boycott of the Moscow Games four years earlier. Professional historians, in lieu of any better explanation and without access to key documents in the Kremlin's archives, have tended to reach the same conclusion.[53]

Whether or not the Soviets would send a team to California was a question that had "loomed over the Olympic movement" ever since US president Jimmy

Carter pressured the USOC—not to mention a host of other countries—into withdrawing its athletes from the Moscow summer Games to punish the Soviet Union for invading Afghanistan in 1979.[54] Fearing a similar outcome, the LAOOC worked hard to avert another mass boycott, with Ueberroth admitting that if the Soviets "didn't come it would make the Games smaller and lessen their importance."[55] Moscow officials, for their part, made it clear that Soviet participation in 1984 hinged upon the US government fulfilling certain demands—including the docking of Soviet ships in Long Beach, the landing of Soviet chartered flights in the United States, and relaxed entry procedures for Soviet athletes and tourists. Yet accepting these demands was made all the more difficult for the Reagan administration after the Soviets shot down a Korean Airlines flight full of American passengers in September 1983, an act the president condemned as "murder." But Reagan, keen to ensure that the country he termed an "evil empire" attended this "special event," instructed a hesitant State Department to cater to the Soviet requests.[56] Although the Soviet media grumbled about the smog in Los Angeles and the rampant commercialism of the Games, and although Soviet Olympic officials justifiably complained about foot-dragging in the State Department, the portents for Soviet participation were still promising as the Olympic year commenced.[57] Many Americans clearly believed the Soviets were still coming. After all, they would not have been so stunned by the boycott if they did not think Soviet attendance in Los Angeles was a distinct possibility.

If the retaliation thesis appears flawed, then what could have caused the Soviets to boycott? Recent scholarship has argued that the decisive challenge to Soviet participation emerged in the form of an innocuous group named the Ban the Soviets Coalition.[58] Started by a bombastic advertising executive named David Balsiger in the aftermath of the Korean Airlines incident, the coalition included in its ranks Eastern European exiles, evangelical Christians, and right wing political activists. This fringe anticommunist group embarked on a resolute mission to stop the Soviets from boarding a plane to California and, if the strategy were to fail, they planned to unsettle and criticize the Soviet team when they reached Los Angeles, and even encourage defections. Clearly unimpressed with the aims of this organization, Ueberroth labeled its participants as "nutty." The Soviets, though, reached a more sinister conclusion. They incorrectly assessed that the group was working in concert with the Reagan administration and that the safety of Soviet athletes could be legitimately compromised. In a statement issued by the Soviet National Olympic Committee on

April 9, Soviet sports officials denounced the "large scale" anti-Soviet campaign in the United States led by various "reactionary political, émigré and religious groupings." More still, the statement charged, this "provocative" campaign had threatened "physical victimization" and made "slanderous allegations" against the USSR and other socialist countries. To his own great surprise and satisfaction, Balsiger had created the impression that the coalition had power and popular support when, in reality, it had neither.[59]

To calm the situation, Samaranch called Soviet and US Olympic officials to the IOC headquarters in Lausanne for an emergency meeting in late April.[60] By all accounts, the gathering was positive and productive. On May 8, 1984, however, the Soviet National Olympic Committee formally announced its decision to boycott the Los Angeles Games. "To act differently," Soviet officials reasoned, "would be tantamount to approving of the anti-Olympian actions of the U.S. authorities and organizers of the Games."[61] Although the Kremlin justified its actions by citing security concerns and the activities of the Ban the Soviets, Western observers retorted that the United States had striven to guarantee the safety of *all* foreign athletes. "The conscious of the United States is clear," said a spokesperson for the State Department. "We have nothing to apologize for."[62] Shocked by the turn of events, representatives of the LAOOC immediately dismissed the Soviet Union's excuses. Yet what Americans believed to be true was irrelevant. In Moscow, they judged the threat to be both immediate and real.[63]

As had been the case for the United States in 1980, the Soviets did not make their stand in isolation. The Kremlin's communist allies in Bulgaria, East Germany, Mongolia, Vietnam, Laos, and Czechoslovakia all fell in line with the boycott. In the coming weeks and months, Afghanistan, Hungary, Poland, Cuba, South Yemen, North Korea, Ethiopia, and Angola pledged their support for the Soviet cause by declining invitations to compete at the Los Angeles Games. For alternative political or financial reasons, Iran, Libya, and Albania also opted not to compete in the Golden State. On May 12, 1984, the LAOOC received more favorable news: the People's Republic of China announced that it would send a team. Several days later Romania, another close communist ally of the USSR, also defied the boycott and began preparing its team for Los Angeles. To avert another potential crisis, the Reagan administration used a persuasive propaganda campaign to urge African and Asian national Olympic committees to send teams to the Games after the Soviet Union had anonymously sent them fake Ku Klux Klan leaflets.[64] Thanks to a twenty-four-hour phone bank to call and persuade national Olympic committees and foreign embassies to agree to officially compete, a record number of 140 nations still took part in the Games; 15 (including the USSR) chose to boycott.[65] Ueberroth was deeply relieved by the strong international participation in Los Angeles. The Soviets "have failed miserably, and they've been given a kick in the backside," he remarked defiantly.[66] Regardless, the standard of competition at the Games was patently weaker.

The Golden Games

For all its controversy, the 1984 Los Angeles Games still provided many memorable sporting moments. The Games officially opened on July 28, 1984, before a capacity crowd of 92,655 at the Los Angeles Memorial Coliseum—a further 2.5 billion viewers watched the event via a live global telecast.[67] Over the next sixteen days of competition, the Los Angeles Games set new standards in sporting excellence. Although any athlete who earns a medal at an Olympic event deserves a hero's recognition, many special performances emerged in Los Angeles. The US sprinter Carl Lewis equaled the record-setting performance of his compatriot, Jesse Owens, by winning four gold medals in the same events (the 100-meter dash, 200-meter dash, 4x100-meter relay, and the long jump). His fellow countryman, Edwin Moses, won his second career Olympic gold medal in the 400-meter hurdles and extended his remarkable winning streak—which would eventually last nine years, nine months, and nine days. Most notably, Chinese gymnast Li Ning was the only athlete of the Games to win six medals.[68]

An incident in the 3000-meter final involving two of the world's premier sportswomen, American Mary Decker (Slaney) and South African–born British teenager Zola Budd, provided the most climatic moment of the Games. In a much anticipated race, the home crowd favorite Decker inadvertently stepped on Budd's left foot, then, shortly after, collided with the British runner again before falling to the curb. Decker lay in anguish on the track, unable to recover from a fall that *Sports Illustrated* described as a "riveting image of Olympic disaster."[69] Budd, who had kept her feet, maintained the lead and increased the pace. But the shy ninety-two-pound teenager, who had only months prior to the 1984 Games circumvented the IOC's expulsion of apartheid South Africa by controversially claiming British citizenship, became the choice target of the partisan Los Angeles crowd.[70] The abuse eventually took its toll. With tears streaming down her face, Budd watched on as Romania's Maricica Puică stormed to the gold medal. Briton's Wendy Sly and Canada's Lynn Williams claimed the silver and bronze medals, respectively. A distraught Budd labored home in seventh place.

Away from the tension-filled Coliseum, the other Olympic sports proved less controversial. Many teams put forward notable performances. Led by future NBA hall of famers Michael Jordan, Patrick Ewing, and Chris Mullin, the USA won the gold medal in basketball. France defeated Brazil to win the Olympic soccer championship in front of a crowd exceeding one hundred thousand people. In fact, the level of support shown to soccer in the United States would pave the way for the US to host the 1994 FIFA World Cup. However, the conspicuous absence of the Soviet bloc teams left its mark on the Games, particularly in the weightlifting events. With the boycott, ninety-four of the world's top-100 ranked lifters were absent along with twenty-nine of the thirty medalists from the recent World Championships. In fact, all ten of the defending World Champions in the ten weight categories boycotted the Games. Although many of the weightlifting medals went to China, this boycott also affected other events. The chief beneficiary appeared to be the United States. The "hometown" team dominated other events that the Soviet bloc countries typically controlled. The US team won nine of the twelve boxing championships, and their men's cycling team won seven medals, including three gold medals, in a sport they had not medaled in since the 1912 Stockholm Games. The US men's gymnastics team won the team gold as well.

The US team not only dominated in the Olympic stadiums and arenas (topping the final medal standings with 174 medals, 115 more medals than their nearest rival, West Germany), but also off it: US sportsmen and sportswomen accounted for 44.7 percent of ABC's total television coverage of the Games. The clear pro-American bias of ABC's television coverage infuriated some foreign athletes, who lodged complaints over the repetitive sight of seeing US Olympians on the television screens within the Olympic village.[71]

Olympic Firsts

Without question, the 1984 Los Angeles Olympics provided many watershed moments in sport history. Most notably, the Games represented an important step on the long path toward female equality in sport. Although the marathon event was introduced in the first modern Olympic Games in Athens in 1896, it was not until 1984 that the IOC included a women's event. It took the efforts of commercial sponsors, the popular media, and a cadre of elite-level female marathoners to accomplish this milestone. The winner of the inaugural women's marathon was Joan Benoit of the United States. Her time of 2:48:45 would have bested the 1952 Olympic champion, Emil Zatopek, and all of the fastest men's times before that. Dramatic images of the event spread around the world when Benoit entered into the Coliseum, her body seemingly invigorated by the wild celebrations of the partisan Los Angeles crowd. Benoit, the eventual gold medalist, cut a stark contrast to the figure of Swiss runner Gabi Andersen-Schiess, who suffered heat exhaustion and stumbled through the last lap of the race. Doctors supervised her as she took nearly six minutes to complete the final lap of the Los Angeles Coliseum, before collapsing after the finish line.[72]

Along with a marathon event, it was a festival of many firsts for women. The Moroccan runner Nawal El Moutawakel became the first female of an Islamic nation—as well as the first Moroccan of either gender—to become an Olympic champion following her victory in the 400-meter hurdles. The female archer, Neroli Fairhall, became the first paraplegic to compete at any Olympic Games since US gymnast George Eyser competed successfully (winning three gold, two silver, and one bronze) at the 1904 St. Louis Games. The American gymnast Mary Lou Retton became the first female outside of Eastern Europe to win the individual all-around competition in gymnastics.

The 1984 Los Angeles Games awarded a spot on the Olympic program to synchronized swimming and windsurfing. Tennis, after a self-imposed exile dating back to the 1924 Paris Games, reappeared on the Olympic program—albeit as a demonstration sport. With Wimbledon and a host of other tournaments around the world, tennis boasted a successful brand that reached an international audience. From its position of prosperity, the International Tennis Federation insisted that the sport would return to the Olympic Games but only on the condition that "professionals" under the age of twenty were granted permission to compete. The IOC faced a philosophical dilemma. Would it continue to insist that the Olympic Games remain open only to "amateur" athletes, or would it make a concession? Ultimately, the lure of television and commercial revenue, as well as a growing desire to ensure that the best possible athletes compete (professional or otherwise), proved too tempting for IOC president Samaranch.[73] Despite concerns about the dangerous precedent of having a demonstration sport with open professionals, tennis returned to the Olympic program in Los Angeles.[74] This return permitted a young West

German teenager named Steffi Graf to achieve the first of many international victories as she won the women's singles event.

The IOC's concession for tennis, as well as its tacit acceptance of professional footballers and ice hockey players, pushed the IOC further toward an "open" Olympics.[75] With its financial coffers now overflowing from record-breaking television contracts and commercial branding, the IOC took further steps to reform "Rule 26" of the *Olympic Charter* concerning amateurism. At the 1987 IOC session in Istanbul, Olympic officials approved a full-medal, professional tennis tournament for the 1988 Seoul Games.[76] The decision to sanction professional tennis players marked the point of no return. In 1990, with tennis having set a successful precedent, the IOC undertook a massive revision of the *Olympic Charter* that ensured professional athletes could, at the decision of their international federation, participate in the Olympic Games. This revised Eligibility Code published in the 1991 *Olympic Charter* marked the end of amateurism as a requirement for an athlete's Olympic eligibility.[77]

The Los Angeles Games also ushered in a new era in US doping history. When Los Angeles received the award for the 1984 Games, the United States had no anti-doping laboratory for running tests on athletes' samples. The high cost of establishing a satisfactory laboratory that could handle the ever-expanding number of athletes, as well as the growing number of substances on the banned list, did not sit well with Ueberroth.[78] His desire to keep costs low meant that he constantly resisted the IOC's desire for expensive testing, especially for the two new substances added to the prohibited substance list for the 1984 Games: synthetic testosterone and caffeine.[79] To solve the problem, Prince Alexandre de Mérode, chair of the IOC Medical Commission, collaborated with Don Catlin, a medical doctor working at the University of California, Los Angeles, to establish the UCLA Olympic Analytical Laboratory in 1982.[80] Although the LAOOC initially objected to the UCLA lab, Catlin's facility eventually oversaw the drug testing for the 1984 Olympic Games. It also made major discoveries in drug testing, most notably the designer anabolic steroid behind the infamous BALCO scandal that later engulfed prominent US athletes Marion Jones and Barry Bonds.[81]

Despite adding caffeine and testosterone to the banned substance list, the IOC failed to include a substance that caused the biggest scandal at the 1984 Olympics. Shortly after the Games, international headlines revealed that roughly half of the US Olympic cycling team had used blood transfusions on their way to winning nine medals. This relatively unknown practice sparked widespread condemnation. USOC team coaches Ed Burke and Eddie Borysewicz both received suspensions, but the IOC conceded the cyclists had not broken any rules. Shortly after the conclusion of the 1984 Games, the IOC Medical Commission banned blood transfusions even though no test existed that could detect the practice.[82]

Olympic Legacies

After sixteen days of enthralling competition, the 1984 Los Angeles Games officially closed on August 12. Aside from the anticapitalist groans of the Soviet Union and its communist allies, the Games were universally heralded as an astounding success. After a decade of political and economic turmoil, the Los Angeles Games restored a sense of legitimacy to the Olympic movement. Boasting a windfall surplus estimated at $223.5 million, the 1984 Games changed perceptions about the value of hosting the Games.

The "Ueberroth Effect" transformed the sputtering Olympic spectacle into an attractive global commodity once again. The post-1984 rise of exclusive corporate sponsorships, expanding television revenue, and the participation of professional athletes rejuvenated the desire of major global cities to host the Olympic spectacle—six cities, including the eventual host Seoul, presented bids for the 1988 Games.[83] As scholars have observed, however, the post-1984 commercial and financial orientation of the Olympic movement under Samaranch's leadership produced a culture of greed and corruption. Lured by the dream of financial success, bid cities—via their army of highly paid lobbyists—employed ethically suspect and even illegal tactics in their desire to win votes and secure the rights to host the Olympic Games. The 2002 Salt Lake City bidding scandal was perhaps the high-water mark of this rotten bidding culture.[84]

Other legacies of the 1984 Los Angeles Games are more favorable but less well known. Southern California's share of the considerable post-Olympics surplus led to the endowment of the LA84 Foundation (formerly the Los Angeles Olympic Committee Amateur Athletics Foundation and later, the Amateur Athletic Foundation of Los Angeles). In the past three decades following the 1984 Games, the LA84 Foundation has funded both the construction or improvement of nearly one hundred sport facilities (serving over five hundred thousand young people annually) and programmatic grants serving over three million youths of Southern California.[85]

The ghost of Los Angeles continues to influence the Olympic movement even three decades after the close of the 1984 Games. The city's continued projection of itself as a young, vibrant, celebrity-fueled mecca for health and fitness conscious global consumers has provided the cultural template for the Olympic movement well into the twenty-first century. Southern California–styled "action" and "extreme" lifestyle sports such as beach volleyball, snowboarding, and BMX cycling have recently become popular commodities at the Olympics. This "Californization" of the Olympic Games signals the IOC's desire to promote a telegenic spectacle that showcases youth, health, beauty, and sporting excellence. The city of Los Angeles, the central incubator of this brand of "California cool," has become inextricably linked with the Olympic movement.[86] Los Angeles's globally appealing lifestyle, coupled with its successful hosting of the Games in both 1932 and 1984, has made the city a forerunner to stage the Olympic festival again in the near future.

CHAPTER TWELVE

Shaping the Boom
Los Angeles Surfing from George Freeth to Gidget

TOLGA OZYURTCU

Sprawling and geographically ill defined, ignoring distinctions of urban and suburban, Los Angeles is the city transformed. It is also the city of transformation: where midwestern hitchhikers become Hollywood stars, where the body you are born with is just a starting point. The effect is not limited to individual change, but historically extends to cultural movements, the city serving as a site of transition from "before" to "after," a place where existing ideas are reconfigured, reimagined, and relaunched into the broader cultural consciousness. In early twentieth-century Los Angeles, entertainment became the entertainment industry; at midcentury, Angelenos at Muscle Beach turned physical fitness from a fringe pursuit into a global obsession.

While the buff denizens of Muscle Beach were reinventing physical culture on the sand, another Los Angeles transformation emerged out of the waves of the Pacific. Surfing was thousands of years old by the time the sport arrived in Los Angeles in 1907, but by the 1950s it was abundantly clear that the city could lay claim to another seismic transformation. Los Angeles shaped surfing throughout the twentieth century, but the city's major impact on the sport came in the aftermath of World War II. Beginning in the late 1940s, Los Angeles surfers revolutionized the sport; over the course of a decade, they reimagined the surfboard itself, created an industry, and laid the ideological blueprint for the surfer's lifestyle. By 1959, the emergent subculture of surfing would intersect with Hollywood and become a cultural phenomenon known as the "surf boom," rendering the surfer a permanent symbol of Los Angeles and Southern California in the popular imagination.

In the ever-growing annals of surfing, considerable attention has been paid to the historical significance of the sport in Los Angeles. The dean of surf historians, Matt Warshaw, argues that by the early twentieth century

> Los Angeles had become an ideal place for the new and offbeat. In terms of surfing basics, it had sunny weather, beautiful beaches, tolerably warm water for most of the year, and consistent waves. Just as important, Los Angeles would try anything; it inhaled people, and exhaled ideas and trends ... by the 1930s, Southern California was uniquely qualified to begin reinventing the sport.[1]

In *Sweetness and Blood*, Michael Scott Moore writes, "Like African music that crossed in ships to America and became the blues, and then jazz, and then rock, surfing would merge with the American landscape and become something new."[2] In this and other volumes, the rich story of Los Angeles surfing has been capably told and rightfully situated in the broader context of the sport's global history.[3] Given this body of literature and the scope of this collection, this chapter provides an overview of how Los Angeles transformed surfing and set the stage for the surf boom. Focusing on the major surfing developments produced by Los Angeles and its surfers between 1907 and 1959, it is part assessment and introduction.[4]

While the surf boom itself is a story for another day, I make reference to its eventuality throughout the chapter, so a few words on the subject are appropriate. The consensus among surf historians is that the boom began in 1959 with the release of Columbia Pictures' *Gidget*, the first Hollywood surf film. Ben Marcus summarizes this view: "Blame it on Gidget. In real life, she was just a perky and pertinacious California teen obsessed with surfing. But when her story was told by her father in the 1957 novel *Gidget* and then made into a 1959 movie starring Sandra Dee, the whole country went crazy for surfing."[5] The success of *Gidget* kicked off the brief, but prolific era of "Beach Party" films that turned California teenagers into a globally recognized symbol of a modern "good life." Cinematically unambitious, but financially successful, the films were campy, goofy affairs—teenage melodramas at the beach. Tony Lisanti writes in his history of Hollywood surf and beach cinema, "Surfers loathed them, teenagers flocked to them, critics dismissed them, and producers laughed all the way to the bank."[6] The boom also played out on vinyl and over the airwaves, most famously in the early songs of the Beach Boys. The Beach Boys did not actually surf very much, but their lyrics propelled surf lingo and geography into the American lexicon; clad in woolen Pendleton shirts lifted off the backs of LA surfers, their look was imitated by teenagers nationwide.[7] Other acts followed, like Beach Boys affiliates Jan & Dean, who achieved chart success singing about surf- and beach-related themes. Hardcore surfers dismissed the poppy Beach Boys and their ilk as posers, preferring the aggressive, instrumental variant of surf music perfected by Los Angeles surfer and guitarist Dick Dale. The instrumental style also enjoyed some mainstream success, with now-legendary groups like the Ventures, Surfaris, and the Champs recording hits like, "Walk Don't Run," "Wipe Out," and "Tequila." The producers of all manner of consumer goods responded to the success of surf- and beach-inspired movies and music, latching on to the craze and imbuing everything from automobiles and clothing to toys and housewares with a distinctly California-via-Hollywood aesthetic. Skateboarding, surfing's terrestrial stepchild, was born during the boom and quickly became a national fad.[8] Given the ongoing legacy of these various strains of boom culture, it is important to note that the boom unfolded within the surfing world as well. As demand for surf equipment and paraphernalia accelerated, it turned surf businesses into the surf industry, from a tiny network of specialist shops into proper manufacturing concerns. The rise in business supported the emergence of sponsored professional surfers, a dedicated surf media, and a broad range of technical and stylistic innovations. That surfing today is a global, multibillion-dollar industry is a direct result of the surf boom.[9]

There were three significant reasons that the surf boom was born in postwar Los Angeles. First, the existence of a small, but influential prewar surf community in the area provided a foundation for later developments. Second, after the war Los Angeles surfers made boards better and more accessible than ever before. Third, as better equipment drove the growth of the sport, the surfing lifestyle emerged. The lifestyle attracted Hollywood; the commodification of the lifestyle sustained the boom. Focusing on the contributions of George Freeth, Tom Blake, and John "Doc" Ball, the first part of the chapter covers the period between 1907 and the start of World War II. In the second part, covering the period between the end of the war to the precipice of the surf boom, my attention shifts to the development of surfboards and the cultivation of the surf lifestyle, primarily in terms of fashion, surf movies, and the emergence of the sport's core values in Malibu. This section also identifies the ways that surfing's development was supported externally in postwar Los Angeles. In a short conclusion, I revisit the boom and examine factors that made the surf lifestyle such a salient commodity for a nationwide audience.

Before proceeding, a couple clarifications of terminology might be useful. First, I use "Los Angeles" as both a geographic constraint and stylistic catchall. To avoid the ongoing debate of what exactly constitutes "LA," I have attempted to rigidly limit this study to the cities and communities of Los Angeles County. Coastally speaking, this translates into the area between Malibu in the north and Long Beach in the south. Most of my attention is focused on the Santa Monica Bay: from Palos Verdes and the beach cities of Redondo, Hermosa, and Manhattan (collectively known as the South Bay), up through Venice Beach and Santa Monica, and the northern terminus of Malibu. Where appropriate, I refer to specific locales, deferring to "Los Angeles" when discussing broader trends and the community as a whole. Second, I use the term "sport" broadly, to capture the act of wave riding—the "doing" of surfing—including both competitive surfing and the notion of surfing as "lifestyle sport." The matter of surfing-as-sport is perhaps the longest standing tension among surfers and like the aforementioned geographic debate, I happily excuse myself from trying to resolve it at this time, especially because large-scale, competitive surfing was a boom-time development.[10]

1907–World War II: The Pioneer, the Tinkerer, and the Organizer

George Freeth: First on the Scene

Before surfing could be transformed in Los Angeles, the sport had to traverse the Pacific. In 1907, Hawaiian George Freeth arrived in Los Angeles, bringing surfing with him from its island birthplace.[11] Part pioneer, part reluctant prophet, Freeth's arrival planted the seed of surfing in the California imagination that would blossom over the course of the twentieth century. Born in Honolulu to an Irish father and half-Hawaiian mother in 1883, Freeth was a renowned swimmer and diver before an uncle introduced him to surfing at the age of sixteen. Emerging as the preeminent surfer on Waikiki beach (the sport's pre-LA mecca), Freeth spearheaded a Hawaiian surfing renaissance, reviving the ancient sport that had all but faded into obscurity in the late nineteenth century. At Waikiki, Freeth reintroduced the somewhat lost art of stand-up surfing, eschewing the prone and kneeling approaches practiced by his contemporaries. Hired by beachfront hotels to perform surfing exhibitions for tourists, Freeth was among the first surfers to earn a paycheck for wave riding. He not only entertained tourists, but set an example for a generation of

Hawaiian surfers, none more notable than his close friend Duke Kahanamoku, an eventual Olympic swimming champion and global surfing ambassador, the man who most surfers still revere as the godfather of the sport.

By 1907, Freeth had made a significant impact on the sport, but his influence was limited to Hawaii. The local legend was at the height of his prowess when he captured the attention of Alexander Hume Ford and Jack London, two mainlanders whose interest in the sport catapulted surfing across the Pacific. A South Carolina plantation heir, Ford was a world traveler, entrepreneur, and journalist who developed a passion for surfing upon his arrival to Hawaii in 1907. In May of the same year, Jack London and his wife, Charmain, also arrived at Waikiki. London was already a successful adventure writer when Ford piqued his interest in surfing, providing the couple with an introductory lesson and an opportunity to see Freeth in action. The convergence of this trio produced two major developments that drove surfing westward. First, in the writings of London and Ford, surfing began its slow paddle into mainstream consciousness.[12] Second, and more importantly, London and Ford encouraged Freeth to head to California. Both men provided Freeth with letters of introduction to facilitate his arrival on the mainland and there is some evidence that Hume's Hawaiian Promotion Committee may have financed Freeth's voyage in an attempt to drive tourist interest in the islands.[13]

Freeth arrived in San Francisco in July 1907. Making his way south shortly thereafter, he became the first surfer in Los Angeles when he rode the waves at Venice Beach. Enjoying a modicum of celebrity thanks to London's article in *Woman's Home Journal*, Freeth became the first, full-time professional surfer by the end of the year, when early Los Angeles developers Abbot Kinney and Henry Huntington hired him to promote their new beachfront suburbs. First at Kinney's Venice Beach, then at Huntington's Redondo Beach, Freeth performed hundreds of surfing demonstrations, introducing thousands to the sport.

Exhibitions brought great attention to surfing, but Freeth was much more than an entertainer. Remaining in the Golden State until succumbing to the Spanish Flu in 1919, Freeth was a one-man grassroots movement for ocean sports. He built surfboards, gave free surf lessons, and founded the mainland's first surfing club at Redondo Beach in 1912. His influence extended beyond surfing: at a time when swimming was beginning to be embraced as healthy recreation, he was among the first swimming instructors in the area, as well as the first professional lifeguard in Los Angeles. He trained the earliest teams of local lifeguards, making the beaches safe for recreation. Ever the well-rounded waterman, he founded the first swim team at the Los Angeles Athletic Club in 1913 and is also credited with introducing water polo to California.

That Freeth found a home for himself and surfing in Los Angeles was the first indication that broader social forces facilitated the embrace of surfing in the area. His experience connects to three of the major factors that undergirded the development of surfing in Los Angeles. First, owing to the relative proximity of California to Hawaii and the advent of steamship travel, Los Angeles was accessible. In the decades that followed, surfers took advantage of affordable air travel between Los Angeles and Hawaii, fostering an exchange of knowledge, innovation, and style between the sport's birthplace and revolutionary outpost. Second, Freeth's ability to financially survive (albeit meagerly) through surfing and related activities presaged the possibility that surfers could earn a living doing what they loved. Later, Los Angeles surfers followed this trajectory, finding ways to keep themselves fed and near the water as lifeguards, Hollywood stuntmen and bit players, and, by the 1950s, as owners and employees of surf industry businesses. Finally, surfing and the beach lifestyle fit firmly into the popular conception of Los Angeles and Southern California as a land of robust health and active leisure. This image of the city only grew stronger in the twentieth century, but can be traced back to the late nineteenth century and the work of early Los Angeles boosters like Harrison Gray Otis and Charles Fletcher Lummis, whose promotional efforts positioned the city as the epicenter of the new, healthy, and bountiful lifestyle on offer in the Southwest.[14]

Tom Blake: Relentless Innovator

While Freeth did much to introduce surfing to the public imagination and make the beaches safe for leisure, the credit for making the sport more widely accessible belongs to Tom Blake. Like Freeth—and so many Angelenos—Blake was a transplant, a champion swimmer originally from Wisconsin, arriving in Los Angeles in 1921.[15] In a chance encounter long-enshrined in surfing lore, Blake was encouraged to move across the country by Duke Kahanamoku after the pair met in a Detroit movie theater. Kahanamoku could not have known it at the time, but in prodding Blake westward, he ensured that his late mentor's efforts to popularize surfing in Los Angeles were not in vain. Blake followed the path blazed by Freeth, earning a paycheck as a Santa Monica beach lifeguard and competing for the Los Angeles Athletic Club swim team. His interest in surfing led to a 1924 trip to Hawaii, where he became a lifelong devotee to the art and craft of wave riding. Granting Blake the title of "the sport's great innovator," surf historian Warshaw describes how Blake's influence spanned the realms of technology and ideology:

> He redesigned the surfboard. He changed the way surfers looked. He transformed wave-riding into something broader and more consuming—what later generations would call the "surfing lifestyle." ... Among all of Blake's many surf-world inventions, this is the one that really counted. Surfers through the decades would think of themselves as different, and more clued-in, than nonsurfers.[16]

While Blake's ultimate legacy may be the blueprint for the surfer's ethos, his efforts following his first visit to Hawaii produced technological innovations in board design and photography that set the stage for the sport's post–World War II acceleration. Blake's foray into surfboard design began with a hand-carved, solid redwood replica of an *olo*, a traditional Hawaiian board enjoying a revival in the early 1920s. Shortly thereafter, Blake began experimenting with methods to make boards lighter. His early attempts at trimming weight involved drilling holes through the entire board and applying a wood veneer as a sealant. By 1930, Blake had moved on to completely hollow boards, supported by a rib-bracing similar to that of an early airplane wing. The result of these experiments was a drastic reduction in board weight: where a solid, fifteen-foot *olo* weighed around one hundred twenty pounds, Blake's rib-braced designs weighed half as much; he eventually produced boards weighing as little as forty pounds. In retrospect, Blake's hollows were more evolutionary than revolutionary. Postwar advances in materials technology rendered hollow boards obsolete, but these new designs could only emerge in a post-Blake paradigm: the midcentury surfers who envisioned new possibilities did so while riding hollow boards.[17]

Another of Blake's innovations—the stabilizing fin or "skeg"—proved to be much more than a historical stepping-stone in the evolution of board design. Trying to achieve a more stable and controllable ride, he found his solution in 1935, affixing a salvaged speedboat fin to one of his boards, leading to what Warshaw has described as "the design advance upon which virtually all future advances were built ... With this breakthrough, all the traction and bite a surfer needed was now available."[18] Within a decade, fins were standard on boards. In the eighty years since Blake's breakthrough, surfers have experimented with variations on fin size, shape, and placement, as well as multi-fin designs, but the basic concept remains unchanged: the fin is as essential to surfing as the wave it was designed to tame.

The fin was not Blake's only major accomplishment of 1935. That same year, he published *Hawaiian Surfboard*, the first book on surfing. Part history, part instruction manual, *Hawaiian Surfboard* depicted surfing as it was in 1935. Blake's photography was the standout feature of the book—images he captured while in the water, using a Graflex camera in a homemade, waterproof wooden housing. Some of Blake's photos also appeared in a 1935 *National Geographic* article, providing a sizable readership base with an introduction to surfing. While Blake was not the first to photograph surfing, Warshaw argues that "the sport's great innovator" is also "rightly noted as the first surf photographer."[19]

Blake continued to bounce between Los Angeles and the Hawaiian Islands through the start of World War II, enlisting in the US Coast Guard as he approached his forties. After serving for three years as a swimming and lifesaving instructor, the second half of his life was driven by wanderlust, from the beaches of California to Florida and eventually back to his native Wisconsin where he passed away in 1994.

John "Doc" Ball: The Organizer

Essential as they were to surfing in Los Angeles, it is unfair to the legacies of Freeth and Blake to cast them as anything less than monumental figures in the global history of the sport. While the story of Los Angeles is oftentimes a tale of immigrants and transplants, it is perhaps fitting that a native is credited for laying the groundwork for the full-fledged Los Angeles postwar surfing scene. The local in question was John "Doc" Ball, a South Bay dentist and acolyte of Blake's, whose contributions to surfing helped to usher in the ideal of the "surfer" as dedicated wave rider, rather than multifaceted "waterman."

Born in Los Angeles in 1907—the year of Freeth's arrival—Ball began surfing in 1929, after enrolling in dental school at the University of Southern California.[20] Ball was a South Bay surfer, primarily spending his time in the waves off Palos Verdes, the southern terminus of the Santa Monica Bay. It is unclear when Palos Verdes was first surfed; local surfer Joe Quigg suggests that it was a (relatively) popular spot by the late 1920s, while Warshaw identifies 1929 as the year that surfers first rode the four different breaks collectively known as "The Cove."[21] What is clear is the appeal of Palos Verdes to the early surfers: an approximation of Waikiki, with gentle, rolling waves, well suited to riding on the Hawaiian-inspired boards of the time. As surfers found Palos

Verdes, Ball found subjects and peers: his greatest contributions to the sport were as a photographer and the founder of the Palos Verdes Surfing Club, a group that included several now-legendary surfers that many surf historians credit as foundational in the emergence of the "surfer" identity.

Ball began dabbling in photography around the same time he started surfing, passions he combined in 1931, after seeing some of Blake's photos in the *Los Angeles Times*. Documenting the surf scene throughout the 1930s, his early work was shot from the sand; in 1937 he took his camera into the waves and exposed the possibilities of surf photography as a discipline unto itself. Making a rubber and wood housing for his Graflex camera, he took photos from the "lineup" (the area in the water where surfers congregate to wait for waves), offering a radical new perspective. Blake's homebrew waterproof camera had gotten him closer to the action, but Ball's got him *into* the action. Ball's work captured the entire surfing experiencing, in and out of the water, offering early evidence of surfing as a "lifestyle" and providing a formula for generations of surf photographers to follow. In national magazines like *Life, Look, Popular Mechanics,* and *National Geographic*, his photographs introduced Los Angeles surfing to readers across the country. After serving as a dentist in World War II, Ball returned to Los Angeles and cemented his legacy with the publication of *California Surfriders* in 1946, a title that remains the preeminent document of prewar surfing in the Golden State.

Founded by Ball in 1935, the Palos Verdes Surfing Club (PVSC) was not the first on the mainland, but it was arguably the most influential, providing a model that was emulated by at least a dozen other clubs along the California coast.[22] Given the eventual perception of surfers as radical, rugged individuals, the importance of the early clubs seems somewhat paradoxical. But, in those early days, with so few surfers and before the emergence of a dedicated surf media, clubs did not obscure the individual—they provided confirmation of a new identity. Taking their cues from fraternal organizations, the PVSC were an impressively organized group of beach bums: dues were paid, meetings were held, minutes were distributed, and members were expected to represent the sport and club positively at their jobs and schools. Connected by their dedication to club and sport alike, the PVSC program of activities was a microcosm of the later, post-WWII Los Angeles surf scene: they hosted contests, held dances and social events, and published a regular newsletter that anticipated the rise of the surf magazine. The club also influenced the way surfers looked and presented themselves, in and out of the water. Club logos were stenciled on boards and jackets; Ball nudged forward the development of surf-specific swimwear by teaching club members how to sew a stronger, longer-lasting swim trunk than what was commercially available. Club members included notable early local surfers like Cliff Tucker, E. J. Oshier, Tulie Clark, and Leroy Grannis.[23] From nearby Hermosa Beach, Grannis became the club's most famous alum, emerging as the master photographer of Los Angeles surfing in the 1960s.[24]

Disbanded by the start of the war, the PVSC and similar clubs were short-lived institutions that did not resurface when surfing picked up again in the late 1940s. Thus, their ultimate legacy is tied to the status they conferred upon surfers as a distinct "in-group." With shared values, beliefs, and a distinct look, the clubs set the tone for the larger "club" of LA surfers that followed. By bringing surfers together under a common banner, the clubs also provide insights into the development of the sport as a socially constructed process. Surfers may be alone in the waves, but the evolution of surf technologies, media, and style are the result of an ongoing process of mutual exchange and influence. Camaraderie in the surf clubs fostered this process before the war; the postwar population boom in Los Angeles provided the platform for an exponential acceleration of the process. I now turn my attention to this revolutionary period.

World War II–Late 1950s: Shaping Boards, Crafting a Lifestyle

The beaches of Los Angeles emptied quickly when the United States entered World War II after the bombing of Pearl Harbor. Most surfers of age enlisted in the war effort, while a combination of a strategic military presence and public fears of a Japanese attack on the California coast rendered beachfront leisure less accessible and appealing to the general public. Early surf demography is not especially reliable, but the rough consensus is that there were fewer than five hundred surfers in all of Southern California before the war. In 1942, despite the rise of surf clubs in the years prior to the war, there was no indication that the sport had reached a critical mass of participants in the area, especially not one big enough to see it through a four-year hiatus. However, instead of arresting surfing's development, the war proved instrumental in the impending surf boom: owing to a host of wartime technological advances and the stratospheric rise of postwar Los Angeles, the prewar headcount doubled to one thousand Southern California surfers by 1950, reached five thousand in 1956, and exploded to one hundred fifty thousand by 1964, with at least another fifty thousand spread throughout the rest of the country.[25]

This section provides an overview of how Los Angeles surfers in the postwar years presaged the surfing boom and how these contributions reflected larger social forces prevalent in Los Angeles at the time. By no means a complete account of the sport in LA in this period, it is an attempt to trace the trajectory of surfing from fringe sport to identifiable lifestyle on the cusp of the mainstream. To follow this path, I begin with the revolution in board design that allowed increasingly large numbers of people to ride a greater number of waves. I then consider how increased participation in the sport cultivated the development of the surfing lifestyle and its related media, styles, and ideals.

Getting Everyone on Board: A Revolution on Chips and Pigs

If war was ever good for anything, it was good for surfing. Peter Westwick and Peter Neushul write, "Surfing, that escapist pleasure, would seem to have little to do with warfare. But from surf forecasting to surfboard production to wetsuits, almost every surfer who paddles out today is using military technology."[26] Military-industrial complex advances in materials technology proved especially important for postwar surfboard makers who turned fiberglass, polyester resins, and various foams into boards that were better and more accessible than ever before. In turn, the postwar population and economic boom in Los Angeles—driven in large part by burgeoning aerospace and defense contractors in the area—provided riders for the boards and human capital for the new surf scene.

Bob Simmons was the first surfboard shaper to experiment with the new materials and the first to apply a rigorous, scientific approach to the craft. Simmons's board making reflected his résumé: he was an engineering student at the California Institute of Technology (Cal Tech) before the war, a machinist during, and a mathematician for Douglas Aircraft after.[27] Warshaw describes Simmons as a visionary, "a primary architect of the modern surfboard who almost singlehandedly brought into play the now-fundamental principles of nose-lift, foil, and finely sculpted rails."[28] Redwood boards had given way to redwood-balsa hybrids prior to the war, but Simmons was the first to make a pure-balsa design and the first to waterproof his board using a fiberglass resin. Speed and buoyancy were Simmons's chief aims; derived from his study of the physics of boat design, Simmons's boards were the lightest and fastest around. A mad genius at heart, Simmons was known as a hard-headed loner, more concerned with pushing the boundaries of design than with promoting his boards. Although relatively few people would ride Simmons's boards, his relentless experimentation and technical skills had a tremendous influence on generations of shapers, from his Los Angeles contemporaries to those born well after his early passing in 1955.

Given his obsession with speed, Simmons's designs were not particularly well suited for maneuverability, nor did they make wave riding easier for novices. Significant progress in these areas arrived in 1950, when shapers like Joe Quigg and Matt Kivlin took Simmons's innovations as the starting point for a shape known as the "Malibu chip." Lighter and shorter than Simmons's designs, the first with a fin as a standard feature, chips were designed for maneuverability. The first boards that could perform turns on the face of the wave, chips led to the development of the turn-heavy "Malibu Style" of riding and early tricks like the "cutback"; it was no longer enough to catch and ride the wave, what you did on the wave also mattered.[29]

The dominant board of Los Angeles surfing in the early 1950s, by 1954 the chip was replaced by an even lighter, faster, and more maneuverable board: Dale Velzy's "pig." Velzy found the name fitting for his unusual board—a reimagined chip with narrower nose, a rounded tail, and an oversized fin.[30] From Hermosa Beach, Velzy was already a well-known board maker by the time he fashioned the first pig, in part because he was the first to hang his shingle, having opened the world's first surf shop in Manhattan Beach in 1949. Chasing customers, he relocated to Malibu in 1951, before settling in Venice Beach in 1954, in a shop co-owned by shaper Hap Jacobs. From their shop, the pig took flight, and became the de facto board shape of the surf boom. Warshaw writes, "By the summer of 1955, the pig was the hottest board on the coast, and the Velzy-Jacobs shop in Venice was taking thirty orders a week . . . Pig boards were about to become so commonplace that the name itself would disappear; by 1957, an American surfboard was a pig by default."[31]

The rapid evolution in board design supports a view of innovation as a social process. Velzy's pig could only come after the chip, the chip after Simmons. Boards reflected the sport's past and the shaper's vision of the present; the performance of the boards suggested new possibilities for future designs. The availability of new, cutting-edge materials played a part in this process, but shifting social norms also helped shape the pig: Quigg's early chip designs were not envisioned for men; they were a result of his efforts to make a manageable board for female surfers.[32] If it was not somewhat socially acceptable for young women in postwar Los Angeles to indulge in beach recreation, the scaled designs may not have emerged when they did. That Velzy could keep a dedicated surf shop in business suggests that demand for boards was not just coming from the burly old surfers returning to the waves, but also from new arrivals to Los Angeles, not to mention children and smaller teenagers who now had boards they could control. Whether they had arrived recently or grown up in the area, two other factors facilitated the adoption of the sport by new surfers. First, the economic bounty of the period led to an increase in leisure time and offered the means to invest in consumptive hobbies. Second, because more Americans were swimming than ever before, surfing was a viable choice to occupy this leisure time. Arguing that swimming ability was a critical prerequisite of the surf boom, Westwick and Neushul attribute the rise in capable swimmers to the federal government's Depression era pool-building efforts, lessons offered by the YMCA and athletic clubs, and the introduction of swimming in school physical education programs.[33]

Los Angeles board design from this period is arguably the most important technological development in the modern history of the sport. It was surfing's tipping point, engendering the rise of the surf boom and all that followed. For new riders, these designs made surfing easier and more fun than ever before. For dedicated surfers, the boards blew open the creative possibilities of wave riding and made distinct, expressionistic styles possible. The quality of the boards and the surfing experience they offered drove demand and led to the birth of the businesses that became the surf industry, especially after 1958, when polyurethane foam replaced balsawood as the primary board-making material.[34] Lightweight and easy to work with, foam allowed for the mass production of boards to meet soaring demand during the surf boom. By the early 1960s, board makers like Hobie Alter, Hap Jacobs, and Greg Noll were churning out hundreds of boards a week.[35]

Out of the Water, a Lifestyle Emerges
With the advent of the pig, Los Angeles surfers changed the performance of the sport and enabled legions of riders to enter the water. Throughout the 1950s and into the surf boom, they also defined what it meant to *be* a "surfer." Call it a "subculture" or a "lifestyle," the notion that being a surfer entails much more than just the act of surfing is a product of Los Angeles during this period. It is impossible to articulate all of the intersecting variables that define the surfing lifestyle, but the basic framework includes a certain set of fashions, slang, and attitudes, along with a healthy dose of suspicion toward non-surfers. Above all, the surfer is defined by single-minded devotion to riding waves and a total—if not coolly detached—commitment to style, both in and out of the water. In

attempts to understand the "soul" of the sport, many surf writers have wrestled with these core values, but I think a pair of fictional surfers from the 1980s distill them with perfect economy. In *Fast Times at Ridgemont High* (1982), Jeff Spicoli explains the surfer's *raison d'être*, "... surfing's not a sport, it's a way of life, it's no hobby. It's a way of looking at that wave and saying, 'Hey bud, let's party!'" Style is similarly all encompassing, you either have it or you don't. Or, as Turtle explains to the kooky Rick Kane in *North Shore* (1987), "I can tell you're lame by the way you wear your shorts."

The surfing lifestyle is at once tangible and intangible. Built over time from shared symbols and values, it eludes easy definition, but its social function is clear: it separates surfers from everyone else. Engaging in a lifestyle requires an active commitment. It is an act of distinction, between in-group and out-group, often communicated through visual style and fashion. Los Angeles surfers were no different in this regard. Out of the water, the uniform was basic and consistent: Levi's jeans or military surplus pants, plain t-shirts and cotton sweaters, the occasional Aloha shirt, canvas sneakers or huarache sandals, and, for chilly coastal mornings and evenings, a Pendleton-brand wool shirt, preferably in plaid. This was the look copied by teenagers across the country during the boom years and is still the foundation of the surfer's off-duty wardrobe. In contrast to the suits and hats favored by men of the era, it is easy to overplay the rebel element in the surf look itself. Surfing *was* the rebellion, the "look" retroactively produced when the boom elevated the status of Los Angeles surfers. They wore things that were affordable and readily available, settling into a standardized look around the time people started paying attention to them. In the water, distinction and function reigned supreme. Disdainful of commercial swimwear, eager to display themselves as a different breed, Los Angeles surfers' standard swimwear through the mid-1950s were predominantly homemade cutoffs and old lifeguard trunks. Commercially available surf-specific swimwear was a boom-era development and Warshaw notes that the finest pre-boom designs were made to order by a cottage industry of surfer's mothers, featuring bold colors, a dedicated pocket for surf wax, and custom embroidery.[36] The now iconic, mid-thigh length of the shorts was a side effect of the board-shaping revolution, as increasingly narrower boards required less fabric to prevent the dreaded thigh chafe. During the boom years, Orange County's Katin emerged as the surfer's brand of choice for Malibu-style trunks and brands like Hang Ten filled department store shelves nationwide with Los Angeles–inspired designs.[37]

Ultimately expressed at the individual level, lifestyles are produced as a collective, negotiated and spread through interaction and communication. In the previous era, an early version of the lifestyle was codified by clubs like the Palos Verdes Surf Club and diffused in the primitive books by Tom Blake and Doc Ball. In 1953, a similar process began to unfold, when Bud Browne, a Santa Monica schoolteacher and lifelong surfer, produced the first-ever surf film, *Hawaiian Surfing Movies*. Browne produced a film every year for the next decade, establishing the genre's basic parameters along the way. Warshaw describes the template:

> Each film cost about $5,000 to make, was a little over an hour long, and consisted mainly of a series of two- or three-minute action sequences focusing on a specific rider or break. Lifestyle vignettes and short comedy sketches were included . . . The soundtracks were all bootlegged jazz or rock, and the music choices as a rule were excellent . . . The movies themselves were more or less all the same.[38]

By the end of the decade, the roster of surf filmmakers adopting this approach included Browne's fellow Los Angeles surfer Greg Noll, and fellow Californians John Severson and Bruce Brown.[39] In the buildup to the boom, the early surf movies offered entertainment, inspiration, and evidence of a growing movement. In footage from Hawaii, Australia, Mexico, and California, surfers encountered new maneuvers and diverse styles of wave riding to attempt and interpret as their own. Previously limited to still photography and oral legends, surfers could now assess the performance of their sport. Because the films captured speed and style within the context of specific locations, they were an approximate scoreboard and record book for the sport. Surfers now had evidence of who had done what where and the means to assess their own performances via comparison.

Surf movies did more than inform and entertain Los Angeles surfers; film screenings gave them something to do with their evenings and provided a setting for the exchanges that shaped the surf lifestyle. A decade before Bruce Brown's *Endless Summer* filled movie theaters across the country, surf filmmakers rented out municipal halls and school auditoriums to showcase their efforts. Browne led the way, debuting *Hawaiian Surfing Movies* at John Adams middle school in Santa Monica, to a packed house of five hundred. It was a scene repeated throughout the decade in Los Angeles and Orange County, mostly in smaller venues like Hermosa Beach's Pier Avenue middle school, occasionally in larger settings, like Santa Monica's three-thousand-seat Civic Auditorium. As with the action on the screen, these gatherings enabled the self-awareness required of a distinct lifestyle, along with a setting to meet and exchange ideas with likeminded beach rats. In darkened public spaces, surrounded by their brethren, surfers forged an identity that was not confined to the waves.[40]

Of course, the waves still mattered, and Malibu had the best waves in Los Angeles. Originally known as Rancho Malibu, a seventeen-thousand-acre private enclave owned by the heirs of oil and insurance magnate Frederick H. Rindge, the beach was still off-limits to the public when a trespassing Tom Blake and his friend Sam Reid became the first to surf the fabled point break in 1927. That same year, the public gained access to Malibu after May Knight Rindge lost a legal battle to keep her late grandfather's ranch private, setting the stage for the surf revolution to come. The epicenter of postwar surfing, Malibu helped crystallize the surfing lifestyle in the 1950s and became ground zero for the surf boom in 1957. Surfers from throughout the area transformed the sport in these years, but in the words of surf journalist Paul Gross, "Malibu is the exact spot on earth where ancient surfing became modern surfing."[41]

Malibu is worthy of a study in its own right, but in the confines of this chapter, it must suffice to identify a few of the major figures and lifestyle considerations that emerged from the Malibu scene. Chips and pigs had been designed with the Malibu wave in mind, and riders of the increasingly maneuverable boards developed the carving approach known as the "Malibu style." To turn up and down the face of the wave, Malibu surfers abandoned the forward-facing parallel stance, instead orienting themselves perpendicularly to the board, allowing for significantly greater control of the board. Surfers have used this stance ever since.

Of all the progenitors of the Malibu style, three are especially notable. Dewey Weber, from Hermosa Beach, was a respected shaper and surfing's original "hot-dogger," a showman known equally for his sharp turning skills and for turning the board into a stage, manically running up and down the deck while riding waves. Weber and his contemporaries pushed the limits of wave riding and made the cultivation of a distinct, individual style one of the sport's loftier ambitions. Standing out was increasingly important; as more and more surfers made their way to Malibu, it became the sport's proving ground. Mickey (or Miki) "Da Cat" Dora added a dose of effortless grace to Weber's frantic footwork, his smooth and daring style earning him the feline nickname. One of the boom's most popular professional surfers, Dora was the sport's original anti-hero. As crowds overwhelmed Malibu toward the end of the decade, Dora's dismissive, exclusionary attitude became the blueprint for the surfer's protectionist ethos of localism, and generations of surfers have since claimed their coveted spots for "locals only." Dora's close friend, the salaciously nicknamed Terry "Tubesteak" Tracy, was perhaps the ultimate embodiment of surfing as lifestyle. Less known for his wave-riding talents, Tracy showed surfers that, at least for long stretches of time, you could abandon mainstream society and commit wholeheartedly to a lifestyle of leisure. During the summers of 1956 and 1957, in a handmade shack, he literally lived on the beach at Malibu. Part court-jester, part master of ceremonies, Tracy was a fixture in the social fabric of the beach, the total "lifer." As the inspiration for the character of Kahuna in *Gidget*, Tubesteak's worldview helped to define the "beach bum" stereotype; Kahuna literally tells Gidget, "I'm a surf bum."[42]

The Los Angeles surf lifestyle bore traces of the sport's prewar roots in the area, but it was also a reflection of its surroundings. Noting the city's history of idealistic self-promotion, historian Lawrence Culver argues that the very idea of "lifestyle" was a Los Angeles invention.[43] After the war, as this affinity for lifestyle combined with economic prosperity and an increased emphasis on leisure, Los Angeles became a hotbed of various subcultures and lifestyles. Along with the surfers, there were bodybuilders at Muscle Beach (Santa Monica), beatniks in Venice, and a group of proto-hippies known as The Nature Boys, walking barefoot in the canyons near Malibu. While there was inevitably some spillover across the subcultures, they mainly supported each other just by existing. A "surfer" was not just defined against the backdrop of mainstream society, he was also clearly *not* a member of these other groups, and vice versa. The surf lifestyle was also facilitated by the thriving automotive culture of the period. Where previous generations of surfers were limited to their local breaks, postwar surfers took to the newly built freeways of Los Angeles and Southern California in pursuit of waves. If one spot was flat or too crowded, they could zip down the coast for something more appealing, then drive back across town to a movie screening. In a time of abundance, the Los Angeles surfer had it all.

Conclusion: Why Surfing?

From swimwear to the world of extreme sports, the legacy of the surf boom remains visible today. But of all of the postwar youth subcultures, why did

Carrying on the legacy of Freeth, Blake, and Ball: a surfer "shoots" the pier, circa *1990*. Photo courtesy of LA*84* Foundation.

Hollywood latch onto surfing and why did the nation embrace it? There is no simple answer, but there were at least three factors that made the surf lifestyle ripe for the picking: the Malibu-Hollywood connection, the longstanding image of California as home of the good life, and the emergence of surfing as a subculture of consumption.

Hollywood stars were among the first settlers at Malibu after the Rindge family land became public. The "Malibu Colony" of the late 1940s included stars like Jackie Coogan and Peter Lawford, and Warshaw notes that interaction between the surfers and residents of the Colony was common on the beach.[44] In the 1950s, Malibu was not just a Hollywood playground, but also a decidedly cool place for local youth to see and be seen. Malibu made *Gidget* possible. Screenwriter Frederick Kohner based the character on his daughter Kathy's experience at Malibu in the summer of 1956; the surf boom followed shortly thereafter. But, as Westwick and Neushul note, Kathy Kohner's very presence on the beach reflected both the allure of the beach and the changing social mores of the time: "She was there because her parents, like countless others along the California coast, thought the beach was a good, healthy place for her and her cousins to spend time."[45]

In *Gidget* and the madness that followed, surfing was a touchstone of a broader California dream-life. In her excellent study of the era, Kirse Granat May argues that this dream-life offered consumptive escapism, no matter where you were:

> This entertainment enabled American teenagers to experience the life of a California teen, and millions tried to buy into it. The California youth culture was important less for its ability to reflect reality and more for its successful creation of an image to which millions of teenagers could respond . . . These images left behind the urban problems of the rest of the country, avoided the growing discussion about civil rights, and domesticated temporarily the more dangerous elements of rock music.[46]

The surface appeal of the image is obvious: the absence of work, pleasure as lifestyle, bikini babes and buff surf dudes, and so on. The image was new and fresh, but its immediate appeal was predicated on previous dreams of Southern California life. In *The Frontier of Leisure*, Lawrence Culver notes that Los Angeles and Southern California had been promoted and sold back to the rest of the United States since the late 1800s.[47] The sales pitch changed over time, but the main themes had long revolved around health, leisure, sunshine, opportunity, abundance, and endless possibility. The surf boom was the first application of the old formula after the dawn of the media age and rise of the teenager, allowing the dream to be bought and sold like never before.

Surfers love nostalgia and nowhere on the American mainland is more romanticized in the surfer's imagination than early 1950s Malibu. Hollywood takes the blame, but the surfers were complicit, even before the crowds showed up. Ultimately, surfing had to be a lifestyle worth commodifying. It had to be cool and it was cool because of the Los Angeles scene. Even before the boom, the emergence of the Los Angeles surfing lifestyle signaled the end of the sport's transition from the prewar fringe activity to a popular leisure subculture. At the risk of offending surfers everywhere, surfing had become what Schouten and McAlexander call a "subculture of consumption":

> a distinctive subgroup of society that self-selects on the basis of a shared commitment to a particular product class, brand, or consumption activity... Other characteristics of a subculture of consumption include an identifiable, hierarchical social structure; a unique ethos, or set of shared beliefs and values; and unique jargons, rituals, and modes of symbolic expression.[48]

Three structural elements explain how these subcultures develop. First, the subculture has a taste-based, legitimating hierarchy, which distinguishes the hard-core inner-circle members from the soft-core secondary members and third-order aficionados who consume the subculture but may not be a member in it. Second, the subculture has a pervasive ethos, or core values, that limits and defines it. Third, the subculture provides opportunities for self-transformation, or the assimilation of new members into the subculture. Schouten and McAlexander derived their theory from an ethnography of motorcycle subcultures, but they might as well have been embedded in the Malibu scene. The pervasive ethos was in place by the mid-1950s. Beaches, film screenings, and surf shops provided points of entry for assimilating new surfers. The social ordering and hierarchy were a survival requirement: first, to deal with crowds and establish a pecking order in the water, and again during the boom, when the non-surfing consumer arrived and it became critical to distinguish the real surfers from the posers, kooks, and flatlanders.

CHAPTER THIRTEEN

The Halcyon Days of Muscle Beach

An Origin Story

JAN TODD

> *Muscle Beach became an international icon, a paradigm of the larger than life Southern California lifestyle, and the larger than life heroes who dominated the stage.*
>
> Mark Sarvas, Santa Monica News[1]

Released in 2009, the oversized, two-inch-thick *Los Angeles: Portrait of a City* contains more than five hundred photographs of life in the City of Angels. Only one image appears on the book's front cover, however, and it shows a group of men, women, and children—all tan and fit—on a raised platform doing acrobatics at the original Muscle Beach in Santa Monica.[2] Off the platform an audience has gathered and their eyes are nearly all focused on a small woman flying through a cloudless blue sky toward the safety of her partner's arms. Some members of the audience are in street clothes, many more in beach wear, and while the vast majority of the audience and all the participants on the platform are white, three African American men are also present, watching the acrobatics demonstration that occurred nearly every weekend at Muscle Beach in midcentury.

If historian Alan Trachtenberg is right and symbols serve a culture by "articulating in objective form the important ideas and feelings of that culture," then the use of Frank Thomas's photo as the cover for a book attempting to capture the essence and spirit of Los Angeles could not be more appropriate.[3] The microsecond captured by the shutter's closing is filled with movement

Frank J. Thomas's cover photo from *Los Angeles: Portrait of a City*. Courtesy of Frank J. Thomas Archives.

and beauty. It reveals Muscle Beach as a cultural nexus where athleticism, fun, fitness, daring, performance, family, and the beach merged. Greater than its disparate parts, the photo presents Muscle Beach as a site where physicality, sensuality, muscle, grace, and the idea of limitless possibility converged. Muscle Beach was unique. At Muscle Beach in the 1930s, 1940s, and 1950s well-conditioned bodies, amazing acrobatic tricks, and demonstrations of physical strength took center stage in a way never before seen in America. Although closed down by the city of Santa Monica in 1958, what started at Muscle Beach served to inspire the fitness revolution of the last half of the twentieth century, and it irrevocably linked the sun, sea, and sand of Southern California with the quest for physical perfection.

In the mid-1950s, when Thomas took his photo, the idea of Muscle Beach as a nonconventional outdoor gym and performance area home to hard-bodied men and women had already spread well beyond the United States. Hundreds of muscle-magazine and wire service stories, several newsreels, and the dozens of public appearances, acrobatic performances, and even the TV and film work by some of the early regulars at Muscle Beach made it so famous that it was admired and emulated as far away as chilly Aberdeen in Scotland.[4]

Despite the importance of this patch of sand and the men and women who flexed, flipped, flew, and lifted there, surprisingly little attention has been paid to Muscle Beach by academic historians. Tolga Ozyurtcu has written the sole dissertation on Muscle Beach and neither that dissertation, nor the few other scholarly articles written to date, have paid much attention to how the original Muscle Beach began and why it evolved as it did.[5] In order to fill at least part of this void, this essay attempts to provide a definitive "origin narrative" for what is now generally referred to as the "original" Muscle Beach—a distinction necessary because three and a half miles south of the Santa Monica pier, another beach-side exercise area favored by the bodybuilding fraternity later became known as "Muscle Beach-Venice." What follows should not be considered as a complete history of Muscle Beach, but as an appetizer or *amuse-bouche* before the full meal to be prepared by future scholars.

Becoming Muscle Beach

In 1916, Santa Monica resident Charles Looff, hoping to make his newly adopted city a more desirable tourist destination, opened a massive amusement pier immediately adjacent to the existing city pier.[6] Looff's new "Santa Monica Pleasure Pier" featured carnival rides, a fun house, a bowling alley, a billiard parlor, and several restaurants.[7] It also created space for fishing and walking, became a concert stage at times, and fundamentally changed the Santa Monica beach experience. As had happened at Coney Island in New York, Looff's new pier proved to be a magnet for the building of restaurants, apartment buildings, and hotels in its close proximity.[8] Muscle Beach's evolution was linked to the pier both because of the site's proximity and because the pier proved to be an excellent vantage point for watching the action on Muscle Beach. Over the years, more than one new member found his or her way to Muscle Beach by being curious about the people they could see from the pier doing acrobatics. And, when Muscle Beach began hosting free public exhibitions on weekends, the amenities offered by the pier and the nearby cafes—where one could buy Muscle Beach burgers—made this unusual outdoor gymnasium an attractive weekend destination even for those who never stepped on the platform.

The pier's involvement in the founding of Muscle Beach is uncontested. Other parts of the story as to how Muscle Beach began have varied widely over the years. According to *Life* magazine in 1946, "Although uninhibited Californians had used the beach for years to display their muscles, it began to be invaded by professionals in 1931, when a Santa Monica high school athletic coach, impressed with the local show of strength, installed playground equipment."[9] *Muscle Power* author Gordon L'Allemand had an entirely different take in a 1949 article, however. He claimed Muscle Beach started when Johnnie Collins and Barney Fry "decided they wanted a place to lift weights, pose with bulging muscles . . . and toss their girlfriends around."[10] Another narrative (a variant on *Life*'s genesis myth) that is still common was first advanced by Joel Sayre in the *Saturday Evening Post* in 1957. According to Sayre, the prime movers who founded Muscle Beach were a "kindhearted widow" named Kate Giroux and a football coach named Vincent Schutt, who began organizing games for children at the beach around 1930.[11]

Those who were actually there, however, tell a rather different story about how—and why—Muscle Beach began in the mid-1930s. According to Relna Brewer McRae, now ninety-six and living in San Diego, the impetus to gather on that hundred-yard stretch of sand just south of the pier and practice tumbling, acrobatics, and adagio was influenced by larger forces—the 1932 Olympic Games in neighboring Los Angeles; a massive 1933 earthquake centered just off the coast of Long Beach; and, of course, the shared need of many Americans to find ways to make ends meet during the Great Depression.[12]

Relna saw the Santa Monica pier—and the sandy beach just south of it that would become known as Muscle Beach—for the first time in the summer of 1926. Her family was in the midst of a move to Northern California from Missouri and they stayed for three months in Ocean Park, Santa Monica's southern neighborhood. Six-year-old Relna and her nine-year-old brother, Paul, were entranced by the pier with its roller coaster and merry-go-round, and she spoke movingly ninety years later of how she loved playing in the sand and wading in the shallow surf under their mother's watchful eye that summer.[13] That same year, significantly, both the Los Angeles schools and the Santa Monica schools added gymnastics to their physical education curriculum and competitive sport offerings.[14] This meant that when the Brewer family moved back to Santa Monica in August 1929, twelve-year-old Paul began learning rudimentary gymnastics and tumbling at John Adams Junior High School. When he entered Santa Monica High three years later he continued to be involved with gymnastics, even though the newly built school had not yet built a boy's gymnasium and the equipment they had to practice on was outdoors and consisted of only a set of parallel bars, a horizontal ladder, and a simple horizontal bar.[15] Although these were less than ideal training facilities, Paul and his friends remained committed to gymnastics and worked out frequently after school. "Paul didn't have the right build for gymnastics," Relna explained in 2016. "But he just loved tumbling and gymnastics, and later found he had better coaches at the beach than he ever did in the schools . . . but it was because of school that first he got interested, and his interest became my interest too."[16]

Paul and Relna were not the only teens in Los Angeles interested in gymnastics in the early 1930s. As the city of Los Angeles began mobilizing to host the 1932 Olympic Games, the greater Los Angeles school gymnastics programs began to be viewed as a potential sources of gymnasts for the American team.[17] Part of the new enthusiasm for gymnastics was undoubtedly caused by the IOC's decision to award individual medals in the sport for the first time. (Previous Olympic Games had only awarded team medals in gymnastics.) The Los Angeles Organizing Committee had requested the change and it had also asked to include three new gymnastics events in which Americans were expected to do well: Indian club swinging, rope climbing, and tumbling.[18]

As the Games drew closer, connections between the schools and the private Los Angeles Athletic Club (LAAC)—already heavily involved in helping prepare athletes for the Games—strengthened when LAAC athletic director Al Treloar let it be known that the club would train any high school boy who showed real talent for the sport.[19] In 1930, the LAAC also hosted the men's national gymnastics championships and sold tickets through the schools at discount prices for students.[20] Student sales jumped significantly when the *Los Angeles Times* reported that two boys from Dallas, Texas—Roland Wolfe and Byrd White—would participate in the men's contest.[21] Fourteen-year-old Rowland Wolfe emerged as a teen sensation from the 1930 nationals. Wolfe easily won the tumbling competition although he was only fourteen, came back and took second in the nationals the following year; and then, at the 1932 Olympics, won the first and only gold medal ever awarded for tumbling, while he was still seventeen.[22] Wolfe became a hero to most would-be gymnasts in the Los Angeles area—including Relna and Paul. Even though they did not attend the Games the Brewers saw the newsreel released after the Games, which showed Wolfe's tumbling routine. "He inspired a lot of us," she reported, "and

I remember us talking about the fact that he was a teenager like we were, and yet he had already done so much."[23]

The final impetus for the founding of Muscle Beach arrived on March 10, 1933, when a massive earthquake shook Southern California for more than ten seconds. Centered just off the coast of Long Beach, the quake was followed by thirty-four aftershocks causing additional damage to many area buildings, including Santa Monica High School.[24] Santa Monica school officials closed several buildings at the high school because of quake damage, moved many classes into tents, and, not surprisingly, decided to hold off on its pre-earthquake plans to build a boy's gymnasium.[25] Harold Zinkin, whose memoir remains the best source on these events, wrote that the Long Beach earthquake was the precipitating event that caused Paul Brewer and some of his Santa Monica High School teammates to turn to the beach for a place to practice.[26] Relna agrees. It was not unusual, she explained, for Paul and some of his friends to horse around and practice some of the tricks he was learning in school when they would go to the beach before 1933. After the quake, however, when he could no longer practice at Santa Monica High School, he and several friends decided that the soft sand at the beach might be their best alternative. Paul and his friends found, however, that the sand got in their eyes when they tumbled. Relna cannot recall where they got it, or whose idea it was, but they acquired a long, heavy rug which they placed on the sand when they trained. According to Relna, the rug's arrival marked the real start of Muscle Beach.[27]

The Magic Carpet

The city of Santa Monica had dedicated an area just south of the pier as a children's playground in the 1920s but in the early 1930s, with Works Progress Administration funding, they hired Kate Giroux as a playground supervisor.[28] In addition to swings, slides, a merry-go-round, and some child-sized gymnastics equipment, Giroux kept bats, balls, nets, and horseshoes for pitching in an old piano box, which she padlocked at the end of each day.[29] As a playground supervisor in charge of small children, Giroux was not happy when Paul and his teen-aged friends began trying to do acrobatic stunts at the playground. Relna still takes umbrage when someone suggests Giroux was responsible for starting Muscle Beach and helping to get the first platform installed. In a letter to the *Smithsonian* following a 1998 article by Ken Chowder, Relna wrote, "Your article on Muscle Beach . . . was great and humorous, but not quite accurate.

Muscle Beach was started in 1933 by Paul Brewer an acrobat and gymnast who wanted to practice on the sand. Katie Giroux... had no interest in the acrobats at all."[30] In interviews in 1997 and in 2016, Relna claimed that Giroux's antipathy toward the teen-aged acrobats went well beyond disinterest. She reportedly told Paul and his teammates, "We don't need or want acrobats down here." Relna remembers Giroux, in fact, as a "mean woman" who went to the city, demanded that acrobatics be banned at the city playground, and reportedly told the city fathers, "This is a children's playground; I want you to get those crazy acrobats off my beach."[31]

Relna claims Giroux was also concerned about the propriety of young men and women doing acrobatics together. The 1930s saw an enormous transformation in terms of what was acceptable as swimwear for both men and women. Both the 1932 and 1936 men's Olympic swimming teams, for example, wore one-piece suits with straps over their shoulders, even though simple trunks were beginning to gain ground. Women in many parts of the United States still wore knee-length skirts over leggings when they entered the water in the mid-1920s, yet by the end of the 1930s the two-piece suit with bare midriff was increasingly accepted.[32] At Muscle Beach, however, even in the photos from the mid-1930s, most men appeared shirtless and wearing simple trunks, while many of the young women, especially those who participated in acrobatics, wore two-piece bathing suits, with no attached legs, and without short skirts to supposedly preserve modesty. For Pudgy Stockton, who became the most famous of these pioneering women, the decision to wear a two-piece suit was based on the desire to be practical, not provocative, even though in Pudgy's case the distinction often had a lot to do with the eye of the beholder. In an interview in 2001, she explained that once she started acrobatics she realized that one-piece swimsuits restricted her movement too much. "Since no one sold two-piece swimsuits at that time," she recalled, "and I was hard to fit in any case, my mother took apart one of my older brassieres and used it to make a pattern. She made all my suits for me in the early days."[33] Relna remembers the exposed flesh of the Muscle Beach gang as a cause of concern for Giroux. "She didn't like us wearing bathing suits all the time," Relna explained, "and I think she didn't like it when the men lifted us and touched our legs and bottoms. She actually told me once that she thought what we were doing was immoral."[34]

While it was not a baseball diamond in a field of corn, the rug on the sand just south of the pier did seem to have some sort of magic, for almost as soon as it was put in place other Los Angeles teens began showing up and wanting to participate. One of the first to arrive was John Kornoff.[35] Kornoff was only thirteen when he saw Brewer and a few other teens practicing on the rug but after wandering over and meeting the group, Kornoff came to the beach as often as he could. According to Zinkin, Kornoff could perform tricks while he was in junior high school that no one at Muscle Beach had yet imagined. He was twice named best high school gymnast in the city of Los Angeles and received a football scholarship to Washington State University starting in 1939.[36]

Randall (Ran) Hall also showed up that summer along with the professional acrobat Johnnie Collins, who became the first unofficial coach at Muscle Beach. Hall had attended Hollywood High where his gymnastics skills brought him an invitation to train at the LAAC in 1931 as a prospective Olympic team member. Although Hall failed to make the Olympic squad, he became friends through the LAAC with a number of professional acrobats who trained there when they were in LA, including the older Collins. Hall and Collins and several other professional acrobats and pro wrestlers sometimes met for outdoor training sessions at the Crystal Pier in Ocean Park. However, after discovering the Brewers and their friends practicing at Muscle Beach in 1933, Collins and Hall became Muscle Beach regulars, and Collins, in particular, began teaching the young teens more advanced acrobatics and adagio and encouraging them to think about becoming performers rather than competitive gymnasts.[37] Adagio is a form of partner acrobatics—often set to music—in which one or more acrobats are supported overhead while performing feats of flexibility or lifting another human. Adagio, hand balancing, and acrobatics are terms used somewhat interchangeably to describe the kinds of physical activities at early Muscle Beach where the building of human pyramids, hand-to-hand balancing, throwing (or catapulting using a teeter board) women through the air, and many other circus-level acrobatic stunts made Muscle Beach a mecca for photographers and "an attraction" that was beginning to draw an audience.[38]

With Collins attending and happy to share his knowledge, interest in the idea of becoming professional acrobats mushroomed, and by the end of the summer there were about twenty men and boys—and Relna—regularly meeting at the playground.[39] One of the new group who found Muscle Beach that summer was a mid-twenties bus mechanic named Al Niederman, who worked for the city of Santa Monica. Niederman had also been introduced to gymnastics in the public schools, and he and Paul became the unofficial leaders of Muscle Beach in its first years.[40] It was Brewer and Niederman, for example, who decided to acquire a large tarp in 1934 and claim more of the playground for their training sessions as numbers continued to grow. And it was Niederman, with his carpentry and welding skills, who built most of the original gymnastics equipment as the beach evolved.[41]

In 1935, Cecil C. Hollingsworth, then the gymnastics coach at the University of California at Los Angeles (UCLA), was hired with WPA funds to teach children's gymnastics classes during the summer.[42] Having Hollingsworth involved with the gymnastics group was helpful on several levels. Kate Giroux liked having him around to keep eye on the teenagers; several of his UCLA gymnasts also began coming to the beach because Hollingsworth was there; and, most important, his presence at Muscle Beach gave Brewer and Niederman additional ammunition when they went back to the city and requested permission to build a small platform, flying rings, and parallel bars at the playground.[43] Although the same request had been turned down the previous year, this time the city agreed as long as Niederman did the welding and directed the construction of the platform. The small platform they built was only three feet by twelve feet and stood barely an inch or so above the ground. However, it was a huge improvement over the carpet and tarp, and when combined with Niederman's newly-built, twenty-five-foot-tall set of rings and his new parallel bars, an adult could at last practice real gymnastics on the beach.[44]

By 1938, the number of people involved with Muscle Beach had risen to about fifty regulars, and the group's training sessions, particularly on the weekends, had begun to attract large crowds. Reporter Joseph Fike, trying to make sense of the rapid growth in the popularity of sport gymnastics in Southern California for the *Los Angeles Times,* wrote in 1938, "It is not altogether a coincidence that local interest in tumbling and apparatus work has grown as the playground has grown until the Los Angeles area today is probably the national center for this type of activity."[45] Fike believed this achievement was no accident and that it was caused by the combination of the Los Angeles City Schools gymnastics program and what was happening at Muscle Beach where annual attendance at the Santa Monica Playground had jumped from approximately 3,500 visitors in 1930 to 1.8 million individuals by 1937.[46]

Despite this enormous growth, participation on the platform at Muscle Beach was still largely a white phenomenon. Historian Alison Rose Jefferson suggests that racial segregation was the norm on most California beaches into the 1960s despite the fact that the California courts had upheld the rights of African Americans to use all beaches in California in 1927. According to Jefferson, African Americans, like other Angelenos, went to the beach in

Santa Monica, but they normally gathered at a two-block-long stretch of sand at the end of Pico Boulevard in Ocean Park that was derogatorily called the "Inkwell."[47] Although the Muscle Beach regulars welcomed African American Olympic weightlifting champion John Davis to the platform when he visited, there is no record of other African Americans participating in the activities at the original Muscle Beach.[48] By the 1950s, when men's bodybuilding contests began being held as part of beach festivities on the Fourth of July, a few African American men did participate in those competitions but they were not "regulars" at Muscle Beach.[49]

For most women, inclusion in the activities at Muscle Beach did not begin with learning gymnastics in school. There were no high school gymnastics programs for girls in the 1930s, the 1932 Olympics did not include women's gymnastics, and the only report in the *LA Times* of women involved with gymnastics prior to the beginning of Muscle Beach discusses a 1908 AAU tournament in which the girls' club will assist and "augment" the boys' team as it competed.[50]

Abbye "Pudgy" Stockton, for example, who was by far the most famous woman associated with Muscle Beach, had no experience with acrobatics until her steady boyfriend, Les Stockton, cajoled her into beginning to train to help her lose weight.[51] She began working out about two years after her 1935 graduation from Santa Monica High School, and at first Stockton would only exercise in the privacy of her bedroom. After losing twenty pounds through a combination of calisthenics, dieting, and light dumbbell training, Pudgy—a nickname her father gave her when she was a small child—agreed to accompany Les to Muscle Beach now that she felt comfortable being seen in a bathing suit. Naturally reserved and somewhat shy, Stockton remembers being overwhelmed at first by the atmosphere at Muscle Beach. Knowing she had no gymnastics background, Stockton said she just tried to stay out of the way in the beginning and began her training by learning to do a handstand. In an autobiographical profile from 1947, Pudgy described her mastery of the handstand as "the main turning point of my life, although at that time I didn't realize it."[52] Years later, Pudgy explained that it took some time for her to get strong enough to hold herself in the handstand position, but being regarded as part of the larger community at Muscle Beach had been her inspiration. Said Pudgy, "We may have been learning our acrobatics from each other, but we still wanted to do things perfectly—to make the movements impressive and beautiful . . . Everyone else was so good, I felt I had to be perfect, too."[53]

Relna Brewer, two years younger than Pudgy, was the first real female star of Muscle Beach and received a great deal of publicity before she married a fellow Muscle Beach regular, Gordon McRae, and moved away during the war years. Petite, blonde, and looking as if she was always just on the edge of mischief, Relna was fourteen when she began tagging along with Paul to Muscle Beach where, rather than being seen as the nuisance "kid sister," she became everyone's favorite adagio partner and grew to become a woman who relished being strong and a focus of the public's gaze. Like many of the young people who came to the beach during the Depression years, Relna dreamed of a career in show business, and was given permission by her mother to take lessons from an older, ex-circus acrobat named Barney Fry, who ran a gym on the second floor of the Elks Lodge in Ocean Park. Fry became a major influence in Relna's life and taught her jiu-jitsu, wrestling, wire walking, and the standard strongman tricks of bending iron bars, tearing phone books, and lifting weights. Strong, agile, and a bit of a showoff, Relna admits she loved the attention her participation in these new activities brought her. Although Relna was still a teenager, Fry began acting as her manager/publicist, and she was soon appearing in variety benefits and other shows where she did strength stunts, performed acrobatics, and often finished by wrestling men much larger than herself. At 5'3" and 115 pounds, with a trim, lithe figure, Relna challenged popular conceptions about strength and femininity and, as would also be the case for Pudgy Stockton, it was her combination of strength, a shapely physique, and facial beauty that sold her photographs to newspapers and muscle magazines. Often referred to as the "strongest girl in America" in the early days of Muscle Beach, Relna's exploits were reported regularly by wire services and appeared as far away as Brazil.[54]

Muscle Beach Comes of Age

The metamorphosis of Muscle Beach from teen hangout/sport camp to the cultural phenomenon that became known around the world began in 1938. It started with the Works Progress Administration's willingness to help build a much larger platform that stood three feet off the ground and was ten feet wide and forty feet long.[55] The new platform with its nearby bleachers was no longer merely a practice space. It was clearly a stage—calling for an audience—and even higher levels of professionalism.[56] Like the rug and the small platform, the big stage at Muscle Beach attracted yet more professional acrobats—and would-be acrobats—so that by 1940 there were about fifty regulars at Muscle Beach and an increasing number of them supported themselves away from Muscle Beach as acrobatic entertainers or stunt performers in the film industry. A 1947 article discussing Muscle Beach as a desirable site for professional photography estimated that as many as fifty different acrobatic acts had emerged from Muscle Beach in just thirteen years.[57]

Another transformational figure at Muscle Beach was Russell (Russ) Saunders, a former diving and gymnastics champion from Winnipeg, Canada, who came to visit his sister in Los Angeles in late 1939 and never really left. Saunders had heard of Muscle Beach before he arrived, but after meeting the people there and seeing how much fun they were having, he decided to find a way to stay. As he was debating whether to enroll in college and continue as a competitive diver, Saunders was offered a chance to play an acrobat in a film starring John Barrymore. That job led to another film job, and that to the next, so that by the time he retired, Saunders had worked as a stuntman in more than one hundred feature films and he had doubled for nearly all of Hollywood's leading men.[58] The likable Canadian became the unacknowledged leader of the acrobatic side of Muscle Beach, as Saunder's acrobatic skills surpassed everyone else's at Muscle Beach. However, he was not a fan of weightlifting. When asked why, his standard reply was that he'd rather lift girls than weights.[59]

Weight training was not fully part of the Muscle Beach scene until the late 1930s. Les Stockton, who married Pudgy in 1941, was among the first to bring weights to the beach but once he started, others followed suit. Stockton began weight training at UCLA and became a convert when he gained twenty solid pounds in six months.[60] The added muscle significantly helped his gymnastics and so Les began *proselytizing* about the benefits of the weight training to all who would listen. Soon most of the men and a surprisingly large number of women at Muscle Beach began incorporating weight training in their workouts and a separate low platform with a locking storage box was created for the activity.[61]

Although it would be after World War II before bodybuilding developed into a major activity at the beach, the group still took pride when one of their own—Harold Zinkin—was named the first Mr. California at a contest organized by Vic Tanny in 1941.[62] Vic Tanny and his younger brother, Armand, were part of the Muscle Beach family, yet both were always more interested in weight training than they were in acrobatics. When he first arrived in Los Angeles to attend UCLA in 1939, Armand Tanny had his eye on making the 1940 Olympic team as a weightlifter, a dream he had to give up when the 1940 Games were canceled. As for Vic, he moved to Santa Monica the following year and opened a small gym close to Muscle Beach.[63] To promote the gym, Vic began organizing strength contests and bodybuilding shows and even large-scale physical culture variety shows. As Vic's gym business began expanding, and as bodybuilding itself became more popular in the 1940s, the Tanny connection brought more lifters and bodybuilders to the beach. By 1955 when the city required the Muscle Beach weightlifters to form an official club so they could purchase insurance in case of accidents, more than one hundred members signed up.[64]

In 1947, a new era began at Muscle Beach with the introduction of the Mr. and Miss Muscle Beach contests. The idea for the contests came from DeForest "Moe" Most, another former LA high school gymnast who became playground supervisor in 1947.[65] Most wanted the new physique contests to serve as the centerpiece of special holiday extravaganzas on the Fourth of July and Labor Day that would showcase Muscle Beach regulars. Although Most had envisioned both the Junior and Senior Mr. Muscle Beach contests as small, local events, an army of photographers and even a newsreel crew showed up for the first one on July 4, 1947.[66]

For the 1947 Miss Muscle Beach contest on Labor Day, Moe had invited neighboring towns to send a representative to the contest, which resulted in some of the contestants being facially pretty but not necessarily in the best physical condition. The following year, Most restricted the contest to women connected to Muscle Beach and this produced a more fit-looking group.[67] Although referred to as a "beauty contest," winning the Miss Muscle Beach title was predicated on the possession of a certain type of beauty. It was a "beauty-muscle" contest, wrote one journalist, and to win you needed to "pour beauty and biceps into the same bathing suit."[68]

Most's decision to begin sponsoring physique contests was part of a postwar shift in emphasis that made the appearance of the body and the ability to lift heavy weights increasingly important to the habitués of Muscle Beach. During World War II, many of the young men involved with Muscle Beach had enlisted in the various armed forces, where their muscular physiques and exceptional fitness caused some of them to be tapped as physical training instructors. Les Stockton, Harold Zinkin, Jack LaLanne, George Redpath, Bert Goodrich, and John Kornoff, for example, all spent part of their war years helping new recruits get quickly into shape via barbell training.[69] The men of Muscle Beach introduced thousands of men to the benefits of weight training and demonstrated that weight training did not make one "musclebound" as was commonly believed in this era. The Beach Bunch also helped build the mystique of Muscle Beach with their tales of the beauty, camaraderie, and great fun to be had just south of the Santa Monica pier.[70] The national impact of these early barbell advocates was further heightened when, on November 17, 1942, a full-color photograph of a formidable looking Johnny Kornoff appeared on the cover of *Look* magazine. Harold Zinkin argued in his memoir that the *Look* cover marked a watershed moment in America's understanding of physical fitness. "Shirtless, muscles rippling, and obviously fit to fight . . . Kornoff depicted the American ideal," Zinkin wrote. "I believe that his photo on *LOOK's* cover was the beginning of a change of attitude regarding fitness, an attitude that culminated years later in President John F. Kennedy's focus on fitness, which even then seemed revolutionary."[71]

Whether Kornoff's cover had the impact Zinkin imagined is not clear. However, both during and after the war dozens of servicemen stopped in Santa Monica on their way to and from the Pacific Theater, and some of them, including future Mr. Americas Steve Reeves and George Eiferman, decided to avail themselves of the military severance package of $20.00 a week for fifty-two weeks and moved to Santa Monica so they could be part of Muscle Beach.[72] The arrival of Reeves in the same year as the first Mr. Muscle Beach contest presaged a discernable rise in the interest paid to bodybuilding and heavy weight training at Muscle Beach.

Acrobatics did not suddenly disappear, of course, but a slow transformation was underway, a transformation precipitated by the fact that the original founders had grown older, married, begun careers, and in many cases no longer lived in Santa Monica. What's more, the shift in emphasis was accelerated in the 1940s and 1950s by specialized magazines like Hoffman's *Strength & Health* and Joe Weider's *Your Physique* and *Muscle Power* that gave much more ink to competitive weightlifters and bodybuilders than they did to pyramid builders.[73] Although many of the original gang returned from time to time, and some—like Les and Pudgy Stockton, Moe Most, Paula Boelsems, and Russ Saunders—continued to live in Santa Monica and frequent the beach, the influx of new people, new interests, and new forms of media, meant the sand on Muscle Beach had begun to shift.

In the 1950s the number of bodybuilders and competitive weightlifters associated with Muscle Beach continued to rise. Olympic champion Frank Spellman, for example, arrived in 1953 and took an apartment on the second floor of a building overlooking Muscle Beach.[74] Several years later, Isaac Berger, the reigning Olympic featherweight champion, and 1956 Olympic silver medalist David Sheppard moved west as well.[75] However, the increasing number of lifters, bodybuilders, and even pro wrestlers then associated with Muscle Beach began to concern some Santa Monica city fathers who viewed this generation of athletes and their more bohemian lifestyle as undesirable. Tolga Ozyurtcu has written an excellent analysis of the various political, social, and commercial forces that converged in 1958 to result in the closing of Muscle Beach, but the trigger that caused it was Isaac Berger's and Dave Sheppard's involvement in a rape case involving two underage African American girls.[76] As Ozyurtcu demonstrates, the rape charges levied at Berger, Sheppard, and several of their male friends provided the city with a so-called reason to bring in bulldozers under cover of darkness—with no public notice or public hearing—and demolish the equipment at Muscle Beach. Although Sheppard and Berger were never found guilty of anything, their case became a tipping point for the raising of broader concerns about what some perceived as a new and inappropriately permissive culture evolving at Muscle Beach—a culture tolerant of out-of-wedlock sex, the use of marijuana, and perhaps even homosexuality. As Ozyurtcu ably demonstrates, the end of the original Muscle Beach is a far more complicated story than space permits here, but I would add that the increasingly prominent identification of weightlifting and bodybuilding with Muscle Beach in the 1950s was a precipitating factor. Consider the words of Mayor Russell K. Hart, who told the *Los Angeles Times* in 1959 that the city planned to strictly enforce the new regulations they'd established for Santa Monica Beach so that "the weightlifters will go someplace else and the name Muscle Beach will be forgotten."[77]

Conclusion

Mayor Hart did not get his wish. Today, just south of the Santa Monica pier, close to the sidewalk, is a sign that reads, "The Original Location of Muscle Beach . . . The Birthplace of the Physical Fitness Boom of the Twentieth Century."[78] There is, admittedly, no weightlifting there, but a large "weight pit" and performance space at Venice Beach is proud to be known as Muscle Beach-Venice, and that space stays firmly in the public's eye because of its close connections to bodybuilder and former California governor Arnold Schwarzenegger.[79]

Beyond Venice, however, the original Muscle Beach lives on in the hearts and imaginations of old and new lifters alike who, through the vast number of photos on the Internet, continue to be inspired by what once was. What the mayor didn't understand was that Muscle Beach wasn't so much about the space as it was about the symbolic importance of the able-bodied men and women who inhabited that space. Like the statues of ancient Greece, photographs of the men and women of Muscle Beach continue to be reinterpreted by new generations of viewers who read them as models for physical perfection and as blueprints for personal transformation. The iconic bodies produced at Muscle Beach, and the worldwide publicity it and its habitués received, created a paradigm for fitness—muscular, tanned, powerful—that is every bit as relevant to the CrossFit/functional training generation as it was when the original Muscle Beach gang showed the world how much fun it was to be fit.

CHAPTER FOURTEEN

I Was Standing There All the While

Jim Murray and the Birth of a Sports Mecca

TED GELTNER

When Jim Murray stepped off the train and set foot on California soil for the first time in 1944, Los Angeles was very much a minor-league sports town. The Dodgers were still firmly ensconced in Ebbets Field at 55 Sullivan Place in Brooklyn; American and National League baseball still only extended as far as the Mississippi River. The professional football team that would eventually become the Los Angeles Rams still had two more years in Cleveland before it would set up shop on the West Coast. The first official NBA basketball game was two years away, and the sport was a decade and a half from coming to Los Angeles. And Murray himself was a twenty-two-year-old northeasterner with six months of journalism experience who had never left New England and had not yet published a single article about sports.

Over the course of the rest of the twentieth century, the city Murray had chosen as his destination would blossom into a sports mecca, and he would become the man to put the story to paper. Eventually, the sports fans of the city would expect to see his bespectacled face staring back at them when they flipped to the sports page, and under his byline they would anticipate sentences born from his "sharp eye and quizzical typewriter,"[1] sentences they knew would entertain them, educate them, and, on most days, make them laugh.

James Patrick Murray was born December 29, 1919, on the eve of America's Golden Age of Sports. He grew up in a house that did its part to celebrate that Golden Age. The Jim Murray story, however, did not have a storybook beginning. The son of a failed druggist and an Irish nurse, he was a sickly child from a broken working-class family in the small suburb of West Hartford, Connecticut. When Jim was three, his father was arrested for selling illegal liquor from his drugstore (this was the age of prohibition) and sent to jail, ending his career as a business owner. At age four, young Jim was struck with Saint Vitus Dance, a disease resulting from streptococcal infection, of which there was little treatment at the time. Jim's medical problems combined with his father's legal ones put a strain on the young family that it could not withstand, and Jim's parents split up. Jim and his two older sisters would spend the rest of their childhood moving from house to house, relative to relative.

For much of Jim's youth, he lived under his paternal grandfather's roof. It was here that his love of sports was born. Jim's father had five brothers, and in happy times, the brothers would sit around the dining-room table, smoking cigars and swapping stories about Golden Age heroes like Babe Ruth and Jack Dempsey and about their own exploits following the local Connecticut sports scene. Most of the brothers usually held down regular day jobs, but it was Uncle Ed who left the most indelible impression on Jim. "My whole life was colored by having an uncle who was a pool hustler," he wrote. "No boyhood should be without one."[2] Ed was a bookie and a pool shark who made his living on the fringes. He showed Jim how to cook dice, how to game the racetrack, and, on the nights he came home with a battered face, the dark side of the gambling life. Uncle Ed's rules would form a code for Jim to live by:

"Never bet on a live horse or a dead woman."
"Never take money from an amateur ... unless he insists."
"Never play cards with a man in dark glasses or his own deck."
"Never play a guy named 'Lucky' ... at anything."[3]

Later, as an adult, Jim would seek out characters in the Uncle Ed vein and populate his columns with men of Ed's ilk.

It was another disease, rheumatic fever, which both cut short Murray's athletic career and at the same time launched him as a writer. At the age of ten, the sickness nearly took his life (at the depths of the illness he was read his last rites), and left him so debilitated that he was unable to attend school regularly for years. Instead, he spent much of his time in his bedroom, reading page after page, volume after volume, of history and literature, and fomenting his own literary dreams. By his teen years, he had recovered enough that he even played baseball competitively, though early on he determined that his own personal contribution to the sporting life would be through observation, not participation.[4]

After graduating with a degree in history from Trinity College in Hartford, Murray landed a job as a general assignment reporter at the *New Haven Register* for the princely sum of $23.50 a week.[5] The year was 1943 and the majority of his peers were fighting World War II, but the remnants of his illnesses left Murray ineligible for military service. So instead, he poured himself into his new career, covering fires and car chases and food shortages, working "67-hour weeks" learning his craft.[6] Into those endless days he somehow managed to fit assignments assisting the *Register* sports editor, and penned his first sports journalism as a cutline writer covering Yale football.[7]

But Murray burned to leave New England and see the world. He vowed to stick it out until the calendar turned to 1944, and then, with what little money he had saved from his reporter's salary, he boarded a train for Los Angeles, hoping to land a job in Hollywood as a screenwriter. His money ran out soon after arrival, and he found himself looking for newspaper work. A Connecticut connection landed him an interview with legendary city editor Jim Richardson at the *Los Angeles Examiner*. Richardson was notorious for chewing up and spitting out reporters, and when Murray showed up in his East Coast attire, complete with overcoat and wing tips, Richardson was ready to send him back out into the street.

> "Do you know where City Hall is?" he demanded.
> "No," said Murray.
> "Do you know where the FBI is?" Richardson asked.
> "No," said Murray.
> "Do you even know where Figueroa Street is, for cryin' out loud?" Richardson barked, his anger rising.
> "No," said Murray.
> Richardson threw his pencil down, stood up and glared at his prey.
> "Well, can you write?"
> "Oh, Mr. Richardson," Murray said. "I can write like a son of a bitch."[8]

The uncharacteristically bold assertion landed him the job, and Murray soon backed it up. He was now a city reporter, covering crime in a town where there was a surplus of it, and where six newspapers battled daily to bring the most lurid, sensational details of those crimes to the Los Angeles readership.

"The competition was fierce," said Melvin Durslag, an *Examiner* reporter when Murray joined the staff. "We used to do all we could think of to get a scoop. We used to fight each other like dogs for stories."[9] Murray joined the fray himself, participating in the coverage of famous crimes of LA lore such as the Black Dahlia case and the Overell Yacht Murders. He covered the Las Vegas murder trial of an Irish war bride, meeting mobster Bugsy Seigel and other members of the Vegas elite. He learned his way around the LA courthouse and the morgue, and picked up the tricks of the trade along the way. His writing stood out even more than his reporting skills, however, and he soon was rewarded with a coveted spot on the rewrite desk, the youngest employee in the Hearst chain to ever earn such a promotion.

The *Examiner* newsroom was a smoke-filled den of yellow journalism and purple prose, and after four years soaking it up, Murray was ready to move on. His next stop was on the opposite end of the spectrum, the pristine, both literally and figuratively, Beverly Hills offices of Time, Inc. *Time* magazine was the pinnacle of American journalism in the late 1940s, a highly profitable enterprise with a worldwide network of writers and editors anonymously bringing the Henry Luce version of the news to millions of subscribers across the continent. Murray took a big raise to join the *Time* network, and traded his beat on the gritty streets of LA for the film lots of Hollywood and mansions of Beverly Hills.

Though his new job involved covering a variety of stories across Southern California, his primary subject for *Time* was the film industry. He developed a wide network of sources, from the producers and directors and grunts of the movie business, to the big names, the ones that lit up the marquee. He profiled John Wayne, Humphrey Bogart, Marlon Brando, Bing Crosby, and many other stars of the day. In the process, he honed the ability to move beyond the reporter-source relationship with his subjects, and developed lasting friendships with them. (Bogart would become a regular poker partner; an engraved money clip from Crosby, a gift after Murray's cover story on the crooner was published, would travel with him for the rest of his life). The New York offices of *Time* had found that magazine covers of Hollywood starlets sold nicely, so Murray was called upon to identify and profile the newest big-screen beauties, from Ava Gardner to Elizabeth Taylor to Marilyn Monroe, whom he would memorably describe in print as "five feet six inches of whipped cream."

Murray discovered Monroe when she was still taking small supporting roles, her dynamic screen presence already overshadowing the leads. One evening,

Murray took her out to dinner. Around the time the waiter was bringing dessert, Monroe became noticeably distracted, her attention focused across the room. As the check was delivered, she asked Murray if he would mind if she went home with somebody else.

"Not at all, as long as you introduce me," Murray replied.
Marilyn waved her arm, and Joe DiMaggio casually strode over to the table.[10]

Meeting Joltin' Joe was a thrill for Murray, and also enhanced the niche he was creating in his role at *Time*. The *Time* editorial staff, according to Murray, was 90 percent Ivy Leaguers with ambitions to cover the State Department or the United Nations, so interest in, and knowledge of, sports was in extremely short supply. The few sports stories that *Time* deemed fit to cover began to fall to him.

In his short time in California he had married, started a family and moved to the Miracle Mile section of Los Angeles, a few blocks away from Gilmore Field, home of the Hollywood Stars minor league baseball team, and walking distance from Pan Pacific Auditorium, where college basketball and semi-pro hockey filled the seats. Murray was a regular attendee at both. At *Time's* Beverly Hills office, he began to make his love and understanding of sports part of his professional life. He wrote about Olympians Bob Mathias and Mel Patton, and took a trip to South Bend, Indiana, to cover a highly anticipated Notre Dame-Navy football game. For *Time's* sister publication *Life*, he penned an editorial about his hatred of the New York Yankees (still coursing through his veins from his New England youth), which included a line that would be quoted for years to come: "Rooting for the Yankees is like rooting for U.S. Steel."[11]

Murray's knack for sports coverage filtered all the way up through Time, Inc., to the company's omnipresent leader, Henry Luce. So when Luce fixated on the idea of creating the first national sports publication under the Time, Inc., banner, Murray was tabbed to join the team that was tasked with formulating the magazine. In the summer of 1953, he hopped a train to New York, where a small group of Time, Inc., editors would plan and design Luce's secret Project X. The fruits of those efforts would take its place on the newsstands in August 1954, with the inaugural issue of *Sports Illustrated*.

Though still officially a writer for *Time*, Murray became the de facto West Coast correspondent for the company's new sports venture. From the outset, the magazine struggled to define itself. Some within its leadership pushed to aim content toward the leisure class and fill pages with yachting and quail-hunting coverage, while others saw the magazine's future among work-a-day sports fans, whose tastes leaned toward baseball, boxing, and horse racing. Murray's early output for *Sports Illustrated* reflected that dichotomy. One issue would include a recap of a UCLA or USC football game, another would feature a yacht race from Newport Beach to Ensenada. Some of the famous names he wrote about in *Time* as the Hollywood correspondent began to appear in *Sports Illustrated* under the James Murray byline: Humphrey Bogart the recreational sailor, Twentieth Century Fox chairman Darryl Zanuck on the croquet wicket, Gary Cooper goes skin-diving.

While Time, Inc., in the form of *Sports Illustrated*, was providing Murray the chance to become a sportswriter, the company also allowed him to write about the evolution of sports in his adopted hometown. He authored a *Time* cover story about Brooklyn Dodger owner Walter O'Malley as O'Malley pondered the Dodgers' move to Los Angeles,[12] and when the move finally occurred in 1958, Murray was at the stadium to report the reception for *Sports Illustrated*. "Angelenos have been deserting their surfboards and barbecue pits under the jacaranda trees in swarms to motor over the freeways to the Coliseum and sit in on the strangest baseball show in the history of the sport. The stands are full of football fans, college and pro, tennis players, shotputters, beach bums, movie stars—even baseball fans," he wrote.[13] Murray also saw fit to acknowledge in print O'Malley's decade-long efforts to keep the team in Brooklyn (he felt Ebbets Field was beyond repair and needed to be replaced) before making the move to California, a fact that was ignored by most East Coast writers. The effort helped develop a close relationship between Murray and O'Malley, one that would last for decades.[14]

Just two years later, the city had another professional sports immigrant. The National Basketball Association's Minneapolis Lakers had settled in Southern California in the summer of 1960. Though few Angelenos paid attention, Murray did. "I was one of the only writers west of the Pecos writing on pro basketball in those days," he recalled later.[15] For *Sports Illustrated*, he spent the holiday season of that year on an eastern road trip with the team as the sole representative of the press. Professional basketball was in its infancy at the time, and the bare-bones travel arrangements offered Murray an intimate view of his subjects. "We used to go on trips in quaking, asthmatic old planes ... and often, the little two-engine wheezer would be occupied by both Lakers and Knicks en route to a doubleheader in Syracuse or Kankakee," he remembered.[16]

On his 1960 road trip, he sat on those planes and in hotel lobbies and coffee shops with Elgin Baylor, Jerry West, Hot Rod Hundley, and the rest of the fledgling Lakers as they made their way through the winter freeze of the northeastern December, "depressed, irritable, and off on the longest trip of their young lives."[17] He would use the trip as an opportunity to bear witness to life as a Laker, at home between the lines but an oddity off the court as they traveled from city to city. Murray found scenes to illustrate the point:

> In the all-night lunchroom a few bleary-eyed refugees from skid row, killing the empty hours until the bars would open again, regarded the entrance of the team with little interest. The tired counterwoman stared as the forest of players queued up. "You must be with some team," she guessed. "Yeah," said Baylor, "the Los Angeles Mothers. We're midget wrestlers."[18]

Murray was by then an experienced magazine writer, with seven years clocked in at Time, Inc. He wasn't concerned with the results of games, but with the personalities that emerged through his own observations and characterizations. The key to his craft, he had determined, was offering readers a window into sports that wasn't open to them as ticket-buying fans. "Readers always get you aside and ask you of an athlete: 'What is he really like?'" he said. "There's a story in every man. The challenge is to find it."[19]

In early 1961, Murray faced a career crossroads. Time, Inc., was notorious for moving its editors around the country like chess pieces. Murray had avoided the fate to that point, but now the home office was calling, and couching a forced move to New York in a promotion to the masthead of *Sports Illustrated*. At the same time, a close friend and former colleague from *Time*, Frank McCulloch, had taken the job of managing editor at the *Los Angeles Times*, and he, too, had a proposition for Murray. The newspaper needed to add some flavor in its sports section. Would Murray like to become the lead sports columnist at the *LA Times*?

The prospect of leaving behind the sun and warmth of Los Angeles for the ice and cold of Manhattan turned out to be the deal breaker. Though he was virtually unknown to Los Angeles newspaper readers, he had lived in the city long enough to become one of them, and to know that he didn't want to leave. Murray made his choice. He would step off the ledge and give up his cushy position at *Time* in favor of the unknown. He would become a columnist, though he'd never published a single column. "The opportunities for falling off a high wire with no net were certainly present . . . but I had been living in L.A. for 17 years when I took the job. I knew the scene. I was no guy fresh off the boat," he wrote.[20]

Despite Murray's complete lack of name recognition, McCulloch and the *Times* didn't hold back on the fanfare when announcing the newspaper's new hire. On February 5, 1961, editors stripped an article across the top of the sports section, headlined "Jim Murray to Write Feature Sports Column in Times." A week later, the first of more than ten thousand Jim Murray columns would grace the *Times* sports front. Under a line drawing of the bespectacled Murray, a sly grin across his face, he introduced himself to an unknowing city: "I've been urged my friends—all of whom mean well—to begin writing in this space without introducing myself, as if I've been standing here all the while only you haven't noticed. But I don't think I'll do that. I think I'll start by telling you a little about myself and what I believe in. That way, we can start the fight right away."[21] What followed were twenty-five column inches of one-liners about the teams and stars of the day across Los Angeles, as well as a self-deprecating analysis of his own athletic and literary career. "I came to Los Angeles in 1944 (the smog and I hit town together and neither one of us has been run out despite the best efforts of public-spirited citizens)," he wrote.

The column made an impact immediately. Peter O'Malley, who would take over for his father as owner of the Dodgers a few years later, remembered the initial appearance of Murray in the *Times*. "My recollection was that it was instant," he said. "Whenever that first column was . . . everybody went 'wow.' It was the cliché of water cooler talk. He had the city instantly, he had the sports fans instantly. From that point on, you had to read Jim Murray's column, because everybody talked about Jim Murray's column, and what he had said that day."[22] The template of a Murray piece had been laid out from the beginning; now the work of refining his style and finding an audience would commence.

In the early 1960s, the sports landscape in America looked about the same as it had fifty years prior. The attention of the sports enthusiast was dominated by baseball, boxing, and horse racing, in that order, and baseball was number one by miles. Murray understood that readers of the *Los Angeles Times* sports pages had an insatiable desire for news and commentary about the national pastime, and he used his space to feed that desire. In 1961, Murray wrote 201 columns, 45 of which were devoted to baseball. The Dodgers were still new, and now contenders, and the Los Angeles Angels were right on their heels as a brand-new American League expansion team. Still, Murray's eclectic tastes steered him toward topics that would not be found in typical sports columns. In the first year, he wrote about rodeo, chess, yachting, bullfighting, and many other oddities. And he peppered his writing with Hollywood references and quotes from his film industry friends, imbuing the proceedings with a uniquely Angeleno feel that quickly caught on with readers. The column mixed humor, history, commentary, and off-beat characters, and took on the personality of its author. But it was in a hotel room two thousand miles away from his home city where Murray truly found his voice.

Six months into his *LA Times* tenure, Murray tagged along on what turned out to be a disastrous, sweaty, tension-filled road trip for the Dodgers. The team pulled into Cincinnati dragging along a ten-game losing streak, with another nine road games in front of them. Most of the players and coaches were in no mood to field questions, and Murray had already written a string of columns about the losing streak and about the life of a ballplayer on the road. As he sat in his hotel room staring at his typewriter, desperate for a fresh topic, he recalled some advice he'd received from an editor many years before: "Son, the best stories are floating right by your front door, if you'll only look out there."[23]

What was out the front door was Cincinnati, and, to Murray, it didn't look like much. He rolled a sheet of paper into the typewriter and took aim. "Now, if you have any sense, you don't want to be in Cincinnati at all," he typed. "Even in daylight, it doesn't look like a city. It looks like it's in the midst of condemnation proceedings. If it was human, they'd bury it."[24] He went on for a few more paragraphs, said the city should be given back to the Indians or bombed by the Russians, until he had tapped out the requisite twenty-five column inches of copy, thinking little of his geographic assault.

The city of Los Angeles had its share of transplanted Cincinnatians, so once it ran in the *Times*, the column quickly was brought to the attention of the residents of the condemnation-worthy trash dump in southwestern Ohio. Safely back in Southern California, Murray began receiving letter after letter defending the city and firing back at him personally. The proverbial light went on in his head.

As luck would have it, the Dodgers losing streak on Murray's interminable road trip had handed over first place to the Reds, and the Reds kept it through the rest of the season, winning the pennant and going on to face the Yankees in the World Series. Murray booked his ticket back to Ohio. Upon landing, he found himself among a populace who knew who he was and didn't like him. A photo of him was published in the *Cincinnati Post and Times Star*, tagged "the most hated man in Cincinnati." At game one of the World Series, fans held up "Boo, Murray!" signs in the outfield at Crosley Field and wore buttons that said "Murray for Idiot." His likeness was hanged in effigy from flagpoles. "I'm so popular in this town, if I'm ever missing, check one of those effigies. If it's got holes in its socks, it's me," he wrote during the series.[25]

Murray's accidental trick had stirred up reader interest to rival that of the town's beloved Reds. *The Post and Times Star* reported receiving more than 250 written responses to Murray's jabs, more than any single article previously.[26] The news made it back to the *Los Angeles Times* leadership, who began shopping Murray's column for syndication. Soon, the column was running in 10 newspapers around the country, a number that would reach 250 within the decade.

The city-assassin shtick was perfect for Murray, a way to entertain and incite, without the necessity of attacking individual players or coaches, a technique favored by many columnists with far greater repercussions and fewer opportunity for laughs. Murray's barbs were largely light-hearted, as were the majority of the civic responses to them. After the back-and-forth with Cincinnati, Murray began to work material about cities into his column on a regular basis. In the winter of 1962, he began scheduling road trips with the Lakers and the Blades, Los Angeles's minor-league hockey franchise, solely for the purpose of traveling to far-flung, ice-choked outposts that he could hammer in print. "The first thing to establish is there really is an Edmonton, Alberta, Canada," he opined. "The tougher part of the question is 'why?'"[27] Pretty soon, Murray decided he didn't need to travel to specific destinations to launch his attacks. Anywhere his plane touched down would do just fine.

On Pittsburgh: "You can tell a native Pittsburgher because he looks as if he's just been rescued from a cave."

On St. Louis: "The city had a bond issue with the campaign slogan 'Progress or Decay,' and Decay won."

On West Virginia: The state is so poor, "it not only didn't know the Depression was over, it didn't even notice when it started."

Louisville "smelled like a wet bar rag."

When pressed, even his beloved Los Angeles absorbed some blows: "It's 400 miles of slide area . . . where you might get run over, incinerated, drowned, buried alive, kayoed by a surfer or speared by a spear-gun. But you'll never get bored."

And on and on it went, in towns large and small across the continent. The entertainment level would only increase when a local columnist, or even a mayor, would choose to engage with Murray. The response would inevitably lead to another round of pot-shots from Murray, and generate more material for the column. More and more, as newspapers signed up to syndicate Murray, he'd arrive in a city and be greeted by locals demanding to know when the attack would commence. "If Jim came to a town, and he wouldn't write about the town right off, somebody in the press box would say 'When are you going to knock our town?'" remembered Murray's friend and colleague at the *Times* Bill Christine. "It was almost a Don Rickles thing. If Rickles didn't make fun of you, you weren't anybody. Well, if Murray didn't knock your town, then there was something wrong with your town."[28]

The civic search-and-destroy tour increased Murray's notoriety tenfold, but it also helped him create his own personal style and persona. Whereas humor was always part of his writing, now he developed a reputation as a humor writer, and devoted full columns to what were essentially a string of one-liners, ala Bob Hope or Jack Benny. On days when the goal was laughs, readers could hear the rim shots after each paragraph. His stock in trade was taking a certain characteristic—a jockey who was tiny, a baseball player who was clumsy—and inflating it up to and beyond its breaking point. Frank Howard, the Dodger's enormously large power hitter, was an early subject of the Murray treatment. Howard was "so big, he wasn't born, he was founded." "Any town not prepared for Howard is apt to declare martial law. He's such a big eater, the smaller players on the team won't sit down at the same table with him. Frank's liable to plunge a fork in them and wash them down with a bottle of ketchup before they can call for help." "When he runs in from right field, seismologists as far away as Johannesburg phone the ballpark in panic as they record an earthquake of the first magnitude." His shoes are so big "shoeshine boys shine them in shifts."[29]

The routine worked especially well in Los Angeles, where entertainment was valued above all else. Only months after his column debuted, Groucho Marx wrote to let Murray know he was a daily, satisfied reader.[30] Many, many other stars of comedy and film would follow. Soon, his reputation grew to include the title of humorist as well as sportswriter. When he had been at the *Times* barely a year, he received an offer to join the writing staff of a new variety program, *The Andy Williams Show*. Veterans of *The Steve Allen Show*, another successful television comedy show, recruited Murray to add laughs to the new program, which was to be built largely around the already established musical abilities of Williams. Murray only stayed a few months (though the show was a ratings success), and the experience taught him that his abilities were better suited to his own typewriter, as opposed to sitting around a table bouncing ideas off of other writers. His jokes would heretofore appear only in newsprint. Steve Allen himself echoed the feelings of many in the industry: "One of my favorite American humorists is Jim Murray of the *L.A. Times*. God, what a gift he has for the funny line. And yet, simply because his field is sports, the so-called experts in humor never bring up his name when the subject of comic writing is under discussion."[31]

Set-ups and punchlines weren't the only tools in Murray's box. He was unafraid to take on social issues as they related to the world of sports. In the early 1960s, the deaths of boxers Benny "The Kid" Paret, Davey Moore, Alexander Lavorante, and others caused a backlash against the sport. Murray, though a lifelong devotee of boxing who wrote about it regularly, condemned the violence and called for the sport's abolition. Outraged readers wrote in by the hundreds, telling him to stick to writing about sports and leave societal issues to the news pages. Murray was unmoved: "The goal of journalism is, or should be, truth. To say a sports writer is supposed to be an apologist for an evil thing is to say a doctor is supposed to defend cancer," he wrote.[32]

Murray felt the same criticism when he delved into civil rights, an unavoidable issue in those years. In his first autumn as a columnist, hometown UCLA appeared to be headed for a Rose Bowl match-up against the segregated University of Alabama, coached by the legendary Paul "Bear" Bryant. Both teams were undefeated. UCLA's black players were threatening to make a statement by boycotting the game. Murray traveled to Alabama and confronted Bryant about the issue in front of a room of Alabama sportswriters, one of whom called Murray a "west coast nigger lover." Bryant avoided the question, but Murray took it head on in print. The columns he filed from Alabama dealt almost exclusively with racial questions, and not a single sentence about the Georgia Tech-Alabama game he had supposedly been there to cover. It was a choice he once again knew would anger a segment of sports-page readers. Many wrote in to call him a communist or worse, but an equal amount rallied in his defense. "I went down to a state in the South which also belongs to the 20th century," he wrote. "Only, it not only doesn't like it, it doesn't know it. Or won't admit it."[33] The federal government would desegregate the University of Alabama by force the following year, but Bryant would not allow a black player to suit up for his football team for nearly a decade.

Murray's most famous line of the hundreds of thousands of words he typed over his career was written while he was taking on another hot-button sports issue, the dangers of auto racing. The Indianapolis 500 had become a national institution, an immensely popular spectacle that could attract four hundred thousand spectators on race weekend. It also left a trail of dead and injured competitors, team members, and even fans. This was a detail that most of the racing community, and the majority of the writers, tended to willfully ignore. "There was a certain aspect of things that you just didn't talk about," said Dan Gurney, a top flight driver during the 1960s and 1970s and a friend of Murray's. "So, here comes Jim, and he's not necessarily under the influence of that traditional way of not talking about it. He just came out, and he really stood on the gas about those issues."[34]

In 1964, Eddie Sachs, a driver Murray had grown particularly close with, was killed in a crash at Indianapolis, along with another driver. The incident accelerated Murray's attacks on auto racing. He wrote direct, stinging columns railing against the sport's dangers, and often felt the negative reaction from drivers and race officials around the track. He also used satire to make his points, often creating absurd scenarios that would demonstrate the sport's denial of the dangers facing its competitors. One such column prior to the 1966 Indy 500 mocked the argument, made by many racing defenders, that auto racing actually advanced the cause of auto safety, through research and development. After setting up a variety of bizarre ways in which the race would test safety, Murray concluded with the four most famous words of his career: "Gentlemen, start your coffins!"[35] He would continue to defy racing officials while defending drivers, making him a hero to some and a pariah to many others.

The combination of humor, passion, and depth quickly catapulted Murray to a level of fame and accomplishment beyond that of all but a select few journalists writing for American newspapers. His syndication numbers went up every year; the *Times* sales staff began building advertising campaigns around him. And, most important to him, he began to earn recognition from those within the profession. In 1964 the National Sportscasters and Sportswriters Association named him the National Sportswriter of the Year at the organization's annual event in Salisbury, North Carolina. It was, he wrote, "one of the great nights of my life. I was signing autographs like Mickey Mantle, everybody laughed at my jokes, and I couldn't buy a drink if I tried—which I didn't."[36] He would win the same award every year, save one, for the next thirteen years. Publishers began to see fit to print his work in book form, too. When one such book was released, his old employer acknowledged his ascension to the top of his profession. "Murray makes his work look easy, which is what Joe DiMaggio used to do," wrote a reviewer for *Sports Illustrated*.[37]

Writing a sports column, Murray wrote, was a useful but limited skill, much like hitting a curveball or lining up a downhill putt. It was one he seemed to have mastered, but in 1979 life, specifically his own body, saw fit to add another level of challenge to the task of sports columnist.

Going back to his childhood, Murray had always had health issues. His vision had never been strong, and by 1979 his right eye was nearly blind thanks to a cataract. He flew to Miami for Super Bowl XIII between the Pittsburgh Steelers and the Dallas Cowboys. He would never make it to the game.

To take a break from the pregame festivities, he went to Gulfstream Park in the middle of the week to watch a few horse races. At lunch, he ordered an egg-salad sandwich, and when it arrived, he looked down in horror at a plate filled with blood-red worms. In actuality, he had suffered four retina tears, the result of an accumulation of damage to his eye.

A series of surgeries and hospital time would follow, but by the summer, he would learn that his left eye was irreparable. Now he had only his right eye, which provided barely any vision at all. There was the possibility of surgical repair, but for the time being, he decided to resume the column. He would attempt to describe to his readers games and athletes and events that he himself would not see.

Upon the announcement, he filed what would turn out to be his single most celebrated column. It ran with the headline "If You're Expecting One-Liners, Wait a Column . . ." In it, he told his readers the story of his lost eye: "I lost an old friend the other day. . . . He stole away like a thief in the night and he took a lot with him. But not everything. He left a lot of memories." Then he recounted what he had seen with the eye, the memorable moments of his life, from the faces of his children on Christmas morning to sunsets over the Pacific. He finished by listing the iconic sports moments and figures, Ali to DiMaggio to Koufax, he had witnessed through his lost friend: "Come to think of it, I'm lucky. I saw all of those things. I see them yet."[38]

Through the fall and winter of 1979, Murray went back to his routine, writing four columns a week without the benefit of sight. His editors at the *Times* assigned a sports-desk employee, John Scheibe, to Murray full-time to chauffer him to events, look up statistics, read him the newspaper, and generally be Murray's eyes. Murray used what little vision he had left to write sentences by hand in large block letters, or he would dictate them into a recorder. The process was tedious and frustrating to him, but nearly invisible to his editors and readers. (Despite his handicap and his six months of medical leave, he would still be named National Sportswriter of the Year for 1979.) Scheibe accompanied him to practices and games and even the World Series in Baltimore and Pittsburgh, where Murray said he couldn't tell if he was interviewing Willie Stargell or Dave Parker. It worked, as Murray knew it would, because his bread and butter lay not in describing specific plays, but in finding angles and characterizations that took readers beyond the literal, and into a realm concocted in his mind, which was still functioning at peak efficiency. So he fought through the difficulties. "It had nothing to do with courage," he wrote later. "When you're in this predicament, what else can you do? It's not 'courage' that makes a cornered animal fight. It's necessity. Desperation."[39]

When the next Super Bowl was being played, Murray was in a hospital recovery room. A new surgical procedure had repaired his right eye, to the point that he would eventually be able to read, type, and even drive. There would be other vision scares, but his year in the dark was over. In the hospital, his bandages were removed, and his new eye focused on the television above, which was showing the Super Bowl. "I will never forget that sight," Murray wrote. "For some men, the most beautiful sight they will ever see in this world is a Canadian sunset or the changing of the leaves of autumn. Not me. For me, it was Craig Morton on Channel 7."[40]

By the decade of the 1980s, Los Angeles had become a professional sports capital. The Dodgers, Lakers, and Rams were all championship contenders, and Murray himself had long been an institution. In the 1980s, Pat Riley was one of the personalities associated with the highest levels of professional-sports success. He would be the head coach on five NBA championships for the Showtime Lakers, a team that took on the personality of the city. But when he first arrived in Los Angeles as a player, a decade earlier, he was a "lowly reserve" overshadowed by stars like Wilt Chamberlain and Jerry West. In fact, his first meeting with Murray came when Murray showed up at practice to interview one of those stars.

> "I read Jim Murray every day," Riley remembered. "It was a different time. When we woke up in the morning, we would all pick up a copy of the *Times* and read Jim Murray."[41]

In the 1971 NBA playoffs, a series of injuries landed Riley in the starting lineup, and he responded with several outstanding performances as the Lakers struggled and eventually lost a series to the Milwaukee Bucks. The effort gave him his first mention in a Murray column, where Murray offered him a "bouquet of flowers" for his efforts. It was, to Riley, an acknowledgment that he had arrived.

A decade later, when Riley was at the helm of the Lakers, the Murray treatment helped create the sleek, corporate CEO image that would stick with the coach for the rest of his career.

> "His style of writing was one of a kind," Riley said. "I remember how he used to characterize me, and how I dressed, if I walked into a room, I'd have my tie and my shoes and my hair in a certain way. And he'd make an example of that, compare me to a general in the army, or Fred Astaire, or whatever he came up with. Then he would add all of the metaphorical layers—he would layer it up and layer it down. He would take that depiction, and make it fun, transform it into entertainment."[42]

Indeed, while sports journalists were granted less and less access to professional athletes as spectator sports became more and more popular and lucrative in American society, just the opposite occurred for Murray. Athletes often treated an interview with Murray as a meeting with the pope. To be profiled by the master could raise one's profile considerably. The portrait he would create would rely little on quotes—"I can write better than they can talk," he liked to say—but instead on his observations and metaphorical comparisons. The result was usually the definitive newspaper profile of a personality and a spot-on read of the athlete's public image. And often the column would bestow upon the subject an unforgettable Murray line:

> Ricky Henderson's strike zone was "as small as Hitler's heart."
> Elgin Baylor was "as unstoppable as a woman's tears."
> John Wooden was "so square he was divisible by four."
> Mark Rypien was "slower than fourth-class mail."

His years at the typewriter had built up a level of trust and a reputation as a writer who wouldn't unfairly criticize athletes or coaches or executives, but who managed to provide objective analysis anyway. Peter O'Malley ran the

Jim Murray, *center*, chats with Los Angeles Dodgers manager Tommy Lasorda, *left*, and general manager Fred Claire, before a game at Dodgers Stadium in Los Angeles. Photo by Jon SooHoo/ Copyright: Los Angeles Dodgers, LLC 2017.

Dodgers through much of Murray's tenure at the *Times*. Murray had earned, through the years, a certain latitude as a writer in the city, he said.

"I can honestly say that I never recall reading anything that Jim wrote that I would have said, 'Son of a gun, that's off the wall,'" O'Malley said. "In other words, it was always fair. And he would take his shots. They weren't all puff pieces. He would criticize when you deserved it. If you made a mistake, he would show it, write about it. But there was never any animosity. I never remember me, or my Dad, reading something and saying 'I need to call Jim about that.' Never."[43]

The easy style and friendly demeanor that came out in his writing was a representation of his personality. The stars and the bit players alike enjoyed his company. And he was as quick with a good line in person as he was in print. One memorable afternoon he was following Arnold Palmer at a golf tournament. Palmer was aware that Ben Hogan was Murray's all-time favorite sports figure.[44] On one hole, Palmer hit an errant drive well off course into a deep ditch, leaving him with an impossible second shot. He walked over to Murray, who was standing behind the ropes.

"Well," Palmer said. "You're always writing about Hogan. What would Hogan do in a situation like this?"

"Hogan wouldn't be in a situation like that," Murray said.

The 1980s also brought tragedy into Murray's life. In 1982, his youngest son, Ricky, whose long-term drug abuse had put the family through years of misery, died of an overdose. The following year, Gerry, Murray's wife of thirty-nine years, was diagnosed with cancer. She died on April 1, 1984. The next day, the editors in the Sports Department at the *Times* received an unexpected column, and soon tears were flowing across the newsroom, as they would be the next day across the city, when the column titled "She Took the Magic and Happy Summer with Her" was published. In any conversation about Jim Murray with those familiar with his work, the column will invariably be mentioned. "I lost my lovely Gerry the other day. I lost the sunshine and roses, all right, the laughter in the other room. I lost the smile that lit up my life," he wrote.[45]

The twin losses sent Murray into a period of depression and loneliness. He talked of retirement, as he had in the past, but his column had become the sole focus of his life, and the task that kept him moving forward. In 1985, he became reacquainted with Linda McCoy, who, as a young Indiana native, had driven Murray around for a week as he covered the Indianapolis 500. Soon, the two were a couple (they would be together for the rest of Murray's life and marry in 1997), and Murray's happiness and energy slowly returned.

The peaks and valleys of his personal life had little effect on his career, however. By the 1990s, the lifetime achievement awards began to roll in. He became what his friend and fellow sports columnist Furman Bisher liked to call "a walking statue," for whom an organization was always at his door with one award or another. Murray was already a member of the National Sportscasters and Sportswriters Hall of Fame, inducted in 1977, to go along with his fourteen annual awards. He received the Red Smith Award from the Associated Press Sports Editors, the year after the award was established and presented to Red Smith. He was elected to various halls of fame from a variety of sports. In 1988, he traveled to Cooperstown to get the J. G. Taylor Spink Award from the Baseball Writers Association of America. He climbed the stage to make an acceptance speech on the sunny summer day that Willie Stargell was also enshrined in the hall. "If I get to heaven and they don't have a pennant chase, magic numbers and a chance to second guess a manager, I'll know I ain't in heaven," Murray told the crowd.[46]

The crowning achievement arrived in 1990, when he became only the fourth sportswriter to receive the Pulitzer Prize, the most coveted award in journalism. Sportswriters across the country wrote columns praising Murray and heralding the fact that one of their own was recognized for achievement. Murray responded with typical modesty and humor: "This is going to make it a little easier on the guy who writes my obit," he joked.

Only a few months into his job at the *Times*, back in March of 1961, Murray had compared writing a daily sports column to riding a tiger. "You may not want to stay on. But you don't dare get off. Either way, it's liable to eat you alive," he wrote.[47] The ride had grown comfortable over the years, and despite protestations that he wanted to get off, he never did. On April 15, 1998, at the age of seventy-eight, he attended the Pacific Classic at Del Mar and watched a horse named Free House win the race. He wrote a column replete with history, charting the champions of twentieth-century horse racing, from Citation to Man O' War to Secretariat, and even found a way to include Babe Ruth. The column, headlined "You Can Teach an Old Horse New Tricks," was published Sunday morning.[48] Murray died of a heart attack at his home Sunday night.

Four days later, on the morning of Murray's funeral, the *Times* printed a four-page extra edition devoted to him, which followed a week-long tribute to his life and work in print. Presidents, athletes, entertainers, writers—dignitaries of all types appeared in the pages of the paper to honor Murray. At his funeral, Murray's friend, broadcaster Jack Whitaker, delivered the eulogy to a standing-room-only crowd, filled with the most famous men and women of Los Angeles sports. "Jim Murray knew better than most that the only proper tools with which to journey through this vale of tears were the generosity of the human spirit and wit and humor," Whitaker told the congregation. "He got through it in great style. If we emulate him, they will get us through too. James Patrick Murray, my, what a grand man you were."[49]

Murray, years before, had made a much less hagiographical attempt at writing leads for his own obituary: "Jim Murray, ticketed for double-parking on a busy thoroughfare in Watchung, N.J., in 1938, died yesterday at the age of 90," was one possibility he tried out in his column.[50] On a day he was feeling more serious, he put his contributions in perspective. "I covered the circus," he wrote. "I felt privileged to have done so. Some of the happiest hours of my life were spent in a press box. Sure, I helped keep the hype going, the calliope playing. I can live with that. It's what I am."[51]

CHAPTER FIFTEEN

Vin Scully

The Voice of Los Angeles

ELLIOTT J. GORN AND ALLISON LAUTERBACH DALE

This chapter combines history and memoir. The authors are both historians and both grew up in Los Angeles as Dodgers fans. Gorn followed the team in the late 1950s and 1960s. Lauterbach Dale became a fan a generation later. With the realization that the voice of Dodgers announcer Vin Scully was their common tie to Los Angeles, they decided to write about his importance to the city.

"A good evening to you wherever you may be." The familiar voice almost sings out of the radio, embracing listeners with the warmth of a soft Los Angeles evening. For more than sixty years, the same greeting has welcomed Dodgers fans to pull up a chair and listen to a baseball game. The man behind those words, Vin Scully, is more than just a well-loved sportscaster. He is the voice of LA.

Born in 1927, Vincent Edward Scully grew up in the Bronx listening to sportscasters on the radio, a career that was barely as old as he was. He took up broadcasting while a student at Fordham University. After graduation, he briefly worked for WTOP in Washington, DC, announcing news, weather, music, and occasionally filling in on the sports desk.[1]

Scully's professional breakthrough came on November 12, 1949, when he was just twenty-two years old, thanks to Brooklyn Dodgers' announcer Red Barber. When Barber needed someone to call the University of Maryland–Boston University football game at Fenway Park for CBS Sports Radio, Barber remembered the red-headed kid he had met months before.

A version of this essay originally appeared in Daniel A. Nathan's *Rooting for the Home Team: Sport, Community and Identity* under the title "The Voice of Los Angeles" (Champaign: University of Illinois Press, 2013), 125–38. It is reprinted here with minor editing changes and a new conclusion.

Scully assumed that he would have a press box from which to do the play-by-play, so he left his coat in the hotel room. But on that frigid November New England night, he was relegated to the roof with nothing but a table and a microphone. Scully never complained. Barber heard the story later and was impressed with the rookie's professionalism. When Ernie Harwell left the Dodgers' broadcasting team two months later, Barber once again thought of Scully.[2]

"I had a feeling for years," Barber later wrote in his autobiography, "it was like a woman who has never had a child. I guess I had never gotten over my early ambition to teach. I always had the dream of taking an untutored kid who showed some promise and of putting him on the air for what he was, a neophyte learning the trade. Scully was a perfect choice." Barber went on to note, though, "Whatever made him the fine broadcaster he is, he had when he started."[3]

Scully joined the Dodgers at spring training in Vero Beach, Florida, in March 1950. More than sixty years later, he is still with the team, the longest tenured announcer in American sports history. When Scully began his career with the Dodgers, sportscasters had been doing regular live coverage for scarcely twenty-five years. Scully, in other words, has been at it for well over two-thirds of sports radio's existence.

Over the course of his six-decade career, Scully has worked in three home stadiums, for five Dodgers owners, during twelve US presidencies, and under eight Major League Baseball commissioners. Dodger Stadium, opened in 1962, is now the third-oldest Major League ballpark (behind Fenway Park and Wrigley Field), and Scully has announced fifty seasons from it. Already a member of the Baseball Hall of Fame, the Radio Hall of Fame, and the American Sportscasters Association Hall of Fame, he is a four-time national sportscaster of the year, an Emmy Award winner, has a star on the Hollywood Walk of Fame, and was elected the American Sportscasters Association's "Top Sportscaster of all time."[4]

While he is the last to flaunt his celebrity status, Scully understands the great platform afforded to him. "Our job is to help people escape, to help them forget their troubles," he once explained.[5] He frequently reminds listeners that they are doing just that. In the fall of 2008, when the California hillsides were once again ablaze, he told fans that baseball was but a child's game. And like he did throughout Korea, Vietnam, the first and second Gulf Wars, and after the World Trade Center towers crumbled, Scully always made it clear that the game was a healthy, even necessary diversion from the real business of life, but a diversion nonetheless.

With a strong sense of perspective—of history—Scully emphasizes to listeners that baseball is a special little world, fascinating to be sure, but not to be overvalued. For example, during an otherwise unremarkable game against the San Diego Padres on June 6, 2010, Scully reminded the audience of life beyond the baseball diamond. Never straying from the task at hand, calling the game, Scully went on to tell the story of D-Day: "Oh yeah, you could just sum it up and say, 'oh sure, Allied Forces invaded Normandy.' There is so much more—as Troy Glaus checks in, Ely's pitch, fastball inside, ball one. First of all, D-Day, the 'D' in front of Day doesn't mean anything. It just meant the day of a military operation—the 1–0 pitch on the way, outside—and it used to be D-Day for any military operation but as the years have gone by when you say 'D-Day,' they're talking about *this* day in 1944. The 2–0 pitch fouled away...."[6]

This is one of the reasons Scully is so successful. Because he eschews hype and bluster, we come to trust him. Scully treats his listeners like adults who understand that the game is a fair-weather pleasure, a moment of grace in a hard world. He doesn't lie to us with apocalyptic intimations of sports' importance. He never exaggerates, either factually or emotionally. The game is enough, the game is the thing, the game unfolds like a nice leisurely story, told by a man who sees it all and speaks it in the cadences of summer.

More than anything, Scully is a storyteller. There is the story of each at bat, merging into the larger narrative of the game, the statistics (Scully's legendary pregame preparation assures that the right statistics are always at hand) that give the still longer view of the season, one of the hundred seasons that preceded it. Scully's flow of words is the flow of baseball history, the fan's history, and against that backdrop—the tale of the player who spent seventeen years in the minor leagues before his call-up, or of the one whose grandmother raised him and watched him pitch a perfect game, or of the players from the far corners of America and the globe, now on the field with the game on the line—he embeds each day's new stories.

Above all—magically, mysteriously—Scully's voice creates a bond of intimacy and community between himself and the fans. Maybe all sports broadcasting strives to accomplish this merging of the personal with the communal, and maybe other broadcasters pull it off sometimes, but Scully has done it for generations.

That closeness became especially visible in the early 1960s. We think of how wired we all are today, but before smart phones and iPods, there were transistor radios. In Los Angeles, one of the most striking things about these portable sets, beginning just a few years after the Dodgers came to town, was how many fans brought them to the ballpark. "The transistor radio was probably the greatest single break that I had in Southern California," Scully once said. "It enabled me to talk more to the fans—and to elicit a response."[7]

But it wasn't just the number of fans who listened; any home radio could do that. When the Dodgers built their new stadium at Chavez Ravine and put together a contending team, the club also secured a loyal fan base. Thousands of fans brought their radios to every Dodgers game. Scully's voice literally echoed throughout the ballpark in the 1960s through the 1980s. Enough fans still bring radios that you often get his running commentary of the live action on the field. This is a metaphor for Scully's place in Los Angeles—the individual radios merging their sound into one big voice, pervading the ballpark, pervading the city.

Angelenos' sense of civic identity resonates with Scully's voice, because some of their most powerful memories are associated with that sound. Scully himself has said, "One of the nicest parts of my job is to have someone come up to me and say, 'When I hear your voice, I think of nights in the backyard with my mom and dad.' It's a wonderful feeling to be a bridge to the past and to unite generations." Always humble, he's quick to add, "The sport of baseball does that, and I am just a part of it."[8]

It is all about baseball, of course, but in Los Angeles, fans know the game through *his* eyes, *his* word-pictures, *his* voice, and it is the voice of intimacy. When Scully described the anniversary of D-Day above, he began, "I don't want this to be an intrusion, but I think we've been friends long enough, you'll understand." And we do. That is why a 2010 *Los Angeles Times* poll found that Scully was tied with former mayor Tom Bradley as the city's most admired citizen of all time.[9]

Many die-hard fans still bring Scully to the games. The rest of us tune in on TV, in the car, and, increasingly for displaced Dodgers fans, online. With the advent of satellite radio, Vin has developed even more of a following. "One of the things we hear from our listeners is how much they love being able to hear Vin Scully," notes David Butler, director of corporate affairs for XM Radio. "Many of them are people who may have seen him on TV or who are baseball fans who have heard about the legend of Vin Scully but had never had the luxury to hear him call a game on the radio."[10] For Los Angelenos spread across the world, online broadcasts offer the ultimate connection back home, whether they are on a military base in the Middle East, in an easy chair in New York, or in a college library in the heartland. Distance need not separate Dodgers fans from the team or city they love. Vin welcomes them back to both. He is attuned to how scattered his audience is, but he also knows that his voice brings them all together. That is his most important role.

Maybe most striking, in a city that routinely destroys all sense of tradition and history, that embraces each postmodern moment as distinct from the last, Scully is all about continuity. For half a century, Los Angelenos have always been able to count on four things: smog, traffic, seventy-degree winters, and Vin Scully. We mark time and the big moments by memories of his broadcasts. Fifty years isn't a long time in the course of human history, but for a town like Los Angeles, it represents the deep past. Not just longevity, but Scully's devotion to baseball, made manifest in his formidable knowledge of the game, matters here, too. He has occasionally announced other sports during his career, but not often. Angelenos' loyalty to Scully was reinforced by his loyalty to baseball.

The children of immigrants from eastern cities, of dust bowl refugees in the 1930s, and of midwesterners whose opportunities on the land closed down as farms consolidated, must have heard him as a voice from home. But others too—African Americans who came from the South in search of equality, jobs, and schools for their children in the 1940s and 1950s; Asian immigrants and their descendants for whom midcentury California began to fulfill earlier promises; Mexican American kids whose parents sought fresh opportunities for their families—all had some familiarity with baseball, but came to think of it as quintessentially American. Scully's easy presentation of the game was tied up with the promise of California life.

Even in the ultimate polyglot city, Scully's voice crosses neighborhood boundaries. In East LA, Gil Reyes, who trained tennis star Andre Agassi, learned English over the radio: "I had a little transistor. KABC every night. Vin Scully was my English teacher."[11] Writing in the *Los Angeles Times* columnist Hector Tobar lists "appreciate Vin Scully" as one of his ten keys to being a "true Angeleno," and Tobar adds, "drop Scully's name into a conversation, and it will instantly identify you as a real Angeleno."[12] Another Dodgers fan who calls himself "Roberto" named his website VinScullyismyHomeBoy.com.[13] A Chinese American blogger, who once taught a constitutional law class at a juvenile detention facility, recalled: "During one of my classes, a Mexican student quipped that though there is tension between blacks and Mexicans on Los Angeles' streets, the one person both groups would unite to defend would be 'the Dodgers announcer.' Scully has such unquestioned respect among people of all races because it is unquestionably evident he respects everyone."[14]

Los Angeles was the first American city to have Major League Baseball games announced in Spanish. Jaime Jarrin, himself a Hall of Fame announcer and a fifty-year veteran of LA Dodgers broadcasts, has a wide following among Spanish speakers, not just in Southern California but in Mexico too. Still, the children of immigrants—the kids we grew up with and now their kids—listen to Scully.[15] Without wishing to dismiss the nostalgia many people have for the Brooklyn Dodgers, the Los Angeles version of the team meant at least as much to the civic identity of the booming new megalopolis as it did in Brooklyn. Every tear shed by a Brooklyn fan watered Angelenos' sense of their town as a big, wide-open place, no mere stepchild to the East Coast. Suddenly, when the team came to LA in 1958, it was a major league city. This was not just a metaphor—we were becoming major league in every way, and for half a century, Vin Scully's voice reminded us that America's best was moving west.

* * *

Elliott recalls: One of my earliest childhood memories is of being at the old Coliseum for a Dodgers game in 1958, the team's first year in LA. I don't recall who the Dodgers played or if we won, I just remember being there. And I remember that a year later, in October 1959 when I was eight years old, I must have been listening to the game at school—it seems amazing that they allowed me to—because my third grade teacher, Mrs. Friedman, let me announce to the class that the Dodgers had just won game six of the Series, making them World Champions. Even then I knew, because I read the backs of my baseball cards, and because our neighbor was from Brooklyn, that that Dodgers came to us with a glorious past. Living gods—Hodges, Snyder, Furillo, Podres—strode the field.

Hearing Scully's voice is also among my earliest LA memories. In the late 1950s, I'd fall asleep with the Dodgers game coming lightly over the radio. Even as a kid, it was impossible not to recognize how good Scully was because the Dodgers had two broadcasters, Scully and Jerry Doggett, the latter perfectly competent at calling the games, but even to a nine-year-old's ear, Doggett was workmanlike, nothing special. The idea always was to stay awake through his innings to get to Scully's.

Maybe it was the radio still murmuring as I slept that indelibly planted Scully's voice in my brain. Radio was everything back in the Dodgers' first couple of decades in LA. The team owner, Walter O'Malley, was convinced that television would kill attendance at the games, so he only broadcast nine games a year on TV, those three 3-game sets they played each season up in San Francisco against the Giants at Candlestick Park, where sometimes the fog was so thick you thought there was something wrong with your television.

It is amazing how powerful the memories are, not so much for the details, which are few, but for the emotions: Winning discount tickets for good grades (a promotion the Dodgers ran year after year in cooperation with the L.A. schools), going to beautiful new Dodger Stadium, which opened in 1962, with my brother and my father, hearing that same voice in the ballpark that I heard at home, and realizing that it was because of the thousands of fans who brought transistor radios to the game. Often in the evening I would go over to my friend Gary White's house, and there in his living room, Mrs. White stood ironing the next day's clothing for the family, always with Vinny's voice pouring out of the radio. He was with me also on many weekend afternoons as I did gardening jobs around the neighborhood. Those were the years of Sandy Koufax and Don Drysdale, of Maury Wills and Tommie Davis. Town and team were in love, and Vinny was the matchmaker.

Most vividly, I remember my father and I pacing the living room, listening to the ninth inning of Koufax's perfect game against the Chicago Cubs in 1965. What made it so memorable was less the game itself than how Scully spoke, never fast or overheated, but relaxed and conversational, yet building tension all the way. This is how he announced the early moments of the ninth inning in what is now an iconic broadcast (note to reader—you have to hear this; it is all about sound, so read it aloud):

> ... Here's the strike one pitch to Krug, fastball, swung on and missed, strike two. And you can almost taste the pressure now. Koufax lifted his cap, ran his fingers through his black hair, then pulled the cap back down, fussing at the bill. Krug must feel it too as he backs out, heaves a sigh, took off his helmet, put it back on, and steps back up to the plate. Tracewski is over to his right to fill up the middle, Kennedy is deep to guard the line. The strike two pitch on the way, fastball, outside, ball one. Krug started to go after it and held up.

> ... One and two the count to Chris Krug. It is 9:41 p.m. on September the 9th. The 1–2 pitch on the way, curve ball, tapped foul, off to the left and out of play.... There are twenty-nine thousand people in the ballpark and a million butterflies.... Koufax into his windup and the 1–2 pitch, fastball, fouled back and out of play.... And it begins to get tough to be a teammate and sit in the dugout and have to watch. Sandy, back of the rubber, now toes it, all the boys in the bullpen straining to get a better look as they look through the wire fence in left field.... One and two the count to Chris Krug. Koufax, feet together, now to his windup and the 1–2 pitch, fastball outside, ball two. A lot of people in the ballpark now are starting to see the pitches with their hearts.... Two and two, the count to Chris Krug. Sandy reading signs, into his windup, 2–2 pitch, fastball got him swinging ... Sandy Koufax has struck out twelve. He is two outs away from a perfect game ...[16]

I left Los Angeles in 1969, but I carried on as a Dodgers fan for twenty more years. I'd listen to games or go to Dodger Stadium on trips home to visit my family. I was back in California in 1988, living up in the Bay Area for a year, and there in October were my Dodgers, seemingly overmatched in the World Series by the Oakland Athletics, a team with some fine pitching and a couple of scary hitters, Mark McGwire and Jose Canseco. With great good fortune, Scully was doing the national broadcast that year. So there I am, lying on the floor of my dingy little Palo Alto apartment, watching game one on a twelve-inch black-and-white TV. I had little hope. The Dodgers' lineup was truly mediocre, especially with the heart and soul of this team, outfielder Kirk Gibson, hobbled by a hamstring pull in one leg and a torn-up knee in the other. Scully had announced before the game began that Gibson would not see action that night. Orel Hershiser led a very tough LA pitching staff, but he didn't start the first game, and Tim Belcher, who did, gave up a grand slam in the second inning to Canseco. Somehow, though, the Dodgers hung in.

Bottom of the ninth, 4–3 A's, and one of the toughest closers in the game, Dennis Eckersley—the Most Valuable Player of the just-completed American League Championship Series—on the mound. Eckersley got two quick outs, and Dodger Stadium grew deathly quiet. But then outfielder Mike Davis worked the count for a walk. The pitcher was due up next, and no one was on deck. To everyone's amazement, Gibson—who had spent the whole game in the training room but had suited up and come to the dugout for the ninth—grabbed a bat and limped to the plate. He fouled off two, and you could see him wince as he tried to drive the ball with his legs. But he stayed alive, fouled off three more pitches and took three balls for a full count. Eckersley's ninth pitch to Gibson was a slider, maybe a little further inside than he wanted, and Gibson reached out and flicked it toward right, much harder than it first appeared.

"High fly ball into right field . . . she is . . . gone!" And then Scully didn't say a word for half a minute as the crowd went wild and Gibson gingerly jogged around the base paths. Scully only broke his silence as Gibson hobbled across home plate into the arms of his teammates: "In a year that has been so improbable, the impossible has happened." There was no grandiosity in his tone but humor, the humor of recognizing that life sometimes plays a little trick then chuckles at our surprise. Scully capped it all with this benediction: "You know, I said it once before a few days ago, that Kirk Gibson was not the Most Valuable Player, that the Most Valuable Player for the Dodgers was Tinkerbell. But tonight, I think Tinkerbell backed off for Kirk Gibson."[17]

One last thing about that moment. When Gibson hit the homer, after a moment of blinking incredulity, I was screaming along with those fans in Dodger Stadium. Screaming until I realized that the apartment building where I lived had gone dead quiet. Of course. I was just across the bay from Oakland. My enthusiasm in that neighborhood was not appreciated.

I never moved back to Los Angeles, and I've since switched my allegiance to other teams. I tried being a Cincinnati Reds fan when I lived there in the early 1990s, but it never took. Something about that bland town and soulless Riverfront Stadium kept those good and exciting Reds teams from capturing my imagination. Then I became a Cubs fan, an addiction to failure that I still fight. I love Chicago, but whatever it is that goes on in that yuppie hell known as Wrigley Field, it isn't baseball.

I often go back to LA because my daughter lives there. There is nothing like hearing Vinny still calling games. I'm not a big fan of Southern California, but his voice somehow captures what is best about the place, the ease and flow of outdoor living, the beauty of mountains and desert and ocean. There is grace in Scully's cadences, just as there is grace in that mellow landscape in the twilight glow.

* * *

Allison recalls: My love of the Dodgers and Vin Scully is not a fleeting affection. I am, in fact, a fourth-generation Dodgers fan. My great-grandfather, Max, loved 'Dem Bums when they still played at Ebbets Field in Brooklyn.

He stayed loyal when the team moved west, introducing my grandmother to Dodgers Blue. After her, my uncle, and finally my little brother and myself, took up the Dodgers legacy. While the Dodgers have changed stadiums and uniforms, lineups and locales, two things have remained constant: Vin Scully and my family's loyalty to the team. Though I never met my great-grandfather, he knew, as I know, the sound of Vin's voice.

So it is against the backdrop of his broadcasts that my family knows Los Angeles. My aunt was literally born to the sound of his voice. A doctor who brought his addiction to the game into the delivery room caught her. My grandmother, of course, didn't mind.

My grandmother would later introduce me to Vinny, too. As a four-year-old, I stood in her kitchen, braiding challah for Shabbat dinner, Scully's voice ever-present in the background. Long before I understood baseball, I knew the sound of his broadcasts, the soundtrack of my childhood. While my grandmother passed away over sixteen years ago, when I hear Vin call a game, I'm instantly transported back to her yellow kitchen. With his help each season, my love of my grandmother and of baseball renews itself over and over again. Years later, sitting in the library reading for my PhD exams, I was still listening to Vinny. The online archive of games kept a constant stream of his trademark anecdotes and stories streaming to my ears.

Although Scully has helped me mark several key milestones in my life, his broadcasts often serve as events in and of themselves. You remember where you were when Kennedy was shot, when the World Trade Center towers fell, or, if you're my mother, when Diana and Charles got married. Baseball fans have their own memorable moments: when Buckner missed the ball, when Larsen was perfect, when Gibson went yard (all of which Scully announced). Vin's 1965 play-by-play of Sandy Koufax's fourth no-hitter and only perfect game is one of those moments. You remember hearing that kind of extemporaneous poetry.

I was eleven in 1994. In the car on the way home from a Red Sox game at Fenway Park, my uncle and I got to talking about Dodgers baseball. Though he had moved to Boston years before, my uncle remained a loyal Dodgers fan, even naming his golden retriever after the team. The conversation inevitably turned to Vin Scully. In the days before Internet broadcasts, my uncle had no way of listening to games on a regular basis. When I asked how he coped, he quickly popped in a cassette tape.

"Three times in his sensational career has Sandy Koufax walked out to the mound to pitch a fateful ninth where he turned in a no-hitter. But tonight, September the ninth, nineteen hundred and sixty-five, he made the toughest walk of his career, I'm sure, because through eight innings he has pitched a perfect game..."

And so Scully and Koufax together began the ninth inning. As the Boston skyline passed by, my uncle and I traveled in time, transported back to the Chavez Ravine, the timeless broadcast echoing in the night air.

Even though I knew how the game turned out, I listened with bated breath. "Two and two to Harvey Kuenn, one strike away. Sandy into his windup, here's the pitch: Swung on and *missed* a perfect game!"

Then the best broadcaster in sports did what only he could do: he went silent. For thirty-eight seconds, all we heard was the roar of the crowd. Vin let the audience tell the story.

Almost thirty years after that broadcast, my uncle and I were united around the radio. A moment my uncle had first shared with his mother, my grandmother, we had made our own.

Koufax's perfect performance was matched by Scully's call. That play-by-play is iconic in Los Angeles, and some even consider it a work of baseball literature. As sportswriter Dave Sheinin once observed, "To hear Scully call the ninth inning... is to make a baseball writer contemplate a career as a roofer. Off the top of his head, without the benefit of a delete button or an editor, Scully composed one of the most gorgeous pieces of baseball literature you will ever encounter."[18]

While several other broadcasts stand out, I remember best those I shared with my family. As a kindergartener, I got to stay up past my bedtime to watch the first game of the 1988 World Series against the Oakland A's. By the ninth inning, Vin was in charge of the television play-by-play. I sat on the couch next to my father and listened to Scully tell us that Kirk Gibson, the 1988 National League MVP plagued by leg problems, was nowhere to be found. Gibson, it turns out, was watching the broadcast from somewhere in the Dodgers' clubhouse while he underwent physical therapy. Legend has it that Vin's observation about Gibby motivated the ailing player to get in the game.

We all watched as Gibby wobbled to the plate. Once he was in the batter's box, Vin, as nobody else could, noted how he was "shaking his left leg, making it quiver, like a horse trying to get rid of a troublesome fly." The count got to three balls, two strikes. And then it happened. Gibson launched a long fly ball just over the right field wall, then he limped around the bases, pumping his fist. While I was screaming, Vin was silent, once again letting the crowd tell the story. And then, perfectly, "In a year that has been so improbable . . . the impossible has happened!" It is impossible for Dodgers fans and Angelenos to recall the home run without also hearing Vin's voice, it is played so often in Los Angeles. And I couldn't not tell it again in these pages.

Twenty-one years later, I sat in the nosebleed seats with my little brother on opening day 2009. My brother clutched his transistor radio (my gift to him for his recent birthday) as we watched the pregame festivities. The Dodgers honored Scully's sixtieth season with the team by asking him to throw out the first pitch (that day we all learned that he is a southpaw). After the ceremonial toss, Scully addressed the fans. "I have needed you a lot more than you have needed me," he told them. I'm confident that all fifty-six thousand fans disagreed with his assessment. And then, like he does before every broadcast, he almost sang the words, "It's time for Dodgers baseball."

The 2011 season was Vin's sixty-second with the Dodgers. For the past few years, he has signed a series of one-year contracts, each time renewing fan loyalties to the Dodgers. Before the 2010 season, however, we got a major scare. That March, one night during spring training, headlines flashed across the Internet announcing that Scully had fallen and hit his head. The news couldn't come fast enough as the City of Angels collectively held its breath. He was, to all of our relief, okay.

The incident was a reminder of the octogenarian's mortality. With each one-year contract, we count our blessings that we get to experience another Scully season, but for how much longer remains unclear. And when he does finally retire, it seems likely that many fans will cut their ties to the team. People move on, find other passions, look to other sports. Scully keeps fans coming back to the Dodgers, at least as much as the other way around. More, much more, without quite realizing it, his voice has become one of those markers of place. Like the sign up in the hills that reads "Hollywood," like the first glimpse of the ocean as you approach Pacific Coast Highway, the timbre and rhythm of Scully's words say, "Welcome to Los Angeles."

* * *

If you grew up in Los Angeles then moved away, especially a generation or two ago, you had to get used to people looking at you and saying, "Huh? LA? No one grows up there, they just move there." One friend actually loved watching others react when he told them he was a fifth-generation Angeleno (he lives in Virginia now).

Why is that? LA has been America's second-largest city for decades, and yet there is something inauthentic about it in our imaginations, as if having roots there was impossible. Of course Hollywood has everything to do with this. Anywhere else in America, the word "industry" conjures images of factories, of hot, cacophonous mills where men pour steel or pound cars together, of women sweating their lives away in textile mills and garment shops, of immigrants and minorities doing the work that the native-born shun, of blue-collar workers either exploited by their bosses or defiantly organized into powerful unions.

But in Los Angeles today, "the industry" means just one thing: the film and entertainment business, whose productions are mere light and sound, fleeting, weightless, insubstantial. We were wrong. It turns out that all of those mines and mills and factories were chimerical. Commercials, television shows, movies, reality TV, the whole image-driven world: That is what's real, that is what lasts. US Steel: Gone. GM: On life support. Pixar: Thriving.

Los Angeles has always seemed to be in the grip of centrifugal forces. Sleepy towns wake up as booming suburbs, whole nations of immigrants pour in, new freeways slither over dry riverbeds. With Angelenos spending so much time in their cars, with new exurbs impossibly far from downtown, with so many immigrants busy becoming new Americans, it makes perfect sense that one of the things holding the town together is a voice on the radio. For more than sixty years Scully's has been *the* voice of LA. And for those of us who no longer live there, what could be better than flying into LAX, renting a car, heading out the 405 freeway, scanning the radio band, and up pops Vinny, still where he's been all these decades, welcoming us back to Dodgers baseball.

Even though we can't imagine the Dodgers without him, he has never ever been a homer like the late Harry Carey, so full of a hypocrite's devotion that he could love both the Cubs *and* the Cardinals. Nor was there ever in Scully's delivery even a trace of that horrible apocalyptic tone we've come to associate with the likes of Bob Costas or Marv Albert, as if they were announcing a Soviet invasion of western Europe. No, Scully is perfect for the Southland, because his voice resonates with that easy, flowing ideal of Southern California life.

Vin Scully broadcast Dodgers baseball for sixty-seven seasons before retiring in 2016. Photo Courtesy of Jon SooHoo/Dodgers.

Scully's persona comes through not in the cheap, overheated, and patronizing tones so common to sports announcing. On the contrary, it's his devotion to his craft—to getting the story right, giving us key statistics, filling in with the back-stories, building drama with his poetic rhythms—that tells us he is LA's own. We love him because, in a city filled with outrageous self-promotion and continual self-regard, here is the real deal—an oasis of understatement, of substance, of art. All elegance and ease and seeming effortlessness, perhaps he is best thought of as a performance artist, without a hint of the pretentiousness that phrase sometimes conjures.

One last thing. Scully has done it in a town dedicated to being forever young. Los Angeles is all about youth, appearances, pleasing surfaces. The town is a living denial of age, of generational continuity. And yet there is Vinny, his shock of red hair now feathered with white, doing his job for more than six decades, offering the city nothing but continuity across generations and ethnic groups and neighborhoods. His are among the better angels of Los Angeles's nature.

Postscript

The 2016 season marked the sixty-seventh and final year Vin Scully invited us all to pull up a chair because "It's time for Dodgers baseball." Before the first pitch on opening day, just outside the ballpark on the newly named "Vin Scully Avenue," the team kicked off a season dedicated to celebrating and thanking Scully. Don Newcombe, who pitched on Scully's first opening day in 1950, was there. So was Sandy Koufax, whose perfect game in 1965 was immortalized by Scully's words. So too was Clayton Kershaw, another brilliant southpaw and the face of today's Dodgers. Master of Ceremonies Al Michaels concluded the festivities with the words, "And now, all Vinny has to do is go to work!"

As in each of the sixty-six prior seasons, go to work he did. By some blessing of fate from the baseball gods, there was a player on the field that day named Socrates Brito, a rookie center fielder for the opposing Arizona Diamondbacks. And so, effortlessly woven into the day's story of strikes and balls, line drives and double plays, Scully told us about the great Greek philosopher from millennia ago, the old man who came down to us as the voice of ancient Athens.

That's one of the keys to Scully. It isn't just the longevity of a gifted announcer. Scully always brought the past into the present, made it alive for us. Stan Kasten, the Dodgers' president, reflected on the historical treasure that is Scully. "Now here's the thing," he told the *New York Times*, "Branch Rickey, before he was an executive, was a major league player. He broke in with the St. Louis Browns in 1905. So Vin Scully has discussed baseball with major leaguers who were here from 1905 through yesterday, O.K.? Who can do that? No one. There's one person on the planet. It's Vin Scully."[19] Scully didn't just know Branch Rickey (and Bill Veeck and Jackie Robinson and the rest); he kept them alive for us.

There are new voices behind the microphones for the Dodgers and Dodgers fans still tune in each night. But Scully will never truly be replaced. And when games are dull or the score lopsided, many of us will sneak away to the audio archives and listen to the real master, his voice and the games he called and the stories he told more alive than ever.

Notes

Introduction

1. Kevin Courrier, *Randy Newman's American Dreams* (Toronto: ECW, 2005), 245–47; "I Love LA" page at "Songfacts" website; http://www.songfacts.com/detail.php?id=4686; "I Love LA" webpage, https://en.wikipedia.org/wiki/I_Love_L.A. The quest to pen a "civic anthem" for Los Angeles dates to the period in which Newman wrote the song. Dennis McDouglas, "L.A: The Spot Is Still without a Song," *Los Angeles Times*, October 6, 1984, J1.

2. Members of the Briggs admitted that they wrote "This Is LA" in 2008 to serve as an urban anthem in response ubiquity of "I Love LA" in serving that role. "The Briggs Chat with Kevin & Bean about How 'This Is LA' Became an Anthem for the LA Kings," June 6, 2012, http://kroq.cbslocal.com/2012/06/06/the-briggs-chat-with-kevin-bean-about-how-this-is-la-became-an-anthem-for-the-la-kings/. Anschutz Entertainment Group, a major sports and rock-and-roll concert promoter, owns both Kings (since 1995) and the Galaxy (since 2007), as well as the Staples Center and Stubhub Center that Kings and Galaxy, respectively, call home. AEG webpage, http://aegworldwide.com/about/companyoverview/companyoverview. My thanks to Wayne Wilson, sports historian, vice president for educational services of the LA84 Foundation, and longtime season ticket holder for the Galaxy for alerting me to the many shifts in the landscape of Los Angeles sports anthems.

3. Gary Klein, "Rams Beat Cowboys, 28–24, in Preseason Opener," *Los Angeles Times*, August 12, 2016; http://www.latimes.com/sports/rams/la-sp-rams-cowboys-20160813-snap-story.html.

4. David Wharton, "2008–09 NBA CHAMPIONS; We Love It! We Love It!" *Los Angeles Times*, June 17, 2009, S4; Bill Plaschke, "Playoffs: LA-6, C-0," *Los Angeles Times*, October 19, 2016, D1.

5. In his rumination "Is Los Angeles a Great Sports Town?" the journalist and Los Angeles native J. A. Adande blames "sniping fans" and "media types" from outside of Southern California for constructing the "tired cliché of fans arriving late and leaving early" but then admits that the stereotype is not entirely undeserved. He insists that Los Angeles has generated passionate fan bases, at least for teams that win with style. "Put a good, entertaining product out there and the city will support it," he insists in making his case. Still, as he notes elsewhere in his meditations on why Los Angeles lost both of its NFL franchises for an extended period, it is hard to draw the local populace to see mediocre teams, a habit that has become a badge of honor in a multitude of other cities where fans turn out regardless of whether the local side wins or even plays entertainingly. J. A. Adande, *The Best Los Angeles Sports Arguments: The 100 Most Controversial, Debatable Questions for Die-Hard Fans* (Naperville, IL: Sourcebooks, 2007), 2–11.

6. Courrier, *Randy Newman's American Dreams*, 245–47. Lyrics for "I Love LA" at Google Music Play; https://play.google.com/music/preview/Ttca7zkgjunufd2ln3newkcxpza?lyrics=1&utm_source=google&utm_medium=search&utm_campaign=lyrics&pcampaignid=kp-lyrics.

7. Contemporary history of sport has made the city the fulcrum of its explorations since the 1970s. Mark Dyreson, "Sport History around the World: The United States of America," in *The Routledge Companion to Sport History*, ed. S. W. Pope and John Nauright (London: Routledge, 2010), 599–623. Among the best urban sport histories are Stephen Hardy, *How Boston Played: Sport, Recreation, and Community, 1865–1915* (Boston: Northeastern University Press, 1982); Roy Rosenzweig, *Eight Hours for What We Will: Workers and Leisure in an Industrial City, 1870–1910* (Cambridge: Cambridge University Press, 1983); Melvin L. Adelman, *A Sporting Time: New York City and the Rise of Modern Athletics, 1820–70* (Urbana: University of Illinois Press, 1986); and Steven A. Riess, *City Games: The Evolution of American Urban Society and the Rise of Sports* (Urbana: University of Illinois Press, 1989).

8. While some have questioned the authenticity of the quip, attributing it instead to Aldous Huxley or H. L. Mencken, the acid-tongue Los Angeles hater Parker generally gets the credit for the infamous line. Adrienne Crew, "Native Intelligence: Misquoting Dorothy Parker," *LA Observed*, August 22, 2013, http://www.laobserved.com/intell/2013/08/misquoting_dorothy_parker.php.

9. David Samuel Torres-Rouff, *Before L.A.: Race, Space, and Municipal Power in Los Angeles, 1781–1894* (New Haven, CT: Yale University Press, 2013); John Walton Caughey, *Los Angeles: Biography of a City* (Berkeley: University of California Press, 1976); Carey McWilliams, *Southern California Country: An Island on the Land* (New York: Duell, Sloan & Pearce, 1946).

10. John E. Ferling, *Whirlwind: The American Revolution and the War That Won It* (New York: Bloomsbury Press, 2015).

11. Caughey, *Los Angeles*; McWilliams, *Southern California Country*; Robert M. Fogelson, *The Fragmented Metropolis: Los Angeles, 1850–1930* (Cambridge, MA: Harvard University Press, 1967); Tom Sitton, *Metropolis in the Making: Los Angeles in the 1920s* (Berkeley: University of California Press, 2001); Kevin Starr, *Material Dreams: Southern California through the 1920s* (New York: Oxford University Press, 1990); David Rieff, *Los Angeles: Capital of the Third World* (New York: Simon & Schuster, 1991); Mike Davis, *City of Quartz: Excavating the Future in Los Angeles* (New York: Verso, 1990); Vincent Brook, *Land of Smoke and Mirrors: A Cultural History of Los Angeles* (New Brunswick, NJ: Rutgers University Press, 2013); Norman M. Klein, *The History of Forgetting: Los Angeles and the Erasure of Memory* (New York: Verso, 1998); Jules Tygiel, *The Great Los Angeles Swindle: Oil, Stocks, and Scandal during the Roaring Twenties* (New York: Oxford University Press, 1994); Bill Deverell, *White Washed Adobe: The Rise of Los Angeles and the Remaking of Its Mexican Past* (Berkeley: University of California Press, 2004).

12. Rieff, *Los Angeles*; Davis, *City of Quartz*; Brook, *Land of Smoke and Mirrors*; Klein, *The History of Forgetting*.

13. UCLA and USC in particular have developed athletic programs that shaped American sports in a variety of ways, by creating dynastic powerhouses on the field and in the gymnasium and by providing spaces for clashes over civil rights and racial equality. See, especially, John Matthew Smith, *The Sons of Westwood: John Wooden, UCLA, and the Dynasty That Changed College Basketball* (Urbana: University of Illinois Press, 2013); Steve Delshon, *Cardinal and Gold: The Oral History of USC Trojans Football* (New York: Crown/Archetype, 2016); Lane Demas, *Integrating the Gridiron: Black Civil Rights and American College* (New Brunswick, NJ: Rutgers University Press, 2011); Kurt Edward Kemper, *College Football and American Culture in the Cold War Era* (Urbana: University of Illinois Press, 2009).

14. Curiously, unlike other American cities, these sporting traditions have not produced an extensive literature, hagiographic or critical. One amusing catalog has appeared, but not a single monograph surveying sport in greater Los Angeles has yet to roll off the press. Steve Hartman and Matt "Money" Smith, *The Great Book of Los Angeles Sports Lists* (New York: Running Press, 2009).

15. Mark Dyreson, "The Republic of Consumption at the Olympic Games: Globalization, Americanization, and Californization," *Journal of Global History* 8, no. 2 (July 2013): 256–78; Mark Dyreson, "World Harmony or an Athletic 'Clash of Civilizations'? Nationalism versus Transnationalism in Olympic Spectacles," *International Journal of the History of Sport* 29, no. 9 (June 2012): 1231–42.

16. Mark Dyreson, "The Endless Olympic Bid: Los Angeles and the Advertisement of the American West," *Journal of the West* 47, no. 4 (Fall 2008): 26–39; Mark Dyreson and Matthew Llewellyn, "Los Angeles Is the Olympic City: Legacies of 1932 and 1984," *International Journal of the History of Sport* 25, no. 14 (December 2008): 1991–2018.

17. For the details of the 2024 Los Angeles bid, which boldly promise that it will focus on events and athletes and use existing venues to run an economically efficient Olympics, see the bid committee's official website at https://la24.org/games-concept.

18. Courrier, Randy Newman's American Dreams, 245–47.

19. M. Azerrad and A. DeCurtis, "100 Best Albums of the Eighties," *Rolling Stone*, November 16, 1989, 53–151.

20. Courrier, Randy Newman's American Dreams, 245–47.

21. Randy Newman, "I Love L.A." (Official Video)—YouTube https://www.youtube.com/watch?v=KcADqxnQA_4.

22. *Down and Out in Beverly Hills*, Paul Mazursky, Buena Vista, 1986; *Naked Gun*, David Zucker, Paramount, 1988; *Chips '99*, John Cassar, Turner Films, 1998.

23. *Volcano*, Mick Jackson, 20th Century Fox, 1997; *Bean: The Ultimate Disaster Movie*, Mel Smith, Gramercy Pictures, 1997; *Escape from LA*, John Carpenter, Paramount, 1996. For an interesting history of this genre in American culture, see Mike Davis, *Ecology of Fear: Los Angeles and the Imagination of fDisaster* (New York: Metropolitan Books, 1998).

24. "I Love L.A." webpage; https://en.wikipedia.org/wiki/I_Love_L.A.

25. Mark Dyreson, "Region and Race: The Legacies of the St Louis Olympics," *International Journal of the History of Sport* 32, no. 14 (August 2015): 1697–1707.

26. Jeremy White, "The Los Angeles Way of Doing Things: The Olympic Village and the Practice of Boosterism," *Olympika: The International Journal of Olympic Studies* 11 (2000): 79–116; Sean Dinces, "Padres on Mount Olympus: Los Angeles and the Production of the 1932 Olympic Mega-Event," *Journal of Sport History* 32, no. 2 (Summer 2005): 137–66; Eriko Yamamoto, "Cheers for Japanese Athletes: The 1932 Los Angeles Olympics and the Japanese American Community," *Pacific Historical Review* 69 (August 2000): 399–429; Mark Dyreson, "Marketing National Identity: The Olympic Games of 1932 and American Culture," *Olympika: The International Journal of Olympic Studies* 4 (1995): 23–48; David Welky, "U.S. Journalism and the 1932 Olympics," *Journal of Sport History* 24, no. 1 (Spring 1997): 24–49. Doris Pieroth, *Their Day in the Sun: Women of the 1932 Olympics* (Seattle: University of Washington Press, 1996).

27. Matthew Llewellyn, John Gleaves, and Wayne Wilson, eds., *The 1984 Los Angeles Olympic Games: Assessing the 30-Year Legacy* (London: Routledge, 2015).

28. Sean Dinces, "The 1932 Olympics and Urban Capitalism in Interwar Los Angeles"; Matt Llewellyn, John Gleaves, and Toby Rider, "The Golden Games: The 1984 Olympics."

29. Dyreson and Llewellyn, "Los Angeles Is the Olympic City"; Dyreson, "The Endless Olympic Bid."

30. Greg Andranovich and Matthew J. Burbank, "Life Cycles of Sports Venues in Los Angeles."

31. See the 2024 Los Angeles bid webpage at https://la24.org/games-concept.

32. Steven A. Riess, "Power without Authority: Los Angeles' Elites and the Construction of the Coliseum," *Journal of Sport History* 8, no. 1 (Spring 1981): 50–65; Michelle L. Turner and the Pasadena Museum of History, *The Rose Bowl* (Charleston, SC: Arcadia, 2010).

33. Robert Smaus, "An Urban Forest by 1984," *Los Angeles Times*, July 25, 1982, M12; Josine Ianco-Starrels, "Frond Memories of L.A.'s Palm Trees," *Los Angeles Times*, July 29, 1984, T84; Cassy Cohen, "Wilshire Boulevard—The Palms," *Los Angeles Times*, November 1, 1984, WS1; Mark Ehrman, "Palm Latitudes," *Los Angeles Times*, September 18, 1991, A8; Peter King, "Under the Unlovely L.A. Palms," *Los Angeles Times*, January 28, 1992, A3; Carolyn S. Murray, "Olympics: An Ongoing Legacy," *Los Angeles Times*, July 25, 1982, M10.

34. Bill Dwyre, "L.A. and the Olympics Were a Golden Match," *Los Angeles Times*, March 20, 2006, S22.

35. Samuel O. Regalado, *Viva Baseball!: Latin Major Leaguers and Their Special Hunger* (Urbana: University of Illinois Press, 1998).

36. Luis Alvarez, "On Los Chorizeros, the Classic, and El Tri: Sports and Community in Mexican Los Angeles."

37. For a lesson in how to avoid this trap, and for the best history of the subject, see Jules Tygiel, *Baseball's Great Experiment: Jackie Robinson and His Legacy*, 25th anniversary ed. (New York: Oxford University Press, 2008).

38. Greg Kaliss, "Never Go Back: Pasadena Racial Politics and the Robinson Brothers."

39. Ted Geltner, "I Was Standing There All the While: Jim Murray and the Birth of a Sports Mecca."

40. For a more extensive biography, see Geltner's *Last King of the Sports Page: The Life and Career of Jim Murray* (Columbia: University of Missouri Press, 2012).

41. Elliott Gorn and Allison Lauterbach, "The Voice of Los Angeles." For a book-length biography of Scully, see Curt Smith, *Pull Up a Chair: The Vin Scully Story* (Washington, DC: Potomac Books, 2009).

42. Ray Schmidt, "Professional Football in the City of Angels."

43. David Wangerin, Soccer in a Football World: The Story of America's Forgotten Game (Philadelphia: Temple University Press, 2008); Jere Longman, The Girls of Summer: The U.S. Women's Soccer Team and How It Changed the World (New York: HarperCollins, 2000).

44. Yuya Kiuchi, ed., *Soccer Culture in America: Essays on the World's Sport in Red, White and Blue* (Jefferson, NC: McFarland, 2014); Gregory G. Reck and Bruce Dick, *American Soccer: History, Culture, Class* (Jefferson, NC: McFarland, 2015); Phil West, *The United States of Soccer: MLS and the Rise of American Soccer Fandom* (New York: Overlook Press, 2016).

45. Kiuchi, ed., Soccer Culture in America; Reck and Dick, American Soccer; West, The United States of Soccer.

46. Jennifer Doyle, "Pitches Less Than Perfect: Notes on the Landscape of Soccer in Los Angeles."

47. Scott L. Bottles, Los Angeles and the Automobile: The Making of the Modern City (Berkeley: University of California Press, 1987); Richard W. Longstreth, City Center to Regional Mall: Architecture, the Automobile, and Retailing in Los Angeles, 1920–1950 (Cambridge, MA: MIT Press, 1997) Cotton Seiler, Republic of Drivers: A Cultural History

of Automobility in America (Chicago: University of Chicago Press, 2008); Clay McShane, Down the Asphalt Path: The Automobile and the American City (New York: Columbia University Press, 1994).

48. Jeremy Kinney, "Sports Car Paradise: Racing in Los Angeles."

49. Tolga Ozyurtcu, "Shaping the Boom: Los Angeles Surfing from George Freeth to Gidget."

50. John D. Fair, *Muscletown USA: Bob Hoffman and the Manly Culture of York Barbell* (University Park: Pennsylvania State University Press, 1999).

51. Jan Todd, "The Halcyon Days of the Original Muscle Beach."

52. See Schwarzenegger's own as-told-to account of the transition from bodybuilder to movie star, written early in his film career. Arnold Schwarzenegger and Douglas Kent Hall, *Arnold: The Education of a Bodybuilder* (New York: Simon and Schuster, 1977).

53. Susan Brownell, "The History of Figure Skating in Southern California."

54. For her own perspective on that transition, see Sonja Henie, *Wings on My Feet* (New York: Prentice-Hall, 1940).

55. For an interesting perspective on the world of figure skating that Kwan and Fratianne inhabited, see Christine Brennan, *Inside Edge: A Revealing Journey into the Secret World of Figure Skating* (New York: Anchor Books, 1997).

56. Michael Freeman, *Jim Brown: The Fierce Life of an American Hero* (New York: William Morrow, 2006).

57. Randy Roberts and James Stuart Olson, *John Wayne: American* (New York: Free Press, 1995).

58. Scott Brooks, "Behind the Curtain: Leadership, Ingenuity, and Culture in the Making of Earvin 'Magic' Johnson, Showtime, and the Laker Dynasty."

59. Bruce Babington, *The Sports Film: Games People Play* (New York: Wallflower, 2014), 3.

60. *The Champion*, Essanay Studios, Charlie Chaplin, 1915.

61. Dan Nathan, "Hollywood Stars at Play in L.A."

62. *Eight Men Out*, Orion Pictures, John Sayles, 1988; *Tin Cup*, Warner Brothers, Ron Shelton, 1996; *The Mighty Ducks*, Buena Vista Pictures, Steve Herek, 1992; *Kingpin*, Metro-Goldwyn-Mayer, Bobby Farrelly and Peter Farrelly, 1996. This is purely my own ranking.

63. *Heaven Can Wait*, Paramount Pictures, Warren Beatty and Buck Henry, 1978.

64. Billy Connolly quotations at https://www.brainyquote.com/quotes/quotes/b/billyconno173621.html.

65. Randy Newman, "I Love L.A." (Official Video)—YouTube https://www.youtube.com/watch?v=KcADqxnQA_4.

66. "I Love L.A." page at "Songfacts" website; http://www.songfacts.com/detail.php?id=4686.

67. Bernice Kanner, "On Madison Avenue: Whispering Campaign—Nike's Dramatic Shift," *New Yorker*, June 25, 1984, 14–15; Robert Passikoff, "Ambush Marketing: An Olympic Competition. And Nike Goes for Gold," *Forbes*, August 7, 2012, http://www.forbes.com/sites/marketshare/2012/08/07/ambush-marketing-an-olympic-competition-and-nike-goes-for-gold/#57dbbfedef87; John Brant, "The 1984 Los Angeles Olympics: A Run to Glory," *Runners World*, July 17, 2014, http://www.runnersworld.com/olympics/. For a broad overview of Nike's corporate empire, see Donald Katz, *Just Do It: The Nike Spirit in the Corporate World* (New York: Random House, 1994).

68. Nike's 1984 "I Love L.A." advertisement, YouTube, https://www.youtube.com/watch?v=po6S8cizOXY.

69. Nike's 1984 "I Love L.A." advertisement, YouTube, https://www.youtube.com/watch?v=po6S8cizOXY.

70. Nike's 1984 "I Love L.A." advertisement, YouTube, https://www.youtube.com/watch?v=po6S8cizOXY.

1. The Life Cycles of Sports Venues in Los Angeles

1. The list of venues is from the Los Angeles Sports Council, accessed September 15, 2015, http://www.lasports.org. The estimate of economic development impact is from an analysis by the Los Angeles Sports Council and the Los Angeles Chamber of Commerce, "Chamber & L.A. Sports Council Release Study Showing a $4.1B Local Economic Impact of the Sports Industry," News Release, August 1, 2013, accessed http://www.lachamber.com/news/2013/08/01/press-release/chamber-l.a.-sports-council-release-study-showing-a-4.1b-local-economic-impact-of-the-sports-industry/.

2. Henry Splitter, "Los Angeles Recreation, 1846–1900, Part I," *Historical Society of Southern California Quarterly* 43 (1961): 35–68; and Henry Splitter, "Los Angeles Recreation, 1846–1900, Part II," *Historical Society of Southern California Quarterly* 43 (1961): 166–99. On the palimpsest of sports facilities, Steven Riess, *City Games: The Evolution of American Urban Society and the Rise of Sports* (Urbana: University of Illinois Press, 1989), 259, examines the effects of three eras of city building on sport, concluding that "sport . . . is not merely a recreational activity that happened to take place in cities, but is an institution that has been shaped, reshaped, and further molded by the interplay of the elements comprising the process of urbanization" and "America's sports institutions have been not simply a product of urbanization but have themselves deeply influenced urban change, usually for the better, in distinctive and visible ways."

3. Nathan Masters, "How Agricultural Park Became Exposition Park," KCET Public Television, November 17, 2011, accessed http://www.kcet.org/updaily/socal_focus/history/la-as-subject/from-agricultural-park-to-exposition-park.html.

4. On the decline of minor league baseball, see Richard Beverage, *The Los Angeles Angels of the Pacific Coast League: A History, 1903–1957* (Jefferson, NC: McFarland, 2011), and Cary Henderson, "Los Angeles and the Dodger War, 1957–1962," *Southern California Quarterly* 62 (1980): 261–89. For a broader perspective, see Joel Franks, "California and Rise of Spectator Sports, 1850–1900," *Historical Society of Southern California* 71 (1989): 287–310.

5. Shav Glick, "End of an Era: Ascot Park to Join Southland Tracks That Have Passed into History," *Los Angeles Times*, November 17, 1990; Danny Jensen, "The Wild History behind the Venue Boxers, Wrestlers, and Punks Called Home," laist, May 13, 2015, accessed http://laist.com/2015/05/13/grand_olympic_auditorium.php, and Bianca Baragan, "Rams' Owner Planning to Build a Stadium in Inglewood," *Curbed LA*, January 5, 2015.

6. Jean Trinh, "When Santa Anita Racetrack Was a Japanese Internment Camp Assembly Center," laist, December 8, 2014, accessed http://laist.com/2014/12/08/when_santa_anita_racetrack_was_a_ja.php.

7. On Pauley Pavilion, see Christelle Snow and Allison Hewitt, "Half a Century of History at Pauley Pavilion," *UCLA Newsroom*, June 10, 2015, accessed http://newsroom.ucla.edu/stories/half-a-century-of-history-at-pauley-pavilion. On the Stubhub Center, see Wayne Wilson, "Sports Infrastructure, Legacy and the Paradox of the 1984 Games," in *The 1984 Los Angeles Olympic Games: Assessing the 30-Year Legacy*, ed. Matthew P. Llewellyn, John Gleaves, and Wayne Wilson (New York: Routledge, 2015), 144–56 and "LA Galaxy Appoint

Design Company to Complete Rebrand of StubHub Center," *PanStadia & Arena Management Magazine*, March 25, 2015, accessed http://www.psam.uk.com/la-galaxy-appoint-design-company-to-complete-rebrand-of-stubhub-center.

8. Rick Orlov, "History of AEG: The Deal That Almost Wasn't," *Los Angeles Daily News*, September 22, 2012.

9. Mark Rosentraub, *Major League Winners: Using Sports and Cultural Centers as Tools for Economic Development* (Boca Raton, FL: CRC Press, 2010), 9.

10. On sports in other nations, see Christopher Gaffney, *Temples of the Earthbound Gods: Stadiums in the Cultural Landscapes of Rio de Janeiro and Buenos Aires* (Austin: University of Texas Press, 2008). On the nature of sports teams and cities in the United States, see Charles Euchner, *Playing the Field: Why Sports Teams Move and Cities Fight to Keep Them* (Baltimore: Johns Hopkins University Press, 1993), and Gerald C. S. Mildner, "Beyond the Major Leagues: Lessons from the Organization of International Sports," in *Sport and Public Policy*, ed. Charles Santo and Gerard C. S. Mildner (Champaign, IL: Human Kinetics, 2010), 23–31.

11. Alan Altshuler and David Luberoff, *Mega-Projects: The Changing Politics of Urban Public Investment* (Washington, DC: Brookings Institution, 2003), 8–44.

12. Benjamin Kleinberg, *Urban America in Transition: Perspectives on Urban Policy and Development* (Thousand Oaks, CA: Sage, 1995), 63–65.

13. Alberta Sbragia, *Debt Wish: Entrepreneurial Cities, U.S. Federalism, and Economic Development* (Pittsburgh, PA: University of Pittsburgh Press, 1996), 77–78.

14. Robert M. Fogelson, *The Fragmented Metropolis: Los Angeles, 1850–1930* (Berkeley: University of California Press, 1993).

15. Amy Bridges, *Morning Glories: Municipal Reform in the Southwest* (Princeton, NJ: Princeton University Press, 1997), 241.

16. Steven P. Erie, *Globalizing L.A.: Trade, Infrastructure, and Regional Development* (Stanford, CA: Stanford University Press, 2004), 46–47.

17. Steven Riess, "Power without Authority: Los Angeles' Elites and the Construction of the Coliseum," *Journal of Sport History* 8 (1981): 50–65.

18. Charles Santo, "Cities, Stadiums, and Subsidies: Why Cities Spend So Much on Sports," in *Sport and Public Policy*, ed. Charles Santo and Gerard C. S. Mildner (Champaign, IL: Human Kinetics, 2010), 69.

19. Altshuler and Luberoff, *Mega-Projects*, 13–21.

20. Peter Eisinger, "The Politics of Bread and Circuses: Building the City for the Visitor Class," *Urban Affairs Review* 35 (2000): 316–33; and Susan Fainstein and Dennis Judd, "Global Forces, Local Strategies, and Urban Tourism," in *The Tourist City*, ed. Dennis Judd and Susan Fainstein (New Haven, CT: Yale University Press, 1999), 1–17.

21. Santo, "Cities, Stadiums, and Subsidies," 70.

22. Janet Abu-Lughod, *New York, Chicago, Los Angeles: America's Global Cities* (Minneapolis: University of Minnesota Press, 1999), 262. On Dodger Stadium, see Henderson, "Los Angeles and the Dodger War," and Don Parson, *Making a Better World: Public Housing, the Red Scare, and the Direction of Modern Los Angeles* (Minneapolis: University of Minnesota Press, 2005).

23. Santo, "Cities, Stadiums, and Subsidies," 71.

24. Altshuler and Luberoff, *Mega-Projects*, 21–27.

25. Jaime Regalado, "Political Representation, Economic Development, Policymaking, and Social Crisis in Los Angeles, 1973–1992," in *City of Angels*, ed. Gerry Riposa and Carolyn Dersch (Dubuque, IA: Kendall/Hunt Publishing, 1992), 159–80.

26. Matthew J. Burbank, Greg Andranovich, and Charles H. Heying, *Olympic Dreams: The Impact of Mega-events on Local Politics* (Boulder, CO: Lynne Rienner, 2001), 18–20, on cities and global economic restructuring and 65–74 on LA's Olympic venues.

27. Altshuler and Luberoff, *Mega-Projects*, 27–42. See also Michael Pagano and David Perry, "Financing Infrastructure in the 21st Century City," *Public Works Management & Policy* 13 (2008): 22–38.

28. Altshuler and Luberoff, *Mega-Projects*, 30–31.

29. Santo, "Cities, Stadiums, and Subsidies."

30. Santo, "Cities, Stadiums, and Subsidies," 74.

31. Santo, "Cities, Stadiums, and Subsidies," 75.

32. Eisinger, "The Politics of Bread and Circuses"; and Mark Rosentraub, *Major League Losers: The Real Cost of Sports and Who's Paying for It*, rev. ed. (New York: Basic Books, 1999).

33. "Coliseum History," Los Angeles Memorial Coliseum, accessed June 11, 2015, http://www.lacoliseum.com.

34. Chris Epting, *Images of America: Los Angeles Memorial Coliseum* (Chicago: Arcadia Publishing, 2002).

35. Information on the use of the Coliseum is from "Memorial Coliseum Commission," Los Angeles Memorial Coliseum Commission, accessed June 11, 2015, http://lamcc.lacounty.gov.

36. "Rome's Colosseum Outdone by Our Football Bowls," *New York Times*, November 5, 1922.

37. "Coliseum History," Los Angeles Memorial Coliseum.

38. "Rome's Colosseum Outdone by Our Football Bowls."

39. Seating and expansion costs are from Michael Benson, *Ballparks of North America* (Jefferson, NC: McFarland, 1989), 212.

40. "Memorial Coliseum Commission," Los Angeles Memorial Coliseum Commission.

41. Rong-Gong Lin II and Paul Pringle, "California Science Center Grants Control of Coliseum to USC," *Los Angeles Times*, September 5, 2013.

42. Information on the lease deal is from Lin and Pringle, "California Science Center Grants Control of Coliseum to USC."

43. Information on renovations to the Coliseum is from Rich Hammond, "USC Embarks on Tough Schedule for Coliseum Facelift," *Orange County Register*, October 22, 2013, "Coliseum History," Los Angeles Memorial Coliseum, and Jordan Moore, "Coliseum On-Field Suites, Club Areas to Be Added at USC Football Games," *USC News*, June 13, 2014.

44. Jordan Moore, "Pat Haden Updates Coliseum Renovation Plans," *USC News*, April 11, 2014.

45. Paul Pringle and Rong-Gong Lin II, "Coliseum Incurred Big Expense in Trying to Keep USC Lease Talks Secret," *Los Angeles Times*, December 28, 2013. Information on the scandal is also drawn from Paul Pringle, Rong-Gong Lin II, and Andrew Blankstein, "Coliseum Had Scant Controls over Spending," *Los Angeles Times*, April 13, 2012; Andrew Blankstein, Paul Pringle, and Rong-Gong Lin II, "Coliseum Probe Brings Three Arrests," *Los Angeles Times*, March 23, 2012, and Andrew Blankstein, Paul Pringle, and Rong-Gong Lin II, "Coliseum Case Widens; Six Charged," *Los Angeles Times*, March 24, 2012.

46. Pringle, Lin, and Blankstein, "Coliseum Had Scant Controls over Spending."

47. Rong-Gong Lin II and Paul Pringle, "Coliseum Faces Million in Losses," *Los Angeles Times*, July 19, 2012.

48. Hammond, "USC Embarks on Tough Schedule for Coliseum Facelift."

49. Rong-Gong Lin II, "USC to take over L.A. Coliseum, Sports Arena on Monday," *Los Angeles Times*, July 25, 2013.

50. Kevin Baxter, "New Soccer Venue in L.A.," *Los Angeles Times*, May 18, 2015.

51. "History," Rose Bowl Stadium, accessed June 23, 2015, http://www.rosebowlstadium.com.

52. "History," Rose Bowl Stadium.

53. "History," Rose Bowl Stadium.

54. Steven Riess, "Historical Perspectives on Sport and Public Policy," *Policy Studies Review* 15 (1998): 4.

55. "Rome's Colosseum Outdone by Our Football Bowls."

56. This information on Rose Bowl renovations is drawn from "History," Rose Bowl Stadium.

57. Joe Piasecki, "Cost of Rose Bowl Renovation Goes Up, Again," *Glendale News-Press*, September 24, 2012.

58. Shawn Hubler, "Aging Rose Bowl Faces Thorny Dilemmas: Sports Boosters Seek a Rehab and NFL Team; Neighbors Dread Crowds," *Los Angeles Times*, August 27, 1995, and Richard Winton, "The Bloom Is off Rose Bowl," *Los Angeles Times*, June 9, 1995.

59. Edmund Newton, "Plan Takes Rose Bowl off Council's Hands," *Los Angeles Times*, October 11, 1992, and Office of the City Manager (Pasadena), "Agenda Report: A Review of the Rose Bowl Operating Company (RBOC)," October 21, 2013, accessed July 9, 2015, http://www.cityofpasadena.net/councilagendas/2014%20Agendas/Feb_03_14/AR%205.pdf.

60. Quoted in Newton, "Plan Takes Rose Bowl off Council's Hands."

61. Newton, "Plan Takes Rose Bowl off Council's Hands."

62. "Rose Bowl Operating Company Board," City of Pasadena, accessed June 29, 2015, http://www2.cityofpasadena.net/commissions/rboc.

63. "Rose Bowl Operating Company Board," City of Pasadena.

64. Lauren Gold, "Rose Bowl, Pasadena Chart Future for Stadium Events Amid Resident Complaints after One Direction Show," *Pasadena Star-News*, September 18, 2014.

65. Joe Piasecki, "A Range of Expectations for Review of Rose Bowl Governance," *Pasadena Sun*, February 12, 2013.

66. Maya Adam, "Rose Bowl Upgrades, Extensions Approved," *Orange County Register*, October 3, 2010, and Brenda Gazzar, "Rose Bowl Renovation Partners 'Thrilled' with Plan's Approval," *Pasadena Star-News*, October 12, 2010.

67. Joe Piasecki, "Premium Seats a Hit at Rose Bowl," *Pasadena Sun*, April 26, 2013, and Lauren Gold, "Iconic Rose Bowl Celebrates Renovation Milestone with Two of College Football's Biggest Games," *Pasadena Star-News*, January 12, 2014.

68. Lauren Gold, "Fitch Rating Downgrades Pasadena to AA+ in part for Rose Bowl Debt," *Pasadena Star-News*, May 28, 2013, and Lauren Gold, "Pasadena Moves to Increase Oversight for Rose Bowl Operating Company," *Pasadena Star-News*, October 31, 2013.

69. Daniel Kaplan, "NFL Sets Stadium Wi-Fi/Cell Standards," *Sports Business Journal*, October 21–27, 2013, 3. For a broader perspective, see George Ritzer and Todd Stillman, "The Postmodern Ballpark as a Leisure Setting: Enchantment and Simulated De-McDonaldization," *Leisure Sciences* 23 (2001): 99–113.

70. "Agenda Report: A Review of the Rose Bowl Operating Company (RBOC)," 4.

71. "Agenda Report: A Review of the Rose Bowl Operating Company (RBOC)," 15.

72. Quoted in Sam Farmer, "Rose Bowl Shoots Down NFL Inquiry," *Los Angeles Times*, July 9, 2015. Since the writing of this chapter the St. Louis Rams and San Diego Chargers

moved to LA and will play in a $2.6 billion shared stadium under construction in the city of Inglewood, to be opened in 2020. The Rams will play home games in the Coliseum and the Chargers in a slightly enlarged for American football StubHub Center in Carson in the meantime. The Oakland Raiders were given permission to move to Las Vegas and are negotiating for a stadium; the Nevada legislature approved a taxpayer subsidy of $750 million toward the $1.9 billion cost (Curtis Kalin, "Oakland Raiders Move to Las Vegas Is One of the Worst Taxpayer-Funded Fiscal Sins of All Time," *Washington Examiner*, April 22, 2017, accessed June 11, 2017, http://www.washingtonexaminer.com/oakland-raiders-move-to-las-vegas-is-one-of-the-worst-taxpayer-funded-fiscal-sins-of-all-time/article/2620935).

2. On Los Chorizeros, the Classic, and El Tri

1. Steve Dilbeck, "Obama Names Fernando Valenzuela Ambassador for Immigration Program," *Los Angeles Times*, September 17, 2005.

2. I use the term Mexican Los Angeles to be inclusive of ethnic Mexicans regardless of citizenship, yet also recognize important historical differences among Mexican nationals, Mexican Americans, and Chicanas/os, and with other Latinas/os in Los Angeles.

3. Jorge Iber, Samuel O. Regalado, José M. Alamillo, and Arnoldo De León, *Latinos in U.S. Sport: A History of Isolation, Cultural Identity, and Acceptance* (Champaign, IL: Human Kinetics, 2011), 225–27.

4. Douglas Monroy, *Rebirth: Mexican Los Angeles from the Great Migration to the Great Depression* (Berkeley: University of California Press, 1999), 47–48.

5. Jorge Iber, "Introduction: Athletics and Chicano/a Life, 1930–2005," in Jorge Iber and Samuel O. Regalado, eds., *Mexican Americans and Sports: A Reader on Athletics and Barrio Life* (College Station: Texas A&M University Press, 2007), 7–8.

6. Jose Alamillo, "Peloteros in Paradise: Mexican American Baseball and Oppositional Politics in Southern California, 1930–1950," *Western Historical Quarterly* 34, no. 2 (Summer 2003): 191–211.

7. Juan Pescador, "Vamos Taximora! Mexican/Chicano Soccer Associations and Transnational/Translocal Communities, 1967–2002," *Latino Studies* 2, no. 3 (December 2004): 352–76.

8. Steve Dilbeck, "Dodgers' Fernando Valenzuela becomes a U.S. Citizen," *Los Angeles Times*, July 22, 2015.

9. Jose Alamillo, "Beyond the Latino Sports Hero: The Role of Sports in Creating Communities, Networks, and Identities," *American Latinos and the Making of the United States: A Theme Study*, National Park Service (2013): 161–83.

10. Natalia Molina, "The Importance of Place-Makers in the Life of a Los Angeles Community: What Gentrification Erases from Echo Park," *Southern California Quarterly* 97, no. 1 (Spring 2015): 71.

11. Samuel Regalado, "Baseball in the Barrios: The Scene in East Los Angeles since World War II," *Baseball History* (Summer 1986); Francisco Balderrama and Richard Santillan, *Mexican American Baseball in Los Angeles* (Mount Pleasant: Arcadia Publishing, 2011); Jose Alamillo, "Peloteros in Paradise: Mexican American Baseball and Oppositional Politics in Southern California, 1930–1950," *Western Historical Quarterly* 34, no. 2 (Summer 2003): 191–211; Douglas Monroy, *Rebirth: Mexican Los Angeles from the Great Migration to the Great Depression* (Berkeley: University of California Press, 1999).

12. Jose Alamillo, "Peloteros in Paradise: Mexican American Baseball and Oppositional Politics in Southern California, 1930–1950," *Western Historical Quarterly* 34, no. 2 (Summer 2003).

13. Jose Alamillo, Samuel Regalado, Richard Santillan, and Francisco Balderrama are among the leading scholars involved. See, for example, "'Neighborhoods of Baseball' Celebrates Community Teams in Multiethnic L.A.," *The Rafu Shimpo: Los Angeles Japanese Daily News*, September 15, 2011; The Baseball Reliquary website accessed October 1, 2015, at http://www.baseballreliquary.org/about/latino-baseball-history-project/.

14. David Wharton, "The Glory of Their Times," *Los Angeles Times*, April 6, 2006.

15. Carmelita Chorizo, accessed October 8, 2015, http://carmelitachorizo.com.

16. Francisco Balderrama and Richard Santillan, "Los Chorizeros: The New York Yankees of East Los Angeles and the Reclaiming of Mexican American Baseball History," *The National Pastime* (Society for American Baseball Research, 2011); Kamren Curiel, "Breakfast of Campeones: How the Lopez Family Made Chorizo Mainstream," *Los Angeles Times*, October 27, 2012; Wharton, "The Glory of Their Times."

17. Wharton, "The Glory of Their Times."

18. Wharton, "The Glory of Their Times."

19. Wharton, "The Glory of Their Times."

20. Eric Avila, *Popular Culture in the Age of White Flight: Fear and Fantasy in Suburban Los Angeles* (Berkeley: University of California Press, 2006); Andy McCue, "Barrio, Bulldozers, and Baseball: The Destruction of Chavez Ravine," *Nine: A Journal of Baseball History and Culture* 21, no. 1 (Fall 2012): 47–52.

21. George Lipsitz, *How Racism Takes Place* (Philadelphia: Temple University Press, 2011).

22. Charles Smith, "The Classic: More than a Football Game," *Los Angeles Times*, October 31, 1993.

23. Iber et al., *Latinos in U.S. Sport*, 203.

24. *Symbol of Heart: The Official Documentary of The East Los Angeles Classic*, Ground-Zero Latino and Carmona Productions, 2003; Mario Villegas, "A Classic for Many Reasons," ESPN.com, November 4, 2010, accessed October 19, 2015, http://sports.espn.go.com/losangeles/news/story?id=5761821.

25. Symbol of Heart.

26. Jeanette Sanchez-Palacios, "Aging Eastsiders Find Strength in Shared Memories," *Los Angeles Times*, December 23, 2000.

27. John Strege, "Garfield, Roosevelt Rivalry Resumes," *Los Angeles Times*, October 28, 1976.

28. Symbol of Heart.

29. Smith, "The Classic."

30. Symbol of Heart.

31. Smith, "The Classic."

32. Smith, "The Classic."

33. Mario Villegas, "A Classic for Many Reasons," ESPN.com, November 4, 2010, accessed October 19, 2015, http://sports.espn.go.com/losangeles/news/story?id=5761821.

34. Smith, "The Classic."

35. George Ramos, "Is Proposed Move of Football Classic a Smart Play?" *Los Angeles Times*, May 8, 1995.

36. Mary Anne Perez, "East L.A. Classic to Move to Rose Bowl," *Los Angeles Times*, November 1, 1992; Lonnie White, "Pride on the Line: Roosevelt and Garfield High

Schools—and Their Fans—Gear Up for the 57th East Los Angeles Classic," *Los Angeles Times*, October 11, 1992.

37. Ramos, "Is Proposed Move of Football Classic a Smart Play?"
38. Ramos, "Is Proposed Move of Football Classic a Smart Play?"
39. Gary Klein, "A Classic Debate," *Los Angeles Times*, November 2, 2000.
40. Klein, "A Classic Debate."
41. Klein, "A Classic Debate."
42. For example, see Joseph Serna and Robert J. Lopez, "Mexico World Cup Fans Arrested; Police Horse Struck in Huntington Park," *Los Angeles Times*, June 24, 2014.
43. Jose Alamillo, "Beyond the Latino Sports Hero: The Role of Sports in Creating Communities, Networks, and Identities," *American Latinos and the Making of the United States: A Theme Study*, National Park Service (2013): 161–83.
44. Ana Gonzalez-Barrera and Mark Hugo Lopez, "A Demographic Portrait of Mexican-Origin Hispanics in the United States," May 1, 2013, Pew Research: Hispanic Trends Project, accessed April 7, 2014, http://www.pewhispanic.org/2013/05/01/a-demographic-portrait-of-mexican-origin-hispanics-in-the-united-states.
45. Gary Hopkins, *Star Spangled Soccer: The Selling, Marketing and Management of Soccer in the USA* (New York: Palgrave McMillan, 2010), 270.
46. Duncan Irving, "Coliseum Rocks as Tricolores Three-Peat," *Soccer America* 53, no. 7 (March 2, 1998): 8.
47. "What's Needed Is Some Civility," *Los Angeles Times*, February 21, 1998.
48. Rueben Navarrette, "Immigrants, Don't Boo U.S. Teams," July 21, 2011, accessed April 8, 2014, http://www.cnn.com/2011/OPINION/07/21/navarrette.soccer/.
49. Patrick Buchanan, "Anti-Americanism in L.A.," accessed January 30, 2015, http://library.flawlesslogic.com/la.htm.
50. "Soccer, Mexico & the US Empire's Breakup," June 29, 2011, Southern Nationalist Network, accessed April 20, 2014, http://southernnationalist.com/blog/2011/06/29/soccer-mexico-the-us-empires-breakup/.
51. George Lipsitz, *Footsteps in the Dark: The Hidden Histories of Popular Music* (Minneapolis: University of Minnesota Press, 2007), 70.
52. Interview with Hercules Gomez by Michael Davies and Roger Bennett, *Men in Blazers*, Grantland Network Podcasts, March 19, 2013, accessed January 30, 2015, http://espn.go.com/espnradio/grantland/player?id=9073010.
53. Mike Jensen, "Mexican Soccer Team Has American Accent, Half of the Improbable Women's World Cup Squad Comes from North of the Border," *Philadelphia Inquirer*, June 17, 1999; Grahame Jones, "Mexico Imports a U.S. Product," *Los Angeles Times*, August 28, 1998.
54. "Michael Orozco Rooting for Mexico," espnfc.com, October 17, 2013, accessed April 10, 2014, http://espnfc.com/news/story/_/id/1585876/us-michael-orozco-says-rooting-mexico?cc=5901.
55. David Davis, "Why Do People Have a Problem with OC-Raised USC Quarterback Mark Sanchez Being Proud of His Mexican Heritage?" *OC Weekly*, August 21, 2008; Jorge Iber, "The Perils and Possibilities of 'Quarterbacking while Mexican': A Brief Introduction to the Participation of Latino/a Athletes in US Sports History," in *More Than Just Peloteros: Sport and US Latino Communities*, ed. Jorge Iber (Lubbock: Texas Tech University Press, 2014).
56. Gustavo Arellano, "A Mouthpiece Says It All," *Los Angeles Times*, October 26, 2007.
57. Davis, "Why Do People Have a Problem with OC-Raised USC Quarterback?"

3. Pitches Less Than Perfect

1. I should address my position as a recreational adult woman player active in soccer scenes dominated by men, and the large histories that haunt questions of field access in Los Angeles. I dedicated several years of my life to playing with men, mostly in pick-up games and then in a men's league, which I cofounded. Women are less out of place in the recreational men's game than one might think. There is a gap between the soccer presented to us on televisions, as "American soccer," and the sport as practiced by ordinary people. The sport spectacle is centered on the male athlete. Corporate, commercial, and national sports organizations have difficulty imagining the women's game as having any commercial appeal. Each successful broadcast of the Women's World Cup, for example, is thus met with surprise. Women, as players and as fans, are positioned outside the commercial sports sphere. With the exception of the four-year cycles of the Olympics and the Women's World Cup, the women's game is rarely broadcast and scarcely covered by sports media. This is a mixed blessing. A woman player-fan like myself finds her relationship to the sport in some senses less mediated, insofar as her involvement in the women's game is staged largely by playing it, and in other senses more mediated, insofar as her relationship to the sport spectacle is routed through the men's game—her relationship to that world is one of either outright exile or marginalization.

2. See David Litterer's website, "History of Soccer in Greater Los Angeles," for an introduction to this subject. Last modified August 12, 2011, accessed November 6, 2015, http://homepages.sover.net/~spectrum/losangeles.html.

3. Kevin Baxter, "Expansion L.A. Soccer Team Plans New Stadium on Sports Arena Site," *Los Angeles Times*, May 17, 2015, accessed November 13, 2015, http://www.latimes.com/sports/soccer/la-sp-la-soccer-stadium-20150518-story.html.

4. This is not true where the women's game is concerned. Most recently, the Women's Professional Soccer League (2007–2012) fielded one team in Los Angeles: the LA Sol. That team folded after one season, in spite of having the best regular season record and a roster packed with some of the world's best players, including Marta (Brazil) and Camille Abily (France). The team was partly owned by AEG (owner of the LA Galaxy). After this one season, AEG withdrew its support without leaving time for another investor to step in. As of this writing, the National Women's Soccer League (run by the United States Soccer Federation) does not have a team in California. The Northwest is a far friendlier home for women's soccer: attendance at Portland Thorns and Seattle Reign matches can hover around twenty thousand.

5. On the subject of this rivalry, see Roberto Donati, Pablo Miralles, and Michael Whalen's excellent documentary, *Gringos at the Gate* (2012).

6. For a more formal analysis of a specific grassroots scene in a different part of Los Angeles, see David Trouille's excellent essays on the Mar Vista Recreational Center: "Neighborhood Outsiders, Field Insiders: Latino Immigrant Men and the Control of Public Space," in *Qualitative Sociology* 36 (2013):1–22, and *Fencing a Field: Imagined Others in the Unfolding of Neighborhood Conflict*. Trouille's essays are grounded in his years playing in a park on Los Angeles's west side, and ethnographic fieldwork exploring this community of players and the park's local context. Trouille also played in the league I managed, which I discuss below.

7. "Silverlake Gang War," Christine Pelisek's October 9, 2003, story for the *LA Weekly* is prescient for its description of the neighborhood's bifurcation. Silverlake was, in the early 2000s, one of the most intensely gentrified zones in Los Angeles, meaning that much of the

neighborhood's working class to working poor have been recently displaced by soaring rents and market pressure. Pelisek writes:

> The level of gang violence occurring in this area, while far from the city's worst, is happening at the same time property values have gone up 33 percent this year alone and "bargain" homes are selling for more than a half-million dollars just north of Sunset. The unexpected rash of violence here illustrates a gangs-versus-gentrification drama that's likely to play out in other neighborhoods across the city as the overheated housing market pushes prospective new homeowners deeper into the fringes of long-held gang turf.

8. See, for example, David Wangarin, *Soccer in a Football World: The Story of America's Forgotten Game* (Philadelphia, PA: Temple University Press, 2008).

9. See Féderation Internationale de Football's *World Football: Big Count* (2006). Accessed November 9, 2015, http://www.fifa.com/worldfootball/bigcount/index.html. Alex Bellos's *Futebol: The Brazilian Way of Life* (London: Bloomsbury, 2002) offers a compelling analysis of the sport's importance to Brazilian culture.

10. For a helpful portrait of the history of the sport in relation to specific ethnic communities, see Derek Van Rheenen's "The Promise of Soccer in America: The Open Play of Ethnic Subcultures," in *Soccer & Society* 10, no. 6 (2009): 781–94, and David Trouille, "Association Football to Fútbol: Ethnic Succession and the History of Chicago-Area Soccer, 1890–1920," *Soccer & Society* 9, no. 4 (2008): 455–76. (Trouille, who received his PhD in sociology from UCLA, played in the league that I discuss below.)

11. See Sean Brown, "Fleet Feet: The USSF and the Peculiarities of Soccer Fandom in America," *Soccer & Society* 8, no. 2–3 (2007): 366–80, and Fernando Delgado's "Major League Soccer, Constitution, and (the) Latino Audience(s)," *Journal of Sport and Social Issues* 23, no. 1 (1999): 41–54.

12. See Gary Armstrong and James Rosbrook-Thompson, "Coming to America: Historical Ontologies and United States Soccer," *Identities* 17, no. 4 (2010): 348–71.

13. On soccer and US exceptionalism, see Andre S. Markovits and Steven Hellerman's *Offside: Soccer and American Exceptionalism* (Berkeley: University of California Press, 2001), and Stefan Szymanski and Andrew Zimbalist's *National Pastime: How Americans Play Baseball and the Rest of the World Plays Soccer* (Washington, DC: Brookings Institute Press, 2006). Publications on soccer as a sport through which we can access the interaction between local and global politics and histories abound. See, for example, Gabriel Kuhn's *Soccer vs. The State: Tackling Football and Radical Politics* (Oakland, CA: PM Press, 2011) and Franklin Foer's *How Soccer Explains the World: An Unlikely Theory of Globalization* (New York: HarperCollins, 2004). Laurent DuBois explores the relationship between immigration and national identity through the recent history of the French national team in *Soccer Empire: The World Cup and the Future of France* (Berkeley: University of California Press, 2010).

For an international history of the women's game, see Jean Williams's *A Beautiful Game: International Perspectives on Women's Football* (New York: Bloomsbury, 2007). A typical anti-soccer, xenophobic polemic: Stephen H. Webb, "Why Soccer Is Un-American," *Politco*, June 12, 2014, accessed November 13, 2015, http://www.politico.com/magazine/story/2014/06/why-soccer-is-un-american-107793#ixzz34WMQFww1.

14. See, for example, Wayne Wilson's writing on fan discourse within the web-based platform BigSoccer.net: "All Together Now, Click: MLS Soccer Fans in Cyberspace," *Soccer & Society* 8, no. 2–3 (2007): 381–98.

15. This data is pulled from the interactive city map, "Mapping L.A.," produced by Data Desk at *The Los Angeles Times*. Accessed November 13, 2015, http://maps.latimes.com/neighborhoods/.

16. See Brown, "Fleet Feet," and Delgado, "Major League Soccer, Constitution, and (the) Latino Audience(s)."

17. For more on the culture and character of MacArthur Park, see Kelly Main's *Place Attachment and MacArthur Park: A Case Study for the Importance of Public Space in an Immigrant Neighborhood and the Implications for Local Planning* (Unpublished diss., University of California, Los Angeles, 2007), which contains a detailed discussion of soccer's importance to the park's character and community. See also Gerardo Sandoval's Immigrants and the Revitalization of Los Angeles: Development and Change in MacArthur Park (Amherst, NY: Cambria Press, 2010).

18. Molly Hennesey Fiske, "Guatemalan Women Kick Aside Constraints in the U.S," *Los Angeles Times*, June 30, 2008, accessed November 13, 2015, http://www.latimes.com/local/la-me-soccer30-2008jun30-story.html.

19. Esmeralda Bermudez, "Soccer Players' Loss Is a Win," *Los Angeles Times*, October 23, 2008, accessed November 9, 2015, http://articles.latimes.com/2008/oct/23/local/me-field23.

20. City of Los Angeles, Department of Parks and Recreation, Press Release: "MacArthur Park Improvement Groundbreaking," November 21, 2008, accessed November 9, 2015, http://www.szone.us/f82/macarthur-park-improvement-project-groundbreaking-28010/.

21. See Ed P. Reyes Council Member, First District, press release: "Reyes Greens 'L.A.s Central Park' with Children's Meadow," October 23, 2008, accessed November 13, 2015, http://lacityorgcd1.blogspot.com/2008/10/reyes-greens-las-central-park-with.html.

22. Daniel Hernandez, "Safari in Los Angeles, in a Home in MacArthur Park," *Intersections: A Blog by Daniel Hernandez*, March 30, 2010, accessed November 9, 2015, http://danielhernandez.typepad.com/daniel_hernandez/2010/03/dissecting-entryway.html. The original blog (Entryway) is no longer accessible.

23. A similar story has been unfolding further east. Open space alongside the LA River was, in the early 2000s, to be developed into playing fields. Although a set of fields ("Taylor Yard") was established in one region, another, closer to downtown Los Angeles ("the Cornfield"), was at first restored as an open green space on which play was welcome, but park officials soon barred people from playing soccer on the park's flat grassy expanse. Then the park was shut down for another redesign. For a period, it has hosted large music festivals. It is now slated to reopen as a passive use park devoid of playing fields. A 2002 Center for Law in the Public Interest report ("Dreams of Fields: Soccer, Community, and Equal Justice: Report on Sports in Urban Parks to the California Department of Parks and Recreation," authored by Robert Garcia, Erica S. Flores, and Elizabeth Pine), captures the optimistic mood that characterized the local community, as politicians promised that the Los Angeles State Historical Park (or, "The Cornfields," as it is known) would host soccer games for area youth, who live in one of the most park-poor sections of Los Angeles. This section of the Los Angeles River will be restored by the city, working with the US Army Corps of Engineers. The land around the river is to be turned into a park designed by Frank Ghery. One senses that those whom soccer fields serve are quickly being pushed out of the area by real estate speculation.

4. Figure Skating in Southern California

1. Guy Price, "Ice Skating," *Los Angeles Evening Herald*, no. 65, January 16, 1917, 7; "Footlights by Guy Price," *Los Angeles Evening Herald*, no. 69, January 20, 1917, 12. Both in California Digital Newspaper Collection, accessed December 13, 2015, http://cdnc.ucr.edu.

2. Tom Miller, "The Lost 1868 Empire Skating Rink—3rd Ave and 63rd Street," The Daytonian in Manhattan, April 29, 2013, accessed January 7, 2016, http://daytoninmanhattan.blogspot.com/2013/04/the-lost-1868-empire-skating-rink-3rd.html.

3. James R. Hines, *Figure Skating: A History* (Urbana: University of Illinois Press and Colorado Springs: World Figure Skating Hall of Fame, 2006), 138–39; Willi Böckl, "Open Air Artificial Ice Rinks," *Skating: Official Publication of the United States Figure Skating Association*, January 1933, 21, archived on the website of the United States Figure Skating Association, www.usfsa.org.

4. "Ice Skaters Will Vie at Bristol," *Los Angeles Evening Herald*, no. 129, March 30, 1916, 10, California Digital Newspaper Collection, accessed December 13, 2015, http://cdnc.ucr.edu.

5. "The Panama-California International Exposition," *The Post Office Clerk: Organ of the United National Association of Post Office Clerks*, 15, no. 1, March 1916, 11.

6. "Twelve Who Shaped San Diego: George Marston," KPBS Aired Program #12, transcribed April 1982 by Tim MacBride. Accessed January 7, 2016, http://library.sdsu.edu/sites/default/files/KPBSMarstonTranscript.pdf.

7. "Lora Jean, Who Says Ice Is Aid to Feminine Beauty," *Los Angeles Evening Herald*, no. 311, October 28, 1916, 3; "Ice Skating Best for Muscles, Says Star at Bristol," *Los Angeles Evening Herald*, no. 297, October 12, 1916, 17. California Digital Newspaper Collection, accessed December 13, 2015, http://cdnc.ucr.edu.

8. *Billboard*, April 28, 1917, 59. Google Books website, accessed December 13, 2015.

9. "Ice Hockey League to Be Formed Here," *Los Angeles Evening Herald*, no. 58, January 8, 1917, 10; "Hundreds Crowd Ice Skating Rink," *Los Angeles Evening Herald*, no. 95, February 20, 1917, 2; "Canadians Lead League with Clubmen Holding Second Place Easily," *Los Angeles Evening Herald*, no. 136, April 9, 1917, 10; all at California Digital Newspaper Collection, accessed December 13, 2015, http://cdnc.ucr.edu. "U.S.C. Hockey Team Plays First Game Next Thursday," *Southern California Trojan*, February 2, 1917, vol. 8, 1, accessed December 13, 2015, http://digitallibrary.usc.edu/cdm/ref/collection/p15799coll104/id/8833.

10. A. Winsor Weld, "Figure Skating in the United States and the United States Figure Skating Association," *Skating*, December 1923, 1; George H. Browne, "The International Skating Union," *Skating*, February 1924, 26.

11. Sylvia Stoddard, "Polar Palace: A Brief History of Lost California Ice Rinks," accessed November 29, 2015, www.squareone.org/PolarPalace.

12. "Lions to Don Skates," *Los Angeles Times*, December 1, 1929, E5. ProQuest Historical Newspapers: Los Angeles Times.

13. "Don Tresidder to Head Loop," *Los Angeles Times*, March 17, 1932, A13.

14. "Los Angelenos Cop Skating Honors," *Los Angeles Times*, February 6, 1933, 10; "Local Skaters Will Compete at Yosemite," *Los Angeles Times*, January 24, 1934, A11.

15. "Southland Folk Watch Sports in Yosemite Snows," *Los Angeles Times*, February 3, 1935, B8.

16. J. M. LeRoy appeared in the society columns of the *Los Angeles Times*, but not as frequently as Mrs. LeRoy, who was labeled a "Hollywood clubwoman" in the society news of the *Los Angeles Times*, October 15, 1913, I14.

17. "Felix Locher New Amateur Skate Chief," *Los Angeles Times*, December 12, 1933, A12.

18. "Rockers and Counters," *Skating*, January 1938. "Felix Locher Biography," IMDb website, accessed December 13, 2015, http://www.imdb.com/name/nm0516646/bio.

19. Extracts from Minutes of Executive Committee Meeting, October 22, 1933, *Skating*, November 1933, 44–48.

20. Yosemite Ranger Notes, "Toboggan Runs, Ice Skating Competitions, and a Bid for the Winter Olympics," February 6, 2014, www.nps.gov/yose/blogs/Toboggan-runs-ice-skating-competitions-and-a-bid-for-the-Winter-Olympics.htm.

21. Extracts from Minutes of Executive Committee Meeting, October 22, 1933, *Skating*, November 1933, 44–48.

22. "Mr. Hapgood Visits California," *Skating*, February 1934, 12–14.

23. "The Skating Club of San Francisco: Club History," club website, reprint of John Rogers, "The Inside Edge, 16, no. 3, accessed December 13, 2015, www.scsf.org/index.php?option=com_content&view=article&id=21&Itemid=156.

24. Edwin F. Washburn, "The 1933 National Championships," *Skating*, May 1933, 1.

25. "Extracts from Report of Annual Meeting," *Skating*, May 1934, 42.

26. Hines, *Figure Skating*, 139–40.

27. "Ice Rink to Expand Space," *Corsair*, 10, no. 23, March 15, 1939, 4. California Digital Newspaper Collection, accessed December 13, 2015, http://cdnc.ucr.edu.

28. Roger F. Turner, "A Trip to the Pacific Coast," *Skating*, April 1939, 9; Pauline K. Newman, "Pacific Coast Championships," *Skating*, April 1939, no. 71, 5.

29. Maribel Y. Vinson, "From Rink to Rink on the West Coast," *Skating*, February 1937, 7–8.

30. Margaretta S. Drake, "The 1937 National Championships," *Skating*, March 1937, 3.

31. The USFS oversees a system of tests that qualify skaters to compete at different levels. The highest and top skill level is labeled "Senior," the second is "Junior," and the third is "Novice."

32. Kathleen Turner, "The New National Champion," *Skating*, March 1940, 18–20.

33. Virginia Vale, "History of the Los Angeles Figure Skating Club," *Bulletin of the L.A.F.S.C.*, April 1982. Posted by Josephine Lawless, Club Historian, accessed January 7, 2016, http://lafsc.org/about/club-history/.

34. Hines, *Figure Skating*, 144.

35. Virginia Vale, "History of the Los Angeles Figure Skating Club," *Bulletin*, April 1982. Posted by Josephine Lawless, Club Historian, accessed January 7, 2016, http://lafsc.org/about/club-history/.

36. "Skating's Family Still Growing!" *Skating*, May 1941, 48–52.

37. Sylvia Stoddard, "Tropical Ice Gardens: A Brief History of Lost California Ice Rinks," accessed November 29, 2015, www.squareone.org/PolarPalace/tropical.html.

38. "Skating's Family Still Growing!" *Skating*, May 1941, 48–52.

39. Scott M. Reid, "Time Hasn't Slowed Down Figure Skating's Nicks," *Orange County Register*, March 27, 2012.

40. "History of Paramount Iceland," website of the Paramount Iceland rink. www.paramounticeland.com/index.php?option=com_content&view=article&id=47.

41. "Breaking of Cable Closes Ice Palace," *Los Angeles Evening Herald*, no. 98, February 23, 1917, 12, California Digital Newspaper Collection, accessed December 13, 2015, http://cdnc.ucr.edu.

42. "The Zamboni Story," website of Frank J. Zamboni and Co., http://zamboni.com/about/zamboni-archives/the-zamboni-story.

43. Katrina Lynn Hawkins, "Utah Inventions: Skating Smoothly with Zamboni," KSL.com, July 8, 2003, accessed December 13, 2015, www.ksl.com/?nid=1012&sid=35384376.
44. Freda Alexander, "Meet the United States Champions," *Skating*, June 1956, 27.
45. Sylvia Stoddard, "In Memoriam: The 1961 World Figure Skating Team." http://www.squareone.org/PolarPalace/usteam.html.
46. Peggy Fleming with Peter Kaminsky, *The Long Program: Skating toward Life's Victories* (New York: Pocket Books, 1999), 36.
47. Lynn Rutherford, "An Unlikely Heroine: A Blend of Beauty and Grace Made Peggy Fleming Unforgettable," *Skating*, November 2009, 31–33.
48. Lawrence, *Skating on Air*, 29–33.
49. E. M. Swift, "Peggy Fleming," *Sports Illustrated* 81, no. 12 (September 19, 1994): 1.
50. "Peggy Fleming Signs $500,000 Pro Contract," *Los Angeles Times*, April 4, 1968, D3.
51. Reid, "Time Hasn't Slowed Down Figure Skating's Nicks."
52. Allison Manley, "Episode 14: Frank Carroll," The Manleywoman Skatecast: Podcasting Skating since 2007, April 14, 2008, accessed December 13, 2015, www.manleywoman.com/episode-14-frank-carroll/.
53. Vale, "History of the Los Angeles Figure Skating Club."
54. Irene West, "Appeal Is Made to Finance Mabel Fairbanks, 'Sepia Queen of Ice,'" *Los Angeles Sentinel*, January 3, 1946, 19, ProQuest Historical Newspapers: Los Angeles Sentinel.
55. "Skater's Skill Breaks Racial 'Ice' at Rink," *Los Angeles Sentinel*, February 7, 1946, 21.
56. Chico C. Norwood, "Creator of Champions," *Los Angeles Sentinel*, July 24, 1980, A2.
57. Stan Chambers, *KTLA's News at 10: Sixty Years with Stan Chambers* (Behler Publications, 2008), Kindle book.
58. Ronald A. Scheurer, "Breaking the Ice: The Mabel Fairbanks Story," *American Visions*; December 1997/January 1998, 12–14, ProQuest Research Library.
59. "Pupil Sues Skate Rink: Polytechnic High Student Charges Rink Wouldn't Permit Him to Skate," *Los Angeles Sentinel*, July 19, 1934, 1; "Skating Rink Fined $200 for Prejudice," *Los Angeles Sentinel*, February 12, 1948, 4.
60. "Skate Carnival Slated Tonight," *Los Angeles Times*, August 3, 1933, A12.
61. Irene West, "Appeal Is Made to Finance Mabel Fairbanks, 'Sepia Queen of Ice,'" *Los Angeles Sentinel*, January 3, 1946, 19.
62. "Mabel Fairbanks Oral History," Sharon Donnan interview with Mabel Fairbanks, Tuesday, January 7, 1999, archives of the LA84 Foundation.
63. "Ice Breakers," *Skating*, March 2005, 9.
64. "Mabel Fairbanks Oral History."
65. Scheurer, "Breaking the Ice."
66. "Mabel Fairbanks Oral History."
67. "Mabel Fairbanks Oral History."
68. "Mabel Fairbanks Oral History."
69. "Mabel Fairbanks Oral History."
70. Tai Babilonia and Randy Gardner, *Forever Two as One* (Jamestown, NY: Martha Lowder Kimball Publishing, 2002), 32.
71. Christine Brennan, "She Is Figure Skating," *USA Today*, March 31, 2000, 1A.
72. Ann Killion, "Kwan Exits Like a Champion, Even without the Gold Medal," *San Jose Mercury News*, February 13, 2006.
73. "Mabel Fairbanks Oral History."
74. Scott M. Reid, "Wagner Coach Nicks Opts to Retire," *Orange County Register*, April 25, 2013, C.

5. Sports Car Paradise

The author would like to acknowledge the following for assistance in the writing of this essay: Jim Sitz, Bill Pollack, R. W. Kastner, Bob Schmitt, the Smithsonian Institution Libraries, the Benson Ford Research Center at the Henry Ford Museum, the Revs Institute, and the editors.

1. Bob Hunter, "Major League Racing," and "Entrant List," in *Official Program: Riverside International Motor Raceway Sports Car Road Races, September 21–22, 1957*, Box 134, Dave Friedman Collection, Accession 2009.158, Benson Ford Research Center, The Henry Ford Museum (hereafter DFC, BFRC), 10, 12–13, 16–17; Racing Sports Cars, "Sports Car Road Races Riverside," 2007, accessed August 1, 2015, http://www.racingsportscars.com/photo/Riverside-1957-09-22b.html.

2. Paul Zimmerman, "Figures Prove L.A. Sports Capital of World," *Los Angeles Times*, December 29, 1958, C1.

3. Scott L. Bottles, *Los Angeles and the Automobile: The Making of the Modern City* (Berkeley: University of California Press, 1987), 4–5, 16, 18, 245.

4. Shav Glick, "Fast Times: From Barney Oldfield to Jeff Gordon, It Has Been Quite a Ride," *Los Angeles Times*, December 29, 1999, accessed September 8, 2015, http://articles.latimes.com/1999/dec/29/news/ss-48667.

5. Robert C. Post, *High Performance: The Culture and Technology of Drag Racing, 1950–1990* (Baltimore: Johns Hopkins University Press, 1994), 9–10, 12.

6. David N. Lucsko, *The Business of Speed: The Hot Rod Industry in America, 1915–1990* (Baltimore: Johns Hopkins University Press, 2008), 6–9, 85–102.

7. Tom McCarthy, *Auto Mania: Cars, Consumer, and the Environment* (New Haven, CT: Yale University Press, 2007), xiii, xix.

8. Thorstein Veblen, *The Theory of the Leisure Class: The Economic Study of Institutions* (New York: MacMillan, 1915), 35, 68.

9. Lawrence Culver, *The Frontier of Leisure: Southern California and the Shaping of Modern America* (New York: Oxford University Press, 2010), 9.

10. Bob Edwards and Ugo Corte, "Commercialization and Lifestyle Sport: Lessons from Twenty Years of Freestyle BMX in 'Pro-Town, USA,'" *Sport in Society: Cultures, Commerce, Media, Politics* 13 (September–October 2010): 1135.

11. John Heitmann, *The Automobile and American Life* (Jefferson, NC: McFarland, 2009), 140–43.

12. Joe Scalzo, *City of Speed: Los Angeles and the Rise of American Racing* (St. Paul, MN: Motorbooks, 2007); Art Evans, *The Fabulous Fifties: Sports Car Racing in Southern California* (Redondo Beach, CA: Photo Data Research, 2002); Michael T. Lynch, William Edgar, and Ron Parravano, *American Sports Car Racing in the 1950s* (Osceola, WI: MBI Publishing, 1998); and Joe Scalzo, "The Way It Was: The Glamour Years of Sports Car Racing on the West Coast," *Automobile Quarterly* 19, no. 2 (1981): 129–30.

13. Pete Hylton, *The Gentlemen's Club: The Growth and Transition of American Sports Car Racing* (n.c.: Heritage Publishing, 2008), 16.

14. Sports Car Club of America, "Definition of a Sports Car," *Sportwagen* 1 (March 1944): 1.

15. Ken W. Purdy, "Racing Car-Mad and Happy," *Vogue* 123 (February 1, 1953): 205.

16. Terry O'Neill, *Northeast American Sports Car Races* (Dorchester, England: Veloce, 2011), 9.

17. Hal Foust, "'52 Good Year, and Bad One, in Auto Racing," *Chicago Daily Tribune*, December 21, 1952, A5; Hylton, *The Gentlemen's Club*, 12.

18. Jim Sitz, e-mail to the author, July 17, 2015.

19. G. N. Georgano, *A History of Sports Cars* (New York: Bonanza Books, 1970), 215–74.
20. Bill Barrett, "John von Neumann," *West Coast Sports Car Journal* 2 (March 1956): 10–11.
21. Roger Barlow, "The Steering Column," *West Coast Sports Car Journal* 3 (February 1957): 24.
22. Bill Pollack, in Evans, *The Fabulous Fifties*, 6–7.
23. Allan Coy, "California Sports Car Club Will Turn 65 Years Old in 2015," 2015, accessed June 14, 2015, http://www.calclub.com/html/html2/archives/2015/PressRelease-Buttonwillow-CalClub.pdf.
24. John R. Bond, "Miscellaneous Ramblings," *Road & Track* 9 (February 1958): 9.
25. Evans, *The Fabulous Fifties*, 7, 148, 150–51, 223.
26. *Official Program: Carrell Speedway Foreign Car Races, July 24, 1949*, accessed July 9, 2015, http://0398ca9.netsolhost.com/covcs0749.htm; Evans, *The Fabulous Fifties*, 8–10, 28–31.
27. "Racing on the Runways: A New Arena," *Sports Illustrated* 1 (September 13, 1954): 56.
28. Jim Mourning, "How It All Began," in *Official Program: 3rd Running Santa Barbara Road Race, May 28–29, 1955*, Box 176, DFC, BFRC; Evans, *The Fabulous Fifties*, 80–81, 84; Dick Hyland, "Hyland Fling," *Los Angeles Times*, March 21, 1953, B2.
29. Mourning, "How It All Began."
30. Evans, *The Fabulous Fifties*, 225–26.
31. Bruce Weber, "Phil Hill, a Racing Legend at Odds with the Sport at Times, Is Dead at 81," *New York Times*, August 28, 2008, accessed July 29, 2015, http://www.nytimes.com/2008/08/29/sports/othersports/29hill.html?sq=phil%20hill&st=cse&adxnnl=1&scp=1&adxnnlx=1221341626-EscZBCokTZE2FOJky33vMQ&_r=0; Scalzo, "The Way It Was," 131–32.
32. W. Lee Tomerlin, "Ken Miles: Outspoken, Outgoing, and Usually Out in Front," *Road & Track* 15 (October 1963): 64–68.
33. Frank Bristow, "Ace Road Race Driver Teaches Others How to Stay Alive on Track," *Los Angeles Times*, October 5, 1959, B1.
34. "Speed Portrait: Richie Ginther," *West Coast Sports Car Journal* 3 (November 1957): 9–11; Bill Barrett, "Meet the Drivers," in *Riverside International Motor Raceway Sports Car Road Races, September 21–22, 1957*; Rex McAfee, "Jack McAfee, 1922–2007," 2007, accessed July 29, 2015, http://www.jackmcafee.com/index.html; Scalzo, "The Way It Was," 130–31, 134.
35. "Carroll Shelby," n.d. [1966], Folder "1963 Correspondence and Reports," Box 160, DFC, BFRC; Scalzo, *City of Speed*, 61.
36. Evans, *The Fabulous Fifties*, 189.
37. "Women in the Sport," in *Official Program: Paramount Ranch Road Races*, March 9–10, 1957, Box 176, DFC, BFRC.
38. Josie von Neumann, "Women's Angle," *West Coast Sports Car Journal* 1 (February 1955): 6; Dusty Brandel, "Women behind the Wheel," in *Official Program: Riverside International Motor Raceway Sports Car Road Races, November 16–17, 1957*, Box 134, DFC, BFRC.
39. Bob Thomas, "Grand Prix Lures Expensive Machines," *Los Angeles Times*, October 11, 1959, A14.
40. Thomas, "Grand Prix Lures Expensive Machines."
41. "Market Place," *Road & Track* 5 (April 1954): 46.
42. An engine's displacement is the total volume of the cylinders that can be filled with a fuel-air mixture and expressed in either cubic centimeters (cc) or liters (l).
43. "A Class for Each Car," in *Official Program: Torrey Pines First National Sports Car Races, July 9–10, 1955*, accessed July 29, 2015, http://0398ca9.netsolhost.com/covtp755.htm; Arthur Evans Jr., "Class Racing," in *Official Program: 4th Running Pomona Road Races, July 27–28, 1957*,

Box 176, DFC, BFRC, 19; "The Car Class," in *Souvenir Program: U.S. Grand Prix for Sports Cars, Riverside International Raceway, October 11–12, 1958*, accessed July 31, 2015, http://0398ca9.netsolhost.com/covtmgp58.htm.

44. Art Lauring, "New Riverside Raceway Unveiled," *Los Angeles Times*, September 12, 1957, C6.

45. "Motor Racing's Finest Groups behind Classic," *Los Angeles Times*, October 12, 1958, D4.

46. Bill Pollack, "Sports Car Racing Comes of Age . . . ," in *Souvenir Program: U.S. Grand Prix for Sports Cars, Riverside International Raceway*, October 11–12, 1958.

47. "Riverside's First 75 Years," *Los Angeles Times*, October 16, 1958, B4.

48. R. W. Kastner, interview by author, digital recording, June 15, 2015.

49. Frank Bristow, "Nine Turns Demanding at Raceway," *Los Angeles Times*, October 11, 1959, A14.

50. Jack Smith, "Of Smith & Cars," *Road & Track* 15 (January 1964): 78.

51. "Saturday's Races Televised—KTTV (11)—1 pm," *Motoracing* 7, no. 16 (April 13–20, 1962): 9.

52. Ken Miles, "Racing Review: What Is Happening to Sports Car Racing?" *West Coast Sports Car Journal* 4 (January 1958): 21; Bill Pollack, interview by author, August 11, 2015.

53. Aston Royce, "The Chronicle of Aston Royce," *West Coast Sports Car Journal* 1 (March 1955): 7; Willard King, "Council Notes," *West Coast Sports Car Journal* 1 (May 1955): 23.

54. John R. Bond, "Miscellaneous Ramblings," *Road & Track* 9 (February 1958): 9; Evans, *The Fabulous Fifties*, 103.

55. Sitz, e-mail to the author; Evans, *The Fabulous Fifties*, 98, 225–26.

56. Dick Sherwin, "The Latest . . . ," *West Coast Sports Car Journal* 1 (May 1955): 17.

57. Willard King, "Council Notes," *West Coast Sports Car Journal* 1 (July 1955): 24; Coy, "California Sports Car Club Will Turn 65 Years Old in 2015," 2015, accessed June 14, 2015.

58. Sitz, e-mail to the author; Evans, *The Fabulous Fifties*, 101.

59. John R. Bond, "Miscellaneous Ramblings," *Road & Track* 9 (February 1958): 9.

60. John R. Bond, "Miscellaneous Ramblings," *Road & Track* 10 (January 1959): 13.

61. Gus V. Vignolle, "SCCA Ousts LA Region; Legal Skirmish Seen!" *Motoracing* 7, no. 3 (November 24–December 1, 1961): 1, 7.

62. "Move Aids Sport—Michelmore," *Motoracing* 7, no. 3 (November 24–December 8, 1961): 3.

63. Pollack, interview.

64. Gus V. Vignolle, "Cal Club Approves SCCA Merger as LA Region Defiant: Cal Club," *Motoracing* 7, no. 4 (December 8–15, 1961): 1, 2, 3.

65. "Quoting Josh Hogue in the *San Francisco Chronicle*," *Motoracing* 7, no. 5 (January 5–12, 1962): 6.

66. "LA Region Demands Hearing," *Motoracing* 7, no. 3 (November 24–December 1, 1961): 3.

67. Art Lauring, "From the Pits," *Los Angeles Times*, May 18, 1958, A18.

68. Gus V. Vignolle, "Ousted LA SCCA Joins USAC," *Motoracing* 7, no. 5 (January 5–12, 1962): 1, 4.

69. Gus V. Vignolle, "45 Pilots Ignore Cal Club Pomona Ban," *Motoracing* 7, no. 8 (February 16–23, 1962): 1.

70. Gus V. Vignolle, "Half Million Suit Hits Cal Club, SCCA," *Motoracing* 7, no. 9 (March 2–9, 1962): 1, 6; Hylton, *The Gentlemen's Club*, 59.

71. Gus V. Vignolle, "Cal Club Flexes Its Muscles," *Motoracing* 7, no. 9 (May 11–18, 1962): 1.

72. Los Angeles Chapter, USSCC, "Open Letter to Sports Car Drivers," *Motoracing* 7, no. 16 (April 13–20, 1962): 8.

73. Gus V. Vignolle, "Rival Cal Club, USSCC Merge!" *Motoracing* 7, no. 17 (June 29, 1962): 1, 4.

74. Gus V. Vignolle, "General Meeting Called for Dec. 13 to Vote on Merger," *Motoracing* 8, no. 1 (November 16–23, 1962): 1, 3; Gus V. Vignolle, "Cal Club, USSCC Move for Merger at Mass Meeting," *Motoracing* 8, no. 3 (December 14–28, 1962): 1, 2; "Zipper New President of Cal Club," *Motoracing* 8, no. 4 (January 11–18, 1963): 4; "Six Definite '63 Races Set by Cal Club," *Motoracing* 8, no. 4 (January 11–18, 1963): 6.

75. "Motor Racing: Record Entry for Amateur Finale at Riverside," *Los Angeles Times*, June 30, 1988, accessed June 14, 2015, http://articles.latimes.com/1988-06-30/sports/sp-7905 _1_amateur-racing; Pete Lyons, "Riverside Requiem," *Autoweek* 38 (July 25, 1988): 25.

76. Coy, "California Sports Car Club Will Turn 65 Years Old in 2015."

6. Professional Football in the City of Angels

1. For a review of Red Grange joining the Chicago Bears in 1925 and the growth of national interest in professional football it triggered, see Raymond Schmidt, *Shaping College Football: The Transformation of an American Sport, 1919–1930* (Syracuse, NY: Syracuse University Press, 2007), 72–77, 79–81. Excellent coverage of the 1925–26 tour by Grange and the Chicago Bears that included Los Angeles can be found in Michael Oriard, "Home Team," *South Atlantic Quarterly* 95, no. 2 (Spring 1996): 479–91.

2. Oriard, "Home Team," 490; Roger Treat, *The Encyclopedia of Football* (New York: A. S. Barnes and Company, 1974), 46; Robert W. Peterson, *Pigskin: The Early Years of Pro Football* (New York: Oxford University Press, 1997), 98–99.

3. George Halas, *Halas by Halas: The Autobiography* (New York: McGraw-Hill, 1979), 159–60.

4. *Los Angeles Bulldogs Official Program*, November 8, 1936; Bob Gill, "The Bulldogs: L.A. Hits the Big Time," *PFRA Annual* 5 (1984): 1. A full page of excerpts from various Los Angeles newspapers after the first two wins against the NFL teams can be found in "Pro-Pigskin Palaver," *Los Angeles Bulldogs Official Program*, November 28, 1936, 8. Frank Finch, "Bears Beat Bulldogs by 7-to-0 Score," *Los Angeles Times*, January 11, 1937; Gill, "The Bulldogs," 3, 12.

5. Treat, *Encyclopedia*, 71; "Pro-Pigskin Palaver," *Los Angeles Bulldogs Official Program*, November 7, 1937, 7; Gill, "The Bulldogs," 4, 13–14. An example of the Cleveland game publicity is in *Los Angeles Bulldogs Official Program*, November 13, 1938. Frank Finch, "Bulldogs Beat Rams, 28–7," *Los Angeles Times*, November 21, 1938.

6. Gill, "The Bulldogs," 7–8, 15; Treat, *Encyclopedia*, 77.

7. The NFL's first-ever Pro Bowl game was played on January 15, 1939—at Wrigley Field, just south of downtown Los Angeles—between the champion New York Giants and the All-Stars before a crowd of 15,000. The NFL All-Stars included three Bulldog players and one member of the Hollywood Stars. Effective with the second of the three Pro Bowl games in Los Angeles the event was moved to Gilmore Stadium, and on December 29, 1940, the game between the Chicago Bears and the All-Stars attracted an attendance of 21,624. Meserole, *Information Please*, 252. David L. Porter, ed., *Biographical Dictionary of American Sports: Football* (New York: Greenwood Press, 1987), 637–38. In 1934, a small California

semiprofessional league included the Hollywood Braves, the Los Angeles Maroons, and the Westwood Cubs. The Westwood team was led by its star halfback, an African American player named Joe Lillard, who had played for the Chicago Cardinals of the NFL in 1932–1933 before the league imposed its unofficial "color barrier." Ray Schmidt, "The Joe Lillard Affair," *College Football Historical Society* (May 2011): 1–4.

8. Bob Gill, "PCPFL: 1940–45," *The Coffin Corner* 4, no. 7 (1982); *Los Angeles Bulldogs vs Hollywood Bears Official Program*, October 12, 1945, 2; Bob Gill, "Jackie Robinson: Pro Football Prelude," *The Coffin Corner* 9, no. 3 (1987). In the 1941 season finale Washington threw a pair of fourth-quarter touchdown passes—including one for 35 yards to Strode to end the scoring—as the Bears escaped with a 17–10 victory over the Bulldogs. Bob Smyser, "Hollywood in 17–10 Victory," *Los Angeles Times*, December 22, 1941.

9. Gill, "PCPFL," *Hollywood Bears vs Los Angeles Bulldogs Official Program*, November 25, 1945; Jack Curnow, "Hollywood Bears Whip L.A. Bulldogs, 24–7," *Los Angeles Times*, November 26, 1945. For highlights and a summary of the Bears' season, see *Los Angeles Bulldogs vs Hollywood Bears Official Program*, January 6, 1946. After the Rams and Dons came to town in 1946, the Los Angeles Bulldogs and the Hollywood Bears continued to field teams through the shortened 1948 season; the Bulldogs winning their final league title in 1946 while the Bears missed playing in 1947. The Bulldogs thus played thirteen seasons (1936–1948) while the Bears fielded six teams (1940–42, 45–46, 48).

10. Stan Grosshandler, "All-America Football Conference," *The Coffin Corner* 2, no. 7 (1980); "Dudley S. DeGroot," *L.A. Dons Press and Radio Guide* (1947): 12.

11. Bob Oates, *The Los Angeles Rams* (Culver City: Murray & Gee Inc., 1955), 16, 22; George Sullivan, "Dan Reeves," *Pro Football's All-Time Greats* (New York: G. P. Putnam's Sons, 1968), 209–13; Steve Bisheff, *Los Angeles Rams* (New York: MacMillan, 1973), 150–51; Treat, *Encyclopedia*, 63; Michael MacCambridge, *America's Game: The Epic Story of How Pro Football Captured a Nation* (New York: Random House, 2004), 7–8, 15–16. Improved commercial air travel by the 1940s, and then enhanced during World War II, was demonstrated in 1940 when the University of Michigan football team flew in two chartered airliners between Detroit and Oakland, California, for their season opening game at the University of California. Richard Cohen, *The University of Michigan Football Scrapbook* (Indianapolis: Bobbs-Merrill, 1978), 100.

12. MacCambridge, *America's Game*, 17–19; Peterson, *Pigskin*, 181; Bisheff, *Los Angeles Rams*, 14; Michael Oriard, *Brand NFL: Making and Selling America's Favorite Sport* (Chapel Hill: University of North Carolina Press, 2007), 211; Peterson, *Pigskin*, 173, 186–88; Oates, *Los Angeles Rams*, 91. By the end of the 1950 season the NFL had only fourteen black players, the number reaching 12 percent of the total players in 1959. After the merger with the AFL the number increased to 28 percent in 1968 and 49 percent in 1982. See MacCambridge, *America's Game*, 71, and Oriard, *Brand NFL*, 210–11. In the 1970 draft the teams of the newly merged NFL selected 135 players from the historically black colleges alone (211). While the Rams broke the NFL's color barrier, the Cleveland Browns of the AAFC in 1946 also signed two excellent African American players named Marion Motley and Bill Willis, thus shattering any color barriers in professional football. Joseph Hession, *Rams: Five Decades of Football* (San Francisco: Foghorn Press, 1987), 25.

13. Oates, *Los Angeles Rams*, 24; Bisheff, *Los Angeles Rams*, 16–17; Treat, *Encyclopedia*, 112–13; Frank Finch, "Eagles Blank Rams," *Los Angeles Times*, December 19, 1949.

14. The majority of serious football historians point to the 1960s as the most notable period in professional football history. With the significant improvements in the game brought about by the increasing numbers of African American players coming into the

league, the merger of the NFL and AFL beginning in 1966, and the continued expansion of television coverage and other media vehicles for the league, the decade of the 1960s unquestionably launched the modern NFL. Among authoritative football historians in support of the major significance of the 1960s, see Oriard, *Brand NFL*, 6–7; MacCambridge, *America's Game*, xvi–xvii; and Bob Carroll, who devoted an entire book to the decade's importance entitled *When the Grass Was Real* (New York: Simon & Schuster, 1993) in which he described the decade as "the best ten years of pro football."

15. Treat, *Encyclopedia*, 103; Ray Schmidt, "Welcome to L.A.," *The Coffin Corner* 25, no. 6 (2003): 5–8. The *Los Angeles Times* described the turnout for the Dons' 1947 home opener as "the largest crowd ever to see a professional league football game." Dick Hyland, "Top Pro Crowd of 82,675 Sees Yanks Topple Dons," *Los Angeles Times*, September 13, 1947. Other than the 1947 home opener, the top Coliseum attendance of the season for the Dons was the 53,726 for the game against the arch rival San Francisco 49ers. The Rams attendance for 1948 appears in Oates, *Los Angeles Rams*, 30. Treat, *Encyclopedia*, 116. The last touchdown ever scored for the Dons was by George Taliaferro on a 52-yard punt return. The game box scores and attendance figures for the Dons are obtained from www.pro-football-reference.com/teams.

16. Hession, *Five Decades*, 45; Peterson, *Pigskin*, 197; Sullivan, *All-Time Greats*, 213; MacCambridge, *America's Game*, 73. In 1951 the DuMont network purchased the rights to present live telecasts nationally of the annual NFL championship game, beginning that year.

17. Bisheff, *Los Angeles Rams*, 34; Hession, *Five Decades*, 45, 50; Frank Finch, "Browns Edge Rams, 30–28," *Los Angeles Times*, December 25, 1950. The Los Angeles Coliseum played host to the NFL's postseason Pro Bowl all-star games from 1951 to 1972. Oates, *Los Angeles Rams*, 49, 51; Finch, "Rams Whip Browns, 24–17, Win Pro Title," *Los Angeles Times*, December 24, 1951.

18. Oates, *Los Angeles Rams*, 74; Hession, *Five Decades*, 56, 62. Fears retired after 1956, Hirsch and Younger after 1957, and Van Brocklin went to Philadelphia for 1958 after continual disputes with Coach Sid Gillman. Treat, *Encyclopedia*, 131; Bisheff, *Los Angeles Rams*, 152–53.

19. Hession, *Five Decades*, 69; Bisheff, *Los Angeles Rams*, 15, 87, 154–55, 157, 161–62.

20. Ed Gruver, *The American Football League: A Year-by-Year History* (Jefferson, NC: McFarland, 1997), 17–20, 41; Treat, *Encyclopedia*, 152; Bob Curran, *The $400,000 Quarterback* (New York: MacMillan, 1965), 89–90; Gruver, *American Football League*, 49.

21. Curran, *The $400,000*, 91; "In the Beginning: They Were the L.A. Chargers," *Los Angeles Times*, September 17, 1985; Braven Dyer, "Chargers Rally, Win, 21–20," *Los Angeles Times*, September 11, 1960; Gruver, *American Football League*, 56, 61. The box scores and attendance figures for the 1960 Chargers are obtained from www.pro-football-reference.com/teams. Treat, *Encyclopedia*, 148.

22. Hession, *Five Decades*, 105, 114–19, 122–25, 128–43; Oriard, *Brand NFL*, 12; Bisheff, *Los Angeles Rams*, 164, 169, 177–78. Dan Reeves, owner of the Rams, was inducted into the Professional Football Hall of Fame in 1967 (Bisheff, 180). *Official National Football League Record & Fact Book* (New York: Time Inc., 2010), 386–88.

23. In 1974–1975, Anaheim was home to the professional Southern California Sun of the new World Football League (WFL). This league's schedule ran from mid-July to mid-November, and, coached by ex-Ram great Tom Fears, the Sun won the west division title in 1974. Severely underfinanced from the start, the WFL and its teams went out of business on October 22, 1975. Tod Maher and Mark Speck, *World Football League Encyclopedia* (Haworth, NJ: St. Johann Press, 2006), 121, 223. Hession, *Five Decades*, 145; "Year of the Ram Belongs to Steelers," *Los Angeles Times*, January 21, 1980.

24. Hession, *Five Decades*, 153–55; Glenn Dickey, *Just Win Baby: Al Davis and His Raiders* (New York: Harcourt Brace Jovanovich, 1991), 151–52, 172; Ira Simmons, *Black Knight: Al Davis and His Raiders* (Rocklin, CA: Prima Publishing, 1990), 205–8, 211–12; Dickey, *Just Win*, 207, 210; Alan Greenberg, "Raiders Send Hogs to Slaughter, 38–9," *Los Angeles Times*, January 23, 1984.

25. Jim Byrne, *The $1 League: The Rise and Fall of the USFL* (New York: Prentice Hall Press, 1986), 24, 47; Chris Dufresne, "Is USFL a One-Man League?" *Los Angeles Times*, March 6, 1983; Dufresne, "Express Escapes with Opening Win," *Los Angeles Times*, March 7, 1983. There were several knowledgeable football observers who were impressed with the level of play in the Express-Generals opener. Jim Murray wrote that "the quality of play may be infinitesimally inferior" to that of the NFL. Overall, Murray was openly hopeful for the new league's chances. Jim Murray, "The Big Test: Can the New League Survive July?" *Los Angeles Times*, March 8, 1983.

26. Byrne, *$1 League*, 79, 103–5, 110; *Sporting News Official USFL Guide and Register* (St. Louis: Sporting News, 1984); Chris Dufresne, "Express Starts Anew, but It's an Old Story," *Los Angeles Times*, February 27, 1984; Byrne, *$1 League*, 173. Scores and highlights for the 1984 season are from the website www.oursportscentral.com/USFL. Also, *Sporting News USFL Guide* (1985).

27. Chris Dufresne, "Fifth Touchdown Pass Beats Express, 34–33," *Los Angeles Times*, February 24, 1985. The 3,059 fans who came to the Coliseum for the final game there by the Express was the smallest crowd in USFL history. Dufresne, "Express Quietly Says Farewell to Coliseum," *Los Angeles Times*, May 31, 1985. Dufresne, "The Result of Express vs Arizona Game: 8,200," *Los Angeles Times*, June 16, 1985.

28. Dickey, *Just Win*, 212, 230–34, 239, 245; Steve Springer, "Raiders Earn Spot in Layoffs," *Los Angeles Times*, December 15, 1994. Al Davis kept a $10 million nonrefundable fee from the town of Irwindale that was paid when their stadium project was first proposed. Also, in late 1990, Davis received up-front and kept a $20 million nonreturnable fee from a company named Spectacor that was going to renovate the Coliseum if the Raiders would sign a twenty-year lease; the deal eventually falling through. Dickey, *Just Win*, 243; Simmons, *Black Knight*, 330.

29. *Football League Record Book*, 380–84; Hession, *Five Decades*, 161, 163; *Football League Record Book*, 378–79; Mike Digiovanna, "St. Louis Rams? Offer Looks Hard to Refuse," *Los Angeles Times*, December 24, 1994; T. J. Simers, "Rams Are All but Run Out of Town," *Los Angeles Times*, December 25, 1994. The last touchdown scored for the Los Angeles Rams came on a 36-yard TD pass catch by Jermaine Ross. Mike Penner, "And So They Leave, With a Whimper, Not a Bang," *Los Angeles Times*, December 25, 1994. The team compiled an overall mark of 377–319–19 through their forty-nine seasons as the Los Angeles Rams. T. J. Simers, "Rams May End on Lowest Note," *Los Angeles Times*, December 24, 1994.

30. By 2015 the field of serious developers willing to start construction of a new Los Angeles stadium to attract an NFL team had been narrowed down to two. In January 2015, St. Louis Rams owner Stan Kroenke announced that he had purchased land and entered into an agreement to build a $2 billion, 80,000-seat stadium with the owners of the adjoining property that included the former site of the Hollywood Park racetrack in Inglewood. Kroenke stressed that this plan was no guarantee that the Rams would be returning to Los Angeles, but he had not been able to reach agreement with St. Louis officials for the adding of major improvements to their stadium. The second major stadium contender was announced in early 2015, with a proposal to build a $1.7 billion multi-team stadium in the town of Carson—about twelve miles south of downtown—to become home to the Chargers and

Raiders. Quickly a referendum was scheduled on a Carson bond issue to build a new stadium. By late May it was reported that the teams had hired a consultant experienced in the financing and planning of sport franchise relocations, and by June the NFL was looking to arrange a temporary stadium venue for use in the 2016 season. Tim Logan, Angel Jennings, and Nathan Fenno, "Inglewood Council Approves NFL Stadium Plan," *Los Angeles Times*, February 24, 2015; Michael R. Blood, "Land Deal Finalized for Planned New Stadium," *Ventura County Star*, May 20, 2015; Sam Farmer, "NFL Pursues Plans for Temporary Venues," *Los Angeles Times*, June 26, 2015.

31. Sam Farmer and Nathan Fenno, "NFL Returns to L.A.: Rams Kick Off in '16," *Los Angeles Times*, January 13, 2016.

7. The 1932 Olympics

I would like to thank Joy Block and Veneesa Cook for their helpful comments on an earlier draft of this chapter.

1. For useful sociological treatments of this issue, see Miriam Greenberg, *Branding New York: How a City in Crisis Was Sold to the World* (New York: Routledge, 2008); John Hannigan, *Fantasy City: Pleasure and Profit in the Postmodern Metropolis* (New York: Routledge, 1998); Dennis Judd and Susan Fainstein, eds., *The Tourist City* (New Haven, CT: Yale University Press, 1999); Costas Spirou, *Urban Tourism and Urban Change: Cities in a Global Economy* (New York: Routledge, 2010).

2. Greenberg, *Branding New York*, 29; Dennis Judd, "Promoting Tourism in US Cities," *Tourism Management* 16, no. 3 (May 1995): 175–87.

3. Greenberg, *Branding New York*, 35–36.

4. Throughout this chapter, I use "neoliberalism" or "neoliberal capitalism" as shorthand for the current historical phase of capitalism, which emerged out of the rightward shifts in the United States and United Kingdom in the late 1970s and early 1980s. It is characterized by the seemingly contradictory combination of "free-market" economic ideology—elites peddle this as a justification for gutting the welfare state—and expanded "corporate welfare" in the form of transfers of public resources to private corporations. What ultimately unites these seemingly incongruous elements is that both yield a result coveted by the capitalist class: the upward redistribution of wealth. See David Harvey, *A Brief History of Neoliberalism* (New York: Oxford University Press, 2007).

5. Steven Riess, "Power without Authority: Los Angeles Elites and the Construction of a Coliseum," *Journal of Sport History* 8, no. 1 (Spring 1981): 51.

6. Riess, "Power without Authority," 51–53; Mark Dyreson and Matthew Llewellyn, "Los Angeles Is *the* Olympic City: Legacies of the 1932 and 1984 Olympic Games," *The International Journal of the History of Sport* 25, no. 14 (December 2008): 1994. On the political economy of Los Angeles tourism and real estate in the late nineteenth century, see Mike Davis, *City of Quartz: Excavating the Future in Los Angeles* (New York: Vintage, 1990), 24–25.

7. Dyreson and Llewellyn, "Los Angeles Is *the* Olympic City," 1993.

8. Riess, "Power without Authority," 58; "Games Fund Suit Decided," *Los Angeles Times*, February 12, 1934, ProQuest.

9. White, "'The Los Angeles Way of Doing Things,'" 83, 88. For more on de Coubertin and modern Olympism, see John MacAloon, *This Great Symbol: Pierre de Coubertin and the Origins of the Modern Olympic Games* (New York: Routledge, 2013).

10. Quoted in Sean Dinces, "Padres on Mount Olympus: Los Angeles and the Production of the 1932 Olympic Mega-Event," *Journal of Sport History* 32, no. 2 (Summer 2005): 140, 143.

11. For more on the absence of reference to actual sport in the official promotional materials, see White, "'The Los Angeles Way of Doing Things,'" 84.

12. Dyreson and Llewellyn, "Los Angeles Is *the* Olympic City," 1992.

13. Quoted in Riess, "Power without Authority," 52.

14. Quoted in Dinces, "Padres on Mount Olympus," 144.

15. Quoted in White, "'The Los Angeles Way of Doing Things,'" 85.

16. Quoted in John Lucas, "Prelude to the Games of the Tenth Olympiad in Los Angeles, 1932," *Southern California Quarterly* 64, no. 4 (Winter 1982): 313.

17. Dinces, "Padres on Mount Olympus," 144.

18. Davis, *City of Quartz*, 25.

19. See, for example, Jefferson Cowie and Nick Salvatore, "The Long Exception: Rethinking the Place of the New Deal in American History," *International Labor and Working-Class History* 74 (Fall 2008): 3–32; David McNally, *Global Slump: The Economic and Politics of Crisis and Resistance* (Oakland, CA: PM Press, 2011), 38.

20. Greenberg, *Branding New York*, 35–36.

21. Riess, "Power without Authority," 51–52; Dyreson and Llewellyn, "Los Angeles Is *the* Olympic City," 1993.

22. Dinces, "Padres on Mount Olympus," 140–42; White, "'The Los Angeles Way of Doing Things,'" 87.

23. Greenberg, *Branding New York*, 35.

24. Riess, "Power without Authority," 53.

25. Judith Grant Long, Public/Private Partnerships for Major League Sports Facilities (New York: Routledge, 2013), 30–31.

26. Riess, "Power without Authority," 54–55.

27. Riess, "Power without Authority," 55, 63.

28. Long, Public/Private Partnerships for Major League Sports Facilities, 35–37.

29. Long, *Public/Private Partnerships for Major League Sports Facilities*, 28–29, 32, 35. Long's periodization applies to stadiums used by professional "major-league" teams. The history of the construction and financing of collegiate football stadiums is somewhat unique. The 1920s witnessed a building boom among universities eager to cash in on the increasing demand for collegiate football, both through increased ticket sales and the purported ability of successful programs to boost the reputation of their school and locale. In this period, universities themselves typically issued bonds to "investors and gridiron boosters" to finance the new facilities. John Watterson, *College Football: History, Spectacle, Controversy* (Baltimore, MD: Johns Hopkins University Press, 2000), 156. See also Raymond Schmidt, *Shaping College Football: The Transformation of an American Sport, 1919–1930* (Syracuse, NY: Syracuse University Press, 2007), ch. 3.

30. Long, Public/Private Partnerships for Major League Sports Facilities, 38; Kevin Delaney and Rick Eckstein, *Public Dollars, Private Stadiums: The Battle over Building Sports Stadiums* (New Brunswick, NJ: Rutgers University Press, 2003), ch. 8.

31. Quoted in White, "'The Los Angeles Way of Doing Things,'" 80.

32. Delaney and Eckstein, *Public Dollars, Private Stadiums*, 38–42.

33. Riess, "Power without Authority," 57–58, 61.

34. Riess, "Power without Authority," 57–58, 60–61.

35. White, "'The Los Angeles Way of Doing Things,'" 100.

36. Riess, "Power without Authority," 59–62; Lucas, "Prelude to the Games of the Tenth Olympiad in Los Angeles, 1932," 314.

37. Carolyn Prouse, "The Jock Doctrine," *Jacobin* 15/16 (Fall 2014), https://www.jacobinmag.com/2014/10/the-jock-doctrine/; Long, *Public/Private Partnerships for Major League Sports Facilities*, 35–38, 88; Delaney and Eckstein, *Public Dollars, Private Stadiums*, 24.

38. David Kotz, *The Rise and Fall of Neoliberal Capitalism* (Cambridge, MA: Harvard University Press, 2015), 191–95. For a helpful review of corporate welfare before 1930, see Charles Beard, "The Myth of Rugged American Individualism," *Harpers*, December 1931, http://classroom.sdmesa.edu/pjacoby/The-Myth-of-Rugged-American-Individualism.pdf.

39. White, "'The Los Angeles Way of Doing Things,'" 100; Riess, "Power without Authority," 61. The $1.5 million figure is cited by Dyreson and Llewellyn, "Los Angeles Is *the* Olympic City," 1996. Robert Barney offers the lowest estimate at $150,000, but does not offer a citation in support. Robert Barney, "Resistance, Persistence, Providence: The 1932 Los Angeles Olympic Games in Perspective," *Research Quarterly for Exercise and Sport* 67, no. 2 (June 1996): 156. Steven Riess indicates a number in between—approximately $430,000—but this excludes disbursements of surplus money to the state. See Riess, "Power without Authority," 62. One conceivable explanation for the wide dispersion of estimates is an inconsistent definition of "surplus" in reporting on the 1932 Games. It is possible that some primary sources equated "surplus" with total revenues rather than with net profits. This would have allowed them to make the figures seem more impressive.

40. This assertion is based on nominal values. In other words, it *is not* based on a "present value" analysis. But such analysis, given the timing of the expenditures, would likely make the gap between expenditures and receipts even wider.

41. Riess, "Power without Authority," 50.

42. Marc Falcous and Michael Silk, "Olympic Bidding, Multicultural Nationalism, Terror, and the Epistemological Violence of 'Making Britain Proud,'" *Studies in Ethnicity and Nationalism* 10, no. 2 (2010): 171. Similar theses can be found in Gordon Waitt, "Playing Games with Sydney: Marketing Sydney for the 2000 Olympics," *Urban Studies* 36, no. 7 (June 1999): 1055–77; Robyn Bourgeois, "Deceptive Inclusion: The 2010 Vancouver Olympics and Violence against First Nations People," *Canadian Woman Studies* 27, nos. 2/3 (Spring 2009): 39–44.

43. Falcous and Silk, "Olympic Bidding," 169.

44. Henry Giroux, *Stormy Weather: Katrina and the Politics of Disposability* (Boulder, CO: Paradigm, 2006), 3.

45. Quoted in Dyreson and Llewellyn, "Los Angeles *Is* the Olympic City," 1995.

46. Mark Dyreson, "Marketing National Identity: The Olympic Games of 1932 and Olympic Culture," *Olympika* 4 (1995): 36.

47. White, "'The Los Angeles Way of Doing Things,'" 81.

48. Quoted in White, "'The Los Angeles Way of Doing Things,'" 95.

49. White, "'The Los Angeles Way of Doing Things,'" 93.

50. Dyreson, "Marketing National Identity," 37; Eriko Yamamoto, "Cheers for Japanese Athletes: The 1932 Los Angeles Olympics and the Japanese American Community," *Pacific Historical Review* 60, no. 3 (August 2000): 415–16.

51. Quoted in Dinces, "Padres on Mount Olympus," 151.

52. Dinces, "Padres on Mount Olympus," 153.

53. Dyreson, "Marketing National Identity," 37; Dinces, "Padres on Mount Olympus," 153.

54. Kevin Starr, *Material Dreams: Southern California through the 1920s* (New York: Oxford University Press, 1990), 137–38.
55. Davis, *City of Quartz*, 162.
56. Yamamoto, "Cheers for Japanese Athletes," 415.
57. Davis, *City of Quartz*, 162–63; John Logan and Brian Stults, "Racial and Ethnic Separation in the Neighborhoods: Progress at a Standstill," *US2010* (December 14, 2010), http://www.s4.brown.edu/us2010/Data/Report/report1.pdf, 8.
58. On the Olympic boosterism that made use of California's "Spanish fantasy past," see Dinces, "Padres on Mount Olympus."
59. Kevin Johnson, "The Forgotten 'Repatriation' of Persons of Mexican Ancestry and Lessons for the 'War on Terror,'" *Pace Law Review* 26, no. 1 (Fall 2005): 5; Francisco Balderrama and Raymond Rodriguez, *Decade of Betrayal: Mexican Repatriation in the 1930s* (Albuquerque: University of New Mexico Press, 2006), 129, 323.
60. White, "'The Los Angeles Way of Doing Things,'" 101; Davis, *City of Quartz*, 28, 32.
61. Barney, "Resistance, Persistence, Providence," 154.
62. Clementina Duron, "Mexican Women and Labor Conflict in Los Angeles: The ILGWU Dressmakers' Strike of 1933," *Aztlan* 15, no. 1 (1984):154–61; Gordon Dillow, "Solidarity Forever: Retired Longshoreman Recalls 1934 Strike That Shaped the Fate of Waterfront Labor," *Los Angeles Times*, September 5, 1993, http://articles.latimes.com/1993-09-05/local/me-32168_1_labor-day.
63. Davis, *City of Quartz*, 26.
64. Neil deMause, "How Boston's Olympic Bid Came Crashing Down," *Vice Sports*, July 28, 2015, https://sports.vice.com/en_us/article/how-bostons-olympic-bid-came-crashing-down; *No Boston Olympics*, accessed August 14, 2015, http://www.nobostonolympics.org/.

8. "Never Go Back"

The author would like to thank Leigh Kaliss and David Schuyler for carefully reading this essay and offering valuable suggestions.

1. Arnold Rampersad, "In Pharaoh's Land: Cairo, Georgia (1919–1920)," 10–17, and "A Pasadena Boyhood (1920–1937)," 18–39, in *Jackie Robinson: A Biography* (New York: Alfred A. Knopf, 1997).
2. Josh Sides, *L.A. City Limits: African American Los Angeles from the Great Depression to the Present* (Berkeley: University of California Press, 2003), 11, 16.
3. Douglas Flamming, *Bound for Freedom: Black Los Angeles in Jim Crow America* (Berkeley: University of California Press, 2005), 36–37.
4. Sides, *L.A. City Limits*, 18–20.
5. Maury Allen, "Pepper Street, Pasadena," in *The Jackie Robinson Reader: Perspectives on an American Hero, with contributions by Roger Kahn, Red Barber, Wendell Smith, Malcolm X, Arthur Mann, and more*, ed. Jules Tygiel (New York: Dutton, 1997), 17.
6. Rampersad, *Jackie Robinson*, 21–22, 64–65.
7. Jackie Robinson, as told to Alfred Duckett, *I Never Had It Made* (New York: G. P. Putnam's Sons, 1972), 17.
8. Robinson, *I Never Had It Made*, 18.
9. Allen, "Pepper Street, Pasadena," 18, 22.

10. Rampersad, *Jackie Robinson*, 60–61. Original citation is *Pasadena Star-News*, April 7, 1987.

11. Jackie Robinson, with Wendell Smith, *Jackie Robinson: My Own Story* (New York: Greenberg, 1948), 8.

12. Rampersad, *Jackie Robinson*, 31.

13. Allen, "Pepper Street, Pasadena," 23.

14. Rampersad, *Jackie Robinson*, 50, 66.

15. David Falkner, *Great Time Coming: The Life of Jackie Robinson, From Baseball to Birmingham* (New York: Simon & Schuster, 1996), 35.

16. Falkner, *Great Time Coming*, 35.

17. Mack Robinson interview, September 4, 1984, Black History Collection, 1984–1999, Pasadena Museum of History, Pasadena, CA.

18. "Robinson Betters 200-Meter Record," *New York Times*, June 28, 1936; Frank Litsky, "Mack Robinson, 85, Second to Owens in Berlin," *New York Times*, March 14, 2000.

19. Arthur J. Daley, "Two World Marks Set as Best U.S. Olympic Track Team Emerges from Trials," *New York Times*, July 13, 1936.

20. Falkner, *Great Time Coming*, 38.

21. For more on black athletes and the 1936 Olympics, see John Gleaves and Mark Dyreson, "The 'Black Auxiliaries' in American Memories: Sport, Race and Politics in the Construction of Modern Legacies," *The International Journal of the History of Sport* 27 (November–December 2010): 2893–2924, and David K. Wiggins, "The 1936 Olympic Games in Berlin," *Glory Bound: Black Athletes in a White America* (Syracuse: Syracuse University Press, 1997), 61–79.

22. Bob Raissman, "Sad Footnote to Jessie and Jackie, *New York Daily News*, February 23, 1997.

23. Rampersad, *Jackie Robinson*, 31.

24. Arthur Pincus, "50 Years Later, Bitter Memories of the Berlin Games," *New York Times*, August 10, 1986; Daley, "Two World Marks Set."

25. Wykoff may have been added to the team because he had won relay gold in the previous two Olympics, and because he had run for the US track team's head coach, Dean Cromwell, at the University of Southern California. Eventually, the track coaches appeared to give in to anti-Semitism by replacing the only two Jewish members of the track team—Stoller and Glickman—with Owens and Metcalfe. For more on this story, see Pincus, "50 Years Later."

26. Falkner, *Great Time Coming*, 38.

27. Mack Robinson interview.

28. Gleaves and Dyreson, "Black Auxiliaries," 2905; "Vezie Will Speak at Men's Stag," *Pasadena Post*, September 24, 1936; "Negro Stars Honored," *Daily Bruin*, September 15, 1936.

29. Rampersad, *Jackie Robinson*, 31, 64.

30. Gleaves and Dyreson, "Black Auxiliaries," 2906.

31. Rampersad, *Jackie Robinson*, 87.

32. Jackie Robinson, with Ed Reid, "Jackie Robinson Tells His Own Story," *Washington Post*, August 21, 1949.

33. Rampersad, *Jackie Robinson*, 27.

34. Allen, "Pepper Street, Pasadena," 19–20.

35. Rampersad, *Jackie Robinson*, 31.

36. Robinson, *I Never Had It Made*, 21.

37. Rampersad, *Jackie Robinson*, 41, 56.

38. See, for example, Shavenau Glick, "Robinson's 104-Yard Run Tops P.J.C. Win," *Pasadena Post*, November 24, 1938, and "Robinson Sparkles in J.C. Finale," *California Eagle*, December 1, 1938.

39. "50,000 Cheer Jack Robinson in Pasadena Rose Bowl Win," *California Eagle*, November 3, 1938; Shavenau Glick, "Robinson Named 'Most Valuable Player,'" *Pasadena Post*, December 7, 1938; "Jackie Robinson to Lead All-Stars," *California Eagle*, December 8, 1938; "Pasadena Civic Groups Honor Jackie Robinson with Loving Cup," *California Eagle*, December 22, 1938.

40. Falkner, *Great Time Coming*, 49.

41. Robinson, *My Own Story*, 9.

42. For more on USC's poor reputation in regards to black athletes, see Woody Strode and Sam Young, *Goal Dust* (New York: Madison Books, 1990), 29, and "Hot Demand for Removal of Dean Cromwell as Troy Track Head," *Pasadena Post*, September 15, 1936. As early as the 1920s, UCLA fielded black athletes on its sports teams, including Ralph Bunche, who would go on to fame as a United Nations ambassador. Bunche was a star basketball player and track athlete for the school from 1925 to 1927. See Andrew Hamilton and John B. Jackson, *UCLA on the Move: During Fifty Golden Years, 1919–1969* (Los Angeles: Ward Ritchie Press, 1969), 172–73.

43. For more on the 1939 UCLA football team, see Gregory Kaliss, "'Harbingers of Progress' and 'The Gold Dust Trio': Washington, Strode, Robinson and the 1939 UCLA Football Team," in *Men's College Athletics and the Politics of Racial Equality: Five Pioneer Stories of Black Men, White Citizenship, and American Democracy* (Philadelphia: Temple University Press, 2012; paperback 2014), 41–73.

44. Kaliss, "'Harbingers of Progress.'"

45. See Bob Hunter, "Overlin Scores Touchdown in Third after Long Drive," *Los Angeles Examiner*, September 30, 1939, and "Cantor Saves Bruins," *Los Angeles Examiner*, November 26, 1939.

46. Lane Demas, "'On the Threshold of Broad and Rich Football Pastures': Integrated College Football at UCLA, 1938–1941," in *Horsehide, Pigskin, Oval Tracks and Apple Pie: Essays on Sports and American Culture*, ed. James A. Vlasich (Jefferson, NC: McFarland and Company, 2006), 86–103. See also Paul Zimmerman, "Sports Post-Scripts," *Los Angeles Times*, October 9, 1939.

47. Letter from Michael Joseph Hart to Robert G. Sproul, Series 359, Chancellor's Office, Box 71, folder 101, December 4, 1939.

48. Strode, *Goal Dust*, 63.

49. Kaliss, *Men's College Athletics and the Politics of Racial Equality*, 59–61.

50. Bob Hunter, "Robinson Hurt in Practice," *Los Angeles Examiner*, November 2, 1939. See also Kaliss, 53–55, 57–58.

51. Robinson, *My Own Story*, 9.

52. "Kenny Signs 3-Year Pact," *California Eagle*, November 21, 1940.

53. Robinson, *I Never Had It Made*, 23.

54. "Pasadena A.C. Members to Sign State Charter," *California Eagle*, February 20, 1941.

55. Robinson's military career—which saw him move to Fort Hood in Texas, nearly ended disastrously. After refusing to move to the back of a bus on his military base, Robinson faced court-martial charges. However, the all-white jury found him not guilty, and he finished his military service without further incident. For more on Robinson's military service, see Rampersad, *Jackie Robinson*, 83–112.

56. Allen, "Pepper Street, Pasadena," 21–23.
57. Allen, "Pepper Street, Pasadena," 24.
58. Robinson, *I Never Had It Made*, 116–19, 275–76.
59. Rampersad, *Jackie Robinson*, 461.
60. Mack Robinson interview.
61. J. Cullen Fentress, "Down in Front: What Now?" *California Eagle*, January 25, 1940.
62. Rampersad, *Jackie Robinson*, 32.
63. Mack Robinson, as told to A. S. "Doc" Young, "My Brother Jackie," *Ebony*, July 1957, 75–82.
64. Robinson, "My Brother Jackie," 76.
65. A. S. "Doc" Young, "Good Morning Sports! Jackie's Brother, Mack," *Chicago Daily Defender*, June 18, 1968.
66. Raissman, "Sad Footnote."
67. Young, "Jackie's Brother, Mack"; Robinson, "My Brother Jackie," 75.
68. Robinson, "My Brother Jackie," 80.
69. Rampersad, *Jackie Robinson*, 461.
70. Gleaves and Dyreson, "Black Auxiliaries," 2907.
71. Rampersad, *Jackie Robinson*, 464.
72. "Opening to Stir Memory," *New York Times*, July 24, 1984.
73. Gleaves and Dyreson, "Black Auxiliaries," 2907.
74. Mack Robinson interview.
75. Allen, "Pepper Street, Pasadena," 21.
76. Raissman, "Sad Footnote."
77. See, for example, Claire Smith, "Jackie Robinson: A Baseball Celebration; A Grand Tribute to Robinson and His Moment," *New York Times*, April 16, 1997.
78. The Jackie Robinson Community Center was dedicated in 1974, two years after Jackie's death. See "Jackie Robinson Community Center," City of Pasadena website, accessed on July 11, 2015, http://bit.ly/1HqMrwH.
79. "Model of Robinson Memorial to Be Unveiled," *Los Angeles Times*, April 15, 1997.
80. "Public Memorials and Monuments," City of Pasadena website, accessed on July 11, 2015, http://bit.ly/1UUXgQX.
81. "Robinson Stadium," Pasadena City College website, accessed on July 11, 2015, http://bit.ly/1eWOGjP.
82. Elizabeth Lee, "Honoring a Champion: Postal Service Names Branch after Athlete Mack Robinson," *Pasadena Star News*, July 4, 2002.
83. Hannah Madans, "Pasadena Praising Robinson Family's Legacy as Pioneers," *Orange County Register*, July 19, 2014.
84. For a persuasive summary of white Los Angeles civic leaders' treatment of people of racial minorities, see Eric Avila, *Popular Culture in the Age of White Flight: Fear and Fantasy in Suburban Los Angeles* (Berkeley: University of California Press, 2004), 20–64.
85. See Gleaves and Dyreson, "Black Auxiliaries," 2899 and Litsky, "Mack Robinson, 85, Second to Owens in Berlin."
86. Raissman, "Sad Footnote."

9. Reel Sports

I need to thank Skidmore College for its generous support of this work, specifically the Faculty Student Summer Research Program; working with Nevon Kipperman on this chapter was a delight. Also, as ever, I am grateful for Greg Pfitzer and Susan Taylor's support.

1. Thomas Doherty, "Film: An Overview," in *Encyclopedia of American Studies*, accessed June 2, 2015, http://eas-ref.press.jhu.edu/view?aid=49.

2. Adam Nagourney, "Hollywood Gets Its Groove Back," *New York Times*, February 12, 2015, accessed January 23, 2016, http://www.nytimes.com/2015/02/15/travel/hollywood-gets-its-groove-back.html.

3. See Celeste Olalquiaga, *Megalopolis: Contemporary Cultural Sensibilities* (Minneapolis: University of Minnesota Press, 1992).

4. David T. Friendly, "Few Sports Films Make a Hit," *Los Angeles Times*, August 14, 1986, Part VI, 1.

5. Angelo Pizzo quoted in Friendly, "Few Sports Films Make a Hit," 1.

6. Aaron Baker, *Contesting Identities: Sports in American Film* (Urbana: University of Illinois Press, [2003] 2006); Seán Crosson, *Sport and Film* (London: Routledge, 2013).

7. Bruce Babington, *The Sports Film: Games People Play* (New York: Wallflower, 2014), 4.

8. *A Personal Journey with Martin Scorsese through American Movies*, DVD, directed by Martin Scorsese and Michael Henry Wilson (Burbank, CA: Miramax Home Entertainment, [1995] 2004).

9. Baker, *Contesting Identities*, 4.

10. *Los Angeles Plays Itself*, DVD, directed by Thom Andersen (New York: Cinema Guild, [2003] 2014).

11. Considering the space allotted to me here, and how many sports films (broadly defined) have been made and set in Los Angeles, I had to be selective. Regrettably, some movies did not make the cut, for different reasons. For example, parts of the Marx Brothers' *Horse Feathers* (1932) and Katherine Hepburn and Spencer Tracy's *Pat and Mike* (1952) were filmed at Occidental College, which is in Eagle Rock, yet neither film evokes a strong sense of geographic specificity or place. The same is true of contemporary movies, such as *Kicking & Screaming* (2005) and *Million Dollar Arm* (2014). A family friendly comedy starring Will Ferrell, *Kicking & Screaming* was filmed in Los Angeles, Sierra Madre, and South Pasadena, but these communities are stripped of most of their local culture and are thus turned into Anywhere-ville, USA. The second half of Disney's *Million Dollar Arm* is set in Los Angeles, however the city is not well developed as a meaningful setting (perhaps the result of some of it being shot in Atlanta). These are, of course, subjective determinations.

12. According to Ray Didinger and Glen Macnow, "*The Karate Kid* is one of the most predictable and implausible sports movies ever made. It's also one of the most enjoyable." Ray Didinger and Glen Macnow, *The Ultimate Book of Sports Movies: Featuring the 100 Greatest Sports Films of All Time* (Philadelphia, PA: Running Press, 2009), 192.

13. Janet Maslin, "Screen: 'Karate Kid,' Bane of Bullies," *New York Times*, June 22, 1984, C16.

14. Jared Cowan, "How a Movie Shot in the San Fernando Valley Made Us All *The Karate Kid*," June 17, 2014, accessed November 30, 2015, http://www.laweekly.com/arts/how-a-movie-shot-in-the-san-fernando-valley-made-us-all-the-karate-kid-4790700; Jared Cowan, "The Valley as Seen in *The Karate Kid*—Then and Now," June 16, 2014, accessed November 30, 2015, http://www.laweekly.com/slideshow/the-valley-as-seen-in-the-karate-kid-then-and-now-4790827.

15. Quoted in Cowan, "How a Movie Shot in the San Fernando Valley Made Us All *The Karate Kid*."

16. Didinger and Macnow, *The Ultimate Book of Sports Movies*, 171.

17. David W. Zang, *Sports Wars: Athletes in the Age of Aquarius* (Fayetteville: University of Arkansas Press, 2001), 141.

18. Hal Erickson, *Baseball in the Movies: A Comprehensive Reference, 1915–1991* (Jefferson, NC: McFarland, 1992), 53.

19. Randy Williams, *Sports Cinema 100 Movies: The Best of Hollywood's Athletic Heroes, Losers, Myths, and Misfits* (Pompton Plains, NJ: Limelight, 2006), 182.

20. Janet Maslin, "Oh Well, Jumping Isn't Everything," *New York Times*, March 27, 1992, C22.

21. Hal Hinson, "'White Men's' Man-to-Man Magic," *Washington Post*, March 27, 1992, B1.

22. Hinson, "'White Men's' Man-to-Man Magic."

23. See http://www.afi.com/members//catalog/AbbrView.aspx?s=&Movie=67158 (accessed December 12, 2015).

24. Lawrence Christon, "Life on a City's Asphalt Stage," *Los Angeles Times*, March 23, 1992, F6.

25. Thomas McLaughlin thinks that *White Men Can't Jump* "has the best cinematic depiction of pickup ball in a mainstream film." According to McLaughlin, "The film beautifully visualizes the interplay on the court, the group improvisations that are pickup ball. There are Hollywood excesses—improbable trick shots, show-off camera angles—but the film does capture the fact that Billy and Sidney understand each other's moves and decisions, that they share a cognitive style." Thomas McLaughlin, *Give and Go: Basketball as a Cultural Practice* (Albany: State University of New York Press, 2008), 220.

26. Actually, the Clippers did not move from San Diego to Los Angeles until 1984.

27. Stephanie Zacharek, "Love and Basketball," *Sight and Sound*, August 2000, 52.

28. Roger Ebert, "Love and Basketball," April 21, 2000, accessed December 19, 2015, http://www.rogerebert.com/reviews/love-and-basketball-2000).

29. Quoted in Lucy McCalmont, "Double or Nothing: An Oral History of 'Love & Basketball,'" June 16, 2015, accessed December 17, 2015, http://www.huffingtonpost.com/2015/06/16/love-and-basketball-oral-history_n_7572140.html.

30. McCalmont, "Double or Nothing."

31. A. O. Scott declares that *Jerry Maguire* was "by far the best romantic comedy of the 1990's." A. O. Scott, "With Sympathy for the Devil, A Rock Writer Finds His Way," *New York Times*, September 13, 2000, E5.

32. David Ansen, "The Jets and the Sharks," *Newsweek*, December 16, 1996, 68.

33. Rachel Abramowitz, "The Z-Boys Are back in Town," *Los Angeles Times*, March 20, 2005, E1.

34. Abramowitz, "The Z-Boys Are back in Town."

35. Abramowitz, "The Z-Boys Are back in Town," E4.

36. A. O. Scott, "When California Started Sliding on Little Wheels," *New York Times*, June 3, 2005, E13.

37. Scott, "When California Started Sliding on Little Wheels."

38. Scott, "When California Started Sliding on Little Wheels."

39. Scott, "When California Started Sliding on Little Wheels."

40. Quoted in Diane Garrett, "Review: 'Lords of Dogtown: Unrated Extended Cut,'" *Variety*, October 2, 2005, accessed January 13, 2016, http://variety.com/2005/digital/features/lords-of-dogtown-unrated-extended-cut-1200521399/.

41. Jack McCallum, "Reel Sports," *Sports Illustrated*, February 5, 2001, 94.

42. William F. Van Wert, "Hollywood," in *Encyclopedia of American Studies*, accessed January 23, 2016, http://eas-ref.press.jhu.edu/view?aid=50.

43. Rob Ryder, Hollywood Jock: 365 Days, Four Screenplays, Three TV Pitches, Two Kids, and One Wife Who's Ready to Pull the Plug (New York: Harper, 2006), 10.

10. Behind the Curtain

1. Harry S. Edwards, "Developing a Championship Culture." Speech given at the University of Washington, Seattle, August 15, 2015.

2. William Oscar Johnson, "Jerry Is Never behind the Eight Ball, Jerry Buss Has Always Had a Way with a Chick, a Cue and a Buck. Now He'll Have His Way with the Lakers, Kings and Forum." *Sports Illustrated*, June 18, 1979. Roland Lazenby, *The Show: The Inside Story of the Spectacular Los Angeles Lakers in the Words of Those Who Lived It* (New York: McGraw Hill, 2006).

3. Scott Ostler and Steve Springer, *Winnin' Times: The Magical Journey of the Los Angeles Lakers* (New York: Collier Books, 1986).

4. Ostler and Springer, *Winnin' Times*.

5. Ostler and Springer, *Winnin' Times*.

6. Ostler and Springer, *Winnin' Times*, 246.

7. Lazenby, *The Show*.

8. Ostler and Springer, *Winnin' Times*.

9. ESPN, "NBA extends television deals," espn.com, October 7, 2014, accessed on September 15, 2015, http://espn.go.com/nba/story/_/id/11652297/nba-extends-television-deals-espn-tnt.

10. Brenton Welling, Jonathan Tasini, and Dan Cook, "Basketball: Business Is Booming," *Business Week* 28 (1985): 74.

11. Martin J. Greenberg and April R. Anderson, "The Name Is the Game in Facility Naming Rights," in *The Business of Sports*, 2nd edition, ed. Scott Rosner and Kenneth Shropshire (Sudbury, MA: Jones & Bartlett Learning, 2010), 243–45.

12. Jerry West, Buss Memorial. Speech given at the Nokia Theater, Los Angeles, California, February 21, 2013, accessed on July 31, 2015, http://www.nba.com/video/channels/nba_tv/2013/02/22/20130221-buss-memorial-west.nba/.

13. UPI, "Magic Johnson Signs $25 Million Contract," *New York Times*, June 26, 1981, accessed July 31, 2015, http://www.nytimes.com/1981/06/26/sports/magic-johnson-signs-25-million-contract.html.

14. Arthur R. Ashe Jr., *A Hard Road to Glory: The African American Athlete in Basketball* (New York: Amistad Books, 1988).

15. Curry Kirkpatrick, "Shattered and Shaken with Rocket Star Rudy Tomjanovich Lost to His Team for the Season and the Lakers' Kermit Washington Fined and Suspended for Decking Him, the Game Faces a Crisis," *Sports Illustrated*, January 2, 1978, accessed September 2, 2015, http://www.si.com/vault/1978/01/02/822276/shattered-and-shaken-with-rocket-star-rudy-tomjanovich-lost-to-his-team-for-the-season-and-the-lakers-kermit-washington-fined-and-suspended-for-decking-him-the-game-faces-a-crisis.

16. Kirkpatrick, Shattered and Shaken.

17. Bloomberg, "Magic Johnson: Basketball & Business," Game Changers at bloomberg.com, January 26, 2015, accessed July 21, 2015, http://www.bloomberg.com/news/videos/2015-01-26/magic-johnson-basketball-business.

18. Ostler and Springer, *Winnin' Times*.

19. Jeff Pearlman, *Showtime: Magic, Kareem, Riley and the Los Angeles Laker Dynasty of the 1980s* (New York: Gotham Books, 2013).

20. Pearlman, *Showtime*.

21. Pearlman, *Showtime*, 34.

22. Pearlman, *Showtime*.

23. Earvin "Magic" Johnson with William Novak, *My Life* (New York: Fawcett Books, 1992); Pearlman, *Showtime*.

24. Johnson, *My Life*; Ostler and Springer, *Winnin' Time*; Lazenby, *The Show*; Pearlman, *Showtime*.

25. Ostler and Springer, *Winnin' Time*, 162.

26. Johnson, *My Life*, 255.

27. Johnson, *My Life*, 255.

28. Johnson, *My Life*; Ostler and Springer, *Winnin' Time*; Lazenby, *The Show*; Pearlman, *Showtime*.

29. ESPN Classic, "Magic Johnson," ESPN Classic presents Vintage NBA, July 22, 1999, accessed July 31, 2015, https://www.youtube.com/watch?v=seZkJXK3QE0.

30. Pearlman, *Showtime*; Ostler and Springer, *Winnin' Times*.

31. Pearlman, *Showtime*, 107.

32. Pearlman, *Showtime*, 118.

33. Mike Littwin, "The Lakers' Other Guard," *Los Angeles Times*, March 31, 1981, quoted in Pearlman, *Showtime*, 117.

34. Pearlman, *Showtime*, 117–18.

35. Pearlman, *Showtime*, 117–18.

36. Pearlman, *Showtime*, 117–18.

37. Johnson, *My Life*.

38. Ostler and Springer, *Winnin' Times*, 202–3.

39. Johnson, *My Life*, 217.

40. Pearlman, *Showtime*, 128.

41. Ostler and Springer, *Winnin' Times*, 209.

42. Lazenby, *The Show*.

43. Pearlman, *Showtime*; Ostler and Springer, *Winnin' Times*.

44. Pearlman, *Showtime*. Worthy also experienced feeling less appreciated than Magic. Worthy was almost traded in 1986 for Mark Aguirre following Magic's suggestion and urging. Buss did not seek the opinion of Jerry West, who would've been dead set against it because of his confidence in Worthy. Worthy took particular offense to the rumor because Aguirre was one of Magic's closest friends.

45. Vincent M. Mallozzi, "30 Seconds with Lisa Leslie," *New York Times*, September 11, 2010, accessed July 21, 2015, http://offthedribble.blogs.nytimes.com/2010/09/11/30-seconds-with-lisa-leslie/.

46. *Jeff Pearlman Blog*, December 11, 2011, accessed July 31, 2015, http://www.jeffpearlman.com/the-quaz-qa-tina-thompson/.

47. Jorge Castillo, "Paul Pierce, Andre Miller Were Teammates Long before Wizards," *Washington Post*, November 27, 2014, accessed on July 21, 2015, http://www.washingtonpost.com/sports/wizards/paul-pierce-andre-miller-were-teammates-long-before-wizards/2014/11/27/2ec0b312-7581-11e4-a755-e32227229e7b_story.html.

48. Jonathan Abrams, "How This Born Laker Became a Celtic: Pierce's 'Birth of Basketball' Meant the Forum and Magic. But Inglewood High's Green Now Suits Him in Boston," *Los Angeles Times*, June 10, 2008, accessed on July 27, 2015, http://articles.latimes.com/2008/jun/10/sports/sp-pierce10.

49. Dr. Jerry Buss, "Dr. Jerry Buss Hall of Fame Speech," Speech given at the Basketball Hall of Fame. Springfield, Massachusetts, August 13, 2010, accessed July 31, 2015, http://www.nba.com/video/channels/hall_of_fame/2010/08/13/20100813_HOF_speech_Buss.nba/.

11. The Golden Games

1. The 1984 Olympic Games in Los Angeles was recently the subject of a special issue of the *International Journal of the History of Sport* 32, no. 1 (January 2015), guest editors, Matthew P. Llewellyn, John Gleaves, and Wayne Wilson.

2. Scarlett Cornelissen, "Resolving 'the South Africa Problem': Transnational Activism, Ideology and Race in the Olympic Movement, 1960–91," *The International Journal of the History of Sport* 28, no. 1 (2001): 153–67; Douglas Booth, "Hitting Apartheid for Six? The Politics of the South African Sports Boycott," *Journal of Contemporary History* 38, no. 3 (2003): 477–93.

3. Nicholas Evan Sarantakes, *Dropping the Torch: Jimmy Carter, the Olympic Boycott, and the Cold War* (Cambridge: Cambridge University Press, 2010).

4. Wayne Wilson, "Los Angeles 1984," in *Historical Dictionary of the Modern Olympic Movement*, ed. John E. Findling and Kimberly D. Pelle (Westport, CT: Greenwood Press, 1996), 169–77; Mark Dyreson and Matthew P. Llewellyn, "Los Angeles Is the Olympic City: Legacies of 1932 and 1984," *The International Journal of the History of Sport* 25, no. 14 (December 2008): 1991–2018.

5. For a fuller discussion of the legacy of the 1984 Los Angeles Olympics, see Stephen Wenn, "Peter Ueberroth's Legacy: How the 1984 Los Angeles Olympics Changed the Trajectory of the Olympic Movement," *The International Journal for the History of Sport* 32, no. 1 (2015): 157–71; Wayne Wilson, "Sports Infrastructure, Legacy and the Paradox of the 1984 Olympic Games," *International Journal for the History of Sport* 32, no. 1 (2015): 144–56.

6. Robert K. Barney, Stephen R. Wenn, and Scott G. Martin, *Selling the Five Rings: The IOC and the Rise of Olympic Commercialism* (Salt Lake City: University of Utah Press, 2004), 153–80.

7. Mark Dyreson, "Global Television and the Transformation of the Olympics: The 1984 Los Angeles Games," *The International Journal for the History of Sport* 32, no. 1 (2015): 172–84; Susan Brownell, "Why 1984 Medalist Li Ning Lit the Flame at the Beijing 2008 Olympics: The Contribution of the Los Angeles Olympics to China's Market Reform," *International Journal for the History of Sport* 32, no. 1 (2015): 128–43.

8. Executive Summary: Community Economic Impact of the 1984 Olympic Games in Los Angeles and Southern California. Los Angeles Olympic Organizing Committee, October 1984. Paul Ziffren Sports Library, LA84 Foundation, Los Angeles, CA. www.la84foundation.org (Hereafter cited as LA84 Archives).

9. For some notably critical examples, see Alan Tomlinson and Garry Whannel, *Five Ring Circus: Money, Power, and Politics at the Olympic Games* (London: Pluto Press, 1984).

10. Christopher A. Shaw, *Five Ring Circus: Myths and Realities of the Olympic Games* (Gabriola Island, BC: New Society Publishers, 2008); Andrew Jennings, The New Lord of

the Rings: Olympic Corruption and How to Buy Olympic Medals (New York: Pocket Books, 1996).

11. Steven A. Riess, "Power without Authority: Los Angeles' Elites and the Construction of the Coliseum," *Journal of Sport History* 8, no. 1 (Spring 1981): 50–65.

12. Dyreson and Llewellyn, "Los Angeles Is the Olympic City."

13. Scholars have pointed out the discrepancies between image and reality created by the 1932 Olympic Games concerning race relations. See David Welky, "'Viking Girls, Mermaids, and Little Brown Men': U.S. Journalists and the 1932 Olympics," *Journal of Sport History* 24 (Spring 1997): 24–49.

14. Barbara Keys, "Spreading Peace, Democracy, and Coca-Cola: Sport and American Cultural Expansion in the 1930s," *Diplomatic History* 28, no. 2 (April 2004): quote on 168; Sean Dinces, "Padres on Mount Olympus: Los Angeles and the Production of the 1932 Olympic Mega-Event," *Journal of Sport History* 32 (Summer 2005): 137–66.

15. Keys, "Spreading Peace, Democracy, and Coca-Cola," 165–96.

16. Jeremy White, "The Los Angeles Way of Doing Things: The Olympic Village and the Practice of Boosterism," *Olympika: The International Journal of Olympic Studies* 11 (2000): 79–116.

17. "In the Matter of the Funds Realized from the Olympic Games Held in California in 1932," LA84 Archives.

18. Richard Mandell, *The Nazi Olympics* (Urbana: University of Illinois Press, 1987); David Clay Large, *Nazi Olympics* (New York: W. W. Norton, 2007); Duff Hart-Davis, *Hitler's Games: The 1936 Olympics* (New York: Harper & Row, 1986); and Arnd Krüger, *Die Olympischen Spiele 1936 und die Weltmeinung* (Berlin: Bartels & Wernitz, 1972).

19. "Palm Latitudes," *Los Angeles Times*, September 29, 1991, 8; "Fond Memories of L.A.'s Palm Trees," *Los Angeles Times*, July 29, 1984, T84; "An Urban Forest by 1984," *Los Angeles Times*, July 25, 1982, M12.

20. Southern California Committee for the Olympic Games, Presentation to the 62nd Session of the International Olympic Committee, Tokyo, Japan, October 4–10, 1964, LA84 Archives.

21. Bill Wise, "After Glow of the Olympiad," *Game and Gossip* 10 (September 1932), 13, 46–48.

22. Brad J. Congelio, "An Odyssey: The City of Los Angeles and the Olympic Movement, 1932–1984," *Southern California Quarterly* 97, no. 2 (2015): 178–212.

23. "The Southern California Committee for the Olympic Games Invites You to Become a Member of the Advisory Board." Pamphlet produced by SCCOG, 1950, LA84 Archives.

24. "About the Southern California Committee for the Olympic Games," accessed August 17, 2015, http://www.sccog.org/webapp/about-us; Southern California Committee for the Olympic Games, Presentation to the 62nd Session of the International Olympic Committee, Tokyo, Japan, October 4–10, 1964, LA84 Archives.

25. Dyreson and Llewellyn, "Los Angeles Is the Olympic City," 2000–2001.

26. Congelio, "An Odyssey," 178–212.

27. International Olympic Committee, 80th Annual Session, May, 1978, Athens, Greece, Olympic Studies Centre, Villa du Centenaire, Quai d'Ouchy 11006 Lausanne, Switzerland (Hereafter cited as IOC Archives).

28. "Bruce Keppel, "Ward Proposes County Vote on Olympic Funds," *Los Angeles Times*, November 16, 1977.

29. Kenneth Reich, "Ordinance to Bar L.A. Funding of Olympics Urged," *Los Angeles Times*, November 22, 1977.

30. Ronald L. Soble, "Olympic Debt: Could It Happen in L.A.?" *Los Angeles Times*, July 1, 1977; Ronald L. Soble, "Huge Deficit: Olympics Still Have Canada Seeing Red," July 1, 1977; Art Seidenbaum, 'Shall We Bear the Torch?" *Los Angeles Times*, August 26, 1977.

31. Kenneth Reich, "Ordinance to Bar L.A. Funding of Olympics Urged," *Los Angeles Times*, November 22, 1977.

32. Kenneth Reich and Bill Boyarskey, "IOC Approves L.A. Bid for '84 Olympics," *Los Angeles Times*, October 10, 1978.

33. As cited in Congelio, "An Odyssey: The City of Los Angeles," 205.

34. Ray Kennedy, "Miser with the Midas Touch," *Sports Illustrated*, November 22, 1982, http://sportsillustrated.cnn.com/vault/article/magazine/MAG1126135/index.htm.

35. Wenn, "Peter Ueberroth's Legacy," 157–71.

36. As cited in Wenn, "Peter Ueberroth's Legacy," 159.

37. For a ghost-written biographical account of the inner workings of the LAOOC, see Peter Ueberroth, *Made in America: His Own Story* (New York: Horizon Book, 1985).

38. Wilson, "Sports Infrastructure, Legacy and the Paradox," 146–47.

39. "LA 84: Games of the XXIII Olympiad," *Design Quarterly* 127 (n.d.), LA84 Archives.

40. Wilson, "Sports Infrastructure, Legacy and the Paradox," 147.

41. For a detailed examination of the LAOOC's commercialization of the 1984 Los Angeles Olympics, see Barney, Wenn, and Martin, *Selling the Five Rings*, 193–202.

42. Wenn, "Peter Ueberroth's Legacy," 160.

43. Moscow Olympic Organizing Committee, "Official Report of the Games of the XXII Olympiad," IOC Archives.

44. Wenn, "Peter Ueberroth's Legacy," 161.

45. International Olympic Committee, 83rd Annual Session, Moscow, July 15–August 3, 1980, IOC Archives.

46. Barney, Wenn, and Martin, *Selling the Five Rings*, 193–202.

47. Ueberroth's idea to have a sponsor pay for the rights to the Olympic Torch relay as well as McDonald's push to be the official Olympic hamburger led many to decry the 1984 Games as the "Hamburger Olympics." See Alan Tomlinson and Christopher Young, *National Identity and Global Sports Events: Culture, Politics, and Spectacle in the Olympics and the Football World Cup* (New York: SUNY Press, 2006), 163.

48. Philip Doughtery, "Chiat/Day Receives Business from Nike," *New York Times*, April 28, 1983.

49. Jube Shiver and Nancy Yoshihara, "Olympic Sponsors See Games as a Mixed Blessing," *Los Angeles Times*, July 28, 1985.

50. Wilson, "Sports Infrastructure, Legacy and the Paradox," 146.

51. "Executive Summary: Community Economic Impact of the 1984 Olympic Games in Los Angeles and Southern California," Los Angeles Olympic Organizing Committee, October 1984, LA84 Archives.

52. Kenneth Reich, "Doleful Days for the Olympic Games," *Sports Illustrated*, May 21, 1984.

53. See, for instance, Christopher Hill, *Olympic Politics: Athens to Atlanta*, 2nd ed. (Manchester: Manchester University Press, 1996), 148; and Allen Guttmann, *The Olympics: A History of the Modern Games* (Champaign: University of Illinois Press, 2002), 159.

54. Sarantakes, *Dropping the Torch*, 247.

55. "After a Month of Hints, Participation Becomes 'Impossible,'" *New York Times*, May 9, 1984.

56. Brad J. Congelio, "Reagan's Rapprochement: A Brief Analysis of the Reagan Administration and the 1984 Olympics," *Journal of Olympic History* 21, no. 3 (2013): 46–50.

57. Evelyn Mertin, "The Soviet Union and the Olympic Games of 1980 and 1984: Explaining the Boycotts to Their Own People," in *East Plays West: Sport and the Cold War*, ed. Stephen Wagg and David L. Andrews (New York: Routledge, 2007), 244–48.

58. See Robert Edelman, "The Russians Are Not Coming! The Soviet Withdrawal from the Games of the XXIII Olympiad," *The International Journal of the History of Sport* 32, no. 1 (January 2015): 9–36. The same argument was also put forward by Alfred Senn in 1985, but Senn did not have access to Soviet archives. See Alfred Senn, "The Soviet Boycott of the 1984 Olympics: The Baltic Dimension," *Baltic Forum* 2, no. 1 (1985): 88–104.

59. Quotes in "Statement of the National Olympic Committee of the USSR," reproduced in Marat Gramov to Juan Antonio Samaranch, April 11, 1984, Radio Free Europe IV, 1977–1984, IOC Archives; Edelman, "The Russians Are Not Coming!"; Senn, "The Soviet Boycott of the 1984 Olympics."

60. Juan Antonio Samaranch to Marat Gramov, April 13, 1984, Radio Free Europe IV, 1977–1984, IOC Archives.

61. "Protests Are Issue: Russians Charge 'Gross Flouting' of the Ideals of the Competition," *New York Times*, May 9, 1984, A1.

62. "Safety Fears Cited in Soviet Games Pullout," *Los Angeles Times*, May 9, 1984, 1.

63. Edelman, "The Russians Are Not Coming!"

64. Nicholas J. Cull, *The Cold War and the United States Information Agency: American Propaganda and Public Diplomacy, 1945–1989* (Cambridge: Cambridge University Press, 2008), 438–39.

65. Harold E. Wilson, "The Golden Opportunity: Romania's Political Manipulation of the 1984 Los Angeles Olympic Games," *Olympika* 3 (1994): 83–97; Nikoletta Onyestyák, "Boycott, Exclusion or Non-participation? Hungary in the Years of the 1920 and 1984 Olympic Games," *International Journal of the History of Sport* 27, no. 11 (2010): 1920–41.

66. As cited in Alfred Senn, *Power, Politics, and the Olympic Games: A History of the Powerbrokers, Events, and Controversies That Shaped the Games* (Champaign, IL: Human Kinetics, 1999), 199.

67. Wilson, "Los Angeles 1984," 169–77; Wayne Wilson, "The Legacy of Raised Expectations: The Impact of Los Angeles 1984 Games," in *The Legacy of the Olympic Games*, ed. Miquel de Moragas, Christopher Kennett, and Noria Puig (Lausanne: International Olympic Committee, November 2002).

68. For a brief overview of the 1984 Los Angeles Games, see Guttmann, *The Olympics*, 157–63.

69. Kenny Moore, "Triumph and Tragedy in Los Angeles," *Sports Illustrated*, August 20, 1984.

70. For more on Budd and the IOC's expulsion of apartheid South Africa, see Matthew P. Llewellyn, "Circumventing Apartheid: Racial Politics and the Issue of South Africa's Olympic Participation at the 1984 Los Angeles Olympic Games," *The International Journal of the History of Sport* 32, no. 1 (January 2015): 53–71.

71. Wilson, "Los Angeles 1984," 169–77.

72. Jaime Schultz, "Going the Distance: The Road to the 1984 Olympic Women's Marathon," *The International Journal of the History of Sport* 32, no. 1 (January 2015): 72–88.

73. International Olympic Committee, Executive Board Meeting, Lausanne, March 9–10, 1979, IOC Archives; International Olympic Committee, Executive Board Meeting, Montevideo, April 3–4 & 6, 1979, IOC Archives.

74. International Olympic Committee, Executive Board Meeting, November 24–25, 1983, IOC Archives.

75. "Confusion Reigns over Issue of Professionalism in Olympic Soccer," *Los Angeles Times*, January 25, 1984, B10; "Norway's Amateur Soccer Players Stand out in an Olympic Field," *Los Angeles Times*, July 31, 1984, H21.

76. International Olympic Committee, Annual Session, Istanbul, August 5–9, 1987, IOC Archives.

77. http://www.olympic.org/Documents/Olympic%20Charter/Olympic_Charter_through_time/1991-Olympic_Charter_June91.pdf (Accessed March 18, 2015).

78. International Olympic Committee, Executive Board Meeting, Lausanne, Switzerland, May 31, 1983, IOC Archives.

79. International Olympic Committee, Executive Board Meeting, Lausanne, Switzerland, May 25–26, 1982, IOC Archives.

80. International Olympic Committee, Executive Board Meeting, Helsinki, Finland, August 5, 1983, IOC Archives.

81. "BALCO Fast Facts," *CNN News Magazine*, May 9, 2015 (http://www.cnn.com/2013/10/31/us/balco-fast-facts/).

82. John Gleaves, "Manufactured Dope: How the 1984 US Olympic Cycling Team Rewrote the Rules on Drugs in Sports," *International Journal for the History of Sport* 32, no. 1 (2015): 89–107.

83. Wenn, "Peter Ueberroth's Legacy," 161–62.

84. Stephen Wenn, Robert K. Barney, and Scott G. Martyn, Tarnished Rings: The International Olympic Committee and the Salt Lake City Bid Scandal (Syracuse, NY: Syracuse University Press, 2011); Helen Lenskyj, Gender Politics and the Olympic Industry (Basingstoke: Palgrave MacMillan, 2013); Gyozo Molnar and Alan Bairner, The Politics of the Olympics: A Survey (London: Routledge, 2010); Dave Zirin, Brazil's Dance with the Devil: The World Cup, the Olympics, and the Fight for Democracy (Chicago, IL: Haymarket Books, 2014).

85. Wilson, "Sports Infrastructure, Legacy and the Paradox," 148–49.

86. Mark Dyreson, "The Republic of Consumption at the Olympic Games: Globalization, Americanization, and Californization," *Journal of Global History* 8, no. 2 (July 2013): 256–78.

12. Shaping the Boom

1. Matt Warshaw, *The History of Surfing* (San Francisco: Chronicle Books, 2010), 100.

2. Michael Scott Moore, *Sweetness and Blood: How Surfing Spread from Hawaii and California to the Rest of the World, with Some Unexpected Results* (New York: Rodale Books, 2011), 4.

3. In addition to Warshaw and Moore, this chapter draws heavily on Drew Kampion, *Stoked: A History of Surf Culture* (Layton, UT: Gibbs Smith, 1997); Leonard Lueras, *Surfing: The Ultimate Pleasure* (New York: Workman Publishing, 1984); Ben Marcus, *Surfing USA!: An Illustrated History of the Coolest Sport of All Time* (New York: Voyageur Press, 2005); Peter Westwick and Peter Neushul, *The World in the Curl: An Unconventional History of Surfing* (New York: Crown, 2013).

4. As an introduction, it is inevitably brief and incomplete, but readers new to the history of the sport will encounter some of the major figures, places, and developments in surfing, as well as the relevant sources for digging deeper into its rich history.

5. Marcus, *Surfing USA!* 59.

6. Thomas Lisanti, *Hollywood Surf and Beach Movies: The First Wave, 1959–1969* (Jefferson, NC: McFarland, 2005), 7. For more on Hollywood surf cinema, see Kirse Granat May, *Golden State, Golden Youth: The California Image in Popular Culture, 1955–1966* (Chapel Hill: University of North Carolina Press, 2002). Also Lueras, *Surfing*, 124; Marcus, *Surfing USA!* 100–06; Warshaw, *The History of Surfing*, 188–92.

7. Fittingly, the Beach Boys were originally known as The Pendletones.

8. Owing to safety concerns and poor technology, it was a short-lived fad, fading away by 1966. A decade later, Los Angeles surfers took advantage of new technology to revive and revolutionize skateboarding; a global industry followed.

9. *Fortune* estimates that the value of the global surf industry will reach $13 billion USD by 2017. Paul Kvinta, "Surfonomics 101" (2013): accessed September 10, 2015, http://fortune.com/2013/06/05/surfonomics-101/.

10. See Douglas Booth, "Ambiguities in Pleasure and Discipline: The Development of Competitive Surfing," *Journal of Sport History* 22, no. 3 (1995).

11. There is no book-length biography of Freeth, but an article by Arthur C. Verge provides a very thorough look at his life. Arthur C. Verge, "George Freeth: King of the Surfers and California's Forgotten Hero," *California History* 80, no. 2–3 (2001). In addition to Verge, this biographical sketch draws from Kampion, *Stoked*, 38–40; Lueras, *Surfing*, 68–73; Marcus, *Surfing USA!* 36–38; Moore, *Sweetness and Blood*, 12–15, 29–31; Warshaw, *The History of Surfing*, 47–55; Westwick and Neushul, *The World in the Curl*, 32–34, 44–50.

12. "Riding the South Sea Surf," London's account of his day in the water with Ford and Freeth was published in the October 1907 issue of *Woman's Home Companion*, before appearing as a chapter in his 1911 travelogue, *The Cruise of the Snark*. Ford followed suit, publishing "Riding the Surf in Hawaii" in the August 14, 1909, edition of *Collier's*, one of the most widely read magazines of the time.

13. Joel T. Smith, "Reinventing the Sport, Part Three: George Freeth," *Surfer's Journal* 12, no. 3 (2003): 92. For more on the impact of Ford and London on surfing, see Scott Laderman, *Empire in Waves: A Political History of Surfing* (Berkeley: University of California Press, 2014), 3, 17–33, 167.

14. For more on Lummis, LA boosterism, and the idealized Southern California leisure culture, see Lawrence Culver, *The Frontier of Leisure: Southern California and the Shaping of Modern America* (New York: Oxford University Press, 2012).

15. For a comprehensive look at Blake, see Gary Lynch and Malcolm Gault-Williams, *Tom Blake: The Uncommon Journey of a Pioneer Waterman* (Newport Beach, CA: Croul Publications, 2013). This biographical sketch also draws from Kampion, *Stoked*, 41–45, 48–56; Lueras, *Surfing*, 80–82, 107–109; Marcus, *Surfing USA!* 28, 46–52; Moore, *Sweetness and Blood*, 18; Warshaw, *The History of Surfing*, 61–65, 72–75; Westwick and Neushul, *The World in the Curl*, 54, 69–74.

16. Warshaw, *The History of Surfing*, 61.

17. They rode these boards in part because they were the best available, but also because they were the first to be mass produced. Blake was granted the first surfing patent for his hollow board (referred to in the patent as a "water sled") in 1932; licensees of his design included airplane and furniture manufacturers, whose distribution of prefabricated boards fostered the early diffusion of the sport beyond the beaches of Hawaii and Southern California

18. Warshaw, *The History of Surfing*, 62.
19. Warshaw, *The History of Surfing*, 94.
20. This biographical sketch of Ball draws from Kampion, *Stoked*, 25,45; Lueras, *Surfing*, 165; Marcus, *Surfing USA!* 38, 161; Warshaw, *The History of Surfing*, 75, 88, 94; Westwick and Neushul, *The World in the Curl*, 269.
21. Steve Pezman, "Turning Points," *The Surfer's Journal* 20, no. 6 (2011), 69; Warshaw, *The History of Surfing*, 75.
22. Freeth led a short-lived club in Redondo Beach early on, and surfers in the Orange County enclave of Corona del Mar had a similarly brief association in the 1920s. See Lueras, *Surfing*, 107.
23. For more on the Palos Verdes Surf Club, see Warshaw, *The History of Surfing*, 74–77.
24. Still revered in in the surfing world, Grannis's work has been recognized by the greater art world as well. Prints of his iconic images fetch thousands of dollars in fine art galleries, and art book publisher Taschen has issued a weighty monograph of his photography.
25. John Irwin, "Surfing: The Natural History of an Urban Scene," *Journal of Contemporary Ethnography* 2, no. 2 (1973), 144; Warshaw, *The History of Surfing*, 198. Both authors note the difficulty in accuracy; the estimates come from board manufacturing and sales.

In 1940, the population of Los Angeles County numbered 2.8 million; by 1950, it was approaching 4.2 million. "Historical Resident Population City and County of Los Angeles, 1850–2010," accessed September 15, 2015, http://www.laalmanac.com/population/p002.htm.
26. Westwick and Neushul, *The World in the Curl*, 82.
27. Westwick and Neushul, *The World in the Curl*, 97–102.
28. Matt Warshaw, *The Encyclopedia of Surfing*, "Bob Simmons" (Boston: Houghton Mifflin Harcourt, 2009).
29. For more on the development of the chip, see: Kampion, *Stoked*, 56, 62–64; Warshaw, *The History of Surfing*, 107–8, 167.
30. Warshaw, *The History of Surfing*, 111–12.
31. Warshaw, *The History of Surfing*, 114. For more on Velzy, see Kampion, *Stoked*, 56, 65; Lueras, *Surfing*, 114,118.
32. Warshaw, *The History of Surfing*, 107.
33. Westwick and Neushul, *The World in the Curl*, 104.
34. Perfected and popularized by Orange County shaper Hobie Alter, foam-cored boards were not an LA innovation per se, but Alter's designs were derived from Velzy's pig. Although Alter mastered the material, Santa Monica surfer and shaper Dave Sweet was also experimenting with foam at this time. Warshaw, *The History of Surfing*, 167–68.
35. Westwick and Neushul, *The World in the Curl*, 108.
36. Warshaw, *The History of Surfing*, 174.
37. Warshaw, *The History of Surfing*, 175.
38. Warshaw, *The History of Surfing*, 138.
39. Severson and Brown would become the preeminent figures in surf media during the boom; Severson launched *Surfer* magazine in 1960, and Brown's *Endless Summer* (1964) was a crossover hit and remains the most successful surf film of all time.
40. For more on Browne and the early surf movies, see Kampion, *Stoked*, 59–60, 96; Lueras, *Surfing*, 50; Marcus, *Surfing USA!* 104, 116.
41. Warshaw, *The Encyclopedia of Surfing*, "Malibu."
42. For more on Weber, see Kampion, *Stoked*, 26, 72, 191; Lueras, *Surfing*, 114; Marcus, *Surfing USA!* 66, 141; Warshaw, *The History of Surfing*, 111–15, 162; Westwick and Neushul, *The World in the Curl*, 108–10, 141. For more on Dora, see David Rensin, *All for a Few Perfect*

Waves: The Audacious Life and Legend of Rebel Surfer Miki Dora (New York: It Books, 2009). Also Kampion, *Stoked*, 25–26, 74–78; Lueras, *Surfing*, 124–29; Marcus, *Surfing USA!* 63–66, 72–73; Warshaw, *The History of Surfing*, 111–22; Westwick and Neushul, *The World in the Curl*, 111, 123–26. For more on Tracy, see Kampion, *Stoked*, 26, 75; Lueras, *Surfing*, 124; Marcus, *Surfing USA!* 64–66; Warshaw, *The History of Surfing*, 111–18.

43. Culver, *The Frontier of Leisure*, 8.
44. Warshaw, *The History of Surfing*, 97.
45. Westwick and Neushul, *The World in the Curl*, 104.
46. May, *Golden State, Golden Youth*, 6.
47. Culver, *The Frontier of Leisure*, 4.
48. John W. Schouten and James H. McAlexander, "Subcultures of Consumption: An Ethnography of the New Bikers," *Journal of Consumer Research* 22, no. 1 (1995): 43.

13. The Halcyon Days of Muscle Beach

The author would like to acknowledge the financial support provided by the LA Sports Foundation for her earlier research on Muscle Beach.

1. Mark Sarvas, "Muscle Beach Getting Back in Shape," *Santa Monica News*, July 1, 1988, 1.
2. Photo by Frank J. Thomas, attributed to 1954. Jim Heimann and Kevin Starr, eds., *Los Angeles: Portrait of a City* (Cologne, Germany: Taschen, 2009), cover.
3. Allen Trachtenberg, *Brooklyn Bridge: Fact and Symbol* (Chicago: University of Chicago Press, 1965), ix.
4. David Webster, "Muscle Beach Comes to Aberdeen," *Health and Strength*, September 30, 1954, 9.
5. Academic scholarship on Muscle Beach is currently limited to a single dissertation: Tolga Ozyurtcu, "Flex Marks the Spot: Histories of Muscle Beach" (PhD diss., University of Texas at Austin, 2014), and several articles: Jan Todd and Michael O'Brien, "Breaking the Physique Barrier: Steve Reeves and the Promotion of Hercules," *Iron Game History: The Journal of Physical Culture* 12, no. 4 (August 2014): 8–29; Jan Todd and Terry Todd, "Steve Reeves: The Last Interview," *Iron Game History: The Journal of Physical Culture* 6, no. 4 (December 2000): 1–14; and Jan Todd, "The Legacy of Pudgy Stockton," *Iron Game History: The Journal of Physical Culture*, 2, no. 1 (January 1992): 5–7.
6. Fred E. Basten, *Santa Monica Bay: The First 100 Years* (Los Angeles: Douglas West Publishing, 1974), 68–73, 76–81; Elizabeth Van Steenwyck, *Let's Go to the Beach: A History of Sun and Fun by the Sea* (New York: Henry Holt and Company, 2001), 78–79, 89–92.
7. James Harris, *Santa Monica Pier: A Century on the Last Great Pleasure Pier* (Santa Monica: Santa Monica Pier Restoration Committee, 2009), 65–66.
8. Harris, *Santa Monica Pier*, 33–38.
9. "Speaking of Pictures . . . Muscle Flexers Show Off Weekly at California Beach," *Life* (August 1946) 14–16.
10. Gordon L'Allemand, "Muscle Beach," *Muscle Power* 7, no 5 (April 1949): 30.
11. Joel Sayre, "The Body Worshipers of Muscle Beach," *Saturday Evening Post* (May 25, 1957), 34–35. Sayre's version was retold in a *Smithsonian* retrospective on Muscle Beach in 1998. See Ken Chowder, "Muscle Beach," *Smithsonian* 29 (November 1, 1998): 124–37.
12. Interview with Relna McRae, February 20, 2016.
13. Paul Brewer, "Muscle Beach Memories: Paul Brewer and Relna (Brewer) McRae," *Santa Monica Muscle Beach Newsletter* 4 (Spring 1990): 1–2.

14. The two districts are now combined in the Los Angeles Unified School District. Gary Klein, "The Best, Bar None," *Los Angeles Times*, December 30, 1999.

15. Brewer, "Muscle Beach Memories," 1; see also Harold Zinkin and Bonnie Hearn, *Remembering Muscle Beach: Where Hard Bodies Began, Photographs and Memories* (Santa Monica, CA: Angel City Press, 1999), 18.

16. McRae, February 20, 2016.

17. At the 1932 Olympics, American athletes won all nine medals in these new events. Frank Roche, "Los Angeles Is Athlete's Mecca: Cream of Nation Head Here for Pre-Olympic Meets," *Los Angeles Times*, February 8, 1931, F5; and "Gymnastics," *Games of the 10th Olympiad Los Angeles; 1932: Official Report* (10th Olympiad Committee, 1933): 653–54.

18. "Gymnastics," *Games of the 10th Olympiad*, 653–54; Roy E. Moore, "Report of the Manager of the American Olympic Gymnastics Team," *Report of the American Olympic Committee* (New York: American Olympic Committee, 1932), 164.

19. Roche, "Los Angeles is Athlete's Mecca," F5; Larry Black, "Heroes without Press Agents," *Los Angeles Times*, December 24, 1939, F6.

20. "Texas Youngsters Arrive for National Gym Meet at Olympic Next Friday," *Los Angeles Times*, June 3, 1930, A17; Jim Thurman, "10"; Joseph Fike, "Athletes Aren't Always Show-Offs!" *Los Angeles Times Sunday Magazine*, August 7, 1938, 9–10.

21. "National Gymnastic Tourney on Tonight: Olympic Stars Show Wares," *Los Angeles Times*, June 6, 1930, A13.

22. Nancy Flake, "Conroe Man's Life One for the Record Books," *Courier of Montgomery County* (Texas), November 16, 2009, 14.

23. McRae interview, February 20, 2016. The Wolfe newsreel does not appear in any film index searched by the author. To view go to http://www.topendsports.com/videos/76/sports/unusual/olympic-tumbler-rowland-wolfe/.

24. Heimann and Starr, eds., *Los Angeles: Portrait of a City*, 183.

25. "Schools at Beach to Be Remodeled: Santa Monica Closes Two Buildings and Will Make Structures Quakeproof," *Los Angeles Times*, May 10, 1933, 10.

26. Zinkin, *Remembering Muscle Beach*, 18; McRae interview, February 20, 2016.

27. McRae interview, February 20, 2016.

28. Rose, *Muscle Beach*, 23–25; McRae interview, October 24, 1997; Zinkin, *Remembering Muscle Beach*, 21–22.

29. Sayre, "The Body Worshippers," *Saturday Evening Post*, 140.

30. Relna Brewer McRae to "Smithsonian Letters Editor," February 1, 1999, copy in author's collection.

31. McRae interview, October 24, 1997; McRae interview, February 20, 2016; and Zinkin, *Remembering Muscle Beach*, 23.

32. Catherine Horwood, "Girls Who Arouse Dangerous Passions," *Women's History Review* 9, no 4 (2000): 653–73; Angela Latham, "Packaging Woman: The Concurrent Rise of Beauty Pageants, Public Bathing, and Other Performances of Female 'Nudity,'" *Journal of Popular Culture* 19 (Winter 1995): 149–67.

33. Interview with Abbye (Pudgy) Stockton, May 10, 2001.

34. McRae interview, February 20, 2016.

35. Zinkin, Remembering Muscle Beach, 27–28.

36. Zinkin, *Remembering Muscle Beach*, 43; "Notable Athletic Alumni of the 1930s," Roosevelt High School website, viewed at https://roosevelths-lausd-a.schoolloop.com/cms/page_view?d=x&piid=&vpid=1441094935558.

37. McRae interview, February 20, 2016.

38. The modern sport of acrobatic gymnastics, now part of the World Games, is reminiscent of the kinds of adagio that happened regularly at Muscle Beach. See "History of Acrobatic Gymnastics," at https://usagym.org/pages/index.html.

39. Johnnie Collins's real last name was Kulikoff. Zinkin, *Remembering Muscle Beach*, 5, 39. See also Rose, *Muscle Beach*, 22–23. Oral history interview by Christine Lazzaretto with Paula Unger Boelsems, July 7, 2010, City of Santa Monica Beach Stories Initiative, typescript in author's collection.

40. Zinkin, *Remembering Muscle Beach*, 20–21, 27; McRae interview, February 20, 2016.

41. McRae interview, February 20, 2016.

42. Oral history Interview . . . with Paula Unger Boelsems; see also Betsy Goldman, "Female Gymnast Once Flew through the Air," *Argonaut Online*, June 10, 2009.

43. McRae interview, February 20, 2016.

44. Paul Brewer, "Muscle Beach Memories," 1; Zinkin, *Remembering Muscle Beach*, 21.

45. Fike, "Athletes Aren't Always Show Offs!" 10.

46. Fike, "Athletes Aren't Always Show Offs!" 9.

47. Allison Rose Jefferson, "African American Leisure Space in Santa Monica: The Beach Sometimes Known as the 'Inkwell,'" *Southern California Quarterly* 91, no. 2 (Summer 2009): 155–89.

48. Davis lived in Northern California for a time and lifted in at least one of the Muscle Beach holiday exhibitions based on surviving photographs. The Abbye (Pudgy) and Les Stockton Papers, H. J. Lutcher Stark Center for Physical Culture & Sports, University of Texas at Austin.

49. Ken Johnson, an African American bodybuilder placed second in the 1951 Junior Mr. Muscle Beach contest, for example, while Leroy Williams was second in the men's contest in 1952. George Bruce, "Ken Cameron—Mr. Muscle Beach 1951," *Strength & Health* (December 1951), 10–11; Eugene Hanson, "Mr. Muscle Beach," *Muscle Power* (December 1952), 18–21.

50. "Gym Clubs to Travel North: L.A. High and 'Poly' Combined Teams to Leave This Week," *Los Angeles Times*, April 5, 1908, VIII-7.

51. Todd, "The Legacy of Pudgy Stockton," 6.

52. Pudgy Stockton, "Abbye (Pudgy) Stockton," unpublished typescript autobiography, author's collection, (1947), 2.

53. Abbye (Pudgy) Stockton interview, September 28, 1991.

54. A full-page wire service article on Relna titled "Strong Women Aren't Freaks," with four photos appeared in many American papers in 1939 and was then translated and printed in Brazil. See "Quando A Beleza Acompanha O Vigor," *Journal do Brazil*, July 9, 19392:1; and Helen Welshiemer, "Strong Women Aren't Freaks," *Salt Lake Tribune* (May 7, 1939), 8.

55. Zinkin, Remembering Muscle Beach, 26–27.

56. The WPA's investment in the new platform was viewed as part of an upgrade of the entire beach area. The following year they built the long, wide sidewalk that runs all the way to Venice and resurfaced the pier. Charles Epting, "Santa Monica's Top Five Landmarks from This Era," *Santa Monica Mirror*, November 4, 2014.

57. Tom Barnett, "Muscle Beach," *U.S. Camera* (August 1947), 28.

58. Myrna Oliver, "Russell Saunders; Muscle Beach Acrobat, Stunt Double in More Than 100 Movies," *Los Angeles Times* (June 6, 2001), B8,

59. Douglas Martin, "Russell M. Saunders, Stuntman in Movies Is Dead at 82," *New York Times*, June 17, 2001, 45.

60. Abbye Stockton, "Glorious Health-Vitality Building," *New Physical Culture* 91, no 6 (June 1947): 29.

61. Interview with Les Stockton, September 28, 1991.

62. Mary Rourke, "Harold Zinkin, 82, Muscle Beach Pioneer Invented Weight Machine," *Los Angeles Times*, September 24, 2004.

63. "Vic Tanny: America's Greatest Physical Educator," *Wisdom* 37 (May 1961): 3–6.

64. Rose, *Muscle Beach*, 127, and Transcript of Interview with Armand Tanny, June 1999, author's collection; see also Jan Todd and Terry Todd, "The Last Interview," *Iron Game History* 6, no. 4 (December 2000): 5.

65. Valerie J. Nelson, "Deforrest 'Moe' Most, 89; Gymnast Was Unofficial Ringmaster at Muscle Beach," *Los Angeles Times*, September 8, 2006.

66. Earle Liederman, "Mr. Muscle Beach," *Muscle Power* 3, no. 6 (November 1947), 10–11; McRae interview, February 20, 2016.

67. Eugene M. Hanson, "Outdoor Health Show: Miss Muscle Beach 1948," *Muscle Power* 7, no. 2 (January 1949): 12.

68. "Bevy of Brawny Beauties to vie for 'Miss Muscle Beach' Title," *Evening Outlook*, August 28, 1947, 1.

69. Les Stockton interview, September 28, 1991; Zinkin, *Remembering Muscle Beach*, 63–68; see also "This and That," Washington State Gymnastics History, viewed at www.wagymnasticshistory.com/history/ thisandthat.html; and Al Thomas, "George Redpath: A Life in the Balance," *Iron Game History* 3, no. 1 (September 1993): 15–17.

70. Hanson, "Outdoor Health Show," 39.

71. Photo of John Kornoff by Leo Aarons, *LOOK* 6, no. 23 (November 17, 1942): cover; Zinkin, *Remembering Muscle Beach*, 68–70.

72. Todd and Todd, "The Last Interview," 5.

73. Rose, *Muscle Beach*, 119–23.

74. Jim Seip, "For 1948 Olympics, Gold Medal Dream Started in York," *York Daily Record*, August 4, 2012.

75. "Musclemen Held on Sex Charges," *Evening Outlook*, December 10, 1958.

76. See, "The Short Goodbye: Scandal, Politics, and the End of Muscle Beach," in Ozyurtcu, "Flex Marks the Spot: Histories of Muscle Beach," 41–75; see also "Musclemen Held on Sex Charges," *Evening Outlook*, December 10, 1958.

77. "Muscle Beach Revival Banned," *Los Angeles Times*, March 29, 1959, WS1, Muscle Beach was referred to as "Santa Monica Beach Playground Number Four" in official correspondence after 1958.

78. "Muscle Beach to Receive Landmark after 30 Years," *Los Angeles Times*, September 2, 1989, 5–16.

79. See, for example, a Muscle Beach video tour Schwarzenegger filmed in 2014 at http://www.dailymotion.com/video/x1fjf6t_arnold-schwarzenegger-venice-muscle-beach-tour-guide-bodybuilding-fitness-celebrity_sport.

14. I Was Standing There All the While

1. "Jim Murray to Write Feature Sports Column in Times," *Los Angeles Times*, February 5, 1961.

2. Jim Murray, "Fats the Pool Hustler," *Los Angeles Times*, December 13, 1966, D1.

3. Jim Murray, *The Sporting World of Jim Murray* (Garden City, NY: Doubleday, 1968), 32–33.
4. Jim Murray, *Jim Murray: An Autobiography* (New York: MacMillan Publishing Company, 1993), 3–4.
5. Jim Murray, unpublished, undated manuscript, private collection.
6. Jim Murray, unpublished, undated manuscript, private collection.
7. "Army vs. Yale," *New Haven Register*, October 24, 1943.
8. Murray, *Jim Murray*, 1–2.
9. Melvin Durslag, interview by author, January 30, 2009.
10. Rick Reilly, "King of the Sports Page," *Sports Illustrated*, April 21, 1986, 82.
11. James Murray, "I Hate the Yankees," *Life*, April 17, 1950, 26–36. The line was later attributed to other writers, most notably Red Smith, a point which Murray had fun with in his own column over the years.
12. "Walter in Wonderland, *Time*, April 28, 1958.
13. James Murray, "Coining Gold in the Cellar," *Sports Illustrated*, June 30, 1958.
14. Peter O'Malley, interview with author, July 30, 2015.
15. Jim Murray, "Remember Those Early Laker Days?" *Los Angeles Times*, June 28, 1985.
16. Murray, "Remember Those Early Laker Days?"
17. James Murray, "A Trip for Ten Tall Men," *Sports Illustrated*, January 30, 1961.
18. Murray, "A Trip for Ten Tall Men."
19. Jim Murray, *The Best of Jim Murray* (Garden City, NY: Doubleday & Company, 1965), xiii.
20. Jim Murray, *Jim Murray*, 133.
21. Jim Murray, "Let's Dot Some 'I's,'" *Los Angeles Times*, February 12, 1961, N1.
22. Peter O'Malley, interview with author, July 30, 2015.
23. Jim Murray, "'That She Blows!" *Los Angeles Times*, January 31, 1962, C1.
24. Jim Murray, "There Are Hardships," *Los Angeles Times*, August 27, 1961, G1.
25. Jim Murray, "Series Fun in Cincy," *Los Angeles Times*, October 9, 1961, C1.
26. Douglass Looney, "Public Snitch Lets Quips Fall Where They May," *National Observer*, August 19, 1972.
27. Jim Murray, "In Deep Freeze," *Los Angeles Times*, March 2, 1962, B1.
28. Bill Christine, interview with author, December 19, 2008.
29. Quotes from Murray, *The Best of Jim Murray*, 150–58.
30. Groucho Marx to Jim Murray, March 17, 1961.
31. Tom Callahan, "Murray Reflecting Truth in Our Age," *Washington Post*, April 15, 1990.
32. Jim Murray, "No Rose for Benny," *Los Angeles Times*, April 5, 1962.
33. Jim Murray, "Living Color," *Los Angeles Times*, November 29, 1961.
34. Dan Gurney, interview with author, September 21, 2010.
35. Jim Murray, "The 500: 'Gentlemen, Start Your Coffins!'" *Los Angeles Times*, May 29, 1966.
36. Jim Murray, "I Finally Won It," *Los Angeles Times*, April 8, 1965.
37. Martin Kane, "Booktalk: Jim Murray Moves Gracefully from Newspaper Column into Hardcover," *Sport Illustrated*, April 12, 1965.
38. Jim Murray, "If You're Expecting One-Liners, Wait a Column," *Los Angeles Times*, July 1, 1979.
39. Murray, *Jim Murray*, 206.
40. Morton was the quarterback of the Denver Broncos, one of the teams competing in Super Bowl XIV.

41. Pat Riley, interview with author, July 29, 2015.
42. Riley interview.
43. O'Malley interview.
44. Prior to his death in 1997, Ben Hogan left a list of people he requested as his honorary bearers at his funeral. Murray and Dan Jenkins were the only two writers on the list. Dan Jenkins, *His Ownself* (New York: Anchor Books, 2014), 121. Murray's remembrance of Hogan was one of only two columns in Murray's career that *Times* editors saw fit to run on the front page. The other concerned the tragedy at the 1972 Munich Olympics.
45. Jim Murray, "She Took the Magic and Happy Summer with Her," *Los Angeles Times*, April 3, 1984.
46. Jim Murray, acceptance speech for J. G. Taylor Spink Award, Baseball Hall of Fame, Cooperstown, New York, August 1, 1988.
47. Jim Murray, "Ride on a Tiger," *Los Angeles Times*, March 12, 1961.
48. Jim Murray, "You Can Teach an Old Horse New Tricks," *Los Angeles Times*, August 16, 1998.
49. Jack Whitaker, "Jim Murray: 1919–1998; Jack Whitaker's Tribute: 'My, What a Grand Man You Were,'" *Los Angeles Times*, August 22, 1998.
50. Jim Murray, "Downing's Epitaph," *Los Angeles Times*, April 10, 1974.
51. Murray, *Jim Murray*, 262.

15. Vin Scully

1. See http://officialvinscully.com/biography.php.
2. Red Barber and Robert W. Creamer, *Rhubarb in the Catbird Seat* (Lincoln: University of Nebraska Press, 1997), 261.
3. Barber and Creamer, *Rhubarb in the Catbird Seat*, 261.
4. Curt Smith, *Pull Up a Chair: The Vin Scully Story* (Dulles, VA: Potomac Books, 2010), xiv.
5. Claire Smith, "Dodgers' Deaths Bring Out the Best," *New York Times*, July 7, 1993, B9.
6. June 6, 2010, about fifty-seven minutes into the broadcast.
7. David Brown, "Answer Man: Vin Scully talks candy, Dodgers and 'Bewitched,'" Yahoo! Sports, September 16, 2010, accessed April 6, 2011, http://sports.yahoo.com/mlb/blog/big_league_stew/post/Answer-Man-Vin-Scully-talks-candy-Dodgers-and-?urn=mlb-270225.
8. Quoted in Michael Connelly, "Conversation with My Hero Broadcaster Vin Scully," *Parade Magazine*, October 18, 2009.
9. Steve Lopez, "From Water Czar to Zorro: Your Votes for Most Admirable Angeleno," *Los Angeles Times*, January 15, 2010, accessed March 31, 2010, http://latimesblogs.latimes.com/lanow/2010/01/best-of-los-angeles.html.
10. Dave Sheinin, "A Legendary Career That Speaks for Itself," July 5, 2005, accessed April 6, 2011, http://www.washingtonpost.com/wp-dyn/content/article/2005/07/04/AR2005070400935_2.html.
11. Quoted in Andre Agassi, *Open: An Autobiography* (New York: Vintage Books, 2010), 138.
12. Hector Tobar, "Some Guidelines on How to Be a True Angeleno," *Los Angeles Times*, May 27, 2011, accessed July 1, 2011, http://articles.latimes.com/2011/may/27/local/la-me-tobar-20110527.

13. See http://www.vinscullyismyhomeboy.com/.

14. See http://www.humanevents.com/article.php?id=42698.

15. Jaime Jarrin is discussed in Samuel O. Regalado's *Viva Baseball: Latin Major Leaguers and Their Special Hunger* (Urbana: University of Illinois Press, 1998), 176–82; Jarrin was interviewed on National Public Radio and spoke of Vin Scully mentoring him; see http://www.npr.org/templates/story/story.php?storyId=106415915.

16. Jane Leavy, *Sandy Koufax: A Lefty's Legacy* (New York: HarperCollins, 2002), 214–16; National Public Radio, "Recorded History: Vin Scully Calls a Koufax Milestone," April 23, 2007, accessed April 6, 2011, http://www.npr.org/templates/story/story.php?storyId=9752592.

17. See http://www.dailymotion.com/video/xd2fhk_1988-world-series-game-1-bottom-of_sport.

18. Sheinin, "A Legendary Career That Speaks for Itself."

19. Tyler Kepner, "A Few Words About Vin Scully, a Storyteller Who Has Seen It All," *New York Times*, April 16, 2016, http://www.nytimes.com/2016/04/13/sports/baseball/a-few-words-about-vin-scully-a-storyteller-who-has-seen-it-all.html?_r=0.

Contributors

Wayne Wilson is vice president, education services at the LA84 Foundation, where he is responsible for digital library development, research projects, conference planning, and the foundation's coaching education program. Wilson is the coeditor of the *Oxford Handbook of Sport History* and the University of California Press book series "Sport in World History."

David K. Wiggins is professor in the School of Recreation, Health, and Tourism at George Mason University. A graduate of San Diego State University and the University of Maryland, he is primarily interested in studying the interconnection among race, sport, and American culture. Among his many publications are *DC Sports: The Nation's Capital at Play*, *Separate Games: African American Sport behind the Walls of Segregation*, and *Glory Bound: Black Athletes in a White America*.

Luis Alvarez is associate professor of history, director of the Institute of Arts and Humanities, and director of the Chicana/o Latina/o Arts and Humanities Program at UC San Diego. He is the author of *The Power of the Zoot: Youth Culture and Resistance during World War II* and coeditor of *Another University Is Possible*. His current book project is *From Civil Rights to Global Justice: Pop Culture and the Politics of the Possible*, an investigation of pop culture and social movements in the Americas since World War II.

Greg Andranovich is professor and chairperson of the Department of Political Science at California State University, Los Angeles. He teaches courses in American government, urban politics, and public administration. His research interests and publications are in two areas—the politics of urban economic development and in the challenges of collaborative decision making. He and Matthew J. Burbank recently published a chapter, "As Olimpiadas e a democracia urbana" (The Olympics and urban democracy) in *Megaeventos, Comunicação e Cidade* (*Mega-events, Communication and the City*), edited by R. Ferreira Freitas, F. Lins, and H. M. Carmo dos Santos.

Susan Brownell is professor of anthropology at the University of Missouri–St. Louis. Her primary research is on Chinese sports, the topic of her two books, *Training the Body for China: Sports in the Moral Order of the People's Republic* and *Beijing's Games: What the Olympics Mean to China*. She edited *The 1904 Anthropology Days and Olympic Games: Sport, Race, and American Imperialism*. She took up figure skating after retiring from track and field, in which she competed internationally. She is a past president of the St. Louis Skating Club, and member of the organizing committee for the 2006 US Figure Skating Championships in St. Louis.

Scott N. Brooks is associate professor of sociology in the Sanford School of Social and Family Dynamics, and associate director of the Global Sports Institute for Social Impact at Arizona State University. He is primarily an ethnographer interested in equity, student engagement, leadership, and community-based learning. Brooks has published in academic journals, edited volumes, and textbooks, including *Black Men Can't Shoot*; been quoted and reviewed by the *Wall Street Journal*, *New York Times*, *Washington Post*, *Der Speigel*, and *SLAM* magazine; and invited to speak on the topic of sport internationally. Additionally, Dr. Brooks has consulted the NFL, MLB, college and high school coaches and athletes; and served as a senior fellow at the Wharton Sports Business Initiative and Yale Urban Ethnography Project.

Matthew J. Burbank is an associate professor in political science at the University of Utah. He teaches courses in American politics, voting and elections, and research methods. His research focuses on political parties, citizen participation in politics, and urban politics and policy. He is the coauthor of *Olympic Dreams: The Impact of Mega-events on Local Politics* and *Parties, Interest Groups, and Political Campaigns*.

Allison Lauterbach Dale is an associate at Morrison & Foerster LLP in San Francisco, where she is the lone Dodger fan among a sea of Giants fans. She received her JD from UC Berkeley, School of Law (Boalt Hall) and her PhD in US history from the University of Southern California, where she specialized in gender and legal history.

Sean Dinces is in the history department at Long Beach City College. He is currently finishing a book on the political economy of stadium development in Chicago since 1980.

Jennifer Doyle is a professor of English at the University of California–Riverside. She is the author of *Campus Sex/Campus Security*, *Hold It against Me: Difficulty and Emotion in Contemporary Art* and *Sex Objects: Art and the Dialectics of Desire*. She has been blogging about sports since 2007, and was briefly the co-organizer of a men's soccer league in Pico Union, Los Angeles. Her sports writing has been published in the *New York Times* and the *Guardian* and on *Deadspin*.

Mark Dyreson is a professor and the director of research and educational programs for the Penn State Center for the Study of Sport in Society. His primary research is on the interconnections between nationalism, cultural patterns, and sport in modern societies. He has published numerous essays and written or edited several books, including *Making the American Team: Sport, Culture, and the Olympic Experience*. He is the coeditor of the Sport in Global Society: Historical Perspectives books series for Routledge Press and a managing editor of the *International Journal of the History of Sport*.

Ted Geltner is a writer and journalism professor at Valdosta State University in Valdosta, Georgia. His most recent book, *Blood, Bone and Marrow: A Biography of Harry Crews*, University of Georgia Press, was chosen by *Publishers Weekly* as one of the best books of 2016. His first book, *Last King of the Sports Page: The Life and Career of Jim Murray*, was published by University of Missouri Press. Before coming to academia, he was a newspaper reporter and editor for seventeen years in California, Florida, and Pennsylvania.

John Gleaves is an associate professor at California State University–Fullerton and codirector for the Center for Sociocultural Sport and Olympic Research. He was the coeditor for *The 1984 Los Angeles Games: Assessing the 30-Year Legacy* and coauthor of *The Rise and Fall of Olympic Amateurism*.

Elliott J. Gorn teaches history at Loyola University–Chicago. He is the author of *The Manly Art: Bare-Knuckle Prize Fighting in America*, and coauthor (with Warren Goldstein) of *A Brief History of American Sports*.

Gregory Kaliss is a visiting assistant professor of history at Towson University. He is the author of *Men's College Athletics and the Politics of Racial Equality: Five Pioneer Stories of Black Manliness, White Citizenship, and American Democracy*, and was coeditor of *The Papers of Frederick Law Olmsted, Volume 9: The Last Great Projects, 1890–1895*. His research interests include sports and race in American history, cultural battles over popular entertainment, and the contested terrain of American public landscapes.

Jeremy R. Kinney is a curator in the Aeronautics Department of the Smithsonian National Air and Space Museum. His numerous publications, exhibitions, and presentations document the history of flight during the first half of the twentieth century. His research interests also include motorsports in the United States and Europe, primarily international air racing during the 1920s and 1930s and the cultural history of the sports car in post–World War II America.

Matthew P. Llewellyn is an associate professor of kinesiology and codirector of the Center for Socio-Cultural Sport and Olympic Research (CSSOR) at California State University–Fullerton. His primary research interests concentrate on the role of sport in the creation of modern societies, as well as the history of the modern Olympic Games. He has published numerous essays and written or edited several books, including *The Rise and Fall of Olympic Amateurism* and *Rule Britannia: Nationalism, Identity and the Modern Olympic Games*. He is the current associate editor of the *Journal of Sport History*.

Daniel A. Nathan is professor and chair of American Studies at Skidmore College, the author of the award-winning *Saying It's So: A Cultural History of the Black Sox Scandal*, and the editor of *Rooting for the Home Team: Sport, Community and Identity* and *Baltimore Sports: Stories from Charm City*. He is past president of the North American Society for Sport History and the recipient of several honors, including a National Endowment for the Humanities Fellowship and a Fulbright Fellowship.

Tolga Ozyurtcu is a clinical assistant professor of sport management and physical culture and sport studies at the University of Texas at Austin. His research examines the intersections of popular culture and sporting subcultures, with an emphasis on lifestyle sport in twentieth-century California. Integrating a historical approach with perspectives from media studies and cultural geography, his scholarly publications and presentations include work on surfing, skateboarding, and bodybuilding. He is currently working, with Jan Todd, on a book about the original Muscle Beach, in Santa Monica, California.

Toby C. Rider is an assistant professor in the Department of Kinesiology at California State University–Fullerton. His current research explores the US government's use of sport in psychological warfare operations during the early Cold War years. He has published multiple articles in peer-reviewed journals, contributed several chapters to scholarly books, and presented his research at numerous conferences. He is also the author of *Cold War Games: Propaganda, the Olympics, and U.S. Foreign Policy* published by the University of Illinois Press.

Raymond Schmidt is an independent historian living in Ventura, California, now retired from his career of over thirty years in computer systems development. He is interested in the history of all major American sports, with particular emphasis on college football, early pro basketball, and golf. Among his book publications are *Two-Eyed League: The Illinois-Iowa of 1890–1892*; *Football's Stars of Summer: A History of the College All-Star Football Game Series*; and *Shaping College Football: The Transformation of an American Sport, 1919–1930*. He has also written many articles for various historical journals and reference works.

Jan Todd, holder of the Roy J. McLean Fellowship in Sport History and Fellow in the National Academy of Kinesiology, is a professor in the Department of Kinesiology and Health Education at the University of Texas at Austin. Todd also directs the H. J. Lutcher Stark Center for Physical Culture and Sports, which contains the papers and personal scrapbooks of Pudgy and Les Stockton, who were friends of Todd's, along with many other books and documents related to the history of physical culture. She has written more than a hundred articles in popular and scholarly journals and two books: *Physical Culture and the Body Beautiful: Purposive Exercise in the Lives of American Women*, and, with Terry Todd, *Lift Your Way to Youthful Fitness*. She is also president of the North American Society for Sport History.

Index

A

Abdul-Jabbar, Kareem, 14, 186, 188–89, 192–98
Abramowitz, Rachel, 179
Academy Awards, 169, 175
Adamic, Louis, 145 Adidas, 64
Admiral Television, 120
African Americans: Robinson Brothers, 9–10, 149–65; in figure skating, 84–88; in football, 114–15, 117–18, 121–23, 125–26; in Hollywood films, 172–77; and Showtime Lakers, 183–200; 1984 Olympic Games, 213–14; at Muscle Beach, 247–48
Agricultural Park, 20
Aguirre, John, 46
Alamillo, Jose, 40
Albert, Frankie, 115
Albert, Marv, 287
Albright, Tenley, 78
Ali, Muhammad, 89, 268
All-American Football Conference (AAFC), 109, 115–19
Allen, Steve, 266
All Year Figure Skating Club, 78, 87
Alter, Hobie, 231
Alvarez, Luis, 9
Ameche, Don, 115
American Broadcasting Company (ABC), 122, 125, 208, 214
American Café, 73
American Football League (AFL), 110–11, 118
American League Championship Series, 282
American Legion, 111–12, 114
American Sportscasters Association Hall of Fame, 276
American Youth Soccer Organization (AYSO), 12, 55, 62, 67
Anaheim Stadium, 124, 127
Anderson-Schiess, Gabi, 215

Anderson, Thom, 169–70
Andranovich, Greg, 8
Andy Williams Show, 265
Angarano, Michael, 179
Anti-African Housing Association, 143
Arciero, Frank, 101
Artic Blades Figure Skating Club, 78–80
Argue, John, 206 Arnett, Jon, 121
Ascot Park, 20
Asian Americans, in figure skating, 88–89
Atwood, Donna, 77–8
Avila, Eric, 43
Avildsen, John G., 170

B

Babich, Lawrence J., 168
Babilonia, Tai, 82, 88
Babington, Bruce, 168
Bad News Bears (film), 168, 171–73, 181
Balchowsky, Ina, 101
Balchowsky, Max, 100–101
Balco, 216
Balderrama, Francisco, 145
Baldwin Hills, 175, 204
Ball Game (film), 168
Ball, John "Doc," 221, 226–28, 233
Balsiger, David, 211
Baltimore Colts, 119, 124
Ban the Soviets Coalition, 211–12
Barber, Red, 275–76
Barlow, Roger, 97, 100
Barnes, Chris, 172
Barrymore, John, 250
Bartlett, Ray, 157
baseball: Jackie Robinson, 9–10, 149–65; Vin Scully, 10–11, 275–89; Jim Murray, 10, 259–60, 262, 265, 267–72; sport venues, 20; Mexican Americans, 37–43; in film, 171–72

Baseball (documentary), 163
Baseball Hall of Fame, 276
Baseball's Reliquary's Shrine of the Eternals, 164
Baseball's Great Experiment: Jackie Robinson and His Legacy (book), 160
Baseball Writers Association of America, 272
basketball: 152, Showtime Lakers, 14, 183–200; in film, 173–75; in Olympic Games, 214; and Jim Murray, 260–61, 269–70
Basketball Hall of Fame, 187–89, 191, 193, 198–200, 214
Baylor, Elgin, 261, 270
Beach Boys, 220–21
Bean: The Ultimate Disaster Movie (film), 6
Beckham, David, 12, 56
Beckham, Victoria, 12
Behra, Jean, 103
Belcher, Tim, 282
Bell, Bert, 120
Bellevue Park, 57
Benny, Jack, 265
Benoit, Joan, 215
Berger, Isaac, 253
Bertelli, Angelo, 119
Beverly Hills, 171, 258–59
Beverly Hills Speedway, 95
Billboard (magazine), 73
Bird, Larry, 183, 187, 190, 199
Bisher, Furman, 272
Black Dahlia, 258
Blake, Tom, 221, 224–26, 233–34
Bloody Christmas, 40
bodybuilding, 13
Boelsems, Paula, 252
Bogaard, Bill, 164
Bogart, Humphrey, 258, 260
Bond, John R., 98, 104
Bonds, Barry, 216
Bonnier, Joakim, 103
Borysewicz, Eddie, 217
Boston Braves, 23
Boston Celtics, 183–84, 187, 189
Boston University, 275
Bowman, Christofer, 84
Boyle Heights, 40, 44, 46, 54
Bradley, Tom, 24, 206, 278

Brando, Marlon, 258
Brewer, Paul, 242–46, 249
Bristol Café, 72–73
Brito, Socrates, 289
Broadway Ice Skating Palace, 73, 79
Brooklyn Dodgers (baseball), 10, 149, 159, 255, 260, 275
Brooklyn Dodgers (football), 112, 119
Brookside Golf Course, 29–30
Brooks, Scott, 14
Brown, Bruce, 233
Browne, Bud, 233
Browne, Devin, 66
Brownell, Susan, 14
Brown, Hubie, 192
Brown, Jim, 14
Brundage, Avery, 205
Bryant, Kobe, 14, 200
Bryant, Paul "Bear," 266
Budd, Zola, 17, 213
Bull Durham (film), 172
Burgueno, Ruben, 47–48
Burbank, Matthew, 8
Burke, Ed, 217
Burns, Ken, 163
Buss, Dr. Jerry, 184–88, 191–93, 195–97, 200
Butler, David, 278
Butler, Niesha, 175
Button, Dick, 82
Buttonwillow Raceway Park, 107

C

California Eagle (newspaper), 143, 159
California Institute of Technology, 229
California Newspaper Publishers' Association, 136
California Skating Association (CSA), 74–75
California Sports Car Club (Cal Club), 93, 97–100, 102–107
California State Chamber of Commerce, 136
Callaghan, Richard, 84
California State University, Los Angeles, 183
California Surfriders (book), 227
Campbell, Elden, 197
Campbell, Hugh, 125
Campbell, Roger, 80
Can-Am Series, 106

Canseco, Jose, 282
Candlestick Park, 281
Cannon, Dyan, 186
Carey, Harry, 287
Carmelita Provision Company, 40–42
Carmen (play), 172
Carpenter, John, 6
Carrell Speedway, 98
Carrier, Dona Lee, 80
Carrillo, Robert, 47
Carroll, Frank, 82–84, 89–90
Carter, Jimmy, 210–11
Casagran, Jose, 47
Catlin, Don, 216
CBS Sports Radio, 275
Cento Miglio, 97–98
Chamberlain, Wilt, 197, 269
Chapel, Bill, 86
Chaplin, Charlie, 15
Charlie's Angels (television show), 179
Chastin, Brandi, 11
Chatmann, Glenndon, 174
Chatsworth, 171
Chavez Ravine, 7, 20, 24, 42–43, 53, 106, 285
Chiat/Day, 209
Chicago Bears, 93, 110, 112, 120
Chicago Cardinals, 112, 121, 287
Chicago Cubs, 281, 287
Chicago Tribune (newspaper), 115
Chicago White Sox, 25
Chicano Moratorium, 43
Chin, Marjorie, 90
Chin, Tiffany, 88
Chips' 99 (film), 6
Chivas USA, 53, 55
Chock Full O'Nuts, 160–61
Chowder, Ken, 244
Cincinnati Post and Times Star (newspaper), 263–64
Claire, Fred, 271
Cincinnati Reds, 283
Clark, Tulie, 228
Cleveland Browns, 119–21
Cleveland Rams, 112, 114, 116
Cohen, Sasha, 82
Cold War, 201
Cole, Natalie, 85

Collins, Johnnie, 242, 246
Columbia Broadcasting Company (CBS), 187, 208
Community Development Association (CDA), 26, 132, 134, 136–40
Community Service Organization (CSO), 42
CONCACAF Gold Cup, 29, 56
Coney Island, 241
Converse, 16
Coogan, Jackie, 237
Cooke, Jack Kent, 185–86, 189, 191
Cooper, Gary, 260
Cooper, Michael, 187, 198
Cooperstown, 272
Corcoran, Jerry, 114
Cosby, Bill, 190
Costas, Bob, 287
Crenshaw, 173, 175
Crenshaw High School, 174
Crisis (magazine), 150
Cronkite, Walter, 189
Crosby, Bing, 115, 258
Crowe, Cameron, 175
Cruise, Tom, 175
Crystal Pier, 246
Culver, Lawrence, 96, 235, 237

D

Daigh, Chuck, 100–101
Daily Bruin (student newspaper), 155
Dale, Allison Lauterbach: recollections of Vin Scully, 11, 284–86
Dale, Dick, 221
Dale Velzy's "Pig," 230–31
Dallas Cowboys, 124, 268
Dallas Texans, 122
Dan Gurney's All American Racers, 95
Daniels, Bill, 125–26
Davis, Al, 125, 127
Davis-Coliseum Anti-Trust Suit, 125
Davis, David, 53
Davis, John, 248
Davis, Mary, 100
Davis, Meryl, 79
Davis, Mike, 143, 145–46
Davis, Ted, 43–44

350 · Index

Davis, Tommy, 281
Decker (Slaney), Mary, 17, 213
de Coubertin, Pierre, 132, 203, 205
Dee, Sandra, 220
de Mérode, Prince Alexandre, 216
DeMornay, Rebecca, 179
DeGroot, Dud, 115
De La Hoya, Oscar, 52
Dempsey, Jack, 256
Department of Parks and Recreation, 64–65
DeStefano, Todd, 28
Detroit Lions, 114, 124
Detroit Pistons, 196
Didinger, Ray, 171
DiMaggio, Joe, 259, 268
Dinces, Sean, 8
Divac, Vlade, 197
Dodger Stadium, 20, 43, 53, 106, 276, 281–82
Doggett, Jerry, 280–81
Dogtown & z-Boys (documentary), 177
Doherty, Thomas, 167
Dora "DaCat" Mickey, 234–35
Dos Santos, Giovanni, 56
Douglas Aircraft, 229
Down and Out in Beverly Hills (film), 6
Doyle, Jennifer, 12
Drake, Dale, 95
Drysdale, Don, 281
DuBois, W.E.B., 150
Dunn, Jack, 76–77
Dyreson, Mark, 132–33

E

East LA Classic, 43–8, 54
East Los Angeles College, 44–45
Ebbets Field, 255, 260, 284
Ebert, Roger, 175
Ebony (magazine), 161
Eckersley, Dennis, 282–83
Economic Research Associates, 210
Edgar, John, 101
Edison, Thomas, 168
Edwards, Dr. Harry, 184
Eiferman, George, 252
Eight Men Out (film), 15
Eldridge, Todd, 84
Elmer, Maxine, 100
El Paso Shoe Club, 40

El Tri, 48–54
Emmy Award, 276
Endless Summer (film), 233
Endow, David, 46
Entertainment and Sports Programming Network (ESPN), 58–9
Epps, Omar, 174
Erickson, Hal, 172
Erving, Julius, 190
Escape from LA (film), 6
Estadio Azteca, 52, 64
European Broadcasting Union, 209
Evergreen Park, 41, 54
Evergreen Rangers, 41
Ewell, Richard, 87
Ewing, Patrick, 214
Exposition Park, 20, 28, 34, 95, 137
Extreme Football League (XFL), 7
Eyser, George, 215

F

Fairbanks, Mabel, 84–90
Fairhall, Neroli, 215
Falcous, Mark, 141
Fassi, Carlo, 81
Fast Times at Ridgemont High (film), 232
Fears, Tom, 118, 120
Fédération Mexicana de Futbol Association (FML), 49
Fédération Internationale de Football Association (FIFA), 58, 214
Fédération Internationale de L'Automobile, 103
Fentress, J. Cullen, 160
Fenway Park, 275–76, 284
Ferraro Fields, 55
Fiesta Bicycle, Motorcycle, and Automobile Meet, 95
FIFA. *See* Fédération Internationale de Football Association.
Figueroa, Armando, 46
figure skating: 14; tank shows, 72–73; East v. West, 73–76; Sonja Henie, 76–77; National Championships, 77–78; Zamboni Machine, 78–79; plane crash, 79–80; Peggy Fleming, 80–82; John Wicks and Frank Carroll, 82–84; Mabel Fairbanks, 84–90

Figure Skating Board, 75
Fike, Joseph, 247
First Outdoor California Figure Skating Championships, 74
Fiscal, Michael Orozco, 52
Fleming, Peggy, 80–82
Flores, Tom, 53, 125
Flowers, Charlie, 122
football: 11; East LA Classic, 43–48, 54; origins of the professional game, 110–11; Los Angeles Bulldogs, 111–15; Los Angeles Dons, 115, 118–20; Los Angeles Rams, 11, 26, 47, 93, 115–24, 127–28; Los Angeles Chargers, 118, 122–23; Oakland Raiders, 125, 127; Los Angeles Express, 125–27; Los Raiders, 125–27; St. Louis Rams, 127
Ford, Alexander Hume, 223
Fordham University, 275
"Foreign Car Races," 98
Fortune, Kristin, 79
Foss, Joe, 122
Fox Sports, 55, 59
Franklin's Gold Dust Soup Powder, 158
Fratianne, Linda, 14, 84
Free House, 273
Freeth, George, 221–24
Friday Night Lights (film), 169
Friendly, David T., 168
From a Left Wing (blog), 55
Frontiere, Georgia, 124, 127
Frontier of Leisure (book), 237
Frosty Frolics (television show), 85–86
Fry, Barney, 242, 249
Furillo, Carl, 280

G
"Gal Fridays," 101
Galindo, Rudy, 88
Gardner, Ava, 258
Gardner, Randy, 82, 88
Garfield High School: Rivalry with Roosevelt High School, 43–48
Garland, John Jewett, 205
Garland, William May, 132, 134, 136, 138, 203, 205
Garrett, Mike, 45–46
Gasol, Pau, 200
Geltner, Ted, 10

Gerrard, Steven, 56
Gibson, Kirk, 282–86
Gidget (film), 220, 235, 237
Gilmore Field, 20
Gilmore Stadium, 20, 95, 112
Ginther, Richie, 100–101
Giroux, Henry, 141
Giroux, Kate, 242, 244–45
Glacier Palace, 74
Gleaves, John, 8
Glickman, Marty, 153–54, 161, 165
Glory Road (film), 169
Goebel, Timothy, 90
Gold Cup, 50
"Gold Dust Trio," 158
Golden Age of Sports, 255–56
Gold, Gracie, 90
Gold's Gym, 13
Gomez, Hercules, 51
Goodell, Roger, 128
Gooding Jr., Cuba, 176
Goodrich, Bert, 251
Goodrich, Gail, 189
Gorn, Elliott: recollections of Vin Scully, 280–83
Graham, Billy, 26
Grambling University, 118
Grand Canyon (film), 180
Grand Prix for Sports Cars, 104
Grange, Harold "Red," 110
Grannis, Leroy, 228
Gray, Mel, 126
Great Depression, 242, 249
Great Western Forum, 7, 175, 180, 186–87, 189
Green, A.C., 197
Green Bay Packers, 112, 124
Greenberg, Miriam, 130, 135–36
Gretzky, Wayne, 89
Griffith Park, 55, 65
Gross, Paul, 234
Guerrero, Lalo, 42
Gulfstream Park, 268
Guthrie, Woody, 170
Gurney, Dan, 100–101, 107

H
Haden, Pat, 27–28
Halas, George, 110, 116

Haley, Jackie Earle, 172
Hall, Arsenio, 14
Hall, Randall (Ran), 246
Hall, Regina, 174
Hang Ten, 232
Hapgood, Richard, 75
Hardwicke, Catherine, 177
Harlem Globetrotters, 198–99
Harlow Café, 73
Harmon, Alan, 125–26
Harper, Harry, 134
Harrelson, Woody, 172, 174
Hart, Michael Joseph, 157–58
Hart, Russell K., 253
Harwell, Ernie, 276
Haupt Jr., Ollie, 77
Hawaii, 22–24, 226, 228, 233
Hawaiian Promotion Committee, 223
Hawaiian Surfboard (book), 226
Hawaiian Surfing Movies (film), 233
Haysbert, Dennis, 174
Haywood, Spencer, 198
Heathcote, Jud, 192
Heaven Can Wait (film), 15
Heffner, Hugh, 191
Heiss, Carol, 80
Heitmann, John, 96
Heller, Randee, 170
Helmick, Ralph, 164
Henderson, Elmer "Gus," 112, 114
Henderson, Ricky, 270
Henie, Sonja, 76–78, 85–86, 90
Hermosa Beach, 222, 228, 230, 234
Hernandez, Daniel, 66
Hill, Phil, 99–101, 103, 107
Hilton, Barron, 122–23
Hinson, Hal, 173
Hirsch, Elroy, 118
Hirsch, Emile, 177
Hitler, Adolph, 154
Hodges, Gil, 280
Hoffmann, Bob, 252
Hogan, Ben, 271–72
Hogue, Josh, 105
Holland, Brad, 187, 192
Hollingsworth, Cecil C., 247
Holloway, Zenobia, 86

Hollywood: figure skating, 74–77, 84; Olympic Games (1932), 133, 136; sports films, 167–81; Showtime Lakers, 186, 188; Olympic Games (1984), 203–204
Hollywood Bears, 114–15, 117
Hollywood Ice Review, 76
Hollywood Jock (film), 181
Hollywood Park, 20
Hollywood stars, 20, 112, 259
Hollywood Walk of Fame, 75, 276
Hoosiers (film), 169
Hope, Bob, 115, 265
Houston Oilers, 122
Houston Rockets, 189
Howard, Frank, 265
Hundley, Rod, 261
Hunter, Bob, 93
Hunter, Tab, 85
Hunter, Wallace, 85
Huntington Beach, 179
Huntington, Henry, 223
Huntington Park, 48–49
Hutton, Betty, 85

I
Ice Capades, 78
Ice Follies, 74
Ice Palace, 73
Ice Rink, 73
Ihmsen, Max, 132
"I Love LA" (song), 3–7, 10, 12–13, 15–17
Indiana State University, 183
Indiana University, 118, 183, 190
I Never Had It Made (autobiography), 156, 158, 160
Inglewood, 199
International Federation of Association Football (FIFA), 214
International Ladies Garment Workers Union, 146
International Motors, 97
International Olympic Committee (IOC), 15–16, 74, 132, 146, 202–203, 205–206, 209–210, 213, 215–18
International Olympic Committee Medical Commission, 216
International Road Racers, 93

International Skating Union (ISU) of America, 72–73
Irsay, Robert, 124
Irving, Julius, 190, 193

J
"Jack Robinson Day," 156
Jackson, Bo, 16
Jackson, Michael, 186
Jacobs, Hap, 230–31
Jan & Dean, 221
Japanese Americans, 142–43
Japan Times (newspaper), 143
Jarrin, Jamie, 37, 280
Jean, Lora, 72–73
Jefferson, Alison Rose, 247–48
Jenkins, David, 80
Jerry Maguire (film), 175–77, 181
J.G. Taylor Spink Award, 272
Johnson, Magic, 14, 89, 175, 180, 183–88, 190–200
Johnson, Marques, 174
Joint Powers Authority, 26
Jones, Marion, 216
Jordan, Michael, 89, 190, 214
Junso, Roland, 79

K
Kahanamoku, Duke, 224
Kaliss, Gregory, 10
Kansas City Chiefs, 127
Kansas City Monarchs, 159
Karate Kid (film), 170–71, 181
Kasdan, Lawrence, 180
Kasten, Stan, 37, 289
Katin, 232
Keane, Robbie, 56
Kelend, Bud, 124
Kemp, Jack, 122
Kennedy, John, 26, 252
Kershaw, Clayton, 289
Kimbrough, John, 119
King, Billie Jean, 81
Kingpin (film), 15
King, Rodney, 8
Kinney, Abbott, 223
Kinney, Jeremy, 12

Kipp, William, 80, 82
Kitt, Eartha, 85
Kivlin, Matt, 230
Klosterman, Don, 126
Knox, Chuck, 124
Kobra Kai, 170
Kohner, Frederick, 237
Kohner, Kathy, 237
Kornoff, John, 251–52
Kotz, David, 140
Koufax, Sandy, 268, 281–82, 284–85, 289
Krause, Bill, 103
Kuchiki, Natasha, 82
Kuenn, Harvey, 285
Ku Klux Klan, 143, 212
Kupchak, Mitch, 198
Kwan, Michelle, 14, 77, 89

L
LA Department of Recreation and Parks, 41
Ladies Figure Skating World Championships, 76
LA 84 Foundation, 8, 15–16, 86, 217
Lafayette Hotel Ballroom, 80
Lafayette Park, 60–61, 173
LaLanne, Jack, 251
L'Allemand, Gordon, 242
LaMarr, Heddie, 85
Lamour, Dorothy, 75
Lancaster, Bill, 171
LaOpinion (newspaper), 37, 56
LA Region, 98, 102–105
Lasorda, Tommy, 271
Lathan, Sanaa, 174–75
Latino Baseball History Project, 40
Lavorante, Alexander, 266
Lawford, Peter, 237
Ledger, Heath, 177
Legion Ascot, 95
LeRoy, J.M., 74
Leslie, Lisa, 199
Levy, Fred, 121
Levy, Ruth, 100
Lewis, Carl, 16–17, 213
Life (magazine), 227, 242
Lipinski, Tara, 89
Lipinski, Jonathan, 176

Lipsitz, George, 47
Lisanti, Tony, 220
Llewellyn, Matthew, 8, 132–33
Locher, Felix (aka John Hall), 74–75, 90
London, Charmain, 223
London, Jack, 223
Long Beach Arena, 79
Long, Judith Grant, 136–37
Looff, Charles, 241
Look (magazine), 161, 227, 252
Lopez, Frank, 42
Lopez, Mario, 40–41
Lord Killanin, 206
Lords of Dogtown (film), 168, 177–80
Los Angeles: founding of, 4; sport venues, 19–35; Mexican Americans and sport, 37–54; soccer, 55–69; figure skating, 71–91; sports car racing, 93–107; professional football, 109–28; Olympic Games (1932), 129–47; Pasadena and the Robinson Brothers, 149–65; Hollywood sports films, 167–81; Showtime Lakers, 183–200; Olympic Games (1984), 201–18; surfing, 219–38; Muscle Beach, 239–54; Jim Murray, 255–73; Vin Scully, 275–89.
Los Angeles Angels, 20
Los Angeles Athletic Club, 224, 243, 246
Los Angeles Buccaneers, 110–11
Los Angeles Bulldogs, 111–16
Los Angeles Chamber of Commerce, 134, 136, 138
Los Angeles Chargers, 118, 122–23
Los Angeles City Council, 29, 137, 206
Los Angeles City Schools, 247
Los Angeles Clippers, 19, 174
Los Angeles County Fairgrounds, 104–105
Los Angeles Dodgers, 9–10, 19, 25–26, 37–39, 42–43, 53, 269
Los Angeles Dons, 115, 118–20
Los Angeles Evening Herald (newspaper), 72
Los Angeles Examiner (newspaper), 93, 132, 157, 257–58
Los Angeles Express, 125–27
Los Angeles Extreme, 7
"Los Angeles Fiesta," 146
Los Angeles Figure Skating Club, 74, 76–79, 84, 86–89

Los Angeles Forty-Sixty, 40
Los Angeles Galaxy, 20, 29–30, 55–56, 128
Los Angeles Lakers, 14, 180, 183–200, 269
Los Angeles Memorial Coliseum, 7, 11, 21, 23, 25–29, 32–35, 45, 48, 50, 110, 118–28, 137–40, 207, 213–15, 260
Los Angeles Memorial Coliseum Commission, 26, 28–29, 34, 117, 125
Los Angeles Mirror (newspaper), 102
Los Angeles Motordrome at Playa del Rey, 95
"Los Angeles 1976 Olympic Committee," 205
Los Angeles Olympic Organizing Committee (LAOOC), 206–12, 243
Los Angeles Plays Itself (documentary), 169
Los Angeles Police Department (LAPD), 63–64, 67–69
Los Angeles: Portrait of a City (book), 239
Los Angeles Raiders, 11, 16–17, 26, 47, 53
Los Angeles Rams, 11, 26, 47, 93, 115–24, 127–28, 255, 269
Los Angeles Rams Football Company, Inc., 121
Los Angeles Sentinel (newspaper), 85
Los Angeles Skating Club, 77
Los Angeles Sparks, 175
Los Angeles Tigers, 110
Los Angeles Times (newspaper), 28, 41, 46–47, 49, 64–65, 93, 102–103, 134, 142, 145, 157, 179, 196, 227, 243, 247–48, 253, 261–73, 278–79
Los Angeles Wildcats, 110–11
Los Chorizeros, 39–43, 46, 48, 52, 54
Love and Basketball (film), 174–75, 181
Lowe, Marion, 100
Lowe, Paul, 122
Lucas, Taylor, 97
Luce, Henry, 258–59
Lucsko, David, 95
Lummis, Charles Fletcher, 224
Lynch, Patrick, 28
Lysacek, Evan, 90

M

Manhattan Beach, 222, 230
May, Kirse Granat, 237
McAdoo, Bob, 198

Index · 355

MacArthur Park, 55, 63–67
Machio, Ralph, 170
Machado, Catherine, 86
Mackie, Bob, 84
"Mack Robinson Day," 164
Macnow, Glen, 171
Main, Kelly, 64
Major League Baseball (MLB), 19, 37, 109, 115, 149, 159–60, 162–63, 276
Major League Soccer (MLS), 19–20, 29, 55, 58–59
Malibu, 221–22, 230, 234–35, 237–38
"Malibu Chip," 230
"Malibu Style," 230, 234
Malone, Moses, 16, 188
Mandela, Nelson, 26
Man O' War, 273
Mantle, Mickey, 267
Manuel Arts High School, 183
Marcus, Ben, 220
Marshall, George, 116
Marston, George, 72
Martin, Dean, 85
Martin, Duane, 174
Marx, Groucho, 265
Marx, Harpo, 172
Maslin, Janet, 170, 173
Mathias, Bob, 259
Matson, Ollie, 121
Matthau, Walter, 171
Mayer, Louis B., 136, 204
McAfee, Jack, 100–101
McAlexander, James, H., 238
McCallum, Jack, 181
McCardle, Leon V., 111
McCladdie, Michelle, 87
McCoy, Linda, 272
McCulloch, Frank, 261–62
McGwire, Mark, 282
McHale, Kevin, 198
McKee, Henry, 134
McKenzie, Sharon, 79
McKinney, Jack, 192
McMinn, Dean, 80
McRae, Gordon, 249
McRae, Relena Brewer, 242–46, 249
McWilliams, Carey, 145
Mears, Kara, 66

Mears, Rick, 95
Medal of Freedom, 162
Meno, Jenni, 82
Men's Junior Championship (figure skating), 77
Merchant and Manufacturers Association, 145
Mercury Figure Skating Club, 77
Metcalfe, Ralph, 154
Metro-Goldwyn Mayer (MGM), 204
Mexican Americans: portrayal of racial harmony, 9; soccer, 11–12, 48–54, 60–69; baseball, 37–43, 53–54; football, 43–48, 52–54; figure skating, 88; Olympic Games (1932), 144–46; Vin Scully, 279–80
Mexican Revolution, 38–39
Meyer, Louis, 95
Michelmore, D.D., 105
Michaels, Al, 289
Michelson, Rhode Lee, 80
Michigan Panthers, 126
Michigan State University, 183, 186, 190
Mighty Ducks (film), 15
Miguel, Nigel, 174
Mikan, George, 189
Miles, Ken, 100–101, 104
Miller, Andre, 199
Miller, Harry, 95
Milwaukee Bucks, 270
Minneapolis Lakers, 24, 260
Miracle Mile, 259
Miss Muscle Beach, 251
Mix, Ron, 122
Mohr, Jay, 176
Molina, Natalia, 38
Moneyball (film), 169
Monroe, Marilyn, 258
Montalban, Ricardo, 85
Montreal Royals, 159
Moore, Davey, 266
Moore, Michael Scott, 220
Morita, Noriyuki "Pat," 170
Morningside High School, 187
Morton, Craig, 269
Moses, Edwin, 213
Most, DeForest (Moe), 251–52
Motion Pictures Producers Association, 136
Motor Racing (magazine), 106

356 · Index

Mount Lee, 167
Moutawakel, Nawal El, 215
Mr. California, 250
Mr. Muscle Beach, 251–52
Muir Tech High School, 153, 156, 162
Mullin, Chris, 214
Murray, Jim: 10, birth and early life, 255–57; career with the *Los Angeles Examiner*, 257–58; covering the film industry and sport for *Time*, 258–61; taking position with *Los Angeles Times*, 261–62; controversy regarding Cincinnati, 263–64; establishing representation as humorist, 265–66; addressing civil rights issues, 266; taking on the sport of car racing, 266–67; health issues, 268–69; profiling Pat Riley, 269–70; writing as representative of his personality, 271–72; tragedy in his life, 272; lifetime achievement awards, 272–73
Muscle Beach: 13, 16, 219, 235, development of 241–44; creating fitness and Exercise space, 244–49; comes of age, 249–53
Muscle Power (book), 242
Myers, Harry, 111–12

N

Nagournwey, Adam, 167
Naked Gun (film), 6
Nater, Swen, 187
Nathan, Dan, 15
National Association for the Advancement of Colored People (NAACP), 151, 155, 160, 165
National Association of Realtors, 203
National Basketball Association (NBA), 14, 19, 24, 53, 174, 183–84, 187–91, 197–98, 255, 260, 269–70
National Broadcasting Company (NBC), 208
National Championships (figure skating), 77–78
National Collegiate Athletic Association (NCAA), 186, 190
National Dance Championship, 80
National Football League (NFL), 7, 19, 26, 33–34, 53, 109–25, 127–28, 176

National Geographic (magazine), 226–27
National Historic Landmark, 26
National Sportscasters and Sportswriters Association, 267
National Sportswriters and Sportswriters Hall of Fame, 272
National Sportswriter of the Year, 267, 269
Navarrette Jr., Ruben, 49–50
Neushul, Peter, 229, 231, 237
Newcombe, Don, 289
New Haven Register (newspaper), 257
New Jersey Generals, 125
Newman, Randy, 3, 5, 7, 10, 12–13, 15, 209–10
Newport Beach, 176, 260
New York Giants, 114
New York Times (newspaper), 100, 173, 189, 289
New York Titans, 122
New York Yankees, 37, 259
Nicholson, Jack, 14, 186
Nicholson, Howard, 85
Nicks, John, 81–84, 87–88, 90
Niederman, Al, 246–47
Nike, 15–17, 209–10
Niky's Sports, 68
Ning, Li, 213
Nixon, Norm, 195–96, 197–98
No Boston Olympics, 146–47, 319
Noll, Greg, 231, 233
North Shore (film), 232
Notre Dame, 28, 45, 53, 259

O

Oakland Raiders, 125, 127
Obama, Barack, 37
O'Brien, Larry, 190
O'Brien, Pat, 115
Ocean Front Walk, 172
Ocean Park, 177, 242, 246, 248–49
O'Connell, Jerry, 176
Oelschlagel, Charlotte, 72
Offenhauser, Fred, 95
Oldenburg, J. William, 126
Oldfield, Barney, 95
Olympic Auditorium, 20
Olympic Charter (official document), 206, 216

Olympic Games (1904), 215
Olympic Games (1908), 74
Olympic Games (1912), 214
Olympic Games (1920), 74, 203
Olympic Games (1928), 76, 203
Olympic Games (1932), 7–8, 25–26, 74, 76, 203–205; Urban Boosterism, 131–35; public-private partnerships, 135–40; "community" as urban façade, 141–46
Olympic Games (1936), 16, 76; and Mack Robinson, 149, 153–55
Olympic Games (Winter 1948), 82
Olympic Games (1952), 205
Olympic Games (Winter 1952), 82
Olympic Games (1956), 205
Olympic Games (1960), 205
Olympic Games (Winter 1960), 79–80
Olympic Games (1964), 205
Olympic Games (1968), 205
Olympic Games (1972), 205
Olympic Games (1976), 201, 205, 208–209
Olympic Games (1980), 201, 205, 207, 210–11
Olympic Games (Winter 1980), 88
Olympic Games (1984), 7–8, 15, 24–26, 29, 33–34, 162, 201–18; making the bid to host, 203–206; making preparations for the games, 206–208; marketing the games, 208–210; boycott, 210–13; athletic performances, 213–14; watershed moments, 214–17; legacy of 217–18
Olympic Games (1988), 216–17
Olympic Games (Winter 1992), 89
Olympic Games (Winter 1994), 89
Olympic Games (Winter 1998), 89
Olympic Games (Winter 2002), 89–90, 217
Olympic Games (Winter 2006), 89
Olympic Games (Winter 2010), 90
"Olympic Partner Programme" (TOP), 202, 210
Olympic Village, 142
O'Malley, Peter, 262, 270–71
O'Malley, Walter, 42, 260, 281
O'Neal, Shaquille, 14, 200
O'Neal, Tatum, 171
One-Round Hogan (film), 168
"Open Letter to Sports Car Drivers," 106
Operation Wetback, 40

Oppegard, Peter, 88
Oregon Sports Hall of Fame, 162
Ornelas Food Market, 41
O'Rourke, Charley, 119
Oshier, E.J., 228
Otis, Harrison Gray, 224
Out of It (film), 168
Outterbridge, John, 164
Overell Yacht Murders, 258
Owens, Jesse, 10, 16, 153–54, 162, 213
Ozyurtcu, Tolga, 13, 241, 253

P

Pacific Classic, 273
Pacific Coast Highway, 286
Pacific Coast League, 40
Pacific Coast Professional Football League, (PCL), 114–15
Pacific Ocean Park, 177
Padilla, Al, 41, 44–46
Palmer, Arnold, 271
Palos Verdes, 222, 226–27
Palos Verdes Surfing Club (PVSC), 227–28, 233
Panama-California Exposition, 72
Pan-Pacific Auditorium, 76
Paramount Iceland, 82
Paret, Benny "The Kid," 266
Parker, Dave, 269
Parker, Dorothy, 4
Parravano, Tony, 101
Pasadena, 29–32, 34; race and the Robinson brothers, 149–65
Pasadena City (Junior) College, 9, 152–53, 155–56, 162, 164
Pasadena City Council, 31–32
Pasadena Community Athletic Club, 159
Pasadena Improvement Association, 151
Pasadena Post (newspaper), 155
Patton, Mel, 259
Paul, III, John, 26
Pauley, Edwin, 118, 121
Paul, Robert, 81
Pauley Pavilion, 20
Pearl Harbor, 228
People's Republic of China, 202
Perez, Manuel "Shorty," 41

Perez, Rosie, 173
Peterson, James E., 105
Philadelphia Eagles, 112, 118
Philadelphia 76ers, 192–93
Philadelphia Skating Club and Humane Society, 78
Pico-Union, 55, 59, 67
Pico/Union Field, 55
Pierce Junior College, 127
Pierce, Larry, 80
Pierce, Paul, 199
Pink Floyd, 179
Pittsburgh Pirates (football), 112,114
Pittsburgh Steelers, 124, 268
Plunkett, Jim, 53
Podres, Johnny, 280
Polar Palace, 74, 76, 78
Pollack, Bill, 101, 103
Pollard, Jr., Fritz, 154
Popular Mechanics (magazine), 227
Porter, John, 142–43, 146
Portland Breakers, 127
Post, Robert, 95
Potzsch, Annett, 84
Pratt, Kyla, 174
Pride of the Yankees (film), 168
Prime Ticket Network (FS West/Prime Ticket), 187
Prince-Bythewood, Gina, 174–75
Pro Football Hall of Fame, 115, 121
Progressive Era, 22
public infrastructure, 21–25
Pulitzer Award, 273
Purdy, Ken, 96

Q
Quigg, Joe, 226, 230

R
racial discrimination: Robinson brothers, 9–10, 150–52, 155, 158, 162, 164–65; Soccer, 50–51; figure skating, 84–86; in football, 114–15, 117–18; at Muscle Beach, 247–48
Radio Hall of Fame, 276
Radio Korea USA, 56
Rafu Shimpo (newspaper), 142–43
Raging Bull (film), 169

Rampersad, Arnold, 152, 161
Ramsey, Dr. Jack, 192
Ramsey, Tom, 126
Rasuk, Victor, 177
Reagan, Ronald, 162, 211–12
Real Madrid, 56
Redondo Beach, 222–23
Redpath, George, 251
Red Smith Award, 272
Reeves, Dan, 109, 116–18, 120–21, 123–24
Reeves, Steve, 252
Reich, Kenneth, 210
Reid, Sam, 234
Reseda, 170–71
Retton, Mary Lou, 215
Reventlow, Lance, 100–101
Reyes, Gil, 279
Richards, Elvin "Kink," 114
Richardson, Jim, 257
Rickenbacker, Eddie, 95
Rickey, Branch, 289
Rickles, Don, 265
Rider, Toby, 8
Riess, Steven, 132, 137, 139
Riley, Pat, 193–95
Right to Play, 125
Rindge, Frederick H., 234
Rindge, Mary Knight, 234
Ritche, Michael, 171
Riverfront Stadium, 283
Riverside International Motor Raceway, 93, 102, 105–107
Road & Track (magazine), 98, 104
Robinson, Edgar, 152
"Robinson Family Weekend," 164
Robinson, Jackie, 9–10, 149–65, 289
Robinson, Jerry, 150
Robinson, John, 177
Robinson, Leslie, 87
Robinson, Mack, 10, 149–65
Robinson, Mallie, 150, 155
Robinson Memorial, 164–65
Robinson Park, 163
Robinson, Rachel Isum, 164
Robinson, Willa Mae, 151–52
Rocky (film), 168–70
Rodriquez, Frank, 49

Rodriquez, Raymond, 145
Rogers Park, 199
Roles-Pursley, Barbara, 80
Rolph, James, 141
Romania, 202
Ronquillo, Henry, 45
Roosevelt High School: rivalry with Garfield High School, 43–48
Rose Bowl, 8, 11, 21, 29–35, 47–49, 52, 54, 56, 123–24, 157, 266
Rose Bowl Operating Company (RBOC), 21, 31–32
Rosenbloom, Carroll, 124
Roulier, Jay, 126
Roybal, Ed, 42
Rozelle, Pete, 121, 123
Russell, Bill, 189
Ruth, Babe, 256, 273
Ryder, Rob, 181
Rypien, Mark, 270

S
Sachs, Eddie, 267
Salcedo, Hugo, 51
Salinas Packers, 112
Salvadori, Roy, 103
Samaranch, Juan Antonio, 202, 209–10, 215, 217
Sanchez, Mark, 53–54
San Diego Chargers, 128
San Diego Clippers, 196–97
San Diego Figure Skating Club, 78, 88
San Diego Padres, 277
Sand, Todd, 82
San Fernando Valley, 170–71
San Francisco, 223
San Francisco Chronicle (newspaper), 105
San Francisco 49ers, 119
San Francisco Giants, 281
San Joaquin Valley Tourist and Travel Association, 74
San Jose State University, 207
Santa Anita Park, 20
Santa Monica, 171, 177, 224, 226, 233–35, 239–54
Santa Monica High School, 244, 248
Santa Monica Mountains, 167

Santa Monica Playground, 247
"Santa Monica Pleasure Pier," 241
Saturday Evening Post (magazine), 242
Saturday Night Live (television show), 189
Saunders, Russell (Russ), 250, 252
Sawyer, Pat, 100
Sayre, Joel, 242
Schecter, Stuart, 164
Scheibe, John, 268–69
Schissler, Paul, 112, 114–15
Schouten, John, 238
Schreiber, Pablo, 177
Schwarzenegger, Arnold, 253
Scorsese, Martin, 169
Scott, A.O., 179–80
Scott, Byron, 187, 196–97, 200
Scott M.E. Church, 156
Scully, Vin: birth and early years, 275–76; joins the Dodgers, 276; broadcasting style, 277–78; transcends ethnic and racial boundaries, 279–80; recollections of Elliott Gorn, 280–83; recollections of Allison Lauterbach Dale, 284–86; persona and postscript, 287–89
Secretariat, 273
Severson, John, 233
Shandling, Gary, 16
Sheinin, Dave, 285
Shelby, Carroll, 100–101, 107
Shell Gasoline, 136
Shelley, Ken, 82
Shelton, Ron, 172–73
Sheppard, David, 253
Sherbloom, Diane, 80
Short, Bob, 185
Showtime Lakers, 180, 183–200
Shue, Elizabeth, 170,
Shutt, Vincent, 242
Silk, Michael, 141
Simmons, Bob, 229–30
Simon, William, 207
Skate and Ski Club, 76
Skating (magazine), 77–78
Sly, Wendy, 214
Smith, Quinn, 172
Smithsonian (magazine), 244
Snider, Duke, 280

Snipes, Wesley, 173–74
Snyder, Meredith, 132
soccer: Mexican Americans, 11–12, 48–56, 59–60; countercultural sport, 58–60; LAPD police, 67–69
South African and Rhodesian apartheid, 201, 213
Southern California Committee for the Olympic Games (SCCOG), 205–206
Southern California Council of Sports Car Clubs, 104
Southern California Hockey League, 73
Southern California Timing Association, 95
Soviet National Olympic Committee, 211–12
Soviet Union, 202, 210–13
Spellman, Frank, 252–53
Sports Arena, 26–27
Sports Authority, 28
Sports Broadcasting: Vin Scully, 275–89
Sports Car Club of America (SCCA), 96–98, 100–107
Sports Car Racing, 12; origins of 96–97; in Southern California, 97–103; Cal Club v. the SCCA, 103–107
Sports Car Racing Association, 99
Sports Film (book), 168
Sports Films, and Hollywood, 167–81
Sports Films: A Complete Reference (book), 168
Sports Illustrated (magazine), 81, 100, 181, 210, 213, 259–61, 268
Sports Management International (SMI), 176
Sports Writing, and Jim Murray, 255–73
Sproul, Robert, 157
Staples Center, 7, 20–21
Starbuck, Jo Jo, 82
Stargell, Willie, 269, 272
Starman (film), 6
State Department, 211–12
Stern, David, 190
Steve Allen Show, 265
St. Louis Rams, 127
St. Moritz Ice Skating Club (Oakland), 76
Stockton, Les, 248, 250–51
Stockton, Pudgy, 245, 248–50, 252
Stoddard, Sylvia, 80

Stoller, Sam, 154
Strength & Health (book), 252
Strode, Woody, 117, 157–58
StubHub Center, 20, 29, 128
Stydahar, Joe, 120
Sunset Boulevard, 171
Super Bowl, 19, 25, 29, 33–34, 47, 53, 123–25, 269
surfing, 13; prior to World War II, 222–28; late 1950s, 228–35; new board designs, 229–31; and lifestyle, 231–35; appeal of the sport, 235–38
Sveum, Dennis, 79
Sweetness and Blood (book), 220
Swift, E.M., 81–82
Symbol of Heart (documentary), 45

T

Tanny, Vic, 250–51
Tarkanian, Jerry, 192
Tarenaka, Shoichiro, 143
Taliaferro, George, 118
Tampa Bay Buccaneers, 124
Taylor, Elizabeth, 258
Ten, Denis, 90
Tennis, 52–53, 133–35, 151, 170, 226
Texaco Gasoline, 136
Texas Christian University, 157
Thomas, Burton, 150
Thomas, Debi, 88
Thomas, Frank J., 240
Thompson, Mychal, 198
Thompson, Tina, 199
Thorpe, Jim, 162
Time (magazine), 258–62
Tin Cup (film), 15
Title IX, 81
Tobar, Hector, 279
Todd, Jan, 13
Tolan, Eddie, 142–43
Toledo, Saul, 40
Tomjanovich, Rudy, 189
"Top Sportscaster of all Time," 276
Tostado, Maria, 45–46
Tournament of Roses, 29–32, 152
Tournament of Roses Association, 30
Trachtenberg, Alan, 239

track and field: Mack Robinson, 10, 149, 153–55; 1984 Olympic Games, 213–15
Tracy, Terry "Tubesteak," 235
Trans-Am Series, 106
Tresidder, Donald, 75
Trinity College, 257
Tropical Ice Gardens, 78
Truax, Eileen, 66
Tucker, Cliff, 228
Turner, Eugene, 77–78
Twentieth Century Fox, 76, 260
Tygiel, Jules, 160

U

UCLA Olympic Analytical Laboratory, 216
"Ueberroth Effect," 217
Ueberroth, Peter, 201, 207–11, 213, 216
Union Football League, 67
United Nations, 259
United States Championships (figure skating), 74
United States Auto Club (USAC), 103
United States Figure Skating Association (USFS), 73–78, 80, 86, 90
United States Figure Skating Hall of Fame, 89
United States Football League (USFL), 125–27
United States Grand Prix For Sports Cars at Riverside, 93, 102–103
United States Men's National Team (USMNT), 48–56
United States Olympic Committee (USOC), 146, 205, 207, 211, 217
United States Postal Service, 164
United States Road Racing Championship, 106
United States Soccer Federation (US Soccer), 49, 58–59, 62
United States Sports Car Club (USSCC), 105
University of Alabama, 266
University of California at Los Angeles, 5, 9, 20, 26, 29–32, 56, 78, 114–15, 117, 153, 155, 157–59, 163, 186–87, 190, 192, 208, 216, 247, 250, 260, 266
University of California, Riverside, 51
University of California, Santa Barbara, 208

University of Illinois, 110
University of Kentucky, 190
University of Maryland, 275
University of North Carolina, 186
University of Oregon, 155–56, 160, 162
University of Southern California, 5, 26–29, 45, 47, 53, 110, 117, 121, 137, 139, 157–58, 174–75, 186, 208, 226, 260
Univision, 59
Urban Branding: Olympic Games (1932), 129–47
US Coast Guard, 226
Usher, Harry, 207

V

Valenzuela, Fernando, 37–39, 46, 48
Van Brocklin, Norm, 118, 120–101
Van Wert, William F., 181
Veeck, Bill, 289
Velzy, Dale, 230
Venice Beach, 16, 64, 172–73, 177, 180, 222–23, 230, 253
Vinson, Maribel, 77, 80, 82, 84–85, 89–90
Vista Hermosa, 65
Volcano (film), 6
Von Neumann, Eleanor, 101
Von Neumann, John, 97, 100–101

W

Waikiki, 222–23, 226
Walker, Herschel, 125–26
Wally Park's National Hot Rod Association, 95
Ward, Arch, 115
Ward, Baxter, 206
Ward, Rodger, 95
Warshaw, Matt, 220, 225–26, 229–30, 232, 237
Washington Junior High School, 153
Washington, Kenny, 114–15, 117, 157–58
Washington, Kermit, 189
Washington Redskins, 125, 127
Washington State University, 158, 246
Waterfield, Bob, 118, 120
Watson, Jill, 88
Watts Giants, 42
Watts Towers, 173
Wayne, John, 14, 258

Weber, Dewey, 234
Weider, Joe, 252
Weingart Stadium, 44, 46–47, 54
West Coast Nascar, 107
Westhead, Paul, 192–93, 195–96
West, Irene, 85
West, Jerry, 187, 191, 195, 261, 269
Westwick, Peter, 229, 231, 237
Whitaker, Jack, 273
White, Byrd, 243
White, Charlie, 79
White, Jeremy, 132, 142, 145
White Men Can't Jump (film), 168, 172–74, 181
Wide World of Sports (television show), 81
Wilkes, Jamal, 186–87, 192, 195, 198
Williams, Freeman, 174
Williams, Lynn, 214
Wills, Maury, 281
Wilson, Atoy, 86–87
Winter Ice Gardens, 86
Wise, Bill, 205
Witt, Katarina, 88
Wolfe, Roland, 243
Wolfe, Rowland, 243
Wolper, David, 207
women: 14, 64, 71–91; sports car racing, 100–101; represented in film, 174–77, 220, 235, 237; accomplishments in 1984 Olympic Games, 213–15; Muscle Beach, 242–54
Women's Home Journal (magazine), 223
Women's National Basketball Association (WNBA), 175
Women's Sports Car Club (WSCC), 100–101
Wonder, Stevie, 186
Woodard, Alfie, 174
Wooden, John, 192, 270
Woodruff, John, 154
Woods, Tiger, 89
Works Progress Administration (WPA), 244, 249
World Cup, 11, 29, 52, 56, 60, 214
World Series, 25
World Trade Center, 276, 284
World War I, 26, 30, 73, 78, 131
World War II, 10, 20, 23, 40, 94–96, 115, 130, 150, 159, 201, 220, 225–28, 250–51, 257, 277
Worthy, James, 186, 197, 199–200
Wright, Bert, 79
Wrigley Field, 20, 276, 283
Wrigley Park, 20
Wykoff, Frank, 154

X

XM Radio, 278

Y

Yale University, 257
Yamaguchi, Kristi, 88–89
Yamamoto, Eriko, 143
Yorty, Sam, 205
Yosemite Park, 74
Yosemite Park and Curry Co., 75
Yosemite Winter Club, 74, 76
Young, A.S., 161
Younger, Paul "Tank," 118
Young Men's Christian Association (YMCA), 231
Young, Steve, 126
Your Physique and Muscle Power (book), 252

Z

Zabka, William, 170
Zacharek, Stephanie, 175
Zamboni, Frank, 78–79
Zamboni, Joan, 79
Zamboni, Lawrence, 78
Zamboni Machine, 78–79
Zang, David W., 172
Zanuck, Darryl, 260
Zatopek, Emil, 215
Zellweger, Renee, 176
Zimmerman, Paul, 157
Zinkin, Harold, 244, 246, 250–52
Zucker, Harvey Marc, 168